THE GERMANIZATION OF
EARLY MEDIEVAL
CHRISTIANITY

The Germanization of Early Medieval Christianity

A Sociohistorical Approach to Religious Transformation

James C. Russell

OXFORD UNIVERSITY PRESS

New York   Oxford

Oxford University Press

Oxford   New York
Athens   Auckland   Bangkok   Bombay
Calcutta   Cape Town   Dar es Salaam   Delhi
Florence   Hong Kong   Istanbul   Karachi
Kuala Lumpur   Madras   Madrid   Melbourne
Mexico City   Nairobi   Paris   Singapore
Taipei   Tokyo   Toronto

and associated companies in
Berlin   Ibadan

First published in 1994 by Oxford University Press, Inc.,
198 Madison Avenue, New York, New York 10016

First issued as an Oxford University Press paperback, 1996.

Oxford is a registered trademark of Oxford University Press, Inc.

Library of Congress Cataloging-in-Publication Data
James C. Russell
The Germanization of early medieval Christianity:
a sociohistorical approach to religious transformation / James C. Russell
p.   cm.   Revision of the author's thesis (Ph.D.)—Fordham University 1990.
Includes bibliographical references and index.
ISBN 0-19-507696-6; ISBN 0-19-510466-8 (pbk.)
1. Church history—primitive and early church, ca. 30–600.
2. Sociology, Christian—History—Early Church, ca. 30–600.
3. Germanic tribes—Religion.   4. Europe—Church history.   I. Title.
BR203.R87   1994   274.3'02—dc20   92-13182

1 3 5 7 9 8 6 4 2

Printed in the United States of America
on acid-free paper

To My Family

Preface

On June 30, 1988, Archbishop Marcel Lefebvre consecrated four priests of his Catholic traditionalist Society of Saint Pius X as bishops, thus triggering a schism within the Roman Catholic Church. Although the theological origins of Lefebvre's disagreement with the Vatican may be traced to his rejection of certain documents promulgated at the Second Vatican Council (1962–1965),[1] a significant degree of his popular support may be attributed to resentment toward the many liturgical changes which followed the Council. The most visible of these was the replacement of the traditional Latin Mass with the *Novus Ordo Missae*.

On a religiocultural level, this schism may be considered the end of the image of the Roman Catholic Church as a popular expression of European Christianity. For at least the preceding millennium, from the coronation of the Saxon King Otto I as Holy Roman Emperor by Pope John XII on February 2, 962, to the opening of the Second Vatican Council by Pope John XXIII on October 11, 1962, the religiocultural orientation of popular Roman Catholicism was predominantly European and largely Germanic.[2] An example of a popular pre–Vatican II Eurocentric view of Christianity has been provided by Avery Dulles in his study *The Catholicity of the Church*, where he cites Hilaire Belloc's affirmation, "The Faith is Europe. And Europe is the Faith."[3]

---

[1] The primary Vatican II documents rejected by Lefebvre were *Gaudium et Spes* (Pastoral Constitution on the Church in the Modern World) and *Dignitatis Humanae Personae* (Declaration on Religious Freedom). Additional information regarding the events and documents preceding the schism may be found in *L'Osservatore romano*, English edition, June 27, 1988 and in François Laisney, *Archbishop Lefebvre and the Vatican* (Kansas City, Mo.: Angelus Press, 1989).

[2] An interesting Russian Orthodox parallel is discussed in Ernest Gordon, "A Thousand Years of Caesaropapism or the Triumph of the Christian Faith," *The World & I*, 3:8 (1988): 681–98.

[3] Hilaire Belloc, *Europe and the Faith* (London: Constable, 1920), p. 331; quoted in Avery Dulles, *The Catholicity of the Church* (Oxford: Clarendon Press, 1985), p. 75. Dulles comments: "Originally centred in the Mediterranean countries, Catholic Christianity later found its primary home in Europe. . . . As a plea to Europeans to recover the religious roots of their former unity, this slogan could be defended. Christianity was in possession as the religion of Europeans, and the Christianity that had united Europe was Catholic. But what about people of different stock? Did Belloc mean to imply that to become Christian they would first have to be

The claim of "catholicity" by the Roman Catholic Church and of universality by Christianity in general is central to the current inquiry. Primarily to advance the perception of its universality, the post–Vatican II Church has sought to shed its predominantly Western, European image. This modification may be witnessed in the Church's ecumenical relationships with representatives of non-European Christianity and non-Christian religions, in its appointment of more non-European prelates, in its canonization of more non-European saints, and in its virtual elimination of Germanic elements from liturgical rites.[4] The increased involvement of the Church in social-justice issues may also reflect an attempt to distance itself from the aristocratic character of a Germanized medieval Church and an attempt to recapture the religiocultural orientation of the early Church of the apostolic and patristic eras. One reason for this current direction may be that the present era, with its densely populated cosmopolitan areas that contain sizable, alienated underclasses, has a social environment somewhat more akin to the urbanized Roman Empire of late antiquity than to the rural-agrarian-warrior societies of early medieval Germanic Europe.

At the same time that this "de-Europeanization" of the Church is being pursued, however, the popularity of Catholic traditionalist movements among persons of European descent suggests that the Germanic elements within Christianity have not lost their appeal. It is hoped that, in addition to contributing to the study of religious transformation, the present inquiry may be of some value to those engaged in pastoral and missiological activities, as well as those pondering the forces involved in the development of their own personal religious identity.

The present book is a revised version of my 1990 doctoral dissertation in historical theology at Fordham University. I wish to thank my mentor, Richard F. Smith, S.J., for his guidance, patience, and kindness. To my readers, Louis B. Pascoe, S.J., and José Pereira, and my examiners, Ewert H. Cousins and Joseph F. Mitros, S.J., I owe much useful advice. To those who have read the manuscript, including G. Ronald Murphy, S.J., C. Scott Littleton, Edward Peters, J. N. Hillgarth, David Harry Miller, Peter Brown, Detlev Brand, Paul Math, and John Van Engen, I am also grateful. I wish to acknowledge my indebtedness to the late Robert E. McNally, S.J., who encouraged me to pursue my interest in the Germanic impact on early

---

Europeanized? If so, his thinking was too particularist." Dulles's thoughts on the catholicity of the Church in the future are the focus of his article "The Emerging World Church: A Theological Reflection," *Proceedings of the Catholic Theological Society of America* 39 (1984): 1–12.

[4] It is noteworthy and perhaps ironic that much of the impetus for this movement came from contemporary Germanic Council Fathers at the Second Vatican Council (e.g., Cardinals Bea, Suenens, Döpfner, Frings, Alfrink, and König) and from Germanic theological consultants (e.g., Karl Rahner, Joseph Ratzinger, Aloys Grillmeier, Otto Semmelroth, and Edward Schillebeeckx). Additional information on the influence of the Germanic Fathers at the Council may be found in Ralph M. Wiltgen, *The Rhine Flows into the Tiber: The Unknown Council* (New York: Hawthorn Books, 1967).

medieval Christianity. The staff of the Fordham University Library also deserves acknowledgment for their many years of professional service.

I wish to thank Robert A. Markus, Patrick J. Geary, G. Ronald Murphy, S.J., James Muldoon, Solomon A. Nigosian, Andrew P. Porter, and Edward C. Hobbs for providing me with pre-publication or unpublished versions of their work. To Cynthia A. Read, Paul Schlotthauer, and Peter Ohlin, my editors at Oxford University Press, I owe assistance and encouragement. My wife, Patricia, and my daughters, Megan and Marie, have patiently endured many sacrifices of time and pleasure to accommodate the completion of this book. Finally, to my parents, Roy and Agnes Russell, and to my aunts, Marie Wilson and Emilie Prucha, I am indebted for the continued support of my academic endeavors over the years.

White Plains, New York J. C. R.
June 1993

Contents

Abbreviations — xiii

Introduction — 3

PART I Toward a Model of Religious Transformation

1. Transformations of Christianity — 11
2. Conversion, Christianization, and Germanization — 26
3. Sociohistorical Aspects of Religious Transformation — 45
4. Sociopsychological Aspects of Religious Transformation — 81

PART II The Germanic Transformation of Christianity

5. Germanic Religiosity and Social Structure — 107
6. Germanization and Christianization: 376–678 — 134
7. Germanization and Christianization: 678–754 — 183

Conclusion — 209

Bibliography — 215

Index — 249

Abbreviations

AHR	*American Historical Review*
ASR	*American Sociological Review*
JEH	*Journal of Ecclesiastical History*
JIES	*Journal of Indo-European Studies*
JL	*Jahrbuch für Liturgiewissenschaft*
MGH	*Monumenta Germaniae Historica*
AA	*Auctores Antiquissimi*
Ep. sel.	*Epistolae selectae*
SRM	*Scriptorum rerum Merowingicarum*
SSrG	*Scriptores rerum Germanicarum in usum scholarum*
PL	*Patrologiae cursus completus, series latina.* J.-P. Migne, ed. (Paris, 1844–)
RBPH	*Revue belge de philologie et d'histoire*
SCH	Studies in Church History
Settimane	*Settimane di studio del centro Italiano di studi sull'alto medioevo* (Spoleto: Centro Italiano di Studi sull'Alto Medioevo, 1954–)
———— 7 (1960)	*Le chiesi nei regni dell'Europa occidentale e i loro rapporti con Roma all'800.*
———— 14 (1967)	*La conversione al Cristianesimo nell'Europa dell'alto medioevo.*
———— 36 (1989)	*Santi e demoni nell'alto medioevo occidentale.*
ZKG	*Zeitschrift für Kirchengeschichte*

THE GERMANIZATION OF
EARLY MEDIEVAL
CHRISTIANITY

Introduction

This inquiry applies recent observations from the behavioral sciences, medieval history, the history of religions, and Indo-European studies, as well as from what has become known as "metahistory,"[1] to the pivotal religious transformation which occurred as a result of the encounter of the Germanic peoples with Christianity. This transformation is examined primarily from the entrance of the Visigoths into the Eastern Roman Empire in 376 until the death of St. Boniface in 754. It is proposed that Christianization efforts among the Germanic peoples resulted in a substantial Germanization of Christianity.

This inquiry is divided into two parts. Part I develops a model of religious interaction between folk-religious societies and universal religions. Part II applies this model to the encounter of the Germanic peoples with Christianity.

In order to provide a basic framework for the study of the Germanization process, Part I focuses on the development of a general model of religious transformation for folk-religious societies that encounter universal religious movements offering this-worldly socialization and other-worldly salvation. Prominent in this model is the association of pre-Christian

---

[1] A somewhat similar approach is advanced by Hans Mol, *Identity and the Sacred* (New York: Free Press, 1976), who describes his general, social-scientific theory of religion as "an attempt to integrate anthropological, historical, psychological, and sociological approaches to religion into one conceptual scheme" (p. ix). Herein, "metahistory" or "megahistory" refers to the effort to establish and systematically apply a paradigm to major historical developments. The metahistorical approach has been encouraged by Katherine Fischer Drew in the opening remarks of her presidential address to the 1987 annual meeting of the Medieval Academy of America, published as "Another Look at the Origins of the Middle Ages: A Reassessment of the Role of the Germanic Kingdoms," *Speculum* 62:4 (1987): 803–12: "Megahistory has not had much appeal to medieval historians, especially in recent years. Most of us are rather tightly bound to a limited body of source material, and we have been able to concentrate on topics of limited scope, expecting to become familiar with all the literature on this subject and to produce an answer to our questions or an interpretation of our problems that takes into account all the relevant evidence. In the process I think that many of us have lost sight of the larger world or even just the world of the Western Roman Empire" (p. 803). The dangers of generalization, superficiality, and pedantry in writing metahistory are aptly discussed by Christopher Dawson, "The Problem of Metahistory," *The Dynamics of World History,* ed. John J. Mulloy (New York: Sheed & Ward, 1956), pp. 287–93, who nevertheless concludes that "metahistory is not the enemy of true history but its guide and its friend, provided that it is good metahistory" (p. 293).

Germanic social structure, religiosity, and ideology with that of other folk-religious Indo-European societies. Thus relevant insights from the study of the transformation of Indo-European Greek and Roman religiosity have been incorporated.

With all due concern for the dangers of overgeneralization, the fundamental postulate derived from this model is that the world-view of the Indo-European Greek, Roman, and Germanic religions was essentially folk-centered and "world-accepting," whereas the world-view of the Eastern mystery religions and early Christianity was essentially soteriological and eschatological, hence "world-rejecting." Equally significant, and related to this distinction, is the assertion that the social structure of the Germanic peoples at the time of their encounter with Christianity reflected a high level of group solidarity, while the urban social environment in which early Christianity flourished was one in which alienation and normlessness or anomie prevailed. It is therefore emphasized that a primary appeal of the early Christian Church was its fulfillment of the need for socialization and its promise of otherworldly salvation.

The Greco-Roman Christianization scenario in which a religious community fulfills the socioreligious aspirations of a highly anomic society would be dysfunctional if applied to a predominantly rural, warrior, pastoral-agricultural society with a high level of group solidarity. For Christianity to be accepted by the Germanic peoples, it was necessary that it be perceived as responsive to the heroic, religiopolitical, and magicoreligious orientation of the Germanic world-view. A religion which did not appear to be concerned with fundamental military, agricultural, and personal matters could not hope to gain acceptance among the Germanic peoples, since the pre-Christian Germanic religiosity already provided adequate responses to these matters. An unintended result of implementing a missionary policy which accommodated Germanic concerns was the Germanization of early medieval Christianity. Although this accommodation apparently was originally intended to have been merely a temporary and regional transition to a more thorough doctrinal and ethical acceptance of Christianity, three factors altered this expectation: an underestimation of the vitality of the pre-Christian Germanic world-view; an overestimation of available instructional resources; and the future religious influence of the Ottonian emperors (962–1002), Henry II (1002–1022), and Henry III (1039–1056) on the papacy and the Church in general. In his study of the Germanic influence on early medieval Christianity, Josef A. Jungmann has concluded that "from the 10th century onwards, the cultural heritage which had accumulated in the Carolingian North, streamed in ever increasing volume into Italy and became the cultural standard in Rome itself," and from there, eventually "became normative for all the West."[2]

---

[2] Josef A. Jungmann, "The Defeat of Teutonic Arianism and the Revolution in Religious Culture in the Early Middle Ages," in *Pastoral Liturgy* (New York: Herder and Herder, 1962), p. 19.

Part II of this inquiry applies the model of religious transformation just discussed to the sociohistorical record of the encounter of the various continental Germanic peoples with Christian missionary efforts. The role of Arianism among the Eastern Germanic peoples and Roman Christianity among the Franks, as well as the methodologies of the Iro-Frankish and Anglo-Saxon missionaries, is examined. Evidence of Christianization and Germanization is identified and analyzed throughout. Outlines of individual chapters follow. Part I comprises chapters 1 through 4, while Part II comprises chapters 5 through 7.

Chapter 1 introduces the basic problems related to Christianization efforts. Examples of cultural conflict encountered during contemporary Christianization efforts are provided and discussed. Basic sociological concepts are introduced and the premises of a model of religious transformation are established.

An inquiry into Christianization efforts among the Germanic peoples and the Germanization of Christianity requires a clear sense of the concepts of religious conversion, Christianization, and Germanization, as well as a working definition of Christianity itself. For this reason, chapter 2 provides a semantic evaluation of the concept of religious conversion, and a historiographical overview of the concept of Christianization. This is followed by the establishment of a reference model of Christianity with which the process of Germanization may be compared. Several examples of the Germanization of Christianity are also provided.

Since pre-Christian Germanic religiosity differed fundamentally from early, pre-Constantinian Christianity, and since reliable source materials that might provide insights into Germano-Christian interaction, particularly from the perspective of the Germanic peoples, are lacking, contributions from the fields of the sociology of religion, the history of religions, and Indo-European studies[3] have been sought to elucidate the nature of the religious transformation which occurred. Chapter 3 establishes the sociohistorical and religious *Sitz im Leben* of the Germanic encounter with Christianity within the larger context of the encounter of an Indo-European folk religiosity with a non-Indo-European, universalist, salvation religion. Indo-European religiosity is generally characterized herein as "folk-

---

[3] The current state of Indo-European studies is greatly indebted to Georges Dumézil, who devoted his career to the comparison of the ideological structures of the linguistically-related cultures of India, Persia, Greece, Rome, and Celto-Germanic Europe, and found them to be remarkably similar. An English-language introduction to his work by his foremost American exponent is, C. Scott Littleton, *The New Comparative Mythology: An Anthropological Assessment of the Theories of George Dumézil*, 3rd ed. (Berkeley: University of California Press, 1982). Mircea Eliade, in *A History of Religious Ideas*, vol. 1, trans. Willard R. Trask (Chicago: University of Chicago Press, 1978), incorporated much of Dumézil's Indo-European vision. While Dumézil's focus had originally been on pre-Christian cultures, his observations have been applied to the medieval West by his colleague at the Collège de France, Georges Duby, in *The Three Orders: Feudal Society Imagined*, trans. Arthur Goldhammer, with a foreword by Thomas N. Bisson (Chicago: University of Chicago Press, 1980).

religious" and "world-accepting," while Christianity and its Hellenistic and Judaic antecedents are generally characterized as "world-rejecting" religions of universal salvation. The historical and socioreligious developments in Greek and Roman religion which evolved into the socioreligious environment of early Christianity are examined from the perspective of a "de-Indo-Europeanization" of the traditional world-accepting Greek and Roman Indo-European folk religiosity. This de-Indo-Europeanization is believed to have occurred in response to a decline in group solidarity and a rise in anomie, which in turn are attributed chiefly to urbanization, territorial expansion, prolonged internal conflicts, invasion, and social heterogenization.

Chapter 4 compares the sociopsychological influences on Roman and Germanic society at the times of their respective encounters with Christianity. The prominent appeal of socialization within the early Christian community and its promise of eternal salvation at a time of general Roman social destabilization is established, and is contrasted with the general absence of the need for such socially stabilizing features in Germanic society, owing to its high level of group solidarity. Contemporary medical evidence is introduced to support a relationship between social destabilization and stress, as well as a relationship between socially induced stress and the appeal of religious socialization.

The Germanic influence on early medieval Christianity may be found in the development of a dramatic-representational interpretation of Scripture and liturgy in which the historical drama of the Incarnation, the Passion, and the lives of the saints came to overshadow the soteriological-eschatological essence of early Christianity. Germanic influence also figured strongly in the development of local proprietary churches or *Eigenkirchen,* chivalry, feudalism, the Crusade ideology, and the cult of relics. However, rather than merely document and discuss the results of Germanization, Part II seeks to more fully explicate the underlying process of religious transformation which precipitated and accompanied these developments.

Chapter 5 provides an evaluation of pre-Christian Germanic religiosity from an Indo-European perspective. After examining the social structure, law codes, and epic literature of the Germanic peoples, it is asserted that for Christianity to have been accepted by the Germanic peoples, it had to be reinterpreted in a primarily heroic and magicoreligious fashion that would appeal to military and agricultural concerns. A general perception of Christianity as primarily a cult dedicated to the most powerful god, however, tended to obscure the soteriological, ethical, and communal dimensions of Christianity which had been preeminent in early Christianity. The anomic socioreligious conditions prevalent in the declining Roman Empire are contrasted with the high level of internal group solidarity which existed among the Germanic peoples during their encounter with Christianity between 376 and 754. The maintenance of this intragroup solidarity through lengthy periods of migration appears primarily due to the operation of the *comitatus* institution and to strong interlocking kinship and community bonds, as well as to a religiosity that provided political reinforcement. Chapter 5 concludes with a discussion of the influence of a society's world-view on its religious development and how this influence may have operated in the encounter of the Germanic peoples with Christianity.

Applying the religious, historical, and behavioral insights gleaned from the preceding chapters to the historical record, chapter 6 presents a sociohistorical analysis of the processes of Germanization and Christianization among the continental Germanic peoples from their entrance into the Eastern Roman Empire in 376 until the Irish missions of the seventh century. The role of Arian Christianity in enhancing a sense of identity and solidarity among the Arian Germanic peoples is discussed, as well as the role of the Gallo-Roman episcopacy in the Christianization of the Franks and in the Germanization of Christianity. The status of catechetical instruction among the Germanic peoples is noted. Also, notice is taken of the metaphysical distinctions between Germanic and Christian notions of time.

Chapter 7 continues the sociohistorical analysis begun in chapter 6 through the period of the Anglo-Saxon missions. The origin and development of the Anglo-Saxon missionary methodology is discussed here with an emphasis on the policy of accommodation. Also, the significance of secular political involvement in the Christianization and Germanization processes is evaluated. It appears that the association of Roman Christianity with Frankish political dominion, while providing Anglo-Saxon missionaries with protection, also served to hinder their Christianization efforts among non-Frankish Germanic peoples. In perceiving the centrality of divine power in Germanic religiosity, the missionaries sought to prove that the power of Christ surpassed that of the local deities, as St. Boniface sought to demonstrate when he chopped down an oak tree dedicated to Thor at Geismar in Hesse. Such emphasis on the superior intercessory power of the Christian God in earthly affairs, and particularly military conflicts, appears to have contributed toward a perception of Christianity as a powerful magicoreligious cult, and thus advanced the Germanization of Christianity. Given the substantial inherent disparity between Germanic and Christian world-views, a missionary policy that encouraged the temporary accommodation of Christianity to a heroic, religiopolitical, magico-religious, world-accepting Germanic world-view appears to have been developed as a more effective approach than straightforward preaching or coercion. Although the accommodation of the Germanic world-view was originally intended to have been a temporary measure, the general lack of post-baptismal religious instruction, complemented by the vitality of Germanic religiosity, resulted in the Germanization of Christianity.

I
TOWARD
A MODEL OF RELIGIOUS
TRANSFORMATION

1

Transformations of Christianity

Each historical instance of an attempt to Christianize a society is unique and dependent upon many factors. Yet in most instances, the fundamental human equation is the same: an individual or small group of highly motivated advocates of Christianity seek to transform the beliefs, attitudes, values, and behavior[1] of a target society. Whether the advocates of Christianity are Anglo-Saxon missionaries in eighth-century Frisia or American missionaries in present-day Uganda, the primary long-term problem is usually one of cultural confrontation.[2]

Distinguishing between that which is essential to Christianity and that which may be modified or omitted to advance the process of Christianization, has always been a major problem for the missionary. When Christian essentials are considered to include substantial elements of the proselytizing party's culture, the potential for alienating the target society is high. When Christian essentials are minimalized, and indigenous cultural and religious customs readily incorporated, the likelihood of religious syncretism increases.

Christian missionaries are thus compelled to take a path between the twin opposing dangers of cultural alienation and religious syncretism. They tacitly presume that such a path exists. However, there is another school of thought on the subject of Christianization—one which challenges the universal or "catholic" character of the Church and of Christianity. Philosophically, its origins may be found in the life and writings of the Emperor

[1] The totality of the belief-attitude-value-behavior construct of a society will hereinafter be referred to as its BAVB.

[2] Some of the eighth-century problems are discussed in David Keep, "Cultural Conflicts in the Missions of St. Boniface," in Stuart Mews, ed., *Religion and National Identity,* SCH, no. 18 (Oxford: Basil Blackwell, 1982), pp. 47–57.

Julian (d. 363), and for that reason it may be referred to as "Julianism."[3] Julian believed that each ethnic and national group had its own unique origin, character, and god, and that it was ill-advised to attempt to modify the cultural and religious traditions derived from this organic uniqueness. Although Julian's view has not been frequently articulated throughout history,[4] and is based upon Julian's personal social observations and religious speculation, Julianism anticipates some contemporary concerns regarding the portability of religion.[5]

The Christianization process is significant from sociological, anthropological, and psychological perspectives. Accounts of Christian missionary efforts constitute some of the earliest and best-documented sources of attempted group BAVB modification.[6] Attempts at Christianization are more unusual than instances of acculturation in which an immigrant group assimilates the cultural characteristics of a much larger host group. In the

---

[3] Recent biographies of Julian include Robert Browning, *The Emperor Julian* (Berkeley: University of California Press, 1976), and Constance Head, *The Emperor Julian* (Boston: Twayne, 1976). An important critique of Browning's work is Peter Brown, "The Last Pagan Emperor: Robert Browning's 'The Emperor Julian,' " in Brown, *Society and the Holy in Late Antiquity* (Berkeley: University of California Press, 1982), pp. 83–102. An evaluation of Julian's religious attitudes may be found in Polymia Athanassiadi-Fowden's analysis of the surviving fragments of his *Contra Galilaeos*, in *Julian and Hellenism: An Intellectual Biography* (Oxford: Clarendon Press, 1981), pp. 161–71.

[4] One who did articulate Julian's position was Oswald Spengler, who stated: "Each Culture possesses its own standards, the validity of which begins and ends with it. There is no general morale of humanity. It follows that there is not and cannot be any 'conversion' in the deeper sense" (*The Decline of the West*, trans. Charles Francis Atkinson, vol. 2 [New York: Knopf, 1926], p. 345). Spengler's explanation of what does occur in certain instances of religiocultural interaction may be found in ch. 7 of vol. 1, which is entitled "Historic Pseudomorphoses."

[5] See, for example, John Hick and Paul F. Knitter, ed., *The Myth of Christian Uniqueness: Toward a Pluralistic Theology of Religions* (Maryknoll, N.Y.: Orbis, 1987). A critique of the pluralistic view is presented by Peter C. Phan, "Are There 'Saviors' for Other Peoples? A Discussion of the Problem of the Universal Significance and Uniqueness of Jesus Christ," in idem, ed., *Christianity and the Wider Ecumenism* (New York: Paragon House, 1990), pp. 163–80. Also of interest in this volume is Joseph H. Fichter, "Christianity as a World Minority," pp. 59–72, who hypothesizes that "the status of Christianity declines with the declining status of the Western nations, while simultaneously the non-Christians of the world are growing in prestige. The religious superiority of Christianity was closely allied with the secular superiority of Western civilization. . . . The importance of Christianity has declined with the decreasing power and influence of the Christian nations" (p. 61). Within Europe today there remain challenges to Christianity that seek the restoration of a pre-Christian religiosity. Representative of these challenges are Sigrid Hunke, *Europas eigene Religion: Der Glaube der Ketzer* (Bergisch Gladbach: Gustav Lübbe Verlag, 1983); and Alain de Benoist, *Comment peut-on être païen?* (Paris: Albin Michel, 1981). An American critique of the effects of Europe's Christianization may be found in Lawrence Brown, *The Might of the West* (New York: Joseph J. Binns, 1963). A recent overview of contemporary Western "neopaganism" from a Christian perspective may be found in Thomas Molnar, *The Pagan Temptation* (Grand Rapids, Mich.: Eerdmans, 1987).

[6] The value of these accounts is emphasized by Jon Miller, "Missions, Social Change, and Resistance to Authority: Notes Toward an Understanding of the Relative Autonomy of Religion," *Journal for the Scientific Study of Religion* 32:1 (1993): 29–50.

Christianization process, it is usually a smaller proselytizing group which seeks to transform the religious attitudes, beliefs, and practices, as well as various cultural characteristics, of the host group. The methodologies of the Christian missionaries should therefore be significant to anyone interested in studying the modification of societal BAVB.[7]

Christianization is neither a process of organic evolution within a society nor of cultural assimilation, although each of these functions is usually operative and may influence the success of Christianization efforts. When a fundamentally non-Christian society is targeted for Christianization, the process is usually led by a small cadre of external agents who ultimately seek to transform not only the society's religious attitudes, but also the underlying ethos and world-view[8] of the society. However, the extent of the Christianizing party's intentions is not always apparent to members of the targeted society. Whether such radical change is possible or even desirable merits serious consideration, for the ethos and world-view of a society constitute the essence of its identity.

Yves M.-J. Congar has suggested that religious conversion may involve a number of factors that reach beyond religion itself:

> It entails an ensemble of psychological and moral changes and of intellectual and affective motivations. Factors dependent upon a milieu may also have an influence, especially an inhibitive one, as can be seen in studies of the psychology of European working classes or of conversions in mission countries, in areas subject to Islam, etc. Certain cases, known to the author of this article, would even lead one to ask whether a certain atavism does not sometimes influence conversions from one religious sect

---

[7] Some of the most interesting American research in this area has been done by Milton Rokeach, and Sandra Ball-Rokeach. For an introduction to their BAVB model, and an account of its experimental application to the controversial area of television programming, see Sandra J. Ball-Rokeach, Milton Rokeach, and Joel W. Grube, *The Great American Values Test: Influencing Behavior and Belief Through Television* (New York: Free Press, 1984).

[8] The terms "ethos" and "world-view" are used here in the sense described by Clifford Geertz in "Ethos, World View, and the Analysis of Sacred Symbols," in *The Interpretation of Cultures* (New York: Basic Books, 1973) pp. 126–41. Geertz states: "In recent anthropological discussion the moral (and aesthetic) aspects of a given culture, the evaluative elements, have commonly been summed up in the term 'ethos,' while the cognitive, existential aspects have been designated by the term 'world view.' A people's ethos is the tone, character, and quality of their life, its moral and aesthetic style and mood; it is the underlying attitude toward themselves and their world that life reflects. Their world-view is their picture of the way things in sheer actuality are, their concept of nature, of self, of society. It contains their most comprehensive ideas of order. . . . The tendency to synthesize world view and ethos at some level, if not logically necessary, is at least empirically coercive, if it is not philosophically justified, it is at least pragmatically universal" (pp. 126–27). The background of world-view analysis is discussed in "World Views and National Souls," in W. Warren Wagar, *World Views: A Study in Comparative History* (New York: Holt, Rinehart and Winston, 1977), pp. 1–14, while contemporary American and Indian world-views are compared in Paul G. Hiebert, *Cultural Anthropology*, 2nd ed. (Grand Rapids, Mich.: Baker Book House, 1983), pp. 355–69. See also "The Structure of Worldviews," in Ninian Smart, *Worldviews: Crosscultural Explorations of Human Beliefs* (New York: Scribner's, 1983), pp. 54–61.

to another. By this I mean that a conversion entails a very complex *human reality,* moral, social, historical, and perhaps even genetic, which it is permissible and very interesting to study.[9]

Recent scientific research has affirmed a genetic component to many individual personality traits such as traditionalism, alienation, and aggressiveness.[10] Genetic factors are now claimed to account for approximately 50 percent of the individual differences in religious attitudes, values, and interests.[11] If combined with the notion of group personality or "syntality,"[12] these findings may contribute toward the development of a genetic approach to societal religious identity.[13]

If a society's religious attitudes, values, and interests are indeed shaped by genetic factors, the attempt by missionaries to alter them becomes more than a matter of religious conversion. Walter Burkert, in his study *Homo Necans: The Anthropology of Ancient Greek Sacrificial Ritual and Myth,* has asserted: "Religious ritual is advantageous in the process of selection, if not for the individual, then at least for the continuance of group

[9] "The Idea of Conversion," trans. Alfeo Marzi, *Thought* 33 (1958): 5–20.

[10] This research has been conducted primarily at the Minnesota Center for Twin and Adoption Research at the University of Minnesota. The most recent results are discussed in Thomas J. Bouchard, Jr., et al., "Sources of Human Psychological Differences: The Minnesota Study of Twins Reared Apart," *Science* 250 (12 October 1990): 223–28. A more general background discussion of twin studies and their results may be found in Thomas J. Bouchard, Jr., "Twins Reared Together and Apart: What They Tell Us About Human Diversity," in Sidney W. Fox, ed., *Individuality and Determinism: Chemical and Biological Bases* (New York: Plenum, 1984), pp. 147–84. An introduction to contemporary evolutionary theory is presented in Richard Dawkins, *The Selfish Gene* (New York: Oxford University Press, 1976), who remarks: "Philosophy and the subjects known as 'humanities' are still taught almost as if Darwin had never lived" (p. 1). Of related interest is Carl N. Degler, *In Search of Human Nature: The Decline and Revival of Darwinism in American Social Thought* (New York: Oxford University Press, 1991); and Horst D. Steklis and Alex Walter, "Culture, Biology and Behavior: A Mechanistic Approach," *Human Nature* 2:2 (1991): 137–69.

[11] Niels G. Waller et al., "Genetic and Environmental Influences on Religious Interests, Attitudes, and Values: A Study of Twins Reared Apart and Together," *Psychological Science* 1:2 (1990): 138–42. While warning against biological reductionism, in a communication to *The American Sociologist* 12 (April 1977): 73–75, Gerhard Lenski urges his colleagues to be more cognizant of biological factors: "Sociologists need to be told . . . that our longstanding opposition to efforts to take biological factors into account in the study of human social systems has become an albatross. If we persist in ignoring or, worse yet, denying the powerful influence of genetic and biochemical factors, we jeopardize sociology's credibility in the scientific community." There is no reason to suggest that the sociology of religion should be exempt from Lenski's advice.

[12] The term "syntality" was introduced by psychologist Raymond B. Cattell in "Cultural and Political-economic Psychology," in idem, ed., *Handbook of Multivariate Experimental Psychology* (Chicago: Rand-McNally, 1966), pp. 769–89, to denote the equivalent of "personality" in an organized group. Cattell has recently described the theoretical framework for a religion focused upon evolutionary progress in *Beyondism: Religion from Science* (New York: Praeger, 1987).

[13] Gene-culture coevolution theory is developed in C. J. Lumsden and E. O. Wilson, *Genes, Mind and Culture: The Evolutionary Process* (Cambridge, Mass.: Harvard University Press, 1981).

identity."[14] The long-term sociological and psychological consequences of modifying a society's BAVB construct have not been thoroughly considered and evaluated. However, by studying historical instances of attempted Christianization, particularly those in which pre-Christian religious attitudes and values were substantially opposed to Christian attitudes and values, useful insights into these consequences may be gained.

Such a study was undertaken by Kenneth Scott Latourette, who, together with Christopher Dawson, pioneered the application of sociocultural analysis to the history of Christianity.[15] By focusing on the interaction between Christianity and non-Christian societies in his comprehensive *History of the Expansion of Christianity,*[16] Latourette derived a methodology for the study of the effects of Christianity on non-Christian societies, and the reciprocal effects of non-Christian societies on Christianity. This methodology is best expressed in the form of the seven questions that he poses in the introduction to his work.

> Of course it must be asked: *What was the Christianity which spread?* . . . Each time that it enters a new territory, we must seek to determine the form and the content of that which was now in process of propagation.
>
> A second question must be raised again and again. *Why did Christianity spread?* . . . What motives led its converts to accept it? To what extent were the methods employed responsible for the successes achieved? How far is the spread attributable to purely religious factors and how far must it be assigned to other circumstances? Again, no one answer can be given which holds true for all times, places, and individuals. The conditions which prepared the ground for the rapid increase of Christianity in the Græco-Roman world were many of them quite distinct from those which paved the way for its triumph among the peoples of Northern Europe. . . . Since Christianity itself is not always the same, the qualities within it which account for its ability to win men and women are not uniform. The methods of its agents have shown great variety.
>
> The obverse of this second main question is another: *Why has Christianity suffered reverses and at times met only partial successes?* . . . Why, in the twentieth century, after being continuously present in India and China for a longer time than was required to win the majority of the population of the Roman Empire does Christianity still enroll numerically only a very small proportion of the peoples of either land?
>
> In the fourth place it must be asked: *By what processes did Christianity spread?*
>
> The fifth, then, of the main questions has to do with results: *What effect has Christianity had upon its environment?* . . . How far was the disappearance

---

[14] *Homo Necans: The Anthropology of Ancient Greek Sacrificial Ritual and Myth,* trans. Peter Bing (Berkeley: University of California Press, 1983), p. 26.

[15] For a current overview and evaluation of this approach, see L. Michael White, "Adolf Harnack and the 'Expansion' of Early Christianity: A Reappraisal of Social History," *The Second Century* 5:2 (1985/86): 97–127.

[16] *A History of the Expansion of Christianity,* 7 vols. (New York: Harper, 1937–45).

of slavery and of gladiatorial contests of the Roman Empire due to Christianity? To what extent are the Crusades to be ascribed to the Christian impulse?

The sixth main question, *the effect of the environment on Christianity,* ... is of similar importance and often equally difficult to answer with accuracy. . . . Shall we appraise the famous saying, "The Roman Catholic Church is the ghost of the Roman Empire," as merely a clever phrase, or does it contain an accurate statement of fact? What effect did that Mediterranean world into which Christianity was born have upon the faith in the years in which its ritual, doctrines and organization were taking form? To what extent, if at all, were the mystery religions which were such prominent rivals copied, either consciously or unconsciously, by the victor?

The seventh and final outstanding question is: What bearing do the processes by which Christianity spread have upon the effect of Christianity on its environment, and of the environment upon Christianity? How far may medieval and modern Europe be ascribed to the methods employed in the conversion of its peoples? . . . To what extent may this often superficial and far from thoroughgoing transformation be traced to the processes by which nominal conversion was accomplished?[17]

These seven questions provide an orientation toward the approach of the present inquiry. The most challenging, according to Latourette,[18] is the seventh and last question, the one with which this inquiry is primarily concerned. That is, this inquiry focuses on the process of the Germanization of Christianity as a consequence of Christianization efforts among the Germanic peoples. Some recent examples of Christianization efforts may serve to more vividly illustrate the forces at play in the processes of Christianization and Germanization.

John B. Kauta, a Ugandan priest, was recently pleased to report that "approximately 16,500 people a day are being converted to Christianity in Africa," although he felt that "the presence of Christianity in Africa has 'more or less left the African in a state of confusion.' "[19] Kauta continued: "The African is like a man straddling two worlds, his two feet resting on his heritage and Christianity. . . . What Africa needs now are experts, anthropologists and theologians who know and understand the Africans, people who are truly Christian and understand what is essential to both Christianity and Africa."[20]

Kauta attributes much of the success of the early Christian missionaries to the educational system that they implemented. They taught "the Africans the basics" and "brought with them medicine, schools and Western

[17] Ibid., pp. x–xv passim.

[18] Ibid., p. xv.

[19] Harriet Rosenberg, "An Act of God," *Reporter Dispatch,* White Plains, N.Y., March 21, 1987, sec. A, p. 7.

[20] Ibid.

civilization."[21] However, Kauta "sounds a note of caution"[22] to contemporary Christian missionaries in Africa:

> There has been a failure to integrate Africa's traditional religions in Christianity and Christian values. I don't blame the early missionaries who came to Africa. I might have done the same thing under their circumstances. But not enough attention has been given to etymological, anthropological and ethnological research. That's where the attitude of what some call arrogance comes in. We need to have a dialogue between the traditional African religions and Christianity.[23]

While there are many substantial differences between the religiocultural climate of twentieth-century Africa and early medieval Europe, similarities do exist in the relationship between the missionary and his mission field.[24] In each case social rewards may contribute significantly toward a non-Christian's motivation to become affiliated with Christianity. In the case of Clovis (d. 511), for example, the potential support of the Catholic Gallo-Roman bishops and aristocracy probably contributed to his decision to be baptized.[25] In the case of contemporary African peoples, the association of Christianity with Western medicine, technology, and education often provides such an impetus. Also, until recently, Christian missionaries in Africa often expressed a less than optimal level of sensitivity and empathy toward the indigenous religiosity of the target population. Similarly, missionaries in early medieval Europe often denigrated the indigenous gods, myths, and cultic practices of the Germanic peoples, sometimes characterizing them as satanic. Such an approach may result in the secret continued adherence by an indigenous population to their pre-Christian religiosity. Commenting on this situation, Paul G. Hiebert notes that:

> In the long run, when pagan customs are practiced in secret, they combine with public Christian teachings to form Christopaganism—a syncretistic mix of Christian and non-Christian beliefs. For example, African slaves in Latin American homes taught the children of their masters the worship of African spirits. When the children grew up and joined the Roman Catholic

---

[21] Ibid.

[22] Ibid.

[23] Ibid. See also Vincent Mulago, "Traditional African Religion and Christianity," in Jacob K. Olupona, ed., *African Traditional Religions in Contemporary Society* (New York: Paragon House, 1991), pp. 119–34.

[24] A discussion of such comparisons is presented in Peter Munz, "Early European History and African Anthropology," *New Zealand Journal of History* 10 (1976): 33–48.

[25] Clovis's role in the attempted Christianization of the Germanic peoples will be discussed in greater detail in chapter 6. The relationship between the Franks and the Gallo-Romans is treated in detail in André Joris, "On the Edge of Two Worlds in the Heart of the New Empire: The Romance Regions of Northern Gaul During the Merovingian Period," in William Bowsky, ed., *Studies in Medieval and Renaissance History,* vol. 3 (Lincoln: University of Nebraska Press, 1966), pp. 3–52.

church, they combined the Catholic veneration of saints and the African tribal religion into new forms of spirit worship that had a Christian veneer.[26]

For contemporary Christian missionaries, Hiebert advocates a middle road between cultural rejection and syncretism, which he terms "critical contextualization."[27]

After Christianity has been introduced into a previously non-Christian population, the process of syncretism often occurs.[28] This process appears to accelerate in those scenarios where the initial impetus is essentially social or political, and is not superseded by deeper religious convictions or enhanced by catechetical instruction. The process of syncretism is especially apparent in the emergence of ethnic forms of Christianity such as voodoo in Haiti,[29] Rastifarianism in Jamaica, santeria in the Caribbean countries, and macumba in Brazil. Examples of medieval European Christo-Germanic syncretism may be found in the development of the concepts of the *Eigenkirche*[30] and of chivalry.[31]

It is from a vastly different environment that a second contemporary example of attempted[32] Christianization is drawn. "Barren Ground: Christian Missionaries Sow the Seed in Japan but Find Little Grows," is the title

---

[26] *Anthropological Insights for Missionaries* (Grand Rapids, Mich.: Baker Book House, 1985), pp. 184–85.

[27] Ibid., pp. 186–92.

[28] A thorough discussion of the process and condition of syncretism is presented in the *Encyclopedia of Religion,* s.v. "Syncretism," by Carsten Colpe, trans. Matthew J. O'Connell. The most recent studies of religious syncretism are contained in Richard Gray, *Black Christians and White Missionaries* (New Haven, Conn.: Yale University Press, 1990); and David J. Hess, *Spirits and Scientists: Ideology, Spiritism, and Brazilian Culture* (University Park: Pennsylvania State University Press, 1991), who suggests an approach which "recognizes that all religion is complex or syncretic, a truism that makes it possible to move on to the idea that religious complexity or syncretism must be broadened to include a broader domain of ideology" (p. 179).

[29] Further syncretic development involving Islam and Hinduism occurred in the early nineteenth century on the west coast of Africa after voodoo was brought there by repatriated American slaves. A thoroughly illustrated documentary of this development may be found in Gert Chesi, *Voodoo: Africa's Secret Power,* trans. Ernst Klambauer (Worgl, Austria: Perlinger Verlag, 1980).

[30] An examination of the development and significance of the *Eigenkirche,* or "proprietary church," may be found in Wilhelm Levison, *Aus Rheinischer und Fränkischer Frühzeit* (Düsseldorf: Verlag L. Schwann, 1948), pp. 323ff.; and Ulrich Stutz, "The Proprietary Church as an Element of Medieval Germanic Ecclesiastical Law," in *Medieval Germany (911–1250): Essays by German Historians,* trans. and ed. Geoffrey Barraclough, Studies in Mediaeval History, vol. 2 (Oxford: Basil Blackwell, 1938), pp. 35–70.

[31] For a more extensive discussion of the development of chivalry, see Richard Barber, *The Knight and Chivalry* (New York: Harper & Row, 1982), especially chapters 2 and 13; and Georges Duby, *The Chivalrous Society,* trans. Cynthia Postan (Berkeley: University of California Press, 1980), especially chapters 11 and 15.

[32] The word "attempted" precedes Christianization here and elsewhere, since the question of how, when, and even if Christianization occurs is central to this investigation. To refer to "Christianization" unqualifiedly, especially at this point, would be inappropriate, since standards by which this process may be defined and measured have not yet been discussed.

of a recent front-page *Wall Street Journal* article.[33] Liam O'Doherty, an Augustinian missionary priest, notes that "we have 10 to 15 adult baptisms a year. . . . Over in South Korea, in a similar operation, they have 40 to 60 a month." Despite the presence in Japan of over 5,200 foreign missionaries, "one of the world's largest concentrations . . . less than 1% of the population is Christian, and despite all the missionary work, the percentage is dropping."[34]

Alden E. Matthews, a United Church of Christ missionary in Japan for thirty-three years, concedes that "there is no way that Christianity will ever take root in Japan," and Campion Lally, a Franciscan priest, concludes that "the day of the foreign missionary in Japan is finished."[35] Several reasons have been offered to help explain this situation. One is that "foreign things tend to succeed in Japan only when they have been 'Japanized,' while Christianity comes to Japan undiluted, unbending and strict."[36] Moreover, "a missionary, in competing with Buddhism and Japanese Shintoism, isn't so much up against their religious as their cultural grip on the Japanese."[37] Japanese religions, unlike early Christianity, possess a significant ethnic component which stresses group loyalty over individual accomplishment. This ethnic or "genetic" loyalty is often expressed by maintaining an altar for ancestor veneration. Furthermore, given Japan's current advanced economic status, missionaries working there cannot benefit from an implicit association of Christianity with a more highly developed civilization.

In a discussion of Japanese religious psychology, Brendan Branley, a Maryknoll missionary to Japan, has noted that "essentially, there is a heightened consciousness of their identity as a distinct people, of their membership in a group whose purposes they are willing to serve at the expense of their own."[38] This observation is supported by Robert Bellah's analysis of the relationship between Japanese religion and economic development. Bellah describes the enduring notion of *kokutai*, which arose during the Tokugawa Period (1600–1868) as "a concept of the state in which religious, political and familistic ideas are indissolubly merged."[39] Jesuit missionaries to China in the sixteenth and seventeenth centuries were similarly con-

---

[33] Bernard Wysocki, Jr., "Barren Ground: Christian Missionaries Sow the Seed in Japan but Find Little Grows," *Wall Street Journal,* July 9, 1986, pp. 1, 20.

[34] Ibid.

[35] Ibid.

[36] Ibid.

[37] Ibid.

[38] Brendan R. Branley, *Christianity and the Japanese* (Maryknoll, N.Y.: Maryknoll Publications, 1966), p. 84.

[39] Robert Bellah, *Tokugawa Religion: The Cultural Roots of Modern Japan* (New York: Free Press, 1985), p. 104. Bellah combines the socioeconomic methodology of Talcott Parsons, his mentor, with the socioreligious methodology of Max Weber to establish the contribution of Japanese religion in the Tokugawa Period toward Japanese socioeconomic modernization.

fronted with a high level of organic unity that was expressed through ances-tor and emperor worship.[40]

A strong sense of social unity and collective security also prevailed among the Germanic peoples in the early Middle Ages.[41] Although they may have been less culturally sophisticated than the contemporary Japanese, like them, the Germanic peoples did not have immediate social or spiritual needs which Christianity might fulfill.[42] Also, the homogeneity of early medieval Germanic society, like that of contemporary Japan, did not predispose it to the Christian message.[43] Christianity tends to flourish in heterogeneous societies in which there exist high levels of anomie, or so-cial destabilization. Since the relationship of social structure to ideological structure and religious expression will play a significant role in this inquiry, a brief discussion of fundamental concepts is presented here.

Thomas O'Dea has summarized Emile Durkheim's concept of anomie as

> *that state of social disorganization in which established social and cultural forms break down.* He [Durkheim] spoke of two aspects of this breakdown.

[40] This problem is discussed from a Catholic perspective in George Minaniki, *The Chinese Rites Controversy from Its Beginning to Modern Times* (Chicago: Loyola University Press, 1985); and from an Evangelical perspective by Ralph A. Covell, "The Conflict of the Gospel and Culture in China: W. A. P. Martin's Answer," in Charles H. Kraft and Tom N. Wisley, *Readings in Dynamic Indigeneity* (Pasadena, Calif.: William Carey Library, 1979), pp. 428–38. The Jesuit missionary role in China has been the subject of renewed interest. Numerous scholarly con-ferences commemorated the four-hundredth anniversary of the arrival of the Italian Jesuit Matteo Ricci in China in 1582. A collection of papers delivered at a symposium at Loyola University on this topic has recently been edited by Charles E. Ronan and Bonnie B. C. Oh, and is entitled *East Meets West: The Jesuits in China, 1582–1773* (Chicago: Loyola University Press, 1988).

[41] An important discussion of Germanic familial and collective security is presented in Katherine Fischer Drew, "Another Look at the Origins of the Middle Ages: A Reassessment of the Role of the Germanic Kingdoms," *Speculum* 62:4 (1987): 803–12.

[42] The Christianization methodology that was implemented where existing non-Christian religious forms seemed to fulfill the socioreligious needs of the target society is significant for the study of historical instances of Christianization, as well as for contemporary missiology. An important analysis of such a situation from a historical perspective is that of C. E. Stancliffe, "From Town to Country: The Christianisation of the Touraine, 370–600," in Derek Baker, ed., *The Church in Town and Countryside*, SCH, no. 16 (Oxford: Basil Blackwell, 1979), pp. 43–59, especially pp. 51–59.

[43] The most recent study of Germanic social structure is Alexander Callander Murray, *Germanic Kinship Structure: Studies in Law and Society in Antiquity and the Early Middle Ages*, Studies and Texts, no. 65 (Toronto: Pontifical Institute of Medieval Studies, 1983), which challenges traditional clan and lineage hypotheses and the notion of a unilineal kinship structure, proposing instead a bilateral kindred structure. Bertha S. Phillpotts, *Kindred and Clan in the Middle Ages and After* (Cambridge: Cambridge University Press, 1917), remains important. Germanic ideological structure is studied in Georges Dumézil, *Gods of the Ancient Northmen*, ed. Einar Haugen, intro. C. Scott Littleton and Udo Strutynski (Berkeley: University of California Press, 1973); Paul C. Bauschatz, *The Well and the Tree: World and Time in Early Germanic Culture* (Amherst: University of Massachusetts Press, 1982); and H. R. Ellis David-son, *Myths and Symbols in Pagan Europe* (Syracuse, N.Y.: Syracuse University Press, 1988).

There is loss of *solidarity;* old groups in which individuals find security and response tend to break down. There is also loss of *consensus;* felt agreement (often only semiconscious) upon values and norms which provided direction and meaning for life tend to break down.[44]

Synthesizing Durkheim's concept of anomie with Max Weber's association of salvation religions with underprivileged classes, O'Dea concludes:

People suffering from extreme deprivation and people suffering from anomie (some groups may be experiencing both) display a considerable responsiveness to religions which preach a message of salvation—that is, which present the world as a place of toil and suffering, and offer some means of deliverance from it. Christianity is a religion of this kind. It offers the believer salvation through participation in Christ's victory over evil and death.[45]

The relative success of Christianization in South Korea may be at least somewhat related to a Korean sense of anomie derived from the protracted military and political conflict which has geographically split the nation in half. Internal political dissension, resulting in frequent public demonstrations, and occasional rioting are symptoms of social destabilization. Japan's previous military occupation of Korea, its current economic primacy, and its generally low regard for Korean immigrants are additional

[44] *The Sociology of Religion* (Englewood Cliffs, N.J.: Prentice-Hall, 1966), p. 56. (Emphases appear in the original.) A further introduction to contemporary concepts in the sociology of religion may be found in Peter L. Berger, *The Sacred Canopy: Elements of a Sociological Theory of Religion* (Garden City, N.Y.: Doubleday, 1967); and Charles Y. Glock, *Religion in Sociological Perspective: Essays in the Empirical Study of Religion* (Belmont, Calif.: Wadsworth, 1973). The application of the sociological concept of anomie to medieval studies has been pioneered by Barbara Rosenwein, *Rhinoceros Bound: Cluny in the Tenth Century* (Philadelphia: University of Pennsylvania Press, 1982), especially pp. 101–12. Further discussion of anomie may be found in Robert K. Merton, "Social Structure and Anomie," in *Social Theory and Social Structure* (Glencoe, Ill.: Free Press, 1949); Renato Poblete and Thomas F. O'Dea, "Anomie and the 'Quest for Community': The Formation of Sects Among the Puerto Ricans of New York," *American Catholic Sociological Review* 21 (1960): 18–36; and Melvin Seeman, "Alienation and Anomie," in John P. Robinson, Phillip R. Shaver, and Lawrence S. Wrightsman, *Measures of Personality and Social Psychological Attitudes,* vol. 1 of *Measures of Social Psychological Attitudes* (San Diego, Calif.: Academic Press, 1991). Of related interest are Karl Mannheim, *Ideology and Utopia: An Introduction to the Sociology of Knowledge,* trans. Louis Wirth and Edward Shils (New York: Harcourt, Brace, 1936); and Peter L. Berger and Thomas Luckmann, *The Societal Construction of Reality: A Treatise in the Sociology of Knowledge* (Garden City, N.Y.: Doubleday, 1966).

[45] O'Dea, *Sociology of Religion,* p. 57. See also Max Weber, "Religion of Non-Privileged Classes," in *The Sociology of Religion,* trans. Ephraim Fischoff, intro. Talcott Parsons (Boston: Beacon Press, 1963); and idem, "Major Features of World Religions," in H. H. Gerth and C. Wright Mills, eds., *From Max Weber* (Oxford: Oxford University Press, 1946). Recent critical applications of the work of Durkheim and Weber include W. S. F. Pickering, *Durkheim's Sociology of Religion: Themes and Theories* (London: Routledge & Kegan Paul, 1984); Wolfgang Schluchter, *Rationalism, Religion, and Domination: A Weberian Perspective,* trans. Neil Solomon (Berkeley: University of California Press, 1989); and Eugen Schonfeld, "Privatization and Globalization: A Durkheimian Perspective on Moral and Religious Development," *Archives de sciences sociales des religions* 69 (1990): 27–40.

factors which may have also contributed to a decline in self-esteem, and a concurrent rise in anomie, among Koreans. O'Dea notes that one response to anomie may be a " 'quest for community' and a search for new meaning. From such quests, movements develop that offer new values and new solidarities."[46] Thus Christianity's appeal to some Koreans may be derived from a desire for relief from frustration through membership in a religious, nonbiological community which promises salvation.

Early nineteenth-century Hawaii provides an example of a society in which the expansion of Christianity appears to have benefited from the disruption of indigenous socioreligious customs.[47] In 1819 Chief Kamehameha II deliberately violated taboos, known as *kapus,* which had functioned to reinforce the dominance of the chief, the nobility, and the priesthood. This action appears to have been taken at least partially to decrease the competing influence of the priesthood and to increase the chief's personal authority, as well as to improve his relationships with European traders who provided him with firearms. Although the weapons that Chief Kamehameha II was able to acquire through European trade may have supplanted the immediate function of the *kapus* for maintaining his dominance, the socioreligious and sociopsychological effects of their abandonment appear to have provoked a widespread condition of anomie. This condition seems to have contributed to the subsequent success of Christian missionaries among Hawaiian villagers.

The last contemporary example of attempted Christianization to be described here is that of the Jews for Jesus. In his column in the New York archdiocesan weekly newspaper, *Catholic New York,* George Higgins has accused this group of unfairly employing "aggressive and deceptive proselytizing tactics."[48] His criticism, and that of the Interfaith Conference of Metropolitan Washington, D.C., which he quotes, is based upon a rejection of "proselytizing efforts which delegitimize the faith tradition of the person whose conversion is being sought."[49] Examples of deceptiveness attributed to the Jews for Jesus by Higgins include concealing their sponsorship by fundamentalist Christians, imitating Jewish liturgical forms, and deliberately avoiding "references to central Christian doctrines such as the Trinity and the crucifixion."[50]

---

[46] O'Dea, *Sociology of Religion,* p. 56. The "alternate community" response to anomie is further developed in Robert Nisbet, *The Quest for Community* (Oxford: Oxford University Press, 1953).

[47] A detailed account may be found in William Davenport, "The 'Hawaiian Cultural Revolution': Some Political and Economic Considerations," *American Anthropologist* 71(1969): 1–20. I am indebted to C. Scott Littleton for bringing this example to my attention.

[48] George G. Higgins, "Jews for Jesus Ignore Church Tradition," *Catholic New York,* January 7, 1988, p. 10.

[49] Ibid.

[50] Ibid.

This last example raises the problem of "accommodating" Christianity to the religiocultural traditions of various ethnic and social groups. May real and fundamental differences between Christianity and non-Christian religions be temporarily misrepresented in order to facilitate initiation into Christianity?[51] May the work of catechesis be postponed until some undetermined time in the baptized individual's future when one may be prodded into conformity with Christian beliefs, values, and practices with admonishments like "If you're a Christian, why don't you act like one"? The Jews for Jesus do not appear to have emphasized the distinctive redemptive core of Christianity, namely, that Jesus Christ, by his suffering and death, has redeemed mankind from their sins. Instead they emphasize Jesus' Jewish heritage and those elements of Christianity that are most clearly derived from Judaism, aspects that one would expect potential converts from Judaism to identify with most closely.

Similarly, the Anglo-Saxon missionaries did not emphasize the central soteriological and eschatological aspects of Christianity. Instead, seeking to appeal to the Germanic regard for power, they tended to emphasize the omnipotence of the Christian God and the temporal rewards he would bestow upon those who accepted him through baptism and through conformity to the discipline of his Church.[52] Other medieval advocates of Christianity, such as the authors of the *Heliand*[53] and *The Dream of the*

[51] Citing the research of John Lofland, "Becoming a World-Saver Revisited," in James T. Richardson, ed., *Conversion Careers: In and Out of the New Religions* (Beverly Hills, Calif.: Sage Publications, 1978), pp. 10f., which deals with the conversion methodology of the West Coast branch of the Unification Church, Eugene V. Gallagher, *Expectation and Experience: Explaining Religious Conversion*, vol. 2 of *Ventures in Religion* (Atlanta, Ga.: Scholars Press, 1990), notes that "new missionary tactics enabled the Unificationists to overcome a persistent dilemma: the more they disclosed their distinctive beliefs at the outset, the less potential converts were likely to join" (p. 74). The new tactics involved the initial formation of close interpersonal bonds between the prospective convert and church members. Gallagher observes: "Commitment and belief travel through a web of social relations. Such relations can be firmly established before any full intellectual acceptance of doctrine; in fact, the development of affective bonds will hasten intellectual assent" (p. 77).

[52] Anton Mayer, "Religions- und Kultgeschichtliche Züge in Bonifatianischen Quellen," in *Sankt Bonifatius: Gedenkausgabe zum zwölfhundertsten Todestag* (Fulda: Parzeller, 1954), pp. 308–9. The most famous instance of an appeal to power is, of course, St. Boniface's felling of the Hessian sacred oak at Geismar in 723 or 724. Although no copies of St. Boniface's actual sermons have been discovered, Thomas Leslie Amos, "The Origin and Nature of the Carolingian Sermon" (Ph.D. diss., Michigan State University, 1983), summarizes the Anglo-Saxon approach to missionary preaching: "The Anglo-Saxons concentrated on stressing the power of the Christian divinity and the positive virtues of Christianity. . . . The Anglo-Saxon missionary preachers always accentuated the positive, emphasizing the power of God and Christ to do things for the faithful in this life and to reward them in the next" (p. 109).

[53] Otto Behaghel, ed., *Heliand und Genesis*, 9th ed., rev. Burkhard Taeger (Tübingen: Max Niemeyer Verlag, 1984); and *The Heliand: The Saxon Gospel: A Translation and Commentary*, trans. G. Ronald Murphy (New York: Oxford University Press, 1992). A few relevant passages from the *Heliand* are translated and analyzed in J. Knight Bostock, *A Handbook on Old High German Literature*, 2nd rev. ed., rev. K. C. King and D. R. McLintock (Oxford: Clarendon Press, 1976), pp. 172–75. For a more detailed analysis, see G. Ronald Murphy, *The Saxon*

Rood,[54] apparently sought to appeal to the Germanic ethos and world-view by portraying Christ as a warrior lord.

These contemporary examples and their early medieval analogues illustrate several important and timeless problems associated with attempted Christianization. The African scenario illustrates the problem of large numbers of potential converts in developing nations who may be attracted as much by the extrareligious aspects of the missionary's culture as by his religious instruction. This may be paralleled by a missionary's tendency to ignore or suppress indigenous religious attitudes. Conversely the Brazilian and Caribbean scenarios demonstrate an allegedly "converted" society's tendency toward religious syncretism. The Korean and Hawaiian examples seem to indicate that social destabilization contributes to the expansion of Christianity, whereas the Japanese example depicts the missiological problem of gaining entrée to a stable and cohesive advanced society in which the missionary's culture has minimal appeal. The Jews for Jesus scenario describes a missionary methodology of initial misrepresentation by obscuring inherent differences in order to gain a foothold. This is apparently followed by a gradual exposure to less compatible Christian beliefs and practices.

After considering these examples, one is tempted to sketch a preliminary model of the religious transformation which may occur as a result of proselytization. The most significant factors in determining an appropriate missiological approach and in predicting missionary success appear to be the prevailing world-view of the target society, the degree of popular satisfaction with the indigenous religion, the level of the target society's sociocultural cohesion, and the target society's levels of scientific and economic development compared to those which exist in the society from which the proselytizing party originates. An anomic society with relatively low levels of scientific and economic development, a prevailing soteriological-eschatological world-view, and an indigenous religion that is waning in popularity, would seem to be the ideal candidate for proselytization by representatives of a universal religion. On the contrary, a cohesive, scientifically advanced, economically stable society with a functional folk religiosity would seem to be the least likely candidate for missionary success.

Just as the field of the scientific study of religion abounds with discussions of the psychosocial stimuli and responses involved in individual

---

Savior: The Germanic Transformation of the Gospel in the Ninth-Century Heliand (New York: Oxford University Press, 1989); Jürgen Eichoff and Irmengard Rauch, *Der Heliand* (Darmstadt: Wissenschaftliche Buchgesellschaft, 1973); " 'Germanisierung' und Akkommodationstendenzen der Kirche," in Johannes Ratofer, *Der Heliand: Theologischer Sinn als tektonische Form,* Niederdeutsche Studien, vol. 9 (Cologne: Böhlau Verlag, 1962); and Wolfgang Huber, *Heliand und Matthäusexegese* (Munich: Max Hueber Verlag, 1969).

[54] Bruce Dickins and Alan S. C. Ross, eds., *The Dream of the Rood* (New York: Appleton-Century-Crofts, 1966).

conversion,[55] the fields of pastoral theology and contemporary missiology abound with discussions of missionary goals and appropriate techniques.[56] Elements of each of the contemporary Christianization scenarios described earlier are present in the historical instances of Christianization efforts in northern and central Europe. Yet the knowledge derived from these contemporary examples has not heretofore been applied to these historical instances. The present inquiry seeks in part to contribute to such an application, as Alan Tippett has urged:

> My contention is that we should turn the information we have on the dynamics of contemporary religious movements and the diffusion of Christianity onto the documents of the middle ages, which so often have been interpreted in the light of the heresies or the politics of Græco-Roman Christendom. . . . Our missiological insights on modern people movements should be brought to bear on the experiences of Boniface and Patrick.[57]

---

[55] See, for example, William James, *Varieties of Religious Experience* (1902; reprint, New York: New American Library of World Literature, 1958); J. H. Leuba, *A Psychological Study of Religion* (New York: Macmillan, 1912); Edwin D. Starbuck, *Psychology of Religion* (New York: Scribner's, 1915); Walter Houston Clark, "William James: Contributions to the Psychology of Religious Conversion," *Pastoral Psychology* 26 (1965): 29–36; Ruth Ann Wallace, "Some Social Determinants of Change of Religious Affiliation" (Ph.D. diss., University of California, Berkeley, 1968); Geoffrey E. W. Scobie, *Psychology of Religion* (New York: Wiley, 1975); Andrew R. Davidson and Elizabeth Thomson, "Cross-Cultural Studies of Attitudes and Beliefs," in *Social Psychology,* Harry C. Triandis and Richard W. Brislin, eds., vol. 5 of *Handbook of Cross-Cultural Psychology* (Boston: Allyn and Bacon, 1980); and Michael A. Persinger, *Neuropsychological Bases of God Beliefs* (New York: Praeger, 1987).

[56] See, for example, William A. Smalley, ed., *Readings in Missionary Anthropology* (Tarrytown, N.Y.: Practical Anthropology, 1967); Johannes Verkuyl, *Contemporary Missiology: An Introduction,* trans. and ed. Dale Cooper (Grand Rapids, Mich.: Eerdmans, 1978); V. Bailey Gillespie, *Religious Conversion and Personal Identity: How and Why People Change* (Birmingham: Religious Education Press, 1979); Robert D. Duggan, *Conversion and the Catechumenate* (New York: Paulist Press, 1984); and Walter Conn, *Christian Conversion: A Developmental Interpretation of Autonomy and Surrender* (New York: Paulist Press, 1986).

[57] Alan R. Tippett, "Christopaganism or Indigenous Christianity?" in Kraft and Wisley, *Readings in Dynamic Indigeneity,* p. 420 n. 8.

2

Conversion, Christianization, and Germanization

"Conversion" and "Christianization" are terms which are used frequently, interchangeably, and inconsistently. This contributes to a considerable degree of ambiguity. When the concepts that these terms represent lie at the center of a religious and historical inquiry, it is particularly important to define the context in which they will be used, as well as to understand the context in which they have been used.

At the conclusion of his Pentecostal discourse, St. Peter was asked by some of his audience what they should do. Peter answered, "Repent and be baptized every one of you in the name of Jesus Christ for the forgiveness of your sins."[1] In his defense before Herod Agrippa II, St. Paul claimed that, in obedience to the vision he experienced on his journey to Damascus, he "set about declaring that they [the people of Damascus and Judea] should repent and turn to God, doing works befitting their repentance."[2] In these passages, and throughout the New Testament, the Greek word *metanoia* is characteristically rendered in the Latin of the Vulgate as *poenitentia,* and in English translations as "repentance" or "penance."[3] Indeed, within a scriptural context, "conversion" implicitly seems to mean "conversion from a state of sinfulness." Aloys Dirksen has concluded that the Church in both the West and the East, from A.D. 200 until the Reformation, has consistently taught that *"metanoia is a conversion* from sin

---

[1] Acts 2:38. The New Testament version cited here and subsequently is the Confraternity of Christian Doctrine Revision (Paterson, N.J.: St. Anthony Guild Press, 1941).

[2] Acts 26:20–21.

[3] The most thorough discussion of the association of both conversion and penance with the term *metanoia* is Aloys H. Dirksen, "The New Testament Concept of *Metanoia*" (Ph.D. diss., Catholic University of America, 1932), particularly pp. 60–69, 96–105. Additional theological interpretations of *metanoia* may be found in *Theologisches Wörterbuch zum Neuen Testament,* s.v. "metaneo, metanoia," by J. Behm and E. Würthwein; *Lexikon für Theologie und Kirche,* s.v. "Metanoia," by R. Schnackenburg; and *Sacramentum Mundi,* s.v. "Metanoia," by Karl Rahner.

which implies contrition, confession, amendment and satisfaction."[4] Consequently, from a semantic perspective, the notions of repentance and conversion are intertwined. Yet "etymologically *metanoia* means a *change of mind*,"[5] and it is this meaning which appears to be the basis of most current notions of conversion. In his discussion of "Conversion" in the *Encyclopedia of Religions,* Lewis R. Rambo states that "recently scholars have argued that conversion is a progressive, interactive process that has consequences in the community. Conversion is thus not a single event, but an evolving process in which the totality of life is transformed."[6]

The association of repentance with conversion can be especially confusing in the current context, given the relative absence of a notion of sinfulness in pre-Christian Germanic religion.[7] If one accepts such an association, it might be difficult to provide substantial evidence of repentance, and hence conversion, among the Germanic peoples in the sixth through eighth centuries. This is one reason why the term "conversion," especially when applied generally and unqualifiedly, seems inappropriate for a study of the effects of Christian missionary activity on Germanic society.

The ambiguity surrounding the term "conversion" increases when it is applied to the experience of an entire society. Studies of individual conversion, whether of saints or political leaders, often carefully analyze an individual's actions and writings for indications and contraindications of conversion.[8] The process of an individual's conversion is not usually considered to consist of baptism alone, but rather presumes a fervent desire to move toward higher levels of Christian perfection: "When Origen speaks of the process of being converted, he speaks not only of a mere purification process, or the need for a group of moral choices, or progress in

---

[4] Dirksen, *"Metanoia,"* p. 69.

[5] Ibid., p. 104. This has most recently been restated by Paul Keresztes, "The Phenomenon of Constantine the Great's Conversion," *Augustinianum* 27 (August 1987): 85: "The meaning of Conversion can probably be best described with the somewhat trite and popular word, the Greek *metanoia,* perfectly expressing the idea of turning around, or a change of mind." This entire issue of *Augustinianum* is devoted to the study of conversion.

[6] See also Lewis Rambo, "Current Research on Religious Conversion," *Religious Studies Review* 8 (1982): 146–59; as well as David A. Snow and Richard Machalek, "The Sociology of Conversion," *Annual Review of Sociology* 10 (1984): 167–90.

[7] See, for example, Hans-Joachim Schoeps, *The Religions of Mankind,* trans. Richard and Clara Winston (Garden City, N.Y.: Doubleday, 1966), pp. 114–15; and Walter Baetke, *Die Aufnahme des Christentums durch die Germanen: Ein Beitrag zur Frage der Germanisierung des Christentums,* special ed. (Darmstadt: Wissenschaftliche Buchgesellschaft, 1962), p. 39. This contrast and others between Germanic and Christian religious ideals will be discussed in greater detail in subsequent chapters.

[8] See, for example, Paula Fredriksen, "Paul and Augustine: Conversion Narratives, Orthodox Traditions, and the Retrospective Self," *Journal of Theological Studies* 37:1 (1986): 3–34; Elisabeth Fink-Dendorfer, *Conversio: Motive und Motivierung zur Bekehrung in der Alten Kirche,* Regensburger Studien zur Theologie, no. 33 (Frankfurt am Main: Verlag Peter Lang, 1986); John Moorhead, "Clovis' Motives for Becoming a Catholic Christian," *Journal of Religious History* 13:4 (1985): 329–39; and Keresztes, "The Phenomenon of Constantine the Great's Conversion," pp. 85–100.

the spiritual life. The process of conversion is not simply purgative, ethical or mystical; it is the continuous result of the coincidence of all three dimensions."[9]

Contemporary authors associate a high degree of ideological and behavioral modification with individual conversion. A. J. Krailsheimer states: "Implicit in the idea of conversion is that of forsaking the past unconditionally and accepting in its place a future of which the one certain fact is that it will never allow the previous patterns of life to be the same again."[10] Hugh T. Kerr and John M. Mulder succinctly summarize: "conversion, however it may be described, involves a complete change from one lifestyle to another."[11] Finally, Charles Y. Glock and Rodney Stark have stated that "conversion . . . may well be defined as the process by which a person comes to adopt an all-pervading world view or changes from one such perspective to another."[12]

One does not expect to find the same level of religious motivation or devotion distributed evenly throughout a social group. It may be assumed that case studies of the religious development of exceptional individuals are not usually representative of the religious development of their peers, especially in regard to the aspect of intensity. Accordingly discussions of historical instances of societal conversion cannot effectively apply standards of religious development as encompassing and rigorous as those applied in discussions of individual conversion.[13] Instead, standards of societal conversion often consist of the number and social status of those persons who are baptized, and the degree to which they accept ecclesiastical custom and discipline.

Historical studies of societal conversion are usually less concerned with theological nuances than are studies of individual conversion.[14] Indeed,

---

[9] John Clark Smith, "Conversion in Origen," *Scottish Journal of Theology* 32 (1979): 240.

[10] *Conversion* (London: SCM Press, 1980), p. 1.

[11] Hugh T. Kerr and John M. Mulder, *Conversion: The Christian Experience* (Grand Rapids, Mich.: Eerdmans, 1983), p. ix. Further discussion of the nature of conversion may be found in the *Catholic Encyclopedia*, s.v. "Conversion," by B. Guldner; *New Catholic Encyclopedia*, s.v. "Conversion, I (In the Bible)," by E. R. Callahan, and "Conversion, II (Psychology of)," by C. Williams; *Sacramentum Mundi*, s.v. "Conversion," by Karl Rahner; *Lexikon für Theologie und Kirche*, s.v. "Bekehrung," by B. Thum and W. Keilbach; *Theologische Realenzyklopädie*, s.v. "Bekehrung," by William H. C. Frend and Michael Wolter; *Dictionnaire de spiritualité*, s.v. "Conversion," by Henry Pinard de la Boullaye; and *The New International Dictionary of New Testament Theology*, s.v. "Conversion," by J. Goetzmann.

[12] *Religion and Society in Tension* (Chicago: Rand-McNally, 1965), p. 6.

[13] Theoretically, an investigation of a contemporary instance of societal conversion might be examined in the same degree of detail as individual conversions often are, if an appropriate battery of religious and other personality surveys could be devised and administered to a representative statistical sample of the affected population.

[14] Welcome exceptions are Birgit Sawyer, Peter Sawyer, and Ian Wood, eds., *The Christianization of Scandinavia: Report of a Symposiun held at Kungälv, Sweden, 4–9 August 1985* (Alingås, Sweden: Viktoria Bokförlag, 1987), which was suggested in correspondence from Peter Brown; and James Muldoon, "Medieval Missionary Efforts—Converting the Infidels to

when theological distinctions are applied directly to historical religious developments, difficulties inevitably arise. A case in point is the classic work of Arthur Darby Nock wherein conversion is defined as "the reorientation of the soul of an individual, his deliberate turning from indifference or from one form of piety to another, a turning which implies a consciousness that a great change is involved, that the old was wrong and the new is right."[15] Ramsay MacMullen notes that Nock's view is based on "the fundamental assumption that religious belief does not deserve the name unless it is intense and consuming."[16] Against this view MacMullen offers an example of the level of religious superficiality which may prevail in a society which presumably had been "converted" to Christianity eight hundred years earlier:

> Discoveries [were] made by church workers in regions and in a period where we would assume particularly deep and well-instructed religiosity: Saxony and the neighboring parts of Germany around 1600. Once out of the upper-class circles, however, and even in a time of bitter theological rivalries to concentrate the greatest possible attention on the faith, the vast bulk of the population are found to have been largely or totally ignorant of the simplest matters of doctrine, rarely or never attending church. . . . [T]hey were given over to "soothsayers, cunning women, crystal-gazers, casters of spells, witches, and other practitioners of forbidden arts."[17]

MacMullen's response to Nock's rigorist definition of conversion is to provide his own liberal definition of conversion as "that change of belief by which a person accepted the reality and supreme power of God and determined to obey him."[18] This approach does not, however, immediately

---

What?" Paper presented at the Twenty-sixth International Congress on Medieval Studies, Kalamazoo, Michigan, May 1991. Muldoon discusses the fundamental questions: "Can a whole society usefully be described as becoming converted? Were Constantine, Augustine and Clovis all converted to the same religion? . . . Can it even be said that these individuals possessed roughly similar or related views of the world, the same starting point so to speak in the process of conversion? In the cases of Constantine and Clovis, can it be said that those who followed their lead and accepted baptism were converted in any meaningful sense—and if so, to whom or to what were they converted?" (p. 5). In addition to this paper, I am grateful to James Muldoon for providing copies of "Conversion of the Barbarians in the Old World and the New," presented at the Conference on the History of Christianity, University of Notre Dame, March 1992, and "Religious Conversion on the Frontier in the Old World and the New," presented at the Twenty-seventh International Congress on Medieval Studies, Kalamazoo, Michigan, May 1992.

[15] *Conversion: The Old and the New in Religion from Alexander the Great to Augustine of Hippo* (Oxford: Clarendon Press, 1933), p. 7.

[16] MacMullen, *Christianizing the Roman Empire* (New Haven, Conn.: Yale University Press, 1984), p. 4.

[17] Ibid., p. 5. MacMullen is citing Gerald Strauss, *Luther's House of Learning: Indoctrination of the Young in the German Reformation* (Baltimore, Md.: Johns Hopkins University Press, 1979). An additional source referred to by MacMullen is J. J. C. von Grimmelshausen, *Simplicius Simplicissimus*, trans. G. Schulz-Behrend (Indianapolis, Ind.: Bobbs-Merrill, 1965).

[18] MacMullen, *Christianizing the Roman Empire*, p. 5.

clarify matters. It is clear from MacMullen's example of seventeenth-century German religiosity that he and Nock are discussing conversion in two different contexts. Although the title of Nock's work might lead one to believe that it is a study in early Christian societal conversion, it is primarily a study of individual conversion within various sociohistorical settings. This is particularly evident in Nock's final chapter, which consists of a comparative study of conversion, not of three societies, but of three individuals: Justin, Arnobius, and Augustine. In contrast, MacMullen's work is a study of the progress of Christianity throughout all levels of Roman society.

This divergence of focus illustrates the need for a more precise terminology. Nock's definition of conversion as "the reorientation of the soul of an individual"[19] is complemented by his definition of adhesion as a form of religious modification which requires a less radical break with one's current beliefs and practices. Adhesion was usually derived from intercultural contact and did not lead "to any definite crossing of religious frontiers, in which an old spiritual home was left for a new once and for all," and "did not involve the taking of a new way of life in place of the old."[20] Adhesion is often the result of "changes in belief and worship due to political development or cultural interplay," and not the result of a "difficult decision to make between two views of life which make its every detail different."[21] Thus it may be surmised that MacMullen would include as converts to Christianity some whom Nock would classify as mere adherents.[22]

For the purpose of historical and religious studies that seek to measure "the degree to which specifically Christian teachings and practices shaped the cultural milieu of medieval folk both high and low,"[23] the use of Nock's strict definition of conversion as radical religious reorientation may be beneficial, since it helps to establish a stable reference system. For this reason, Nock's definition of conversion, despite its orientation toward the experience of individuals rather than groups, will be accepted herein. However, it is essential that a term be introduced which spans Nock's notions of adhesion and conversion and connotes a sense of progression from "non-Christianity" through adhesion to conversion and does not necessarily imply radical religious reorientation.

Such a term would overcome the inherent semantic limitations of the term "conversion" when it is applied societally. It would also convey the complexity of the interactive process which ensues when a non-Christian

---

[19] Nock, *Conversion,* p. 7.

[20] Ibid., pp. 6–7.

[21] Ibid., p. 5.

[22] The views of Nock and MacMullen are discussed further in "Understanding Conversion in Late Antiquity," in Eugene V. Gallagher, *Expectation and Experience: Explaining Religious Conversion,* vol. 2 of *Ventures in Religion* (Atlanta, Ga.: Scholars Press, 1990).

[23] John Van Engen, "The Christian Middle Ages as an Historiographical Problem," *AHR* 91 (1986): 537.

society and Christianity encounter each other. A suitable term for this process is "Christianization."[24] The concept of Christianization suggests a societal process that optimally could be studied and measured in a more rigorous manner, somewhat like that in which a psychologist or theologian may study the religious belief and behavior of an individual who claims to have undergone a personal religious conversion. The study of a historical instance of attempted societal Christianization may be aided by the application of concepts from the sociology of religion to the transformation of the beliefs, attitudes, values, and behavior (BAVB) of the society. As Christopher Dawson has noted, to understand the religion of "periods like the Middle Ages, when religion and civilization were so closely united . . . it is not enough to study it theologically in its essential dogmas and religious principles; it is also necessary to study it sociologically with reference to the changing complex of social traditions and cultural institutions into which it became incorporated."[25]

Although carefully researched studies of the process of religious conversion in individuals are not uncommon,[26] similar studies of societal conversion are less common, and usually concentrate on contemporary missionary efforts by Christians[27] and proselytizers of the various "new religions,"[28] rather than on historical instances of attempted Christianization. The primary socioreligious treatments of historical instances of Christianization appear to be Richard E. Sullivan's studies of early medieval missionary activity,[29] Peter Brown's article "Aspects of the Christianisation

[24] Comparing the papers presented at the 1966 and 1980 Spoleto conferences on the early Middle Ages, John Van Engen, "The Christian Middle Ages," has observed an increasing reluctance to accept the finality implied in the terms "conversion" and "Christianization." He notes that "the official christening of a king or people hardly produced deep faith or organized practice overnight; in anthropological terms, it did not in itself transform a customary culture" (p. 542).

[25] "The Sociological Foundations of Medieval Christendom," in Christopher Dawson, ed., *Medieval Essays* (New York: Sheed & Ward, 1954), pp. 54–55. Other relevant works by Dawson include *Religion and Culture* (New York: Sheed & Ward, 1948), *The Making of Europe: An Introduction to the History of European Unity* (1932; reprint, New York: World, 1952), and *Religion and the Rise of Western Culture* (1950; reprint, Garden City, N.Y.: Doubleday, 1958).

[26] Contemporary studies include Robert D. Duggan, *Conversion and the Catechumenate* (New York: Paulist Press, 1984), and Joseph F. Byrnes, *The Psychology of Religion* (New York: Free Press, 1986).

[27] For examples of such studies, see W. Harold Fuller, *Mission Church Dynamics: How to Change Bicultural Tensions into Dynamic Missionary Outreach* (Pasadena, Calif.: William Carey Library, 1940); and Charles H. Kraft and Tom N. Wisley, ed., *Readings in Dynamic Indigeneity* (Pasadena, Calif.: William Carey Library, 1979).

[28] See especially the extensive treatment presented in four articles under the entry "New Religions" in the *Encyclopedia of Religions*. Also of interest are Jacob Needleman, *The New Religions* (Garden City, N.Y.: Doubleday, 1970); Charles Y. Glock and Robert N. Bellah, eds., *The New Religious Consciousness* (Berkeley: University of California Press, 1976); and Irving Hexman and Karla Poewe, *Understanding Cults and New Religions* (Grand Rapids, Mich.: Eerdmans, 1986).

[29] "The Carolingian Mission and the Pagan," *Speculum* 28 (1953): 705–40; "Early Medieval Missionary Activity: A Comparative Study of Eastern and Western Methods," *Church History*

of the Roman Aristocracy,"[30] Henry Mayr-Harting's study of the coming of Christianity to Anglo-Saxon England,[31] C. E. Stancliffe's analysis of the Christianization of the Touraine region,[32] Ramsay MacMullen's recent work *Christianizing the Roman Empire,*[33] to which reference has been made above, Peter Munz's study of early European history and African anthropology,[34] Hans-Dietrich Kahl's phenomenological assessment of early medieval Christianization efforts,[35] and the recently published report of a 1985 symposium on the Christianization of Scandinavia.[36] As the current inquiry was being completed, three books and two articles appeared which are noteworthy for their incorporation of a socioreligious approach to religious transformation. The books are by Robert A. Markus,[37] Ronald Hutton,[38] and Valerie I. J. Flint.[39] The articles appear as chapters in the *Oxford Illustrated History of Christianity.*[40] They are by Robert A. Markus[41] and Henry Mayr-Harting.[42] Finally, notice should be taken of the recent publication of a paper presented by Robert A. Markus.[43]

---

23 (1954): 17–35; "Carolingian Missionary Theories," *Catholic Historical Review* 42 (1956/57): 273–95; "The Papacy and Missionary Activity in the Early Middle Ages," *Mediaeval Studies* 17 (1955): 46–106; and, of special interest for its systematic approach, "Khan Boris and the Conversion of Bulgaria: A Case Study of the Impact of Christianity on a Barbarian Society," in *Studies in Medieval and Renaissance History,* vol. 3, William Bowsky, ed. (Lincoln: University of Nebraska Press, 1966). Of related interest is Sullivan's recent historiographical analysis: "The Carolingian Age: Reflections on Its Place in the History of the Middle Ages," *Speculum* 64 (1989): 267–306.

[30] *Journal of Religious Studies* 51 (1961): 1–11.

[31] *The Coming of Christianity to Anglo-Saxon England,* 3rd ed. (University Park: Pennsylvania State University Press, 1991).

[32] "From Town to Country: The Christianisation of the Touraine, 370–600," in Derek Baker, ed., *The Church in Town and Countryside,* SCH, no. 16 (Oxford: Blackwell, 1979), pp. 43–59.

[33] Of related interest is his study *Paganism in the Roman Empire* (New Haven, Conn.: Yale University Press, 1981).

[34] "Early European History and African Anthropology," *New Zealand Journal of History* 10 (1976): 37–50.

[35] "Die ersten Jahrhunderte des missionsgeschichtlichen Mittelalters: Bausteine für eine Phänomenologie bis ca. 1050," in Knut Schäferdiek, ed., *Die Kirche des früheren Mittelalters,* first half of vol. 2 of *Kirchengeschichte als Missionsgeschichte* (Munich: Chr. Kaiser Verlag, 1978), pp. 11–76; and "Bausteine zur Grundlegung einer missionsgeschichtlichen Phänomenologie des Hochmittelalters," in *Miscellanea Historiae Ecclesiasticae,* vol. 1 (Louvain: Publications Universitaires de Louvain, 1961), 50–90.

[36] Sawyer, Sawyer, and Wood, eds., *The Christianization of Scandinavia.*

[37] *The End of Ancient Christianity* (Cambridge: Cambridge University Press, 1990). I am indebted to Edward Peters for bringing this work to my attention.

[38] *The Pagan Religions of the Ancient British Isles: Their Nature and Legacy* (Oxford: Basil Blackwell, 1991).

[39] *The Rise of Magic in Early Medieval Europe* (Princeton, N.J.: Princeton University Press, 1991).

[40] John McManners, ed., *Oxford Illustrated History of Christianity* (Oxford: Oxford University Press), 1990.

[41] "From Rome to the Barbarian Kingdoms (330–700)," ibid., pp. 62–91.

[42] "The West: The Age of Conversion (700–1050)," ibid., pp. 92–121.

[43] "From Caesarius to Boniface: Christianity and Paganism in Gaul," in Jacques Fontaine

MacMullen's *Christianizing the Roman Empire* constitutes the first systematic book-length historical study of an instance of Christianization, and is thus valuable in the current development of a model of religious transformation. His penetrating analysis of the sociocultural forces at work is in many ways reminiscent of Latourette's *History of the Expansion of Christianity.*[44] MacMullen's chapter titles include: I. Problems of Approach, II. What Pagans Believed, III. Christianity as Presented, VI. Nonreligious Factors in Conversion, IX. How Complete Was Conversion? and X. Conversion by Coercion.[45] The present inquiry will seek to address these key topics as they apply to the Christianizing of the Germanic peoples and the Germanization of Christianity.

Before proceeding further, it may be beneficial to devise working definitions of Christianity and Christianization for the purpose of this inquiry. A popular perception of the attempted Christianization of the Germanic peoples includes the baptism of Clovis, the missionary efforts of the Irish monks, the mission of St. Boniface, and the coerced baptism of the Saxons by Charlemagne, after which the Germanic peoples are considered "converted to Christianity." Studies of medieval Christianity generally concede that the initial results of Christianization efforts were largely superficial, and that many pagan practices and attitudes remained for centuries, but such studies seldom analyze the sociohistorical and sociopsychological aspects of the process of religious transformation which occurred as a result of the encounter of the Germanic peoples with Christianity. It is hoped that the model of religious transformation developed here in Part I will provide a structural reference that will assist in interpreting the historical record in Part II.

Regarding the conversion of Clovis, Patrick J. Geary has recently remarked: "From what Clovis was converted is not certain. . . . To what he was converted is equally problematic."[46] Many attempts have been made throughout history to distill the "essence of Christianity."[47] Christianity

---

and J. N. Hillgarth, eds., *The Seventh Century: Change and Continuity* (London: Warburg Institute, University of London, 1992), pp. 154–172. Appreciation is extended to Robert A. Markus for providing a pre-publication copy of this paper which was presented at the Warburg Institute in 1988.

[44] See above, pp. 15–16, 15 n. 16.

[45] MacMullen, *Christianizing the Roman Empire*, p. v. Related articles by MacMullen include "Conversion: A Historian's View," *The Second Century* 5:2 (1985/86): 67–81; "Two Types of Religious Conversion to Early Christianity," *Vigiliae Christianae* 37(1983): 17–92; and " 'What Difference Did Christianity Make?' " *Historia* 35 (1986): 322–43. A critique of MacMullen's approach with methodological considerations for the study of Christian religious transformation may be found in the first chapter of Markus, *The End of Ancient Christianity*. Additional critiques published in *The Second Century* 5:2 (1985/86) are William S. Babcock, "MacMullen on Conversion: A Response," pp. 82–89; and Mark D. Jordan, "Philosophic 'Conversion' and Christian Conversion: A Gloss on Professor MacMullen," pp. 90–96.

[46] *Before France and Germany: The Creation and Transformation of the Merovingian World* (New York: Oxford University Press, 1988), pp. 84–85.

[47] The most famous such effort was that of Adolf Harnack, entitled *Das Wesen des*

may be defined according to a rigorist, historicist paradigm in which the religiosity of a particular era, individual, or council is considered to epitomize "true Christianity." One form of the historicist approach is the "oldest is best" assertion: the older a belief or custom may be shown to be, the greater is its proximity to an immutable core or essence of Christian dogma or tradition. As time goes on and societies deviate from this exemplary instance of Christianity, reforms are regularly required to restore conformity with an ancient ideal.

An objection to this approach from within the context of the history of ideas has been made by Jeffrey Burton Russell:

> I propose that a concept is *not* best understood in light of its origins, but rather in light of the direction in which the tradition is moving. To take Christianity as a notorious example: I do not believe that the truth of Christianity will best be elucidated by a search for its *origins,* but rather by an observation of its development in tradition. This approach is a reversal of the assumption that has dominated Christian and much other religious scholarship for a very long time, an assumption characterized by the genetic fallacy: that the true meaning of a word—or of an idea—lies in its pristine state.[48]

Such a position may be considered a relativist one. Even less stable may be a subjectivist definition of Christianity based upon the self-identification of individuals or a society as "Christian."

A generally relativist approach to the problem of the differentiation of Christian belief and practice has been advanced by William A. Clebsch, who asserts that "changing cultures and differing aspirations produced a variety of Christianities, evinced in various manifestations of Christ, over the centuries of European History."[49] In a manner which recalls Latourette's fifth and sixth main concerns, which are, "what effect has Christianity had upon its environment" and "the effect of the environment on Christianity,"[50] Clebsch claims that "the task . . . is to make sense of the mutually dependent relation between the Christian religion and European culture by illustrating how the culture has been religiously shaped and how the religion, including its deity and savior, has been culturally conditioned."[51]

Christentums, translated as *What is Christianity?* intro. by Rudolf Bultmann, trans. and ed. T. B. Saunders (1902; reprint, New York: Harper, 1957). A discussion of the validity of the notion of an ideological core within Christianity is presented in Stephen Sykes, *The Identity of Christianity: Theologians and the Essence of Christianity from Schleiermacher to Barth* (Philadelphia: Fortress Press, 1984).

[48] *The Devil: Perceptions of Evil from Antiquity to Primitive Christianity* (Ithaca, N.Y.: Cornell University Press, 1977), pp. 49–50.

[49] William A. Clebsch, *Christianity in European History* (New York: Oxford University Press, 1978), pp. v–vi. Clebsch, long a student of Church history, has "over the last two decades . . . tried to rethink and relearn this field in the interest of religious history rather than church history" (ibid. p. viii). His first chapter, "Introduction: History and European Christianity," is devoted to distinguishing between the two areas.

[50] See above, pp. 15–16.

[51] Clebsch, *Christianity in European History,* p. 6.

While Clebsch's view of Christianity is appealing, a particular problem with relativist perceptions is that their instability further complicates comparisons between Germanic and Christian socioreligious BAVB constructs. If the essence of Christianity is always in a state of flux, how can any particular form of belief or observance be deemed "non-Christian"? This absence of well-defined religious standards inevitably leads to imprecision and confusion, particularly since the characterization of any aspect of a religious development as "non-Christian" is usually interpreted as a negative value judgment and therefore only made reluctantly.

How, then, are the boundaries to be drawn in order to distinguish among those attitudes, beliefs, and practices which appear to be traditionally Christian, those which appear to be "borderline" Christian, and those which appear not to be Christian at all? It must be acknowledged beforehand that any definition of Christianity may be criticized as artificially static or exclusive. Even so, for the purpose of this inquiry an objectivist definition of Christianity and Christianization will be adopted, only because a well-defined standard permits more reliable measurement and comparative analysis of various aspects of religious development. This approach may eventually lead to conclusions similar to those asserted by Clebsch above. However, instead of proceeding from the assumption that "changing cultures and differing aspirations produced a variety of Christianities," it is sought here to evaluate the religiocultural interaction between the Germanic peoples and Christianity from within the larger context of the interaction between Indo-European societies and universal religious movements. After comparing the religious, cultural, and behavioral aspects of the early Christian and Germanic expressions of Christianity, the magnitude and the nature of the disparity between them may be evaluated. Then it may be possible to determine with some accuracy the extent of reciprocal acculturation between Germanic religiosity and Christianity, and the path this acculturation followed.

For the purpose of this comparison it is helpful to isolate the most distinctive and essential characteristic of Christianity that predominated prior to Constantine and Licinius's Edict of Milan, which officially legitimated Christianity in 313. Nearly all world religions share certain fundamental characteristics. Individuals and groups generally seek to guarantee their basic requirements for survival. A fruitful harvest and physical security are often foremost among the favors sought from supernatural entities. It is not in the realm of supplication for survival, then, that the unique characteristics of Christianity are to be located. Rather, it is in the belief in individual redemption through the suffering and death of Jesus Christ.[52]

---

[52] That this soteriological focus of Christianity was prevalent in the Apostolic Church, and paramount in the New Testament, is argued by Arland J. Hultgren, *Christ and His Benefits: Christology and Redemption in the New Testament* (Philadelphia: Fortress, 1987).

Therefore, whenever the notion of Christianization is discussed, a thorough effort should be made to determine the extent to which the distinctive soteriological-eschatological core of Christianity is consciously accepted. If Christianization efforts in a folk-religious society do not result in a substantial and discernible reorientation of the world-view of that society toward a Christian soteriological-eschatological world-view, then Christianization cannot be said to have occurred. In addition, it is helpful to evaluate a society's degree of conformity in each of the following areas: the reception of baptism and other sacraments, doctrinal assent, ethical conformity, liturgical usage, and ecclesiastical discipline. The extent to which the epic literature of a society reflects Christian ethical ideals is another measure of the degree to which that society has been Christianized. The notion that baptism alone may be equated with conversion or Christianization is not considered acceptable from the perspective of this inquiry.[53]

The most significant conceptual discussion of medieval Christianization is contained in a recent article by John Van Engen.[54] In it, he discusses the current debate among historians as to whether or not "medieval culture was essentially 'Christian' or 'Catholic.' "[55] As Van Engen notes, some historians now claim that, outside of a minuscule clerical elite, "the great mass of medieval folk lived in a 'folklore' culture best likened to that observed by anthropologists in Third World countries."[56]

Van Engen attributes the origin of this debate to "the emergence of medieval religious life as a field of historical inquiry fully as legitimate as medieval politics, warfare, and economics."[57] He traces this development from Herbert Grundmann's focus on popular medieval religious movements[58] and Etienne Delaruelle's focus on popular piety,[59] through Jean Leclercq's work in bringing monastic piety into the mainstream of secular

---

[53] Gabriel Le Bras, "The Sociology of the Church in the Early Middle Ages," in Sylvia Thrupp, ed., *Early Medieval Society* (New York: Appleton-Century-Crofts, 1967), has stated: "We meet peculiar difficulties in the problem of conversion. It is impossible to tell how many of those who were baptized became Christians" (p. 52).

[54] John Van Engen, "The Christian Middle Ages," 519–52.

[55] Ibid., p. 522.

[56] Ibid., p. 519. For an overview of works by supporters of this general view, see Thomas Tentler, "Seventeen Authors in Search of Two Religious Cultures," *Catholic Historical Review*, 71 (1985): 248–57.

[57] Van Engen, "The Christian Middle Ages," p. 522.

[58] Ibid., p. 523. Herbert Grundmann, *Religiöse Bewegungen im Mittelalter*, 3rd ed. (Hildesheim: Georg Olm Verlagsbuchhandlung, 1961), is considered by Van Engen to have become "the foundation for the study of medieval religious life" (ibid.). Other related works by Grundmann are *Ketzergeschichte des Mittelalters*, 2nd ed. (Göttingen: Vandenhoeck & Ruprecht, 1967), and "Neue Beiträge zur Geschichte der religiösen Bewegungen," *Archiv für Kulturgeschichte* 37 (1955): 129–82.

[59] Van Engen, "The Christian Middle Ages," p. 524. Several of his recent articles are reprinted in Etienne Delaruelle, *La piété au moyen âge* (Turin: Bottega d'Erasmo, 1975).

historical research[60] and Gabriel Le Bras's sociology of religion.[61] From the work of these historians, each of whom possessed some degree of personal interest in medieval Christianity, emerged a new school which "approached medieval life as historical anthropologists investigating a native culture subjected to the propaganda of Christian missionaries."[62] The leading exponents of this school, according to Van Engen, are Jacques Le Goff and Jean-Claude Schmitt, both of whom "have now set out to draw far more systematically on structural analysis as a way of getting at a submerged popular culture in which religion—that is, a religion common to Indo-European peoples—played a cohesive force."[63]

Van Engen seeks to temper Le Goff's view of a Christian clerical elite religious culture which coexisted with a predominantly Indo-European popular religious culture, and argues for an ongoing synthesis, a slow "transition from one customary religious culture to another," concluding when "at some undeterminable point most people in Europe came to consider themselves 'Christian.' "[64] The self-perception of a majority of Europeans that they were Christian is not, however, equivalent to a more objective test of their beliefs, attitudes, values, religious practices, ethics, and behavior. Van Engen notes elsewhere that Jean Delumeau, Keith Thomas, Carlo Ginzburg, Gerald Strauss, and several others have argued "that medieval folk were at best only superficially Christianized," and that "Christian faith and practice first took hold among the European masses during the Reformation and Counter Reformation movements."[65]

In his rejection of a religious dichotomy between early medieval clerical and popular elements, Van Engen notes that "influence cut both ways . . . . [w]ritten clerical culture, however, also absorbed a great deal from popular religious culture, as demonstrated plainly and most obviously in the

[60] Van Engen, "The Christian Middle Ages," p. 525. See Jean Leclercq, *The Love of Learning and Desire for God: A Study of Monastic Culture,* trans. C. Misrashi, 2nd ed. (New York: Fordham University Press, 1974), and *Monks and Love in Twelfth-Century France: Psycho-Historical Essays* (Oxford: Clarendon Press, 1979).

[61] Van Engen, "The Christian Middle Ages," p. 525. For an introduction to his approach, see Gabriel Le Bras, "The Sociology of the Church in the Early Middle Ages," in Thrupp, ed., *Early Medieval Society,* pp. 47–57; or Henri Desroche, "Areas and Methods of a Sociology of Religion: The Work of G. Le Bras," *Journal of Religion* 35 (1955): 34–47.

[62] Van Engen, "The Christian Middle Ages," p. 528.

[63] Ibid., p. 529. Recent representative works of these authors are Jacques Le Goff, *Time, Work and Culture in the Middle Ages,* trans., Arthur Goldhammer (Chicago: University of Chicago Press, 1980), and Jean-Claude Schmitt, *The Holy Greyhound: Guinefort, Healer of Children Since the Thirteenth Century* (Cambridge: Cambridge University Press, 1983). Of particular relevance to the present study are two articles contained in Le Goff's work: "Labor, Techniques, and Craftsmen in the Value Systems of the Early Middle Ages (Fifth to Tenth Centuries)," pp. 71–86; and "Clerical Culture and Folklore Traditions in Merovingian Civilization," pp. 153–58.

[64] Van Engen, "The Christian Middle Ages," p. 550.

[65] Ibid., p. 521. The general approach leading to this view and Markus's critique of it may be found in *The End of Ancient Christianity,* pp. 10–13.

various reform movements."[66] One need not, however, wait until the various reform movements of the twelfth century to discover the influence of popular religious culture on written culture. Its beginnings were coincidental with the first attempts to Christianize the Celtic and Germanic peoples of northern and central Europe, and is evident in the epic literary, dramatic, and liturgical developments of the early Middle Ages, that is, the seventh through tenth centuries. Indeed, occurring simultaneously with the Christianization efforts of the missionaries was the less obvious process of the Germanization of Western Christianity.[67]

This Germanization process is often overlooked.[68] Studies of the interaction between Christian and Germanic religion and culture customarily focus upon the Christianization process as the active force and Germanic paganism as a passive or reactionary phenomenon. This is understandable, since there is no evidence of a major drive by non-Christian Germanic peoples comparable to that of the Emperor Julian to restore or advance pre-Christian Roman religion. Yet there did exist a subtle but pervasive Germanizing force which resulted primarily from a missionary policy of accommodation and gradualism, instead of a policy requiring preliminary doctrinal and ethical inculcation.

This observation is not intended to detract from the overall effectiveness of the Church's missionary policy. In fact, it is quite possible that if doctrinal assent and ethical modification had constituted a prerequisite for baptism, those Celtic and Germanic leaders whose own baptism often

---

[66] Van Engen, "The Christian Middle Ages," p. 550.

[67] The expression "the Germanization of Christianity" was popularized by Arthur Bonus in *Von Stöcker zu Naumann: Ein Wort zur Germanisierung des Christentums* (Heilbronn: Eugen Salzer, 1896), and in *Zur Germanisierung des Christentums* (Jena: Eugen Diederichs, 1911). Although Bonus coined the expression in the context of the then emergent "Deutsche Christen" movement, which sought to eliminate un-Germanic elements from Christianity, Heinrich Böhmer, "Das germanische Christentum," *Theologische Studien und Kritiken* 86 (1913): 165–280, responded by reformulating the notion of the "Germanization of Christianity" as a subject meriting historical inquiry. Particularly significant is Kurt Dietrich Schmidt, "Die Germanisierung des Christentums im frühen Mittelalter," in idem, *Germanischer Glaube und Christentum* (Göttingen: Vandenhoeck & Ruprecht, 1948). Additional background is contained in *Die Religion in Geschichte und Gegenwart*, 3rd ed., s.v. "Germanisierung des Christentums," by Kurt Dietrich Schmidt, and *Theologische Realenzyklopädie*, s.v. "Germanisierung des Christentums," by Knut Schäferdiek.

[68] One who has not overlooked the significance of the process of Germanization is Erwin Iserloh, who has stated: "Für den Kirchenhistoriker . . . erhebt sich die Frage, ob das Christentum in seinem vollen Wesensbestand von den germanischen Völkern angenommen wurde oder ob die Germanen auf Grund ihrer Art und gemäß ihrer damaligen Reife nur bestimmte Seiten der christlichen Lehre und des christlichen Lebens zu realisieren vermochten und dadurch andere wesentliche Elemente zunächst nicht oder künftig überhaupt nicht mehr in Erscheinung traten. Brennender als die Frage nach der Christianisierung der Germanen ist also für den Kirchenhistoriker die nach der Germanisierung des Christentums" ("Die Kontinuität des Christentums beim Übergang von der Antike zum Mittelalter im Lichte der Glaubensverkündigung des heiligen Bonifatius," in Klaus Wittstadt, ed., *Verwirklichung des Christlichen im Wandel der Geschichte* [Würzburg: Echter Verlag, 1975], p. 12).

precipitated that of many of their kinfolk might well have rejected Christianity outright owing to its obvious ideological opposition to their Indo-European warrior code. Thus the Christianization policies of accommodation and gradualism[69] were effective in incorporating the Germanic peoples into the Roman Catholic Church, but at the same time they led to a substantial Germanization of Western Christianity.

The early medieval Germanization of Christianity, in most cases, then, was not the result of organized Germanic resistance to Christianity, or of an attempt by the Germanic peoples to transform Christianity into an acceptable form. Rather, it was primarily a consequence of the deliberate inculturation of Germanic religiocultural attitudes within Christianity by Christian missionaries. This process of accommodation resulted in the essential transformation of Christianity from a universal salvation religion to a Germanic, and eventually European, folk religion. The sociopsychological response of the Germanic peoples to this inculturated form of Christianity included the acceptance of those traditionally Christian elements which coincided with Germanic religiosity and the resolution of dissonant elements by reinterpreting them in accordance with the Germanic ethos and world-view. The profundity of the resulting transformation of Christianity is attested to by Josef A. Jungmann, who notes: "we may safely assert that in all the two thousand years of the Church's history, no period has ever seen a greater revolution in religious thought and institutions than that which took place in the first five centuries between the close of the patristic age and the dawn of scholasticism [600–1100]."[70]

The general imperceptibility of this transformation may be due to two reasons. The first is that theologians and church historians are accustomed to locating developments in Christianity in such matters as doctrinal debates, heterodox formulations, Church-State controversies, spiritual treatises, the founding of religious orders, and conciliar pronouncements. However, the order of magnitude of the development being considered here is far greater than any of these. For example, the Germanic peoples did not bother to object to individual dogmas, because dogmatic orthodoxy was not central to their notion of religion. The second reason that the Germanization of Christianity is seldom acknowledged may be that now, when syncretic developments are usually associated with "developing nations," there may exist at least a sub-conscious reluctance by Western Christians to accept the notion that their mainstream religious tradition is itself the result of a syncretic development which eventually became normative.

---

[69] A more detailed discussion of the development of these policies will be presented in chapter 7.

[70] "The Defeat of Teutonic Arianism and the Revolution in Religious Culture in the Early Middle Ages," in *Pastoral Liturgy* (New York: Herder and Herder, 1962), p. 1; originally published as "Die Abwehr des germanischen Arianismus und der Umbruch der religiösen Kultur im frühen Mittelalter," *Zeitschrift für katholische Theologie* 69 (1947): 36–99.

However, such reluctance among Christians may be somewhat ironic, since, were it not for its Germanization, Christianity might never have spread throughout Northern and Central Europe.

One of the most obvious examples of the Christian accommodation of Germanic religiocultural attitudes may be found in the medieval Church's attitude toward warfare. In a study of this subject, J. M. Wallace-Hadrill has noted:

> Germanic pagan peoples had a clear sense that war was a religious under-taking, in which the gods were interested. At once one thinks of Woden as a God peculiarly, though not exclusively, connected with warfare. . . . Pagan and pagan-transitional warfare, then, had its religious facet. Not surprisingly, Christian missionaries found this ineradicable, though not unadaptable to their own purposes. Christian vernacular makes considerable use of the terms of pagan warfare. . . . Why, then, did the men who converted the Anglo-Saxons differ so sharply [in their apparent indifference toward the warrior code] from Wulfila? The Anglo-Saxons were not less bellicose than the Goths. The answer may lie in the prudent spirit of accommodation shown by Gregory the Great. More than that, the pope was an ardent supporter of warfare to spread Christianity and convert the heathen, and this last is, I think, the more important consideration. So far from rejecting the Germanic war-ethos the pope means to harness it to his own ends, and the evidence is that he succeeded. The barbarians may fight to their heart's content in causes blessed by the Church, and this is made clear not only in the matter of vocabulary. *It is the position of the Church rather than of the Germans that had undergone modification.* As Erdmann showed, the Church subsumed and did not reject the warlike moral qualities of its converts. Who shall say that St. Michael of later days was not Woden under fresh colors?[71]

The apotheosis of the Christian assimilation of the Germanic warrior code may be found in St. Bernard of Clairvaux's "recruitment tract" for the military order of the Knights Templars, *De laude novae militiae,* in which the killing of non-Christians in battle is justified, if not encouraged.[72]

---

[71] "War and Peace in the Early Middle Ages", in *Early Medieval History* (Oxford: Basil Blackwell, 1975), pp. 29–30 (emphasis added). Carl Erdmann's *Die Entstehung des Kreuzzugs-gedankens* (Stuttgart: W. Kohlhammer, 1935), to which Wallace-Hadrill refers, contains a thorough discussion of the development of medieval military ethics, and has since been translated by M. W. Baldwin and Walter Goffart as *The Origin of the Idea of Crusade* (Princeton, N.J.: Princeton University Press, 1977). Further discussion of the tension between the Germanic warrior code and Christian pacifism may be found in Clinton Albertson's introduction to his edition of *Anglo-Saxon Saints and Heroes* (New York: Fordham University Press, 1967), pp. 1–28. The prominence of the Germanic warrior code in medieval literature is documented by Mary Crawford Clawsey, "The Comitatus and the Lord-Vassal Relationship in the Medieval Epic" (Ph.D. diss., University of Maryland, 1982).

[72] *De laude novae militiae,* in *Sancti Bernardi Opera,* ed. J. Leclercq, C. H. Talbot, and H. Rochais, vol. 3 (Rome: Editiones Cistercienses, 1959), pp. 213–39. Additional information on the Templars may be found in Edith Simon, *The Piebald: A Biography of the Knights of*

To further validate the assertion of the Germanization of medieval religious culture, it is useful to consider the principle *lex orandi, lex credendi*. Van Engen advances this notion when he states that "the real measure of Christian religious culture on a broad scale must be the degree to which time, space, and ritual observances came to be defined and grasped essentially in terms of the Christian liturgical year."[73] Similarly, it may be presumed that the real measure of the Germanization of medieval religious culture must be the degree to which time, space, and ritual observances came to be defined and grasped essentially in terms of the Germanic ethos and world-view.

The succinct outline of early medieval liturgical history provided by Cyrille Vogel in his guide to medieval liturgical resources ascribes a major role to Germanic influence in the formation of early medieval religious culture. He states:

> The period that extends from Gregory the Great [590–604] to Gregory VII [1073–1085] is characterized by the following facts regarding liturgy:
>
> a) the systematization of the liturgy of the City of Rome and of the papal court (the *Roman* liturgy in the strict sense);
>
> b) the spread of this liturgy into the Frankish kingdom through the initiatives of individual pilgrims and, after 754, with the support of the Carolingian kings;
>
> c) the deliberate Romanization of the ancient liturgy of Northern Europe (Gallican) at the behest of Pepin III and Charlemagne;
>
> d) the progressive creation of a "mixed" or "hybrid" set of new rites in the Carolingian Empire through the amalgamation of the Roman liturgy with indigenous ones;
>
> e) the inevitable liturgical diversification resulting from these Romanizing and Gallicanizing thrusts;
>
> f) the return of the adapted Romano-Frankish or Romano-Germanic liturgy to Rome under the Ottos of Germany, especially after the *Renovatio Imperii* of 962;
>
> g) the permanent adoption of this liturgy at Rome because of the worship vacuum and the general state of cultural and religious decadence which prevailed in the City at that time.
>
> This long period which we have just outlined is one of major importance in the history of Christian worship. The Latin liturgy which came into being in this era and which continued to be the liturgy for centuries to come, was not a purely Roman one; as a result of its long and turbulent history, it is better characterized as Romano-Frankish or even as Romano-Germanic.[74]

Templars (Boston: Little, Brown, 1959). Information regarding other medieval military religious orders as well may be found in Desmond Seward, *The Monks of War: The Military Religious Orders* (Hamden, Conn.: Archon, 1972); and Alan Forey, *The Military Orders from the Twelfth to the Early Fourteenth Centuries* (Toronto: University of Toronto Press, 1992).

[73] Van Engen, "The Christian Middle Ages," p. 543.

[74] *Medieval Liturgy: An Introduction to the Sources,* trans. and rev. William Storey and Niels Rasmussen (Washington, D. C.: Pastoral Press, 1986), p. 61. Of related interest by Vogel

Vogel is not alone in attributing great significance to the evolution of the official Roman Catholic liturgy into a Romano-Germanic form. Jungmann likewise viewed this development as portending momentous consequences, not only for the future of Christian worship, but for Western religious culture in general:

> As is well known, in Church life, in forms of worship, in canon law, in monastic life, and, not least, in theological science, from the 9th century it was the countries north of the Alps that took the lead, while Italy suffered a period of set-back. From the 10th century onwards, the cultural heritage which had accumulated in the Carolingian North, streamed in ever increasing volume into Italy and became the cultural standard in Rome itself. . . . Ultimately it was from Rome that the new spirituality and new ways spread to the Church at large. What had been established in the Carolingian empire now became normative for all the West. The structure of the liturgy is but the most outstanding example.[75]

Some examples, derived by Jungmann from a Germanic over-reaction against Arianism, are a decline in Christ's mediative role, an increase in private votive Masses commemorating Mary and the saints, the multiplication of signs of the cross in the Mass, and the introduction of silent prayer with hands folded, which was derived from the posture of a vassal pledging fealty to his lord. Germanic influence was largely responsible, according to Jungmann, for an increased emphasis upon the dramatic and allegorical representation of events from the life of Christ in the Mass and in Scripture, as well as in the weekly liturgical cycle, and a simultaneous decline in soteriological-eschatological emphases in the liturgy and in artistic expression. Also related to Germanization was the emergence of the Christmas festival cycle as a rival to the Easter cycle, and an increased stratification of clergy and laity, represented by the growing distance between the altar and the faithful, as well as by the introduction of a communion rail boundary at which communicants knelt. Although Jungmann believed that the primary cause of these developments was an anti-Arian response which emphasized Christ's power and glory, given the generally low level of the perception and significance of doctrinal subtleties among the Germanic peoples in the early Middle Ages, it seems more likely that these developments were the expression of a Germanic ethos and worldview.[76]

---

are "Les Echanges liturgiques entre Rome et les pays francs jusqu'à l'époque de Charlemagne," *Settimane* 7 (1960), pp. 185–295; and *Le Pontifical romano-germanique*, 3 vols., Studi e Testi, nos. 226, 227, and 269 (Vatican City: Biblioteca Apostolica Vaticana, 1963–72).

[75] Josef A. Jungmann, "The Defeat of Teutonic Arianism and the Revolution in Religious Culture in the Early Middle Ages," pp. 18–19.

[76] This position may be reinforced by the observation that the Franks, who did not become affiliated with Arianism, do not appear to have differed significantly in their interpretation of Christianity from their formerly Arian Germanic neighbors. Josef A. Jungmann, "The Defeat of Teutonic Arianism and the Revolution in Religious Culture in the Early Middle Ages," chapters

As Jungmann observed, liturgy was not the only aspect of medieval religious culture which was Germanized. In his *History of Christian Spirituality*, Urban T. Holmes notes that Germanic spirituality "tended more toward objects—e.g., the Cross, the Real Presence in the Eucharist, the Blessed Virgin, the Scriptures—than the subtleties of process—e.g., growth in perfection. *The whole shape of Western spirituality is a function of this radically new Germanic culture with a strong addition of Celtic culture.*"[77]

Drawing upon evidence from the Germanic law codes, Katherine Fischer Drew has recently sought to "reemphasize the importance of the role played by the Germanic kingdoms . . . [in] the period from about A.D. 500 to 800."[78] A common feature among the Germanic peoples is "the development of a concept of collective security. This was closely related to two Germanic institutions: The family and kin group on the one hand and personal lordship on the other."[79] Collective security may be considered the antithesis of anomie. The social and spiritual needs of the Germanic peoples were being adequately fulfilled from sources within their own societies. A religious movement which had flourished in the anomic urban quarters of a declining society,[80] was not likely to meet with immediate success in a rural emerging society with a high level of collective security, unless that religious movement was represented in a manner which was compatible with the world-view of the latter society. Only then could an alien religious movement effectively compete with the internal sources of stability.[81] A noteworthy example of such accommodation was the portrayal of Christ as a victorious Germanic warlord.[82]

The gradual Germanization of Christian ethics, liturgy, religious culture, and ecclesiastical organization which occurred contemporaneously with Christianization efforts,[83] provides an alternate explanation for the

---

9 through 11 of idem, *The Mass of the Roman Rite: Its Origins and Development*, vol. 1 (New York: Benziger Brothers, 1951), and chapter 5 of Raymond E. McNally, *The Unreformed Church* (New York: Sheed and Ward, 1965), which generally follows Jungmann's exposition, provide additional discussion of the developments mentioned here.

[77] *A History of Christian Spirituality: An Analytical Introduction* (New York: Seabury Press, 1980), p. 50 (emphasis in the original). See also Oliver Davies, *God Within: The Mystical Tradition of Northern Europe*, with a foreword by Rowan Williams (New York: Paulist Press, 1988).

[78] "Another Look at the Origins of the Middle Ages: A Reassessment of the Role of the Germanic Kingdoms," *Speculum* 62:4 (1987): 803.

[79] Ibid., p. 804.

[80] For additional information on the socioeconomic background of the Roman Church, see Mikhail Rostovtzeff, *Social and Economic History of the Roman Empire*, 2 vols., 2nd rev. ed., rev. P. M. Fraser (Oxford: Clarendon Press, 1957); A. Judge, "The Social Identity of the First Christians: A Question of Method in Religious History," *Journal of Religious History* 11 (1980): 201–17; and W. A. Meeks, *The First Urban Christians: The Social World of the Apostle Paul* (New Haven, Conn.: Yale University Press, 1983).

[81] This situation is discussed in Stancliffe, "From Town to Country," pp. 43–59, especially pp. 51–59.

[82] See above, pp. 23–24, 23 n. 53.

[83] These and other examples of Germanization will be discussed within their historical contexts in Part II.

observation that "medieval folk were at best only superficially Christianized," and that "Christian faith and practice first took hold among the European masses during the Reformation and Counter Reformation movements."[84] Depending on how one defines "masses," it might be that "Christian faith and practice first took hold among the European masses" during the Commercial Revolution of the twelfth century, as may be evidenced by the emergence of such expressions of organized lay piety as the Humiliati and the Waldensians, culminating in the Order of Friars Minor. If the first major episode of Christian response to anomie occurred in late antiquity, and the second may have occurred during the Commercial Revolution,[85] a third may be occurring in the present era in response to the Industrial Revolution, a response that may have been formally initiated by Leo XIII's 1891 encyclical *Rerum Novarum*.

Neither Le Goff and the "new school" nor Van Engen focus on the sociocultural dynamics that operate during the process of Christianization. Le Goff's arguments for a "two-tiered" clerical-popular dichotomy in medieval religious culture are fundamentally class-based, and allow only for a stubborn retention of pre-Christian Indo-European religious expressions by popular elements, while the "clerical elite" was a source of Christianization. However, the Germanizing liturgical contributions of an Alcuin or an Amalar of Metz, for example, do not fit easily into a schema wherein a clerical elite is seeking to impose orthodox Roman Christianity upon the native populace. Neither Le Goff and the "new school" nor Van Engen explicitly attribute a substantial role to the Germanic ethos and world-view in the development of medieval religious culture. Instead of a class-based approach to the problem of medieval Christianization, this inquiry takes an ethnocultural approach in which the Germanization of Christianity is the primary feature.

---

[84] Van Engen, "The Christian Middle Ages," p. 521. Here Van Engen is summarizing the views of Jean Delumeau, Keith Thomas, Carlo Ginzburg, Gerald Strauss, and several others.

[85] For an important socioreligious analysis of the Commercial Revolution, see Barbara H. Rosenwein and Lester K. Little, "Social Meaning in the Monastic and Mendicant Spiritualities," *Past and Present* 63 (1974): 4–32, especially 16–20. Little further develops his analysis of the mendicant orders, and credits them with providing the necessary spiritual response to the new economy, in *Religious Poverty and the Profit Economy in Medieval Europe* (London: Paul Elek, 1978). See also Robert S. Lopez, *The Commercial Revolution of the Middle Ages, 950–1350* (Englewood Cliffs, N.J.: Prentice-Hall, 1971). Additional information on the Waldensians and other prototypes of the Franciscan movement is contained in Grundmann's *Ketzergeschichte des Mittelalters,* pp. 28–34.

3

Sociohistorical Aspects of Religious Transformation

To better understand the religious transformation which resulted from the encounter of the Germanic peoples with Christianity, it is useful to become familiar with other instances of pre-Christian and non-Christian religious transformation, particularly those in which a folk-religious society encountered a universal religious movement. Of special interest is the religious transformation which occurred when the folk-religious Indo-European societies of ancient Greece and Rome encountered "proto-Christian" mystery cults during the Hellenistic age. An examination of Hellenistic and Jewish religious and philosophical currents should contribute toward the development of a general model of the interaction between folk-religious societies and universal religions, and of the religious transformation which stems from it. This model will then be applied to the encounter of the Germanic peoples with Christianity.

Several approaches from the comparative study of religion are utilized this chapter. These include the distinction between folk and universal religions, the analysis of that which is considered sacred by these types of religion, and a comparison of the prominence of political, magical, ethical, and doctrinal elements in each type of religion. It is understood that in certain instances the application of such comparative structures may temporarily obscure some of the subtle distinctions that exist in the multi-dimensional matrix of religious characteristics, and, given the limitations of dualistic and tripartite classifications, may even occasionally lead to forced generalizations. However, it is believed that the benefits to be derived from careful typological comparisons outweigh the dangers.[1]

---

[1] Talcott Parsons, in his introduction to Max Weber, *The Sociology of Religion,* by trans. Ephraim Fischoff (Boston: Beacon Press, 1963), pp. lxiii–lxvii, criticizes Weber's implementation of his concept of the "ideal type," since Parsons believes it has contributed toward "typological rigidity and trait atomism." Given this danger, in the current inquiry the attribution of a particular characteristic to a religious phenomenon does not imply an exclusive association, nor does it imply that antithetical characteristics may not also exist within the same phenomenon, albeit less prominently. Notice is also taken of the likelihood of a range of variation within most characteristics.

To successfully develop a general model of religious transformation for the encounter of folk-religious societies with universalist religious movements, it is important, first, to avoid attributing preconceived Christian notions of religion to non-Christian religions,[2] and second, to consider the categorization of religions into two types based upon fundamental structural differences. These two types may be described as "folk," "ethnic," or "natural," religions, and "universal," "revealed," "prophetic," or "historical" religions.[3] Indo-European religions may be placed in the category of folk religions, whereas, for the purpose of this inquiry, the category of universal religions will comprise Buddhism, Christianity, Islam, and the mystery cults of Isis, Cybele, Sarapis, Mithras, Eleusis, and Dionysus.

By placing the Christianization of the Germanic peoples and the Germanization of Christianity within the larger context of the relationship between Indo-European folk religions and the universal religious movements that developed in their midst, one may carefully draw analogies regarding the development and expansion of Christianity. The sociohistorical analogies and hypotheses drawn from Indo-European studies and the sociology of religion, which are advanced in this chapter and elsewhere, are intended to contribute toward a deeper insight into the ideological and cultural transformations that accompanied Christianization efforts among the Germanic peoples. Also, in those areas where serious lacunae occur in the historical record, carefully drawn analogies and inferences from the fields of Indo-European studies and the sociology of religion may at least provide a reasonable interpolation of what may have transpired, not, of course, insofar as actual historical events are concerned, but rather as regards ideological and cultural transformations. In this way, certain patterns derived from the study of the Indo-European religions of India, Persia, Greece, Rome, Scandinavia, and Ireland may be carefully applied

---

[2] A succinct discussion of this prerequisite is contained in Ernest Benz, "On Understanding Non-Christian Religions," in *The History of Religions: Essays in Methodology,* ed. Mircea Eliade and Joseph M. Kitigawa (Chicago: University of Chicago Press, 1959), pp. 115–31.

[3] A good introduction to this schema of categorization may be found in Gustav Mensching, "Folk and Universal Religion," trans. Louis Schneider, in *Religion, Culture and Society: A Reader in the Sociology of Religion,* ed. Louis Schneider (New York: Wiley, 1964), pp. 254–61. Of related interest, particularly for the student of popular religion, and those who, like Jacques Le Goff, prefer to approach the process of medieval Christianization with a class-based paradigm, is Mensching's "The Masses, Folk Belief and Universal Religion," trans. Louis Schneider, in *Religion, Culture and Society,* pp. 269–73. See also Ugo Bianchi, *The History of Religions* (Leiden: E. J. Brill, 1975), p. 53, in which the author, though he advocates caution in classifying "Types of Religion" (pp. 36–44), appears to consider the classifications of "ethnical and 'founded' " religions to be a valid one. He states: "One must first of all distinguish between those religions which have an 'ethnic' character, and those which were 'founded', a distinction of primary importance in the typology of religions." Bianchi continues: "The former have their roots in the pre-history of a people. . . . The religious qualification of a member of the group will generally coincide with his ethnical, cultural and political status." Bianchi considers Hinduism to be primarily an ethnical religion, while in Judaism he notes the coexistence of the universalism usually associated with founded religions, together with an ethnical-national character.

to the Indo-European religion of the Germanic peoples.[4] When they pertain to the interaction of Indo-European religion with proto-Christian or early Christian religion, they may be particularly valuable. They are not intended to substitute for the historical record, but to supplement and enhance it, when it is beneficial and possible to do so.

The responses of non-Christians to Christianization efforts have only recently become the focus of scholarly analysis. Claiming that Adolf von Harnack's classic study, *The Mission and Expansion of Christianity in the First Three Centuries,* contains no reference "to a pagan source and hardly a line indicating the least attempt to find out what non-Christians thought and believed,"[5] Ramsay MacMullen comments that "to ignore the prior views of converts or to depict the Mission as operating on a clean slate is bound to strike an historian as very odd indeed."[6] It would seem to be just as odd if the historian of medieval Christianity were to ignore those developments in the sociology of religion and in Indo-European studies which may compensate for the dearth of reliable extant sources for the study of pre-Christian Germanic religion, and particularly its interaction with Christianity.[7]

An appropriate starting point for studying the encounter between folk-religious societies and universal religions may be an examination of the concept of religion itself. The most common contemporary focus in informal comparative discussions of religion appears to be on belief. One Christian sect differs from another in its beliefs. Christianity differs from Judaism

---

[4] The application of Indo-European studies to Germanic religiosity is considered essential by Jan de Vries, "Der heutige Stand der germanischen Religionsforschung," *Germanisch-romanische Monatschrift,* series 2 (1951–1952): 1–11.

[5] Ramsay MacMullen, *Paganism in the Roman Empire* (New Haven, Conn.: Yale University Press, 1981), p. 206 n. 16; quoted in Robert L. Wilken, *The Christians as the Romans Saw Them* (New Haven, Conn.: Yale University Press, 1984), p. xiv. While in general agreement with the point made by MacMullen, L. Michael White, "Adolf Harnack and the 'Expansion' of Early Christianity: A Reappraisal of Social History," *The Second Century* 5:2 (1985/86): 105 n. 39, cites seven references by Harnack to Pliny, Celsus, and Porphyry.

[6] MacMullen, *Paganism,* p. 206 n. 16.

[7] An important discussion of the advantages and limitations of applying sociological or anthropological theories to the history of Christianity is contained in Wayne A. Meeks's introduction to *The First Urban Christians: The Social World of the Apostle Paul* (New Haven, Conn.: Yale University Press, 1983), pp. 2–7. An anthropological perspective on this subject is presented in George R. Saunders's preface, introduction, and concluding article entitled "Transformations of Christianity: Some General Observations," in *Culture and Christianity: The Dialectics of Transformation,* ed. idem (Westport, Conn.: Greenwood Press, 1988). Speaking for the contributors to this work and other colleagues at the University of California at San Diego, Saunders recalls that "we were mystified by the paucity of serious anthropological studies of Christianity, and particularly the lack of systematically comparative work" (p. xi). Recent applications of sociological theory to early Christian religious development include Howard Clark Kee, *Christian Origins in Sociological Perspective: Methods and Resources* (Philadelphia: Westminster Press, 1980); idem, *Miracle in the Early Christian World: A Study in Sociohistorical Method* (New Haven: Yale University Press, 1983); and idem et al., *Christianity: A Social and Cultural History* (New York: Macmillan, 1991).

and Islam in its doctrine that Jesus Christ is the Son of God. An approach to comparative religion which focuses on doctrinal beliefs is certainly valid when describing the distinguishing characteristics of revealed, universal religions, and particularly forms of Christianity. Such a doctrine-centered approach is not, however, well suited to discussions of folk religions, or to comparisons of folk religions and universal religions, since folk religions tend to identify themselves primarily in an ethnocultural sense rather than in a doctrinal sense. Consequently, when one proposes to discuss a folk religion, or to compare a folk religion with a universal religion, or especially when one proposes to discuss the attempted transformation of a society from a folk religiosity to a universal religion and the concurrent transformation of a universal religion into a folk religion, one must carefully consider the method to be used in studying the interaction between two inherently dissimilar phenomena. In his discussion "Problems of Approach," the first chapter of his study *Christianizing the Roman Empire*, Ramsay MacMullen stresses the importance of this consideration:

> Generalizing may conclude that all forms of religion have one common structure: so a person's shift of allegiance toward Christianity need have involved only the exchange of one theology or theodicy or liturgy or system of morals for some other that was seen as preferable. Perhaps no one today is likely to make so strange an error, but it is not hard to find it in older authorities otherwise deserving of great respect. Granted, some variations of the generalizing fault are hard to avoid. Even to be recognized, they need a certain degree of detachment from our own ways. We ourselves naturally suppose, immersed as we are in the Judeo-Christian heritage, that religion means doctrine. *Why* should we think so? In fact, "that emphasis is most unusual as seen from a cross-cultural perspective."[8]

The first step in studying the interaction between a folk-religious society and a universal religion is to acknowledge that the fundamental distinction between a folk religion and a universal religion is one of kind, and not merely of degree. The next step is to devise a comparative methodology that recognizes this distinction. Rudolf Otto's pioneering approach to the study of religion through the study of that which manifests a sacred character in a particular culture is helpful in this regard.[9] It appears that the primary sacral locus of most folk religions, including Indo-European religions, is the folk community itself. The sacrality of the community is expressed in ritual ceremonies that celebrate its relationship with its own exclusive gods and that "promote a strong sense of in-group identification and loyalty."[10] In contrast, the primary sacral locus of universal religions, such as early

---

[8] *Christianizing the Roman Empire (A.D. 100–400)*, (New Haven, Conn.: Yale University Press, 1984), p. 8. The quotation in the last sentence is taken from Clyde Kluckhohn, "Myths and Rituals: A General Theory," *Harvard Theological Review* 35 (1942): 53.

[9] Rudolf Otto, *The Idea of the Holy*, 2nd ed. (London: Oxford University Press, 1950).

[10] Roger Pearson, *Introduction to Anthropology* (New York: Holt, Rinehart and Winston, 1974), p. 269.

Christianity, appears to be the salvation of the individual by access to an existence which transcends that normally associated with a biological view of human life. According to most universal religions, this existence is attainable by all mankind through initiation into a community of belief and adherence to a universal ethical code.[11]

Historically, folk religions have usually been succeeded by universal religions. Gustav Mensching suggests three ways in which this has occurred: (1) a prophet-figure within the folk religion proclaims a universal religion based upon the older folk religion, as in prophetic Judaism and early Zoroastrianism; (2) contact with a foreign universal religion is established which complements or replaces the original folk religion, as in the case of those mystery religions from Egypt and Asia Minor that expanded into post-Alexandrian Greco-Roman society; and (3) a "supra-national *world religion*" is established by a religious leader, who is in some degree of tension with his native folk religion, as in the case of Christianity and Islam.[12] Mensching attributes change in religious structure to "structural change in the mode of existence of men themselves and thus upon *anthropological* presuppositions."[13] Accordingly, universal religions are perceived as "a response to a newly arisen need of man awakened to self-consciousness,"[14] a need that folk religions did not address.

While Mensching implied a natural progression from folk to universal religion, Robert Bellah has advocated a thesis of "religious evolution."[15] Conceding first that the "construction of a wide-ranging evolutionary scheme . . . is an extremely risky enterprise,"[16] Bellah categorizes religions into two types: those that are "world-accepting"—generally, primitive and modern religions; and those that are "world-rejecting"—generally, the "historic religions" that emerged in the first millennium B.C. and the first millennium A.D.[17] Bellah's description of "historic" religions corresponds to Mensching's description of "universal" religions. This categorization does not, of course, deny that primitive and archaic religions may exhibit

[11] Gustav Mensching, "Folk and Universal Religion," pp. 257–61.

[12] Ibid., p. 256.

[13] Ibid., p. 257.

[14] Ibid., p. 261. In the section "The VIth century B.C.: An 'Axial Epoch,' " in the chapter "Studies and Problems in the History of Religions," in Ugo Bianchi, *The History of Religions,* the following questions are posed: "To what extent did the tendency towards a 'spiritualistic' interpretation, with a particular fondness for dualist concepts, prevail in this epoch and spread across the world between the Mediterranean and India? To what extent and in what way could analogous circumstances produce analogous developments?" (pp. 142–43).

[15] "Religious Evolution," in Roland Robertson, ed., *Sociology of Religion: Selected Readings* (Baltimore: Penguin Books, 1969), pp. 262–92, first published in *ASR* 29(1964): 358–74.

[16] Ibid., p. 291. Bellah continues: "Nevertheless such efforts are justifiable if, by throwing light on perplexing developmental problems they contribute to modern man's efforts at self interpretation" (ibid.).

[17] Ibid., pp. 264–65. Bellah's overall schema, including his association of world-rejection with historic religions, is assessed in M. H. Barnes, "Primitive Religious Thought and the Evolution of Religion," *Religion* 22:1 (1992): 21–46, especially 25–31.

some world-rejecting characteristics, or that "historical," universal religions, which for the purpose of this discussion have been limited to Buddhism, Christianity, Islam, and several mystery cults, may exhibit some world-accepting characteristics, particularly after they are accepted by ruling elites.

The primary appeal of a universal religion to a ruling elite may be its potential as a force for enhanced social cohesion. Although further research into this area of sociopolitical and religious interaction is necessary before an informed appraisal may be rendered, it appears that this utilitarian view contributed toward the popularization of Zoroastrianism throughout the Persian Empire by King Cyrus (d. 431 B.C.), in Alexander the Great's advocacy of Hellenistic ecumenism, in the expansion of Hinayana Buddhism during the reign of the Indian Emperor Asoka (d. 232 B.C.), in the expansion of Mahayana Buddhism throughout China during the T'ang dynasty (620–907), in the legitimizing of Christianity by Constantine in 313, and in the military-religious expansion of Islam under the Caliphate (632–661) and the Umayyad Dynasty (661–750). Also, as will be discussed in Part II, some Germanic leaders appear to have utilized Arian Christianity to preserve their ethnocultural identity, while others utilized Roman Christianity to enhance the level of social cohesion throughout their realms.

It seems that the tendency of folk religions to be supplanted by universal religions occasionally may be reversed by the imposition of a folk-religious world-view which, in turn, reinterprets the universal religion in a folk-religious mode. This seems to occur when universal religions spread to areas where folk-religious attitudes are solidly entrenched. Such appears to have been the case in Buddhism's expansion into China and Japan, as well as in Christianity's expansion into the early medieval Germanic kingdoms.

The primary contribution of Bellah to the current inquiry is his analysis of "the phenomenon of religious rejection of the world characterized by an extremely negative evaluation of man and society and the exaltation of another realm of reality as alone true and infinitely valuable."[18] This world-rejecting orientation tends to be manifested in universal religions and is contrasted by Bellah with the world-accepting orientation of primitive religion, which is "concerned with the maintenance of personal, social and cosmic harmony and with attaining specific goods—rain, harvest, children, health—as men have always been. But the overriding goal of salvation that dominates the world-rejecting religions is almost absent in primitive religion, and life after death tends to be a shadowy semi-existence in some vaguely designated place in the single world."[19]

---

[18] Ibid., p. 264.
[19] Ibid., p. 265.

To determine the nature and consequences of the Germanization of early medieval Christianity, it is not necessary to establish an evolutionary model of religious development, nor is it necessary to establish a taxonomy of religious movements. However, since the current inquiry is primarily concerned with the interrelationship between a predominantly world-accepting folk religiosity and a predominantly world-rejecting universal religion, it would be beneficial if observations could be made regarding the reception of expanding world-rejecting religions in various types of societies. It is in this regard that Mensching's and Bellah's sociological approaches are useful.

Between primitive and historic religions Bellah places archaic religions. They differ from primitive religions primarily in their degree of complexity, systematization, and hierarchical differentiation, but not in their world-accepting ideological core, which tends "to elaborate a vast cosmology in which all things divine and natural have a place."[20] Both primitive and archaic religions in Bellah's system may be included in Mensching's designation of folk religions. In each of these types, religion is an intrinsic component of the predominant culture and as such reinforces the social order. When the social order is disrupted by internecine rivalry, political change, or military conquest, attempts to provide religious rationalization for these developments may provoke "new modes of religious thinking."[21] In certain instances, "the breakdown of internal order led to messianic expectations of the coming of a savior king."[22] These destabilizing social developments seem to have contributed to the emergence of the historical, universal religions, which are distinguished from the archaic, folk religions by their transcendental, world-rejecting character. Bellah explicates:

> For the masses, at least, the new dualism is above all expressed in the difference between this world and the life after death. Religious concern, focused on this life in primitive and archaic religions, now tends to focus on life in the other realm, which may be either infinitely superior or, under certain circumstances, with the emergence of various conceptions of hell, infinitely worse. Under these circumstances the religious goal of salvation (or enlightenment, release and so forth) is for the first time the central religious preoccupation. . . .
> . . . From the point of view of these religions a man is no longer defined chiefly in terms of what clan he comes from or what particular god he serves but rather as a being capable of salvation. . . .
> *Religious action* in the historic religions is thus above all action necessary for salvation.[23]

This description of historical, universal religions is significant, since it also describes the ideological milieu from which Christianity emerged. It may be compared with the earlier observations of Ernst Troeltsch:

[20] Ibid., p. 273.
[21] Ibid., p. 275.
[22] Ibid.
[23] Ibid., pp. 276–77.

A new era of creative religious experience and sensitiveness to religious influences characterized the close of the ancient world. The way had been prepared for this change by a number of factors, which may be briefly enumerated: the destruction of national religions, which was a natural result of the loss of national independence; the mingling of races, which led naturally to the mingling of various cults; the rise of mystery religions with their exclusive emphasis upon the inner life, and their independence of questions of nationality and birth; the fusion of various fragments of religion which had broken away from their national foundation; the philosophical religion of culture with its varied forms of assimilation to the popular religions; the need of a world empire for a world religion, a need which was only partially satisfied by worship of the Emperor.[24]

The consequence of these sociohistorical developments was an increased concern regarding "the supreme question of eternal salvation."[25] Whereas Bellah tends to attribute the emergence of world-rejecting religious forms primarily to internal forces of socioreligious evolution, Troeltsch tends to associate the popularity of Christianity with specific sociohistorical developments. While the current inquiry follows Bellah's application of a "response to the world" taxonomy to folk and universal religions, his notion of religious evolution has not been incorporated. Instead, religious transformation is attributed herein more to ethnocultural forces than to evolutionary patterns.[26]

It is always important to recognize the existence of many subtle nuances within religious attitudes and behavior—nuances which may be temporarily obscured in an attempt to develop a general model of religious transformation. It is similarly important to reiterate that characterizations such as "world-rejecting," when made regarding a particular religion, reflect an attempt to designate what appears to be its predominant emphasis, and does not deny that opposite emphases may coexist within that religion. An example of such coexistence is found within early Christianity, which may be characterized as predominantly "world-rejecting," given its strong soteriological-eschatological orientation epitomized by the transcendent act and notion of Redemption. However, such a characterization does not exclude a coexisting emphasis on the immanent sanctification of matter epitomized by the act and notion of the Incarnation.

It may be helpful to provide a more precise definition of what is meant by "world-rejecting" and "world-accepting" within the scope of the current

---

[24] *The Social Teaching of the Christian Churches,* vol. 1, trans. Olive Wyon, intro. H. Richard Niebuhr (1931; reprint, New York: Harper & Row, 1960), p. 43.

[25] Ibid., p. 40.

[26] Robert Wuthnow, "Perspectives on Religious Evolution," in *Rediscovering the Sacred: Perspectives on Religion in Contemporary Society* (Grand Rapids, Mich.: Eerdmans, 1992), has commented that since Bellah's essay on religious evolution was first published in 1964, he "has at times appeared to abandon even the premises of progress and linear development on which evolutionary theories are based" (p. 88).

inquiry.[27] Although the use of these categories in the current inquiry has been inspired by Bellah, their meaning for this inquiry differs somewhat from Bellah's. "World-rejection," as used herein, is broadened to include not only an "extremely negative evaluation of man and society and the exaltation of another realm of reality as alone true and infinitely valuable,"[28] but also attitudes of general indifference or opposition toward the sociobiological principle of group survival through in-group altruism.[29] World-

[27] Before deciding upon a "response to the world" taxonomy of "world-accepting" versus "world-rejecting" to describe folk and universal religions respectively, consideration was given to the following alternative taxonomies: monist versus dualist, collectivist versus individualist, polytheist-pantheist versus monotheist, and immanent versus transcendent. While each of these provides some degree of insight into the distinctions between folk and universal religions, and more particularly, between pre-Christian Germanic religiosity and early Christianity, it was felt that the classifications of world-accepting versus world-rejecting, as defined herein, provoked the least number of exceptions and most productively elucidated the relationships in question. The classification of religions is discussed in "The 'Structures' of Religion and the Historical Typology of Religions," and in "Types of Religion," sections in Ugo Bianchi, *The History of Religions*. Studies in the sociology of religion which employ a "response to the world" taxonomy include B. R. Wilson, "An Analysis of Sect Development," *ASR* 24 (1959): 3–15; idem, "A Typology of Sects in a Dynamic and Comparative Perspective," *Archives de Sociologie de Religion* 16 (1963): 49–63, trans. Jenny M. Robertson, in Robertson, *Sociology of Religion: Selected Readings*, 361–83; idem, *Religious Sects* (London: Weidenfeld, 1970); idem, *Magic and the Millenium* (London: Heinemann, 1973); and Roy Wallis, *The Elementary Forms of the New Religious Life* (London: Routledge & Kegan Paul, 1984). Aware of the limitations inherent in applying ideal-type models to religious sects, Wilson, *Religion in Sociological Perspective* (New York: Oxford University Press, 1982), has proposed a tripartite "response to the world" taxonomy which is comprised of three basic categories: "world-denying, world-indifferent, and world-enhancing" (pp. 111–13). I am grateful to Solomon Nigosian for a copy of his paper, "Eliade, Bellah and van der Leeuw on Classification of World Religions," presented at the annual meeting of the Eastern International Region of the American Academy of Religion, Toronto, April 1991, in which he proposes a system of classification which distinguishes between those religions "originated by a founder and those originated by a group" (p. 6).

[28] Bellah, "Religious Evolution," p. 264.

[29] Sociobiology has been defined in E. O. Wilson, *Sociobiology: The New Synthesis* (Cambridge, Mass.: Harvard University Press, 1975), as the "systematic study of the biological basis of all social behaviour" (p. 4). To Wilson, the central theoretical problem of sociobiology is: "How can altruism, which by definition reduces personal fitness, possibly evolve by natural selection?" He responds: "The answer is kinship: if the genes causing the altruism are shared by two organisms because of common descent, and if the altruistic act by one organism increases the joint contribution of these genes to the next generation, the propensity to altruism will spread through the gene pool" (pp. 3–4). In an article entitled "Ecology and the Evolution of Social Ethics," in J. W. S. Pringle, ed., *Biology and the Human Sciences* (Oxford: Oxford University Press, 1972), V. C. Wynne-Edwards states: "From the biological point of view, his [the individual's] overriding duty should be to ensure the survival of the stock to which he belongs and whose torch he temporarily bears. That is the primary purpose toward which his moral or altruistic behaviour ought therefore be directed" (p. 68). The sociobiological notion of in-group altruism may be translated into the sociological concept of group solidarity. The successful operation of in-group altruism, and hence group solidarity, is dependent upon a high degree of genetic homogeneity within the group, whereas an increase in social heterogenization, such as that which often accompanies urbanization and imperial expansion, may act to impede the operation of altruism, and hence result in a decline in social cohesion. Wilson has commented that "the rate of gene flow around the world has risen to dramatic levels and is accelerating, and

rejection implies a desire to transcend or substantially transform one's current earthly existence, whether through asceticism, meditation, or sociopolitical action during one's lifetime, or through eternal life after death. In this regard a universal religion, in which the primary condition for membership is orthodox religious belief rather than ethnocultural identity or class status, may be considered truly world-rejecting.

It is appropriate at this point to consider some examples of world-rejection and their relationship to sociohistorical factors in various religious traditions. Perhaps the closest parallel to the expansion of Christianity in the Roman Empire can be found in the expansion of Mahayana Buddhism in China. In his discussion "Otherworldliness," Hajime Nakamura describes the sociohistorical climate which accompanied this expansion:

> In the China of early centuries A.D., the confidence of the declining aristocrats was shaken and could not be restored. Men began to seek something immutable in a time of disaster, or perhaps an escape into nature from an inhuman scene they found intolerable. . . . Among the literati, the early optimism reflected in classical Chinese literature yielded to a generally more pessimistic view of life during and after the Han dynasty (from about the second century B.C.). The experience of early Chinese buoyancy and the onset of a more pessimistic mood sensitized the Chinese to Buddhism, making them more receptive to this foreign religion in the third and fourth centuries than they had been earlier or were to be much later.
>
> Gradually more and more Chinese came to subscribe to Buddhism, a religion at first alien to them; many even eventually believed that conformity to the Buddhist way of celibacy and ritual acts of bodily mortification rendered a higher service to their parents than the Confucian ideals of preservation of the body and perpetuation of the family.[30]

---

the mean coefficients of relationship within local communities are correspondingly diminishing. The result could be an eventual lessening of altruistic behavior through the maladaption and loss of group-selected genes" (*Sociobiology,* p. 575). Wilson cites I. Eshel, "On the Neighbor Effect and the Evolution of Altruistic Traits," *Theoretical Population Biology* 3:3 (1972): 258–77. For a summary of recent research, see J. Phillipe Rushton, "Genetic Similarity, Human Altruism, and Group Selection," *Behavioral and Brain Sciences* 12:3 (1989): 503–18, with "Open Peer Commentary" and an "Author's Response," pp. 518–59. Particularly noteworthy is the comment of Douglas T. Kenrick that "Christianity began to develop in the rapidly overpopulating Middle East only 2,000 years ago, and may have been a cultural adaptation to the novel experience of living among closely allied nonkin" (p. 532).

[30] "Otherworldliness," a section in the chapter "Features of Medieval Thought," in *A Comparative History of Ideas* (London: KPI, 1986), p. 356. Nakamura illustrates Buddhist otherworldliness by citing the following parable: "In medieval Japan a disciple asked Master Dogen, 'My mother is very old, and I am the only son. If I should become a recluse [i.e. Buddhist monk], she cannot live for even one day. What shall I do?' The master replied, 'If you are surely aspiring for the Way of Buddha, you should take (the Buddhist) orders, having prepared for the livelihood of your mother. However, if it is difficult, you should take orders immediately. Even if your old mother should starve to death, her merit of letting her only son enter the Way of Buddha is very great, isn't it? Her merit will cause her to attain Enlightenment in an after-life in the future.' " (p. 359). Buddhism's tendency toward world-rejection is documented throughout the *Dhammapada,* and particularly in chapter 13, "The World," where

The world-rejecting tendency of Mahayana Buddhism in its sociohistorical context has also been observed by Ninian Smart in "The Appeal of Buddhism":

> The spread of Buddhism was assisted by the disintegration of the Han empire toward the latter part of that century [second century A.D.]. In a time of turbulence, civil war, and unrest, the official Confucian doctrines were bound to seem ineffective and inadequate, and the way was open for a faith which had more personal and individual concerns. . . .
>
> The appeal of the new faith was various. First, the monastic order—the Sangha—presented an idea of the contemplative and religious life that could command respect. Moreover, the order was open to all, and thus provided a peaceful haven for many for whom the bloodshed and distresses of the period had become intolerable. The notion that a person should forsake his kith and kin to lead a religious life undoubtedly encountered considerable resistance in a culture where family ties, reinforced by the cult of ancestors, were so strong. Nevertheless, the Sangha gradually made headway.[31]

In China, resistance to the world-rejecting elements of Buddhism was centered in the world-accepting, socially-reinforcing Confucian notions of ancestor and emperor worship, while in Japan, adherence to the predominantly folk-centered Shinto world-view functioned similarly.[32]

In the initial expansion of Islam, one may also find indications of the destabilizing sociohistorical circumstances which tend to predispose a community to the reception of a prophetic, revealed, religious movement with

---

one is admonished: "Do not follow the evil law! Do not live on in thoughtlessness! Do not follow false doctrine! Be not a friend of the world. . . . Look upon the world as you would on a bubble, look upon it as you would upon a mirage: the king of death does not see him who thus looks down upon the world. Come, look at this world, glittering like a royal chariot; the foolish are immersed in it, but the wise do not touch it." This excerpt is from "The Dhammapada," trans. Max Müller, in Lin Yutang, ed., *The Wisdom of China and India* (New York: Modern Library, 1942), pp. 338–39. See also the section "An Eastern Example of a Universalist Religion: Buddhism," in the chapter "Studies and Problems in the History of Religions," in Ugo Bianchi, *The History of Religions,* where Bianchi states: "Pettazzoni has pointed out that Buddhism, in its historical dynamism, was somewhat similar to Christianity in the West. Both were rejected by the religion and the people of their own land, of which the respective founders were nevertheless very eminent personages, and both were widely diffused, with a universalist trend, because of their appeal to the individual, for they preached a doctrine, or rather a way, of salvation. Yet, Pettazzoni observes, these two religions are very dissimilar. Christianity is antisyncretical whereas Buddhism comes to terms with gods and rites of different cults." (p. 161). The degree to which Christianity was syncretized or otherwise transformed through its relationship with the Germanic peoples remains at the crux of this inquiry.

[31] "The Appeal of Buddhism," in the chapter "Chinese and Japanese Religious Experience," in Ninian Smart, *The Religious Experience of Mankind,* 3rd ed. (New York: Scribner's, 1984), pp. 181–82.

[32] Hans-Joachim Schoeps, *The Religions of Mankind,* trans. Richard and Clara Winston (Garden City, N.Y.: Doubleday, 1966), has written of Shintoism: "It differs from most other religions in having no founder, no dogmatic scriptures, and in being a pure religion of this world, concentrating upon the family and the national community. The closest historical parallel to it is to be found in the folk religions of the ancient Greeks, Romans and Teutons" (p. 213).

world-rejecting tendencies. Ninian Smart has observed that the Arab world at the time of Muhammad suffered from urban decay, a lack of irrigation and control of flooding, and frequent involvement in military conflicts between the Byzantine and Persian Empires.[33] Also, in the city of Medina there existed a large Jewish community "whose prosperity contrasted with the relative poverty of the Arabs."[34] It was here that Muhammad came after spending several years in Mecca and Taif without success. As Smart notes:

> Medina, three hundred miles north of Mecca, offered more hope. Some of the Medina citizens, concerned at the internal strife which plagued that city, were attracted to Muhammed as a leader who might bring peace and a reordering of the community. . . . The situation at Medina gave the Prophet remarkable opportunities. . . . He had to reconcile the many tensions which grew up. . . . The brotherhood of those who acknowledged Islam, or obedience to Allah, was stressed. Almsgiving was introduced as a method of alleviating the lot of the poorer members of the new community. This strong sense of brotherhood under God was an important factor in the religious and military successes of the faith in later years.[35]

It was not only in this initial expansion of Islam that sociohistorical factors appear to have played a contributing role. After Muhammad's death in 632, Arab armies, inspired by "the unity of purpose imparted by Islam,"[36] conquered extensive Persian and Byzantine territories.

Smart attributes the success of Islamic expansion in these territories largely to the fact that "great numbers of people among the populations of the countries which they first overran were disaffected."[37] The relationship between their alienation and their acceptance of Islam is addressed by Smart: "The substratum of the population was Semitic, and on it was superimposed Hellenistic and Byzantine culture and rule. The Semitic peoples still retained enough consciousness of their origins and traditions to welcome the Arab invasion and the overthrow of their Greek masters. Also, divisions and subsequent persecutions had weakened Christianity: and many were happy to escape the tensions by accepting the undoubtedly monotheistic faith of Islam, and the new brotherhood which it seemed to offer."[38] Additionally, Islam's world-rejecting tendency offered its faithful adherents, including its warriors, the soteriological-eschatological benefits of an afterlife replete with earthly joys, while sinners would experience eternal torment.[39]

---

[33] *The Religious Experience of Mankind,* 3rd ed., pp. 390–91.
[34] Ibid., p. 391.
[35] Ibid., p. 397.
[36] Ibid., p. 411.
[37] Ibid., p. 412.
[38] Ibid.
[39] Ibid., p. 400.

Although the previous survey of the apparent role of sociohistorical factors in the expansion of religions with world-rejecting tendencies is not an exhaustive examination of the topic, it is hopefully sufficient to postulate a relationship between the sociohistorical status of a folk-religious society and its propensity toward accepting a world-rejecting religious movement. Briefly stated, it is suggested here that the prolonged existence of anomic social conditions in a folk-religious society predisposes that society to religious movements with prominent world-rejecting tendencies. Conversely, it is suggested that the presence of a high level of group solidarity in a society impedes the acceptance of a religious movement with prominent world-rejecting tendencies, unless these tendencies are initially obscured from potential converts. This sociohistorical postulate will be utilized later to assist in comparing the reception of Christianity by the urban communities of the Roman Empire in the first through fourth centuries, and the reception of Christianity by the Germanic peoples in the fourth through eighth centuries.

The interrelationship between anomic social conditions and world-rejecting religious tendencies forms the core of Arnold Toynbee's study "The Epiphany of the Higher Religions":

> An historian's first approach to the higher religions [here comprising Judaism, Zoroastrianism, Buddhism, Christianity, and Islam] will be by way of the social milieu in which they make their epiphany. They are not the product of their social milieu. . . . Nevertheless, an examination of the social milieu will help us to understand the nature, as well as the rise, of religions in which this experience of meeting God is commended to Mankind as the inspiration for a new way of life.
>
> The founders of the higher religions have mostly arisen in the ranks of the vast majority of the members of a disintegrating society whose normal human sufferings have been intensified to an abnormal degree by the social breakdown and disintegration resulting from the failure of parochial-community worship. In the successive degrees of this abnormal suffering the last turn of the screw, short of physical extermination, is the experience of being uprooted from one's home and becoming a refugee, exile, or deportee who has been wrenched out of his ancestral framework. . . .
>
> This has been the human seed from which the higher religions have sprung. . . .
>
> The epiphany of these new higher religions in the souls of the *déracinés* was neither quick nor easy. The breakdown and disintegration of Society and the victims' consequent loss of their ancestral heritage, including their physical home in which their lives had their roots, was a challenge of unusual severity.[40]

According to Toynbee, the spiritual response to the social disintegration which characterizes the "time of troubles" tends to be one in which "men's

---

[40] *An Historian's Approach to Religion,* 2nd ed. (Oxford: Oxford University Press, 1979), pp. 76–77.

and women's hearts ... transfer their religious allegiance to some object of worship that will give them peace by uniting them, and that will unite them in virtue of being, itself, unitary and universal."[41]

If the predominant world-view of early Christianity is considered to be one of world-rejection, and if the predominant world-view of the traditional Indo-European religions is considered to be one of world-acceptance, the northwestward expansion of Christianity may be viewed as an encounter between opposing world-views. Sociohistorically speaking, early Christianity emerged from the predominantly world-rejecting religious environment of Palestinian Judaism and Hellenism, and subsequently encountered the predominantly world-accepting religiosity of the Roman, Celtic, Germanic, and Slavic branches of the Indo-European peoples. The Greek branch has been purposefully excluded here since, by the time of Christianity, Greek religiosity had become so thoroughly "de-Indo-Europeanized" by centuries of contact with world-rejecting religious and philosophical movements that it no longer exhibited a predominantly world-accepting character.

The traditional Indo-European religions in their early stages exhibited characteristics which may be expected of a pastoral, nomadic, warrior people who conquered agrarian peoples. The Indo-Europeans "had a patriarchal social organization"[42] and tended to impose an aristocratic feudal social structure upon the indigenous peoples whom they conquered.[43] Indo-European society was usually organized into "three social strata, which

---

[41] Ibid., p. 35. In an important discussion of contemporary religious responses to societal anomie, which refers to the research of Renato Poblete, "Puerto Rican Sectarianism and the Quest for Community" (M.A. thesis, Fordham University, 1959), Hervé Carrier, *The Sociology of Religious Belonging,* trans. Arthur J. Arrieri (New York: Herder and Herder, 1965), describes the psychosocial reaction of an immigrant to a large city: "He experiences his first shock when he suddenly becomes aware of his unadaptability, his insecurity, and what the author calls his 'state of anomie.' A parallel reaction accompanies the first; it expresses a basic need for identification; it is fostered by the kindness of numerous compatriots sharing the same fate and speaking the same language. This experience is described by the author as the 'quest for community.' The immigrant arriving without resources and being harshly subjected to contact with a complex culture which seems hostile to him, has the feeling of no longer belonging to anything; he has lost his frame of reference with its natural supports; even the Catholic Church seems a stranger to him. The invitation to join a small religious group where he will meet his fellow countrymen, will pray with them and will be understood, answers his craving for affiliation" (p. 89). For the Puerto Rican immigrants in Poblete's study, "the small religious groups" to which they were attracted were the myriad Pentecostal sects of New York City.

[42] R. A. Crossland, "Immigrants from the North," *Cambridge Ancient History,* 3rd ed., vol. 1 (Cambridge: Cambridge University Press, 1971), p. 861. See also, idem, "Indo-European Origins: The Linguistic Evidence," *Past and Present* 12 (1957): 16–46; P. Friedrich, "Proto-Indo-European Kinship," *Ethnology* 5 (1966): 1–23; and Emile Benveniste, *Indo-European Language and Society,* trans. Elizabeth Palmer (Coral Gables, Fla.: University of Miami Press, 1973). The strength of the evidence for Indo-European patrilineal descent has been questioned by Alexander Callander Murray in "Introduction and Indo-European Background," in *Germanic Kinship Structure: Studies in Law and Society in Antiquity and the Early Middle Ages,* Studies and Texts, no. 65 (Toronto: Pontifical Institute of Mediaeval Studies, 1983). Murray suggests the possibility of patrilocal residences and bilateral kindreds (p. 37).

[43] Crossland, "Immigrants from the North," pp. 863–65, 874–76.

included, in order of precedence, a priestly stratum, a warrior stratum, and a herder-cultivator stratum."[44] It has been the contribution of Georges Dumézil to show that the hierarchic tripartite social organization of the Indo-Europeans was reflected in their mythology and ideology. Given the significant role of the warrior in Indo-European societies, it is not surprising that the warrior ideology is "perhaps the most distinctive feature of the Indo-European worldview."[45]

While Indo-European societies were being Christianized, Christianity itself was being "Indo-Europeanized."[46] However, by the time of their encounter with Christianity, the Indo-European ideological core of the older Indo-European societies of Greece and Rome had been substantially diluted through the assimilation of the religiosity of the indigenous non-Indo-European Mediterranean inhabitants of Greece, and, following the conquests of Alexander the Great, particularly through the religiosity of many non-Indo-European immigrants.[47] For the purpose of comparison, W. K. C. Guthrie's description of Hellenic, pre-Alexandrian, Greek religious attitudes is provided:

> To appreciate the situation, we must realize how completely identified were the state and its religion. It was not a case of making the Church subordinate to the State. There was no word for church at all, nor did such a thing exist apart from the state itself. The gods were worshiped at

[44] C. Scott Littleton, *The New Comparative Mythology: An Anthropological Assessment of the Theories of Georges Dumézil*, 3rd ed. (Berkeley: University of California Press, 1982), p. 4.

[45] *Encyclopedia of Religion*, s.v. "War and Warriors: Indo-European Beliefs and Practices," by C. Scott Littleton.

[46] The concept of "Indo-Europeanization," as applied here, is restricted to the acculturation of those expressions which appear to be grounded in a common Indo-European ideology, and thus are likely to have had their origin in a period of proto-Indo-European unity. It does not automatically apply to those random features of an individual Indo-European society which cannot be derived from a common Indo-European tradition. The methodology of comparative Indo-European studies will be discussed in greater detail in chapter 5.

[47] Expressions of indigenous, non-Indo-European Greek religiosity may include the Eleusinian and Dionysiac mysteries, for which, according to Walter Burkert, *Greek Religion*, trans. John Raffan (Cambridge: Harvard University Press, 1985), "a Neolithic basis may be assumed" (p. 278). He continues: "Both the [Eleusinian] Demeter and Dionysos mysteries show specific relations to the ancient Anatolian Mother Goddess." See also Part 1, ch. 3, "The Minoan-Mycenaean Religion." In a chapter entitled "The Religion of Eleusis," in *Greek Folk Religion* (1940; reprint, Philadelphia: University of Pennsylvania Press, 1984), Martin P. Nilsson proposes that this pre-Indo-European vegetation cult was transformed into a cult of individual immortality in the Hellenistic period (pp. 63–64). A discussion of the relationship between the Indo-European and non-Indo-European sources of Greek religion may be found in Raffaele Pettazzoni, "Les Deux Sources de la religion grecque," *Mnemosyne* 4 (1951): 1–8. Non-Indo-European elements are the focus of Marija Gimbutas, *The Goddesses and Gods of Old Europe: 6500–3500 B.C.: Myths and Cult Images* (Berkeley: University of California Press, 1982); and idem, *The Language of the Goddess: Unearthing the Hidden Symbols of Western Civilization*, with a foreword by Joseph Campbell (New York: Harper & Row, 1989). The most recent discussion of the Indo-European immigration to Greece is Robert Drews, *The Coming of the Greeks: Indo-European Conquests in the Aegean and the Near East* (Princeton N.J.: Princeton University Press, 1988).

festivals which were state occasions, and participation in them was part of the ordinary duties of a citizen as such. Although many gods were worshipped at Athens, the patron of the city, and the deity nearest to every Athenian's heart, was of course Athena, and the coincidence of the name is significant. Religion and patriotism were the same thing. . . . Such a thing as personal and individual religion was unknown to the great majority of citizens. The sects which attempted to introduce it never achieved much influence so long as the city-state held together, and in so far as they had any success, were definitely subversive of the established order.[48]

It should be noted that, despite significant differences, there existed fundamental similarities between the manifestations of Indo-European religiosity and social structure found in Hellenic Greece and the Roman Republic. Notwithstanding his criticism of comparative Indo-European studies in general, and his observation that "we cannot but be struck by a decided difference between them," H. J. Rose acknowledges "real and considerable resemblances," since

> both Greek and Roman cults were polytheistic, both were creedless, neither was attached to any system of ethics, both admitted, though neither required, the use of cult images and other visible objects of worship, both had priests and priestesses, yet neither developed a powerful priesthood which could, as such, make its influence felt in politics or even in governing the life of the individual in any great detail; and, perhaps most important of all, both were closely attached to the organization of the State, and before that existed, to the family, clan, or tribe.[49]

Together with the social and intellectual characteristics described in the preceding paragraphs, this description of Hellenic Greece and the Roman Republic forms a model of what may be designated as "traditional," "classical," or "authentic" Indo-European religiosity.

Interestingly, the timetable and geographic pattern of Christian expansion resulted in its interaction with successively younger, more homogeneous, and more authentically Indo-European societies.[50] Despite the

---

[48] *The Greek Philosophers: From Thales to Aristotle* (New York: Harper & Row, 1960), pp. 82–83.

[49] *Religion in Greece and Rome* (New York: Harper & Row, 1959), p. ix.

[50] The socioreligious relationship of Greek and Roman religion vis-à-vis Christianity has been discussed in Franz Cumont, *Oriental Religions in Roman Paganism* (1911; reprint, New York: Dover, 1956); Arthur Darby Nock, *Conversion: The Old and the New in Religion from Alexander the Great to Augustine of Hippo* (Oxford: Clarendon Press, 1933); Alain Hus, *Greek and Roman Religion,* trans. S. J. Tester (New York: Hawthorn Books, 1962); John Holland Smith, *The Death of Classical Paganism* (New York: Scribner's, 1976); Ramsay MacMullen, *Paganism in the Roman Empire* and *Christianizing the Roman Empire;* Robert L. Wilken, *The Christians as the Romans Saw Them;* Stephen Benko, *Pagan Rome and the Early Christians* (Bloomington, Ind.: Indiana University Press, 1984); and Robin Lane Fox, *Pagans and Christians* (New York: Knopf, 1987). Unfortunately, comparable scholarship regarding the early medieval interaction between pre-Christian Celto-Germanic religion and Christianity does not yet exist. The only recent works which focus on this area appear to be J. N. Hillgarth, ed.,

diluted state of Indo-European ideology in the Roman Empire during the early Christian period, some of the older Indo-European sociocultural forms appear to have endured. They contributed to a gradual Indo-Europeanization of various aspects of early Christianity, even prior to its contact with the Germanic peoples. Some of the most prominent examples of pre-Germanic Indo-Europeanization include the adoption of a Greek philosophical method in Christian apologetic literature and the emulation of Roman hierarchical and legal structures by the Church. The most significant effects of the subsequent Celto-Germanic Indo-Europeanization of Christianity were the emergence of a sense of Euro-Christian religiopolitical complementarity and a magicoreligious reinterpretation of Christianity, both of which figured prominently in medieval Europe.[51]

Frederick Copleston in his *History of Philosophy* has summarized the Christian debt to Greek philosophy:

> As Christianity became more firmly established and better known and as it became possible for Christian scholars to develop thought and learning, the philosophical element tended to become more strongly marked, especially when there was question of meeting the attacks of pagan professional philosophers. . . . As the Christians had no philosophy of their own to start with (i.e. in the academic sense of philosophy), they very naturally turned to the prevailing philosophy, which was derived from Platonism but was strongly impregnated with other elements. As a rough generalisation, therefore, one may say that the philosophic ideas of the early Christian writers were Platonic or neo-Platonic in character (with an admixture of

---

Christianity and Paganism, 350–750: The Conversion of Western Europe, rev. ed. of *The Conversion of Western Europe, 350–750* (Philadelphia: University of Pennsylvania, 1986); Gale R. Owen, *Rites and Religions of the Anglo-Saxons* (New York: Dorset Press, 1985); Valerie I. J. Flint, *The Rise of Magic in Early Medieval Europe* (Princeton, N.J.: Princeton University Press, 1991); and Ronald Hutton, *The Pagan Religions of the Ancient British Isles: Their Nature and Legacy* (Oxford: Basil Blackwell, 1991). Two recent works which focus on the later Christianization efforts among the Scandinavians, but which contain valuable observations regarding the Christianization process, are Régis Boyer, *Le Christ des Barbares: Le Monde nordique, IXe–XIIe siècles* (Paris: Cerf, 1987); and Birgit Sawyer, Peter Sawyer, and Ian Wood, eds., *The Christianization of Scandinavia: Report of a Symposium held at Kungälv, Sweden, 4–9 August 1985* (Alingås, Sweden: Viktoria Bokförlag, 1987).

[51] See "Men Bound by Ties of Service and Fidelity," in vol. 1 of *The Cambridge Illustrated History of the Middle Ages,* ed. Robert Fossier, trans. Janet Sondheimer (Cambridge: Cambridge University Press, 1989), pp. 83–84; Georges Duby, *The Three Orders: Feudal Society Imagined,* trans. Arthur Goldhammer, with a foreword by Thomas N. Bisson (Chicago: University of Chicago Press, 1980); Mircea Eliade, "The Assimilation and Reinterpretation of Pre-Christian Traditions: Sacred Kingship and Chivalry," sect. 267 of *A History of Religious Ideas,* vol. 3, *From Muhammed to the Age of Reforms,* trans. Alf Hiltebeitel and Diane Apostolos-Cappadona (Chicago: University of Chicago Press, 1985), pp. 89–92; and "Indo-European Christianity," in Larry Caldwell, "The Indo-European Context of *Beowulf*" (Ph.D. diss., University of Nebraska, Linclon, 1983). Caldwell does not differentiate between various stages of Indo-European socioreligious development and hence, includes certain "later stage" phenomena such as Persian dualism and Greco-Roman neo-Platonism as authentically Indo-European, whereas in the current inquiry they are considered to be the results of de-Indo-Europeanization.

Stoicism) and that the Platonic tradition continued for long to dominate Christian thought from the philosophic viewpoint.[52]

The assertion that there was an Indo-European Greek influence on early Christianity is limited here to the categorical, logical *form* of most apologetic literature. As R. T. Wallis has concluded: "Neoplatonism thus stands not as an abandonment of Greek rationalism, but as an adaptation of the categories of Greek thought to the world of inner experience."[53] The apparent decline in the Indo-European ideological orientation of the *content* of Greek philosophy through the process of "Hellenistic transformation"[54] will be developed as this chapter progresses. These assertions are not intended to in any way diminish the profound influence of the predominantly non-Indo-European content of Hellenistic philosophy on Christianity, examples of which appear to include the influence of Neoplatonism among the Alexandrian apologists, and their development of allegorical exegesis.[55]

A religious movement is unlikely to gain adherents if it does not respond to a prevalent social aspiration. Two of the most prevalent social aspirations have been the desire among "out-groups" to improve their social status and the desire among "in-groups" to retain and rationalize their social

---

[52] *A History of Philosophy,* vol. 2 (Garden City, N.Y.: Doubleday, 1950), pp. 28–29.

[53] *Neoplatonism* (New York: Scribner's, 1970), p. 6.

[54] Since the term "Hellenization" inherently emphasizes the assimilation of Hellenic Greek culture by non-Greeks, the term "Hellenistic transformation" is employed here to include the reciprocal assimilation of non-Hellenic religiocultural attitudes and practices by the Greeks themselves. Many of these non-Hellenic religiocultural influences originated in Egypt and Babylon. However, some originated in pre-Hellenic, non-Indo-European, Minoan Greece. Jaan Puhvel, *Comparative Mythology* (Baltimore: Johns Hopkins University Press, 1987), provides a helpful model of these cultural forces: "The three main ingredients of ancient Greek culture in general, and of myth in particular, may be described as substratal ('Aegean,' 'Pelasgian,' 'Minoan' in Crete), superstratal (Indo-European Greek), and adstratal (the steady seepage from Asia Minor and points farther east). Indeed the substratum and early adstratum may have been in considerable measure a continuum" (pp. 127–28). One example of this continuum may have been the development of substratal pre-Hellenic cults of seasonal vegetative rejuvenation into adstratal Hellenistic cults of individual immortality, as asserted by Nilsson, *Greek Folk Religion:* "So it was possible to develop on the foundation of the old agrarian cult a hope of immortality and a belief in the eternity of life, not for the individual but for the generations which spring from one another. Thus, also, there was developed on the same foundation a morality of peace and good will, which strove to embrace humanity in a brotherhood without respect to state allegiance and civil standing. The thoroughly industrialized and commercialized citizens of Athens in its heyday had lost understanding of the old foundation of human civilization—agriculture—and at the end of the fifth century B.C. the individual was freed from the old fetters of family and tradition. . . . Man was no longer content with the immortality of the generations but wanted immortality for himself" (pp. 63–64). The term "Hellenism," as used herein, refers to the syncretic product of the Hellenistic transformation.

[55] An important treatment of the role of Hellenistic philosophy in the development of Christian doctrine is found in Jaroslav Pelikan, *The Emergence of the Catholic Tradition (100–600),* vol. 1, *The Christian Tradition: A History of the Development of Doctrine* (Chicago: University of Chicago Press, 1971), pp. 27–55.

dominance.[56] Among the Indo-European peoples, who were the in-groups in the societies that they conquered, dominance was often expressed in the mythological theme of a "war of foundation," in which the Indo-European invaders absorbed their defeated subjects into the lowest stratum of society.[57] The existence of ancestor worship among the Indo-European conquerors also served to reinforce their social dominance, since "those who are most closely related to the original heroic or legendary ancestors are likely to rank more highly than those with more remote kinship affiliation."[58]

Christianity was not alone in providing solace for those members of out-groups who sought to transcend the anomic conditions of the Hellenistic world. Ideologies of world-rejection and individual salvation began to become popular in Greece following the devastating internecine Peloponnesian Wars,[59] and their popularity accelerated during the reign of Alexander the Great. His conquest of the Persian Empire, which included Egypt, Syria, Assyria, and Babylon, resulted in extensive social amalgamation and ultimately contributed to the destabilization of Hellenic culture and traditional Indo-European Greek religion. Samuel Angus has observed:

> The national character of Greek religion disappeared. The Greeks began to abandon their religion, which they believed came from the North, and to look with favourable regard upon religions coming from the East. Hence, particularly from the fourth century B.C. onwards, Oriental cults gained access into Greece....

[56] Max Weber, *The Sociology of Religion*, trans. Ephraim Fischoff, intro. Talcott Parsons (Boston: Beacon Press, 1963), pp. 106–8; the entirety of chapter 7, "Religion of the Non-Privileged Classes," is relevant. See also the discussion of Thomas F. O'Dea, *The Sociology of Religion* (Englewood Cliffs, N.J.: Prentice-Hall, 1966), pp. 57–61.

[57] Littleton, "War and Warriors: Indo-European Beliefs and Practices." This absorption of conquered peoples is evident in the Roman mythological portrayal of the subjugation of the Sabines by Romulus and his companions, as well as the Homeric Greek portrayal of the victory over the Trojans. It should be noted that these mythological portrayals are not considered by Littleton to have been derived from historical occurrences, but rather constitute expressions of a central Indo-European mythologem.

[58] Pearson, *Introduction to Anthropology*, p. 270.

[59] In a chapter entitled "Anomie and Arms: Toward a Sociology of War," Elwin H. Powell, *The Design of Discord: Studies of Anomie* (New Brunswick, N.J.: Transaction Books, 1988), theorizes: "When the state is weakened by anomie, i.e. internal discord, the power of the military grows because a lack of cohesion invites attack by outsiders and undermines the authority of the ruling class, which then resorts to force, terror, and intimidation to maintain its position of dominance. Times of anomie are times of war" (p. 141). Strains of world-rejection emanating from this period are reflected in the growing popularity of the Orphic mysteries, Pythagorean dualism, Sophist relativism and skepticism, as well as the Platonic concept of the individual, immortal soul. These and other indications of a growing tendency toward world-rejection in the fifth and fourth centuries B.C. are discussed in the chapter "Mysteries and Asceticism" in Walter Burkert, *Greek Religion*. Elizabeth K. Nottingham, *Religion and Society* (New York: Random House, 1954), has observed that "historical evidence indicates that new religious movements are best able to make a lasting imprint on human societies if they are born when civilizations are in turmoil," (p. 64), and that "extensive anomie is a fertile breeding ground for new types of religious organization" (p. 66).

Greek religion was doomed in the collapse of the *polis* which had given it life and form.[60]

A primary factor in the emotional and spiritual reorientation toward individual salvation may be traced to Alexander's policy of cosmopolitanism, or *oikoumene*. When a cohesive society is destabilized by invasion, immigration, or civil strife, it seems likely that those citizens who formerly derived a sense of unity, stability, and even immortality from their common ancestral religion may begin to feel alone, alienated, and threatened. In such a psychological state, the appeal of mystery cults that offer individual salvation and a sense of community is likely to increase. This societal "failure of nerve," as it was coined by J. B. Bury,[61] may be contrasted with the heroic, Homeric attitude of courageously facing and accepting one's destiny, no matter how tragic it may be. Although he is describing the early Christian era, the contrasts which Gilbert Murray has drawn in the following excerpt succinctly summarize the effects of the Hellenistic transformation as well:

> Any one who turns from the great writers of classical Athens, say Sophocles or Aristotle, to those of the Christian era must be conscious of a great difference in tone. There is a change in the whole relation of the writer to the world about him. The new quality is not specifically Christian: it is just as marked in the Gnostics and Mithras-worshippers as in the Gospels and the Apocalypse, in Julian and Plotinus as in Gregory and Jerome. It is hard to describe. It is a rise of asceticism, of mysticism, in a sense, of pessimism; a loss of self-confidence, of hope in life and of faith in normal human effort; a despair of patient inquiry, a cry for infallible revelation; an indifference to the welfare of the state, a conversion of the soul to God. It is an atmosphere in which the aim of the good man is not so much to live justly, to help the society to which he belongs and enjoy the esteem of his fellow creatures; but rather, by means of a burning faith, by contempt for the world and its standards, by ecstasy, suffering and martyrdom, to be granted pardon for his unspeakable unworthiness, his immeasurable sins. There is an intensifying of certain spiritual emotions; an increase of sensitiveness, a failure of nerve.[62]

It is particularly the world-rejecting tendency to focus on a life after death that distinguishes the new Hellenistic religiosity from the traditional world-accepting Indo-European Hellenic religiosity. The ancient Greeks

[60] *The Mystery Religions and Christianity: A Study in the Religious Background of Early Christianity* (New York: Scribner's, 1925), pp. 11–15.

[61] This description of the Christian era was suggested by J. B. Bury to Gilbert Murray, who used it for the title of chapter 4 of his *Five Stages of Greek Religion,* 3rd ed. (1925; reprint, Garden City, N.Y.: Doubleday, 1955). Murray recalls his conversation with Bury in his preface, p. xiii.

[62] *Five Stages of Greek Religion,* p. 119. Robert K. Merton, *Social Theory and Social Structure,* enlarged ed. (New York: Free Press, 1968), believes that Murray's chapter on "The Failure of Nerve," from which this excerpt is taken, "must surely be ranked among the most civilized and perceptive sociological analyses in our time" (p. 202).

were not as concerned with their posthumous status, nor did they attempt to construct a system of posthumous reward and punishment. Rather, they regarded any posthumous existence as an undesirable shadowy replica of their current existence. Even in Thucydides' account of Pericles' funeral oration to the families of slain Athenian warriors, "there is no suggestion anywhere of a personal existence continued after death; the dead live only in their deeds; and only by memory are the survivors to be consoled."[63] G. Lowes Dickinson further elaborates on the Indo-European Greek attitude toward life after death:

> From such a conception of the life after death little comfort could be drawn; nor does it appear that any was sought. So far as we can trace the habitual attitude of the Greek he seems to have occupied himself little with speculation, either for good or evil, as to what might await him on the other side of the tomb. He was told indeed in his legends of a happy place for the souls of heroes, and of torments reserved for great criminals; but these ideas do not seem to have haunted his imagination. He was never obsessed by that close and imminent vision of heaven and hell which overshadowed and dwarfed, for the medieval mind, the brief space of pilgrimage on earth. Rather he turned, by preference, from the thought of death back to life, and in the memory of honourable deeds in the past and the hope of fame for the future sought his compensation for the loss of youth and love.[64]

In searching for the source of this apparent disinterest in the prospect of life after death, one cannot overlook the possibility that a strong sense of group solidarity may have contributed to a feeling that one attains some degree of immortality through the ongoing life of one's polis, particularly when one performs heroic deeds to guarantee its continued existence. The Greek polis embodied far more than the common notion of a "city-state" suggests. According to H. D. F. Kitto, "the Greeks thought of the polis as an active, formative thing, training the minds and characters of the citizens."[65] "The polis was a living community, based on kinship, real or assumed—a kind of extended family, turning as much as possible of life into family life."[66] "Religion, art, games, the discussion of things—all these were needs of life that could be fully satisfied only through the polis."[67] According to the idealized description of the polis contained in Plato's *Laws*, the traditional polis religion "is not tuned to the religious needs of the individual."[68] Rather, "it shapes the community of the polis, pointing out and verbalizing its functions through its gods. To have Hestia, Zeus,

---

[63] G. Lowes Dickinson, *The Greek View of Life*, preface E. M. Forster (1896; reprint, Ann Arbor: University of Michigan Press, 1958), p. 36.

[64] Ibid., pp. 35–36.

[65] *The Greeks* (Harmondsworth: Penguin Books, 1957), p. 75.

[66] Ibid., p. 78.

[67] Ibid.

[68] Burkert, *Greek Religion*, p. 335.

and Athena on the acropolis means having the hearth as the centre of the community, and the highest god and the representative of the city in proximity."[69] It is significant that Gregory Nagy has recently concluded that "the Greek *polis* grew out of tribal institutions that reflect, albeit from a distance, an Indo-European heritage."[70]

The apotheosis of the ancient Greek ideal of familial unity and security, and a resulting sense of immortality, may be found in Sparta, where "the family-state raised kinship relations to a more universal level. Whatever helped the family-state was regarded as good, whatever injured it as bad."[71] The religious effect of such strong endogamous reinforcement was that "the individual Spartiat, at any rate, no longer faced fate alone; the enlarged household gave a greater sense of social solidarity; it removed the sting of death, and gave every loyal Spartiat a sense of immortality in the survival and security of the family-state."[72]

While granting the existence of multiple influences, one may yet propose a relationship between social heterogeneity, anomie, and the prospects for expansion of universal world-rejecting religions within a given society. As natural biological solidarity is perceived to diminish and traditional social institutions decline, individuals may tend to focus more upon their own personal existence and seek membership in nonbiologically related universal cults that provide opportunities for socialization and a promise of individual salvation. Oswald Spengler, in his discussion of the "world-city," of which Rome and Alexandria were examples, postulated: "The last man of the world-city no longer wants to live—he may cling to life as an individual, but as a type, as an aggregate, no, for it is a characteristic of this collective existence that it eliminates the terror of death. That which strikes the true peasant with a deep and inexplicable fear, the notion that the family and the name may be extinguished, has now lost its meaning."[73] As the destabilization of a society becomes more apparent, and the anxieties of everyday life become less bearable, the appeal of universal, world-rejecting religions which promise idealistic solutions seems likely to increase. Since socioreligious destabilization often follows a period of imperial expansion,[74] it is not surprising to find civil

---

[69] Ibid.

[70] "The Indo-European Heritage of Tribal Organization: Evidence from the Greek *polis*," in Susan Nacev Skomal and Edgar C. Polomé, eds., *Proto-Indo-European: The Archaeology of a Linguistic Problem: Studies in Honor of Marija Gimbutas* (Washington, D.C.: Institute for the Study of Man, 1987), p. 262.

[71] John W. Richards, "The Evolution of the Spartan Social System," *Mankind Quarterly* 20 (1980): 339.

[72] Ibid.

[73] *The Decline of the West*, vol. 2: *Perspectives of World History*, trans. Charles Francis Atkinson (New York: Knopf, 1928), pp. 103–4.

[74] The existence of such a relationship between political and socioreligious developments is advanced by Eric Voegelin, *Order and History*, vol. 4: *The Ecumenic Age* (Baton Rouge: University of Louisiana Press, 1974), pp. 21–22, in his discussion of the expansion of Gnosticism.

rulers advocating the acceptance of universalist world-rejecting religions among their diverse subjects, at least partially to impose a sense of unity.[75]

When Christianity is viewed from the historical perspective of the Hellenistic mystery cults, its subsequent expansion becomes more understandable. From Egypt came the cults of Osiris and Sarapis, from Asia Minor came the cult of the Great Mother goddess Cybele, and from Syria came that of Atargatis and Adonis.[76] The cults of Dionysus and Eleusis appear to have originated in pre-Hellenic, Minoan, Greece,[77] while the cults of Jupiter Doliche and of Mithras appear to have originated in the West.[78] Although each originated in a different geographical area, they all appealed to a general sense of individual alienation that seems to have pervaded the Mediterranean region during the Hellenistic age. After discussing the cults of Osiris and Serapis, Cybele, and Atargatis and Adonis, Karl Baus concludes:

> The three mystery cults have, in spite of differences of detail, one basic idea in common. The death and constant renewal observed in Nature were symbolically crystallized in the myth of a young god of vegetation, who is torn from the side of the goddess by a tragic death but rises again to new life. By this is represented the fate of man, whose strange and sometimes incomprehensibly tragic death weighed like a dark burden upon the thought and feeling of Antiquity. Should there not be for him also, as for the god in the myth, a resurrection into a mysterious hereafter? The mere possibility, hinted at in the myth, of such an eschatological hope was bound to appeal to Hellenistic man. Precisely because the old religions of Greece and Rome knew no encouraging answer to this exciting question, people turned to these new forms of religious faith, whose attraction was increased by the mysterious and outlandish nature of the initiation ceremonies, which seemed like an echo from beyond the grave. The hymns and prayers, with their intensity of feeling, caught in their spell many an anxious and excitable mind.[79]

While the mystery cults appear to have appealed primarily to middle-class elements of Hellenistic society, the upper classes turned to the new

---

See also, Paul M. Kennedy, *The Rise and Fall of the Great Powers: Economic Change and Military Conflict from 1500 to 2000* (New York: Random House, 1988).

[75] Toynbee, *An Historian's Approach to Religion*, pp. 105–13, discusses what he refers to as "the capture of higher religions for political purposes," noting: "So long as a Church is proscribed and is exposed to the peril of being persecuted at any moment, its membership is likely to be limited to a spiritual élite who are both disinterested and courageous. As soon as it is taken into partnership by the powers that be, its moral quality is likely to be diluted through mass-conversions of time-servers eager to jump on the victor's band-wagon. . . . The Church can be captured and converted into an instrument for the furtherance of the old order's interests if the manoeuvre is not advertised or avowed" (pp. 106–7).

[76] Karl Baus, *From the Apostolic Community to Constantine*, vol. 1 of *History of the Church*, ed. Hubert Jedin and John Dolan (New York: Crossroad, 1982), p. 90.

[77] Burkert, *Greek Religion*, p. 278.

[78] MacMullen, *Paganism*, pp. 118–30.

[79] Baus, *From the Apostolic Community to Constantine*, pp. 92–93.

philosophical schools of Cynicism, Skepticism, Stoicism, and Epicurean-ism.[80] Rather than appeal directly to a desire for immortality, the Epicu-reans and Stoics succeeded because their philosophies satisfied a desire for individual happiness and self-fulfillment: "they offered a conception of the world and human nature which drew its support from empirical obser-vations, reason and recognition that all men have common needs; . . . both systems adopted the important assumption that happiness depends upon an understanding of the universe and what it is to be a man."[81] While the Skeptics challenged the validity of philosophical inquiry and the Cynics challenged societal norms of behavior, both schools espoused individual freedom and were critical of the traditional values of the polis. The focus on an ethical pursuit of self-fulfillment in each of the major Hellenistic philosophies differs significantly from the focus on metaphysical inquiry found in the traditional Hellenic, and particularly pre-Socratic, Greek philosophy of the "world of the polis," which had prevailed during the pre-Alexandrian period.[82] In contrast to the Hellenistic quest for new paths to individual happiness or salvation, Walter Burkert has noted that "the pre-Christian [and in this context 'pre-Hellenistic'] religions proclaimed with the utmost conviction that only ancestral tradition could guarantee the legitimacy of religion."[83]

---

[80] Of these philosophical schools, Alain Hus, *Greek and Roman Religion,* pp. 77–78, observes that the Stoics predominated in their acceptance among the elite, while A. A. Long, *Hellenistic Philosophy: Stoics, Epicureans, Sceptics,* 2nd ed. (Berkeley: University of California Press, 1986), has noted that "in the Roman world during the first two Christian centuries Stoicism was the dominant philosophy among educated pagans" (p. 232). Its adherents included Seneca, Epictetus, and Marcus Aurelius.

[81] Long, *Hellenistic Philosophy,* pp. 6–7. Edward McNall Burns, *Western Civilizations: Their History and Their Culture,* 7th ed. (New York: W. W. Norton, 1969), has noted that, "despite the differences in their teachings, the philosophers of the Hellenistic Age were generally agreed upon one thing: the necessity of finding some way of salvation for man from the hardships and evils of his existence" (p. 193). Guthrie, *The Greek Philosophers: From Thales to Aristotle,* con-cludes his work with the following comments: "Aristotle's philosophy represents the final flowering of Greek thought in its natural setting. . . . He was the teacher of Alexander, the man who finally swept away that compact unit in which everyone could play an active part, and substituted for it the idea of a great kingdom which should embrace the world. . . . The help-lessness of man before great powers brought philosophy of a different type. It brought intense individualism, and the conception of philosophy not as an intellectual ideal but as a refuge from impotence and despair. It might be the quietism of Epicurus or the fatalism of the Stoa. The old Greek spirit of free and fearless inquiry was gone, and Aristotle's order was inverted. Some theory of conduct, something to live by, came first, and the satisfaction of the intellect was a secondary consideration. The Hellenistic world has its own achievements, but they are largely the outcome of an increased mingling of Greek with foreign, and particularly with Oriental elements. If what we want to discover is the mind of Greece, there is perhaps some excuse for stopping here" (p. 161).

[82] See Eric Voegelin, "From Myth to Philosophy," part 2 of *The World of the Polis,* vol. 2 of *Order and History* (Baton Rouge: Louisiana State University Press, 1957).

[83] *Homo Necans: The Anthropology of Ancient Greek Sacrificial Ritual and Myth,* trans. Peter Bing (Berkeley: University of California Press, 1982), p. xxii. Burkert notes further that "through his oracle, the Delphic god always sanctioned rites 'according to the custom of the

Although Stoicism was characterized by reason and restraint and did not focus on otherworldly yearnings as did later Neoplatonist and Neo-pythagorean philosophical movements, it did possess certain inclinations which conform to the description of world-rejecting tendencies stated earlier in this chapter. Primary among these were the notions of individualism and universalism, each of which may be viewed as a rejection of the world-accepting sociobiological principle of group survival through in-group altruism. Instead of reinforcing group solidarity, "stoicism provided a theoretical basis for self-sufficiency and for universal brotherhood, thus fulfilling two essential aspirations of the uprooted individuals of the Hellenistic Age."[84]

While the upper class became attracted to the new philosophical schools which extolled individualism and universalism and the middle class became attracted to various mystery cults, "the great mass of simple folk . . . turned towards the lower kinds of superstition, which in Hellenistic times especially were very widespread in numerous forms."[85] Among these people the most attractive forms of religious behavior involved astrological speculation and magic. Franz Cumont sought to explain why astrological tendencies, which had their origin in Babylon, were not expressed among the Greeks prior to the Hellenistic era.

---

city'; and the Boeotian [the second century B.C. Greek author, Agatharchides] was speaking for many when he remarked, in regard to a strange fish sacrifice at Lake Copais, 'There is just one thing I know: that one must maintain the ancestral customs and that it would be improper to excuse oneself for this before others' " (ibid.). In an observation which challenges the notion that cultural advancement is necessarily accompanied by a movement toward a universalist religious perspective, Burkert maintains that "only in ancient Greek religion do we find an uninterrupted tradition of the greatest antiquity in a highly refined culture, unsurpassed in its intellectual and artistic achievement" (p. xxiii). He also maintains that "it was due to this union of antiquity with sophistication that the Greeks were the first systematically to call religion into question" (ibid.).

[84] James L. Price, *Interpreting the New Testament*, 2nd ed. (New York: Holt, Rinehart and Winston, 1971), p. 342. In his discussion "Alexander's Influence," Everett Ferguson, *Backgrounds of Early Christianity* (Grand Rapids, Mich.: Eerdmans, 1987), notes an "increase of individualism" following his conquests, and observes: "Individualism may seem a paradox alongside universalism, but the two are corollaries. The breaking of traditional patterns of inherited conduct in the enlarged world of the Hellenistic age threw men back upon themselves and gave opportunity for individual expression. Chosen things became more important than inherited things. As one example, personal religion stems from the philosophical individualism of Socrates. It is hard to imagine Christianity succeeding in any other environment than that which resulted from the conquests of Alexander" (p. 9). This last sentence is particularly noteworthy when the anomic, individualistic, sociocultural conditions of the Hellenistic age are juxtaposed with the high level of group solidarity which existed among the Germanic peoples at the time of their encounter with Christianity.

[85] Baus, *From the Apostolic Community to Constantine*, p. 94. The appeal of astrology was not, of course, limited to the lower class. As Rome became Hellenized, its emperors and upper class also succumbed to the influences of astrology and magic. These developments are discussed in greater detail in J. H. W. G. Liebeschuetz, *Continuity and Change in Roman Religion* (Oxford: Oxford University Press, 1979), pp. 119–39.

The insatiable curiosity of the Greeks, then, did not ignore astrology, but their sober genius rejected its hazardous doctrines, and their keen critical sense was able to distinguish the scientific data observed by the Babylonians from the erroneous conclusions which they derived from them. . . .

But after the conquests of Alexander a great change took place. The ancient ideal of the Greek republic gave way to the conception of universal monarchy. Thenceforth municipal cults disappeared before an international religion. The worship of the stars, common to all the peoples, was strengthened by everything that weakened the particularism of cities. In proportion as the idea of "humanity" spread, men were the more ready to reserve their homage for those celestial powers which extended their blessings to all mankind.[86]

Thus Alexander's conquests and ecumenical pursuits appear to have contributed toward religious syncretism, the popularization of astrology and the advancement of the notion of a universal brotherhood of man. This notion later became a central and distinctive feature of Christianity. According to W. W. Tarn, Alexander "declared that all men were alike sons of one Father, and when at Opis he prayed that Macedonians and Persians might be partners in the commonwealth and that the peoples of his world might live in harmony and in unity of heart and mind, he proclaimed for the first time the unity and brotherhood of mankind. . . . He, first of all men, was ready to transcend national differences, and to declare, as St. Paul was to declare, that there was neither Greek nor barbarian."[87]

It has thus far been asserted that each class of Hellenistic Greek society tended toward its own form of world-rejecting religiosity: the upper class tended to be attracted to world-rejecting philosophical schools,[88] the middle class to mystery cults, and the lower class to astrology and magic. Following the conquest of Greece by Rome in 146 B.C., Oriental mystery cults, and Hellenistic religiosity in general, achieved greater acceptance within the Roman Republic. When these cults "threatened to break the exclusive control of the political authorities over religious activities" and "threatened to undermine rather than supplement the ancestral religion," the Roman government's "official response to innovation was either negative, or more often passive."[89] Contributing to the spread of the general

---

[86] *Astrology and Religion among the Greeks and Romans,* trans. J. B. Baker (1912; reprint, New York: Dover, 1960), pp. 31–32.

[87] *Alexander the Great* (1948; reprint, Boston: Beacon Press, 1956), p. 147. The relevant scriptural passages are Galatians 3:26–29 and Colossians 3:10–11.

[88] Since the implicit inclusion of Epicureanism here may be challenged, it should be recalled, as Everett Ferguson, *Backgrounds of Early Christianity* (Grand Rapids, Mich.: Eerdmans, 1987), does that: "Epicurus was not (in its modern connotation) an Epicurean. . . . Both Epicureans and Stoics sought to liberate humans from fate, to make them self-sufficient and indifferent to externals" (pp. 300–1).

[89] Peter Garnsey and Richard Saller, *The Roman Empire: Economy, Society and Culture* (Berkeley: University of California Press, 1987), pp. 170–74. Garnsey and Saller also note that

Hellenistic quest for individual salvation was the socioeconomic upheaval which resulted from the protracted Punic Wars (264–146 B.C.). Of particular significance for the success of the mystery cults was "the growth of a helpless city mob composed of impoverished farmers and workers displaced by slave labor."[90]

The first official reception of an Oriental mystery cult in Rome was that of Cybele, also known as the Great Mother, which was introduced in 204 B.C. The reception provoked substantial opposition from the republican Senate, which "objected to the ecstatic nature of the cult in which there was scope for self-mutilation by males, and practice of the cult was at first restricted to the natives who had come with the 'image' from Pessinus."[91] The next major Roman encounter with an Oriental cult was in 186 B.C. The Dionysiac Bacchanalia was viewed by the Roman authorities as "a cult which allowed meetings by night of both sexes, made a pretext of ecstasy and was on the side of public disorder." They therefore "decided to forbid the cult to their citizens and to license it only for those who could show it was their traditional religion."[92] Burkert, who views the Bacchanalia as an atypically well-organized cult, has noted that the essence of the case against it was largely sociopolitical:

> The accusation was that there had been a huge conspiracy (*coniuratio*) that was to overthrow the existing *res publica;* "another people is about to rise," *alterum iam populum esse.* This vision of "another people" that is to oust the *populus Romanus Quiritium* is a frightening one which in a strange way foretells the proclamation of a new *politeia,* a new *civitas* by later Christians. This may also explain why repression was so cruel and radical, with some 6,000 executions at a time. There is nothing comparable in religious history before the persecution of Christians.[93]

In addition to the suppression of the cults of Cybele and Bacchus, later in the first century B.C. "consular officials destroyed a temple of Isis and Sarapis which had been put up 'on privately owned land.' "[94] Although there were sporadic attempts to bolster the status of the traditional religion by Augustus and other emperors, the absence of a vigilantly enforced policy of opposition to the introduction of alien ideological and religious influences resulted in the gradual permeation of the Hellenistic mysteries and their ideal of individual salvation throughout all levels of Roman society.

"this attitude falls far short of the policy of toleration with which the Roman state is usually credited" (ibid.), and refer the reader to Peter Garnsey, "Religious Tolerance in Classical Antiquity," in *Persecution and Toleration,* ed. W. J. Sheils, SCH, no. 21 (Oxford: Basil Blackwell, 1984), pp. 1–28.

[90] Burns, *Western Civilizations,* p. 217.

[91] Alan Wardman, *Religion and Statecraft among the Romans* (London: Granada Publishing, 1982), p. 112.

[92] Ibid., p. 113.

[93] *Ancient Mystery Cults* (Cambridge: Harvard University Press, 1987), p. 52.

[94] Wardman, *Religion and Statecraft,* p. 113.

Coincidentally, in the single career of the emperor Caracalla, who reigned from A.D. 198 to 217, may be found actions which epitomized the Hellenistic transformation of the traditional Indo-European Roman religion. After Commodus (reigned A.D. 176–192) "had represented himself as Hercules, participated fully and openly in the festivals of the Egyptian gods, incorporated a prayer to Sarapis in the official prayers of the new year, and saluted Sarapis *Conservator Augusti* on his coins, all that was left for Caracalla to do was to introduce the Egyptian gods into the sanctuaries within the sacred boundary of Rome (the pomerium) and reconstruct the official Pantheon around them."[95] In addition to this act of religious innovation, Caracalla advanced the egalitarian and individualistic ideological components of Hellenism by his "Antoninian Constitution," an edict issued in A.D. 212 which conferred citizenship upon nearly all free inhabitants of the Roman Empire.[96] The effect of this edict was greatest in the eastern areas of the empire, where few inhabitants had previously possessed citizenship. As an indirect consequence, nontraditional Oriental cults gained in their level of acceptability and prestige.

In examining the effects of this process of Hellenistic transformation upon the Indo-European classical religiosity, Solomon Katz has noted that "the Græco-Roman spirit of rationalism was being buffeted and broken by waves of religious enthusiasm," and that "of all the many changes occurring in the Roman Empire, this change from a scientific, objective, and rational basis of thought and life to a way of life based upon faith and dogma is perhaps the most revolutionary."[97] While acknowledging that the intellectual and psychological aspects of the decline of Rome are "extremely difficult to assess," Katz speculates on the causality of the ideological developments which accompanied the Hellenistic transformation:

> As a result of the chaos and dislocation of life, there was a growing note of pessimism and despair which led to apathy and inertia. A reflection of this was the shift of interest from the here to the hereafter. We have seen how, under the stress of political, economic and social ills, men turned to otherworldly religions, the Oriental mystery cults and Christianity. As they lost confidence in the Empire and in their own power to alter conditions, they tried to find inner security as compensation for a world which was grim and uncertain. This groping for salvation in new religions is one aspect of the psychological change; another is the resignation to the misfortunes of this world; to a totalitarian regime, a collapsing economy, and the barbarian invaders themselves. There was a "loss of nerve," as it has been called,

---

[95] Garnsey and Saller, *The Roman Empire,* p. 172.

[96] This action appears to have been motivated primarily by economic concerns rather than by sociopolitical ideology. To support his profligate reign, Caracalla sought to increase the revenue which accrued from inheritance taxes. Only Roman citizens were required to pay these taxes.

[97] *The Decline of Rome and the Rise of Mediaeval Europe* (Ithaca, N.Y: Cornell University Press, 1955), p. 53.

a breakdown of morale, a defeatist mentality. Even if they had the means, men no longer had the will to maintain the Empire against invasion and dissolution.[98]

When considering the significance of the expansion of Hellenistic religious attitudes for the expansion of Christianity, it may be helpful to distinguish between the two. The foremost distinction was the lack of any formal socioreligious organization or *ekklesia* among the mystery cults, philosophical schools, astrologers, or magicians, whereas "with Christianity there appeared an alternative society in the full sense of potentially independent, self-sufficient, and self-reproducing communities."[99] Another distinction lay in the generally ambiguous notion of salvation in Hellenism, where it referred to a wide spectrum of actions including recovery from illness and the immortality of one's soul, whereas within the context of early Christianity, salvation referred primarily to the bodily resurrection of the faithful.[100] One might add that a distinctive aspect of Christian salvation is the notion of atonement by the savior figure for individual and corporate sinfulness.

Kurt Aland has asserted that "the only thing the mystery religions and Christianity have in common is the term [salvation, resurrection and immortality], but the things that really matter are fundamentally different."[101] Furthermore, the historicity of the person of Jesus is unparalleled in the myths surrounding the central characters of the mystery cults. However, what is most significant for the present study is not the extent to which Christianity may have been influenced by Hellenistic religious developments, but rather, the extent to which Christianity and the mystery cults responded to the same fundamental socioreligious aspiration. This may be summarized as a world-rejecting desire for personal salvation from an earthly existence fraught with uncertainty, dissatisfaction, and the dissolution of old

[98] Ibid., p. 83. This general sociopolitical apathy, and particularly the reluctance to risk personal physical injury for the preservation of the empire, may be considered a primary indicator of social decadence. Indeed, Robert M. Adams, *Decadent Societies* (San Francisco: North Point Press, 1983), has claimed that "the simplest definition of decadence . . . is not failure, misfortune, or weakness, but deliberate neglect of the essentials of self-preservation—incapacity or unwillingness to face a clear and present danger" (p. 36).

[99] Burkert, *Ancient Mystery Cults*, p. 51.

[100] Ibid., p. 28.

[101] *A History of Christianity*, vol. 1: *From the Beginnings to the Threshold of the Reformation*, trans. James L. Schaaf (Philadelphia: Fortress Press, 1980), p. 24. Aland cites the study of Greek religion by Martin Nilsson, *Geschichte der griechischen Religion*, 2 vols., 3rd ed. (Munich: Beck, 1961), to buttress his assertion. Also noteworthy in the attempt to dissociate Christianity from the influence of the mystery cults is Hugo Rahner, *Greek Myth and Christian Mystery*, trans. Brian Battershaw, intro. E. O. James (1963; reprint, Cheshire, Conn.: Biblo & Tannen, 1971). The influential and provocative work which sought earlier in this century to attribute the development of early Christianity to the mystery cults, and ultimately to Persian religious concepts, is Richard Reitzenstein, *Hellenistic Mystery Religions: Their Basic Ideas and Significance*, 3rd ed., trans. John E. Steely, Pittsburgh Theological Monograph Series, no. 15 (Pittsburgh: Pickwick Press, 1978), published in German in 1926.

communal bonds. Karl Baus has provided the following important synopsis in "The Religious Situation in the Graeco-Roman World at the Time of Its Encounter with Christianity":

> Political developments in the eastern Mediterranean area also played their part in furthering the decline of the classical Greek religion. The period of rule of the Diadochs [successors of Alexander who fought among themselves from 323 to 280 B.C.] involved in Greece itself the final dissolution of the old city-states, and this in turn was a death-blow to the religious cults which had been maintained by them or their associations of noble families. The newly founded Hellenistic cities in the East, with their commercial possibilities, enticed many Greeks to emigrate, so that the homeland grew poorer and many ancient sanctuaries fell into ruin. Of much more far-reaching effect was the exchange of religious ideas and their liturgical forms of expression, which was brought about by the hellenization of the East, an exchange in which the gods of Greece and the Orient were to a great extent assimilated to one another but lost many of their original attributes in the process. . . . Oriental cults streamed into Greece and beyond to the western parts of the empire, effecting there a decline of old beliefs and, even in spite of new forms, a loss of religious content.
>
>   The ancient Roman religion was also subjected to the same process of dissolution. Since the Second Punic War there had been a steadily growing hellenization of Roman religion. . . . When towards the end of the Second Punic War the Sibylline books demanded the introduction of the cult of Cybele from Asia Minor, the gods of the East began their triumphal entry into Rome and contributed to the disintegration of the ancient Roman faith. All attempts to stem the invasion on the part of the Senate and of those circles in Rome which viewed these developments with anxiety were in the long run unsuccessful.[102]

Baus has also noted within Hellenistic religion certain predispositions that were conducive to the subsequent arrival of the Christian message. Among these were "the feeling of emptiness which had undeniably arisen among men of more thoughtful nature on account of the failure of the ancient religions, . . . a deep desire of redemption in the men of that time which was also bound to be quickened when eternal salvation was offered by a Savior," and "finally, the strong tendency to monotheism, so apparent in the religions of the Hellenistic period."[103] These Hellenistic religious attitudes "provided the Christian missionaries with an ideal bridgehead in the pagan lands."[104]

Thus far, the transformation of the traditional world-accepting Indo-European classical religions into the potpourri of Greco-Roman and Oriental cults and unlimited syncretic variations that existed in the Roman Empire by the third century A.D. has been surveyed. This development is

---

[102] Baus, *From the Apostolic Community to Constantine,* pp. 87–88.
[103] Ibid., pp. 97–98.
[104] Ibid., p. 98.

significant not only because it relates to the decline of Indo-European religiosity, but also because the resulting Hellenistic religiosity formed one of the two major environmental, if not ideological, influences upon early Christianity. The other major influence was Palestinian Judaism. Since Indo-European Greco-Roman and Hellenistic religiosities were compared earlier from the perspective of a world-accepting folk religiosity versus world-rejecting universal religions, Palestinian Judaism will be examined similarly.

The socioeconomic environment of Palestine in the time of Jesus and the apostolic Church was one of urban disenchantment:

> Everyone was dissatisfied with the existing political and social conditions, with the exception of the wealthier families, many of whom were priests, known as the Sadducees. This ruling faction kowtowed to their overlords. Fear, hatred, and bitter resentment were in evidence everywhere; and, on top of these things, there was much poverty. In spite of recurrent warfare, the population had increased during these centuries [63 B.C. to A.D. 135]. Declining food supplies and wasteful governments made desperate the plight of all citizens, except for some of the provident and hard-working peasants and artisans. Commercial and maritime trade had greatly increased during the era of the Hasmoneans and the Herods, but this influx of wealth had not improved conditions among the masses. It had tended rather to uproot them from their lands and, in chaotic times, to make them a restless group of malcontents.[105]

The religious attitudes which accompanied this socioeconomic situation, and which were probably reinforced by it, may be characterized as "Jewish 'apocalypticism,' a movement and a literature . . . which had a decisive influence on early Christianity."[106] Incorporated into the Jewish apocalyptic world-view were the eschatological beliefs that "history is the arena of God's activity," that Israel was "destined to serve the divine purpose in a special way," and that this service would soon be facilitated through a messiah figure.[107]

---

[105] James L. Price, *Interpreting the New Testament,* 2nd ed. (New York: Holt, Rinehart and Winston, 1971), pp. 45–46. Additional socioeconomic details of this period are discussed in Joseph Klausner, *Jesus of Nazareth: His Life, Times and Teaching,* trans. H. Danby (1929; reprint, New York: Macmillan, 1959); Frederick C. Grant, *The Economic Background of the Gospels* (London: Oxford University Press, 1926); and Joachim Jeremias, *Jerusalem in the Time of Jesus,* trans. F. H. Cave and C. H. Cave (Philadelphia: Fortress Press, 1969).

[106] Price, *Interpreting the New Testament,* pp. 75–76.

[107] Ibid., pp. 75–82. Jewish apocalypticism and related topics are discussed further by D. S. Russell, *The Method and Message of Jewish Apocalyptic* (1964; reprint, Philadelphia: Fortress Press, 1978); Amos N. Wilder, *Eschatology and Ethics in the Teaching of Jesus,* rev. ed. (New York: Harper & Row, 1950); and Joseph Klausner, *The Messianic Idea in Israel: From Its Beginning to the Completion of the Mishnah,* trans. W. F. Stinespring (New York: Macmillan, 1955). An interesting study which follows the development of apocalyptic thought through the Middle Ages is Norman Cohn, *The Pursuit of the Millennium,* rev. and expanded ed. (New York: Oxford University Press, 1970).

These prominent apocalyptic and messianic notions of Palestinian Judaism, which also permeated early Christianity, shared with contemporary Hellenistic religiosity a fundamentally world-rejecting character. This is an important assertion for the current inquiry, given the relative absence of the world-rejecting notions of salvation, astrology, magic, messianism, apocalypticism, and dualism in authentic Indo-European religiosity. It is contended here that the Hellenistic transformation process was also a "de-Indo-Europeanization process," insofar as the core world-accepting Indo-European folk ideal of familial and communal solidarity as exemplified in the life of the polis was gradually displaced by an individualist and universalist religiosity.

The idea of salvation is central to this inquiry. In the preceding chapter it was stated that belief in redemption through the suffering and death of Jesus Christ constitutes, at least for the current inquiry, the ideological core of the Christian ethos and world-view.[108] It has been noted by S. G. F. Brandon that "Christianity, which is the salvation-religion par excellence, stemmed from Judaism; but its soteriology was profoundly influenced by ideas current in the Greco-Roman world, in which it spread during the formative centuries of its growth."[109] Since Palestinian Judaism and Hellenism were both essentially world-rejecting and salvation-oriented, it is not surprising that these themes were incorporated into early Christianity. While Christianity's Hellenistic heritage contributed toward the notion of individual salvation, Christianity's Judaic heritage advanced notions of both individual and group salvation, as well as the associated concepts of eschaton and messiah. The transformation of "this-worldly" Judaic group salvation into "other-worldly" Christian universal salvation may be credited to sociopolitical factors, as well as to the Pauline initiative. Vittorio Lanternari has developed an interesting theory regarding this transformation:

> The transcendental nature of Christianity sets it historically apart both from the messianic movements that preceded it and from those arising among primitive peoples which strive equally for human salvation on earth.
>
> One may wonder what caused Christianity to so transform the values inherent in the earlier prophetic messages. A determining factor is the

[108] See above, p. 35.

[109] *Dictionary of the History of Ideas,* s.v. "Sin and Salvation." Brandon has also edited a collection of essays entitled *The Savior God: Comparative Studies in the Concept of Salvation Presented to Edwin Oliver James* (1963; reprint, Westport, Conn.: Greenwood Press, 1980). Also related to this topic are idem, *Man and His Destiny in the Great Religions* (Manchester: Manchester University Press, 1962); idem, *History, Time and Deity* (Manchester: Manchester University Press, 1965); idem, *The Judgement of the Dead* (London: Weidenfeld & Nicholson, 1967). Further discussion of the concept of salvation may be found in the *Encyclopedia of Religion,* s.v. "Soteriology"; *Encyclopedia of Religion and Ethics,* s.v. "Sin" and "Salvation"; *Reallexikon für Antike und Christentum,* s.v. "Erlösung"; *Religion in Geschichte und Gegenwart,* s.v. "Erlöser" and "Erlösung."

endogenous nature of the Christian movement, which developed from an urban society overburdened by hierarchical structures. Christianity arose and grew as a "popular" manifestation in reaction to the presence within its society of two oppressive forces, the Jewish priesthood and the Roman Empire, which could be fought on religious grounds only if the existing values of that society were rejected and others of purely spiritual and nonworldly significance were adopted in their stead. The redemptive message of Christianity—opposing the form and nature of both church and state at that time—was obliged to offer, as it did, a total escape from reality by holding out the promise of a kingdom able to overthrow all the worthless institutions which sustained society.[110]

Although the internal scriptural evidence of early Christianity's world-rejecting orientation is probably most convincing,[111] the discovery of the Nag Hammadi Library in 1945 and the Dead Sea Scrolls in Qumran in 1947 may contribute additional credibility to such a characterization. If Jesus was associated with an Essene community, and if the Qumran scrolls depict such a community, there exist grounds for suggesting that the ascetic, messianic, eschatological, and proto-Gnostic orientation expressed in the scrolls may have influenced Jesus and the early Christian community.[112] The Christian subject matter of many of the Nag Hammadi Library

[110] Vittorio Lanternari, *The Religions of the Oppressed: A Study of Modern Messianic Cults,* trans. Lisa Sergio (New York: Knopf, 1963), pp. 312–13. By referring to the "endogenous nature of the Christian movement," Lanternari is asserting that Christianity is a movement "produced to meet critical conditions of purely internal origin." Salvation is sought "through spiritual, cultural, or ethical channels," and is eschatologically directed toward "life in the hereafter, where the individual may truly achieve liberation." This form of salvation is to be contrasted with the more sociopolitical form of "immediate action through militant struggle" (pp. 310–13).

[111] The rather consistent use of the term "world" in a perjorative sense in each of the Gospels, which can be documented with the aid of a scriptural concordance (e.g., *The Eerdmans Analytical Concordance to the Revised Standard Version of the Bible,* compiled by Richard E. Whitaker, with James E. Goehring [Grand Rapids, Mich.: Eerdmans, 1988], pp. 1237–38), especially when combined with the Pauline spirit-flesh dichotomy, seems to generally coincide with the first half of Bellah's description of world-rejection as "an extremely negative evaluation of man and society" ("Religious Evolution," p. 264), whereas Jesus' proclamation of the "kingdom of God," whether it is interpreted in a historical or eschatological sense, seems to generally coincide with the second half of Bellah's description of world-rejection as "the exaltation of another realm of reality as alone true and infinitely valuable" (ibid.). Furthermore, scriptural injunctions to leave one's family to follow Christ, such as those found in Luke 10:28–31, are inherently opposed to the fundamental world-accepting sociobiological principle of group survival.

[112] A concise analysis of the philosophical and religious views of the authors of the Qumran scrolls is contained in ch. 9, "The Doctrines of the Sect," and ch. 13, "The Messianic Conceptions of Qumran and the Early Church," in John Allegro, *The Dead Sea Scrolls: A Reappraisal,* 2nd ed. (Harmondsworth: Penguin Books, 1964), as well as in Price, *Interpreting the New Testament,* pp. 72–76. Allegro's personal impression is worth noting: "My own opinion is that the scrolls prompt us increasingly to seek an eschatological meaning for most of Jesus' reported sayings: More and more become intelligible when viewed in the light of the imminent cataclysm of Qumran expectations, and the inner conflict in men's hearts as the time drew near" (p. 175).

texts tends to associate them, at least peripherally, with early Christianity. Their Gnostic orientation has been viewed by James M. Robinson as constituting a developmental continuum with the Dead Sea Scrolls.[113]

Although Gnosticism may have been a more radically world-rejecting religious movement than mainstream early Christianity, it may also be viewed as a quasi-intellectual response to the same problems of social destabilization and alienation to which mainstream Christianity advocated a response of faith. J. N. D. Kelly has surmised that Gnosticism "was neither religion in the strict sense nor philosophy pure and simple; it is best described as a species of theosophy."[114] In its "bizarre mixture of speculation, fantasy and mysticism, interspersed with Scriptural reminiscences,"[115] Gnosticism may be considered the apotheosis of the world-rejecting religious outlook. If, as Elaine Pagels has suggested, the Gnosticism presented in the Nag Hammadi texts represents an "alternative form of early Christianity,"[116] its significance for a fuller comprehension of early Christianity is substantially increased. However, even if this is not the case, an understanding of Gnosticism is important for this inquiry because it may be considered to constitute the antithesis of Indo-European religiosity, and particularly its Hellenic and Germanic manifestations.

Historically the origins of Gnosticism, like dualism, have been attributed by some to Zoroastrian influence.[117] However, since the discovery of the Nag Hammadi texts, a consensus appears to be developing which places the origin of Gnosticism within the Jewish community.[118] In addition to studying the historical origins of Gnosticism and other world-rejecting religious movements, it also may be fruitful to consider them from an existential perspective. This approach has been taken by Hans Jonas, who views Gnosticism as an escapist response by those who felt alienated by the sociopolitical disintegration of the Eastern Roman Empire.[119] Eric Voegelin

[113] James M. Robinson, introduction to idem, ed., *The Nag Hammadi Library in English,* trans. Members of the Coptic Gnostic Library Project of the Institute for Antiquity and Christianity (San Francisco: Harper & Row, 1977), p. 7. This work, which is an indispensable resource for analysis of the texts, has been completely revised in a third edition published in 1988.

[114] *Early Christian Doctrines,* 2nd ed. (New York: Harper & Row, 1960), p. 24.

[115] Ibid.

[116] *Gnostic Gospels* (New York: Random House, 1979), p. xxiv.

[117] J. Duchesne-Guillemin, *The Western Response to Zoroaster* (Oxford: Clarendon Press, 1958), particularly ch. 6, "Iran, Israel, Gnosticism."

[118] *Encyclopedia of Religion,* s.v. "Gnosticism," by Gilles Quispel. However, Rodney Stark, "Christianizing the Urban Empire: An Analysis Based on 22 Greco-Roman Cities," *Sociological Analysis* 52:1 (Spring 1991): 77–88, supports "the thesis that while Christianity arose as a 'Jewish heresy,' Gnosticism arose as a Christian 'heresy,' rather than constituting a Jewish movement with origins parallel to those of Christianity" (p. 77).

[119] *The Gnostic Religion: The Message of the Alien God and the Beginnings of Christianity,* 2nd rev. ed. (Boston: Beacon Press, 1963), is the popular English introduction to Jonas's work. A recent overview of the history and historiography of Gnosticism may be found in the *Encyclo-*

has pursued the existential approach further toward the realm of psychohistory. His analysis of Gnosticism is important because it posits a relationship between sociopsychological development and religious orientation, and contributes to an understanding of possible sociopsychological factors involved in the expansion of universal, salvation-oriented, world-rejecting religions:

> The knowledge, the Gnosis, . . . is the precondition for engaging successfully in the operation of liberating the pneuma in man from its cosmic prison. The imaginative game of liberation derives its momentum from an intensely experienced alienation and an equally intense revolt against it; Gnostic thinkers, both ancient and modern, are the great psychologists of alienation, carriers of the Promethean revolt.
>
> The futility of existence in a time of imperial expansion, however, can find less-complicated ways to vent itself, as the history of zealotism and apocalyptic movements shows. Alienation and revolt, though they provide the momentum, do not alone produce a Gnostic system that, with considerable speculative effort, tries to comprehend the whole of reality and its process. The additional factor is a consciousness of the movement toward the Beyond of such strength and clarity that it becomes an obsessive illumination, blinding a man for [to] the contextual structure of reality.[120]

In chapter 1 it was suggested that social and ideological structure may predispose a society to one or another form of religious expression.[121] More particularly, Thomas O'Dea's conclusion that "people suffering from extreme deprivation and people suffering from anomie (some groups may be experiencing both) display a considerable responsiveness to religions which preach a message of salvation" was noted.[122] Conversely, it was suggested that a social structure which provided a strong degree of cohesiveness and security, like that which prevailed within the Germanic societies of the early medieval period, might not be conducive to the social and ideological messages of salvation expressed by Christianity.[123] Powell, Lanternari, and Voegelin have supplemented this model by suggesting conditions which may cause stable, cohesive societies to become destabilized, anomic ones. The

---

pedia of Religion, s.v. "Gnosticism," by Gilles Quispel. Additional research on Gnosticism is contained in Ugo Bianchi, ed., *Le Origini dello Gnosticismo: Colloquio di Messina, 13–18 Aprile 1966,* Numen Supplement, no. 12 (Leiden: Brill, 1967), particularly E. M. Mendelson, "Some Notes on a Sociological Approach to Gnosticism." An important resource for Gnostic as well as other studies in Hellenistic and Oriental religiosity is the ongoing work of Maarten J. Vermaseren, ed., *Etudes préliminaires aux religions orientales dans l'Empire romain* (Leiden: Brill, 1967–81), which contains over a hundred volumes.

[120] *The Ecumenic Age,* pp. 19–20. Acknowledgment is due Ellis Sandoz, Director of the Voegelin Institute at Louisiana State University in Baton Rouge, for suggesting the clarifying interpolation in the last sentence.

[121] See above, pp. 20–21.

[122] *The Sociology of Religion,* p. 57, quoted and cited above on p. 21.

[123] See above, p. 20.

most comprehensive survey of the social, political, psychological, and historical factors which appear to contribute to the development of world-rejecting religious movements may be found in a series of articles by Noel W. Smith.[124]

After commenting on the insecure sociopolitical conditions which precipitated the Christianization of Egypt in the second century, Smith concludes: "Egypt was only one of many cultures that underwent a revolution in social and psychological concepts at that time. Under the same insecure and debilitating conditions as the Egyptians faced, Greece and other nations in much of the Mediterranean and in regions eastward also shifted their psychological concepts. . . . Under conditions of fear, debasement, and enslavement, naturalism gave way to supernaturalism. . . . The internal/external or mind/body dichotomy which did not exist in earlier Egypt or in Homeric or Hellenic Greece has remained a legacy of psychology to the present day."[125]

---

[124] "The Distant Past and Its Relation to Current Psychology: A Tour of Psychophysical Dualism and Non-Dualism," *Mankind Quarterly* 32:3 (1992): 261–73; "The Evolution of Psychophysical Dualism in Ancient India: From the *Rig Veda* to the *Sutras,*" *Mankind Quarterly* 31:1/2 (1990): 3–15; "Psychological Concepts Under Changing Social Conditions in Ancient Egypt," *Mankind Quarterly* 30:4 (1990): 317–27; "Indo-European Psychological Concepts and the Shift to Psychophysical Dualism," *Mankind Quarterly* 30:1/2 (1989): 119–27; "Belief Systems—A Psychological Analysis," *Mankind Quarterly* 25:3 (1985): 195–225; and "The Ancient Background to Greek Psychology," *Psychological Record* 24 (1974): 309–24.

[125] "Psychological Concepts Under Changing Social Conditions in Ancient Egypt," pp. 324–25.

4

Sociopsychological Aspects of Religious Transformation

A comparison of the sociopsychological forces operating within the anomic urban centers of the Roman Empire, and those operating among the predominantly rural societies of the Germanic peoples, will aid in understanding the different responses to Christianity in each of these disparate social environments.

A recent social history of Pauline Christianity by Wayne A. Meeks provides important insights into the social structure and social psychology of the early Christian community. He notes that "the image of the initiate being adopted as God's child and thus receiving a new family of human brothers and sisters is a vivid way of portraying what a modern sociologist might call the resocialization of conversion. The natural kinship structure into which the person has been born and which previously defined his place and connections with the society is here supplanted by a new set of relationships."[1] Meeks contrasts the spontaneous, ad hoc nature of the Christian community and its "regular use of terms like 'brother' and 'sister,' [and] the emphasis on mutual love," both of which "reinforce the *communitas* of the Christian groups," with the society "of 'the world,' " exemplified by "the closely structured, hierarchical society of the Greco-Roman city."[2] The attempt of the early Christian communities to emulate and eventually supplant the natural sociobiological relationships of the family unit and the larger ethnic community contributed to a perception of them by some non-Christian Roman citizens as "a disruptive social phenomenon and a danger to the security of the state."[3] This perception is at least partially attributable

[1] Wayne A. Meeks, *The First Urban Christians: The Social World of the Apostle Paul* (New Haven, Conn.: Yale University Press, 1983), p. 88.

[2] Ibid., p. 87. For the use of a surrogate family model in contemporary alternative religious movements, see Robert H. Cartwright and Stephen A. Kent, "Social Control in Alternative Religions: A Familial Perspective," *Sociological Analysis* 53 (1992): 345–61.

[3] Stephen Benko, *Pagan Rome and the Early Christians* (Bloomington: University of Indiana Press, 1984), p. 21. The most notable exponent of this view was Celsus, whose critique of Christianity, entitled *The True Word* (c. 180), expressed concern regarding the effect of Christianity on Roman family life. Perhaps this concern had been heightened by scriptural passages

to the novel universalist form which Christianity took. Robert L. Wilken has examined this fundamental distinction in form as it appears in Celsus's critique of Christianity:

> There is another dimension to this exchange between Celsus and the Christians. It is not simply a debate between paganism and Christianity, but a debate about a new concept of religion. Celsus sensed that Christians had severed the traditional bond between religion and a "nation" or people. The ancients took for granted that religion was indissolubly linked to a particular city or people. Indeed, there was no term for *religion* in the sense we now use it to refer to the beliefs and practices of a specific group of people or of a voluntary association divorced from ethnic or national identity. . . . The idea of an association of people bound together by a religious allegiance with its own traditions and beliefs, its own history, and its own way of life independent of a particular city or nation was foreign to the ancients. Religion belonged to a *people,* and it was bestowed on an individual by the people or nation from which one came or in which one lived.[4]

The eschatological orientation of early Christianity as expressed in the Pauline exhortation to celibacy,[5] contributed to the frequent attraction of individuals who had left their families. The early Christians gathered in nonbiological communities that tended to emulate familial bonds. The novel and socially dysfunctional nature of these communities, when judged by contemporary Roman standards, incurred substantial criticism. As Elaine Pagels has recently noted: "In a sense such critics were right; for Christians did threaten the social and ethical system of the ancient world in ways that eventually would alter the structure of the empire itself."[6]

Those who were attracted to such alternative communities were not exclusively from the lower classes of the empire, as was once thought.[7]

---

such as Luke 14:26: "If anyone comes to me and does not hate his father and mother, and wife and children, and brothers and sisters, yes, and even his own life, he cannot be my disciple"; and Luke 18:29–30: "Amen I say to you, there is no one who has left house, or parents, or brothers, or wife, or children, for the sake of the kingdom of God, who shall not receive much more in the present time, and in the age to come life everlasting." See also Celsus, *On the True Doctrine: A Discourse Against the Christians,* trans. R. Joseph Hoffmann (New York: Oxford University Press, 1987).

[4] Robert L. Wilken, *The Christians as the Romans Saw Them* (New Haven, Conn.: Yale University Press, 1984), pp. 124–25.

[5] See, for example, 1 Corinthians 7:29–35.

[6] *Adam, Eve, and the Serpent* (New York: Random House, 1988), p. 32. The socially disruptive effect of early Christianity is conveyed by the legend of Thecla, an attractive adolescent girl who rejected an arranged marriage to a wealthy man, left home, and joined a Christian community. Pagels surmises: "Whether or not she in fact heard Paul himself preach, she—and thousands like her—welcomed such radical versions of the gospel. Following Jesus' advice, these young disciples broke with their families and refused to marry, declaring themselves now members of 'God's family.' Their vows of celibacy served many converts as a declaration of independence from the crushing pressures of tradition and of their families, who ordinarily arranged marriages at puberty and so determined the course of their children's lives" (p. 20).

[7] Influential in advancing this view has been Abraham Malherbe, *Social Aspects of Early Christianity* (Baton Rouge: University of Louisiana Press, 1977). However, this should not be

However, although "the most active and prominent members of Paul's circle" may be classified as "upwardly mobile," they may also be classified as "people of high status inconsistency" because "their achieved status is higher than their attributed status."[8] The sociopsychological significance of this condition is discussed by Meeks:

> A series of studies has demonstrated that, in present-day American society, persons of low status crystallization, that is, those who are ranked high in some important dimensions but low in others, tend to behave in certain predictable ways. Some may take political action favoring change in the society. Some may withdraw from groups and tend to become unsocial. Others may develop psychophysiological symptoms of stress. All these kinds of behavior, some sociologists believe, show that a high degree of status inconsistency produces unpleasant experiences that lead people to try to remove the inconsistency by changing the society, themselves, or perceptions of themselves.[9]

Related to the concept of social inconsistency is that of "relative deprivation," according to which "it is not the absolute level of poverty or powerlessness [of a group] that counts, but the way in which they perceive their status relative to significant other groups."[10]

---

taken to exclude the observation of Celsus, recently concurred in by Stephen Benko, *Pagan Rome and the Early Christians,* p. 157, that "the uneducated were attracted in great numbers to the church." Also commenting upon Celsus, Ramsay MacMullen, *Christianizing the Roman Empire, A.D. 100–400* (New Haven, Conn.: Yale University Press, 1984), notes that "the church's teachings were offered most often to the unsophisticated or uneducated, and by people of low standing in the community" (p. 37). In this regard, see also 1 Corinthians 1:26–29. After noting that in "all but the largest cities," there was an "absence of clearly defined middle or 'merchant' classes," Robin Lane Fox, *Pagans and Christians* (New York: Knopf, 1986), states: "The hard core of these churches' membership lay in the humbler free classes, people who were far removed from higher education and at most controlled a very modest property of their own. It is against this silent majority that the exceptions should be seen, although the exceptions generally wrote the surviving texts and addressed exceptional Christians" (pp. 299–301).

[8] Meeks, *The First Urban Christians,* p. 73. The studies on "status inconsistency" cited by Meeks were provoked by Gerhard E. Lenski, "Status Crystallization: A Non-vertical Dimension of Social Status," *ASR* 19 (1954): 405–13, which "stimulated a series of responses and further investigations which has probably still not come to end" (p. 215 n. 24). These responses and further investigations include Irwin Goffman, "Status Inconsistency and Preference for Change in Power Distribution," *ASR* 22 (1957): 275–81; Gerhard E. Lenski, "Social Participation and Status Crystallization," *ASR* 21 (1956): 458–64; Elton F. Jackson, "Status Consistency and Symptoms of Stress," *ASR* 27 (1962): 469–80; Elton F. Jackson and Peter J. Burke, "Status and Symptoms of Stress: Additive and Interaction Effects," *ASR* 30 (1965): 556–64; Herbert M. Blalok, "Status Inconsistency, Social Mobility, Status Integration, and Structural Effects," *ASR* 32 (1967): 790–801; Carlton A. Hornung, "Social Status, Status Inconsistency, and Psychological Stress," *ASR* 42 (1977): 623–38; and M. S. Sasiki, "Status Inconsistency and Religious Commitment," in *The Religious Dimension: New Directions in Quantitative Research,* ed. Robert Wuthnow (New York: Academic Press, 1979), pp. 135–56.

[9] *The First Urban Christians,* p. 55.

[10] Ibid., p. 172. This concept, which appears to have developed from the Weberian concept of "nonprivileged classes," has been further examined and applied by David Aberle, "A Note on Relative Deprivation Theory as Applied to Millenarian and Other Cult Movements," in

While "cautious in applying to ancient society a theory that has been empirically generated from observations about a modern society," Meeks believes that in investigating the social status of the early Christians, theories of status inconsistency "can have great heuristic power."[11] Among the early Christians, intellectuals who were not accepted into the predominantly pagan social structure, may have been forced to accept careers as artisans or laborers. Feeling thwarted by the existing socioeconomic system, they may have experienced that sociopsychological condition of alienation variously described as "cognitive dissonance" or "status dissonance."[12] Persons affected by status inconsistency also often develop feelings of resentment toward a society in which they are not permitted to enjoy the influence and prestige they feel they are entitled to. For example, a well-educated Syrian immigrant who performed menial tasks in a Greek city no longer enjoyed the esteem accorded him in his native land. He may therefore have been attracted to a socioreligious community in which all members were considered equal, and enjoyed the mutual respect and intimacy of brothers and sisters, regardless of their status outside the community. The promise of "the forgiveness of sins and life everlasting" also probably figured in the decision of status-inconsistent individuals to become members of the local Christian community. It is likely that the alienation and resentment felt by many status-inconsistent individuals was shared by a substantial percentage of more "consistently low status" individuals such as uneducated slaves.

Although Meeks does not speculate on the historical origins of widespread status inconsistency, some attempt at explanation is in order. One may theoretically trace its impetus to the social destabilization of the entire Mediterranean region by the Peloponnesian Wars and the conquests of Alexander the Great, which were discussed in the previous chapter in connection with the emergence of Hellenistic mystery cults. To more fully convey the magnitude of the "heterogenization" process that accompanied the Hellenistic transformation, a demographic summary of Alexander's empire is provided:

> Alexander's empire was basically the old Persian Empire plus Greece and must be accounted an Asian state in terms of population:

Sylvia L. Thrupp, ed., *Millennial Dreams in Action: Studies in Revolutionary Religious Movements,* Comparative Studies in Society and History, supp., 2 (The Hague: Mouton, 1962), pp. 209–14.

[11] Meeks, *The First Urban Christians,* p. 55.

[12] Ibid., p. 173. For a further discussion of "cognitive dissonance," Meeks suggests Leon Festinger, *A Theory of Cognitive Dissonance* (Stanford, Calif.: Stanford University Press, 1957). More recent discussions may be found in Lawrence S. Wrightsman, *Social Psychology,* 2nd ed. (Belmont, Calif.: Wadsworth, 1977), pp. 364–73; and Neil R. Carson, *Psychology: The Science of Behavior* (Boston: Allyn and Bacon, 1984), pp. 583–87. For Robin Lane Fox's response to Meeks and the application of the concept of cognitive dissonance to the early Church, see his *Pagans and Christians,* pp. 317–22.

Macedonian Empire in Europe (Greece)	3.0m [million]
in Africa (Egypt)	3.5
in the Near East (less Arabia)	12.0
in Central Asia and India	1.5
TOTAL	20.0
Number in Asia	13.5, or two thirds

However, if the demographic centre of the Empire lay in Asia its driving force was clearly European and its conscious aim was to promote the Greek way of life. The number of Greek settlers was, in absolute terms, insignificant—no more than 0.25m—but as agents for the spread of Hellenism they proved sufficient. Later the Romans took over the Greek role and for the rest of the classical period the western Near East was part of their Empire.[13]

Despite the intentions of these "agents of Hellenism," the ultimate result was not cultural conformity but syncretism, cultural confusion, and the loss of cultural identity by native and immigrant alike. Not only were the cultures of the conquered territories "syncretized" with Greek culture, but native Greek culture itself was gradually transformed and "de-Hellenized." Mircea Eliade has summarized the key socioreligious aspects of this social, historical, cultural, and religious transformation:

> From whatever point of view Alexander's campaigns are judged, there is agreement that their consequences were profound and irrevocable. After Alexander the historical profile of the world was radically changed. The earlier political and religious structures—the city-states and their cult institutions, the *polis* as the "center of the world" and reservoir of exemplary models, the anthropology elaborated on the basis of a certainty that there was an irreducible difference between Greeks and "barbarians"—all these structures collapse. In their place the notion of the *oikoumene* and "cosmopolitan" and "universalistic" trends become increasingly dominant....
>
> ... What has been called the "Hellenistic Enlightenment" encouraged individualism and at the same time cosmopolitanism. The decadence of the *polis* had freed the individual from his immemorial civic and religious ties; on the other hand, this freedom showed him his solitude and alienation in a cosmos that was terrifying by its mystery and vastness.... But it was the Stoics who popularized the idea that all men are *cosmopolitai*—citizens of the same city, i.e., the cosmos—whatever their social origin or geographical situation.[14]

As Eliade has observed, the de-Hellenizing effects of the Hellenistic transformation were particularly directed against the traditional Greek polis. Persian, Syrian, and Egyptian immigrants to Greek cities and towns often established their own communities and shrines. Eventually, "as their numbers

---

[13] Colin McEvedy and Richard Jones, *Atlas of World Population History* (Harmondsworth: Penguin Books, 1978), pp. 125–26.

[14] Mircea Eliade, *A History of Religious Ideas,* vol. 2: *From Gautama Buddha to the Triumph of Christianity,* trans. Willard R. Trask (Chicago: University of Chicago Press, 1982), pp. 203–8 passim.

and solidarity grew to the point that they could demand some civic recognition, their cult, by now usually housed in a proper Greek temple and assimilated in many other ways as well to the Greek urban environment, became part of the municipal religious establishment."[15] Native Greeks then became attracted to the new religious forms. That the process of demographic heterogenization and religious syncretism initiated by Alexander did not end with the Roman conquest of Greece in 197 B.C., is made clear by George La Piana in his study of foreign groups in Rome.[16]

An understanding of the socioreligious dynamics of urbanization is vital to this inquiry. The differences between the rural environment of the Germanic peoples and the urban environment where early Christianity thrived constitute the single most salient social distinction between the two societies. Rodney Stark has recently confirmed that not only was Christianity "first and foremost an urban movement," but that city size and the degree of Christianization are positively correlated.[17] He relates this observation to a "well-known subcultural theory of urbanism" which asserts that "the larger the population, in absolute numbers, the easier it is to assemble a 'critical mass' needed to form a deviant subculture."[18] Stark suggests that the high levels of social disorganization and ethnic heterogeneity in Greco-Roman cities contributed toward their high levels of Christianization.[19]

---

[15] Meeks, *The First Urban Christians,* p. 18. The "de-Hellenization" or "Orientalization" of the Greek cities is discussed in detail in chs. 3 and 4 of Nock, *Conversion: The Old and the New in Religion from Alexander the Great to Augustine of Hippo* (Oxford: Clarendon Press, 1933), while the expansion and appeal of the Oriental cults are discussed in chs. 6 and 7.

[16] *Foreign Groups in Rome During the First Centuries of the Empire* (Cambridge, Mass.: Harvard University Press, 1927). Commenting on this work, Elizabeth K. Nottingham, *Religion and Society* (New York: Random House, 1954), remarks: "La Piana . . . has shown how the contacts and conflicts of the foreign groups in the tenement quarters of Rome's vast immigrant areas furnished a haven for a great variety of cults and oriental mystery religions. His descriptions remind us of immigrant areas in New York City or Chicago, with their converted down-at-heel brownstone houses, many of which are meeting places for Rosicrucians, spiritual or oriental churches, or more ephemeral cults. According to La Piana, one of the reasons that Christianity—itself a mystical oriental import to the Roman scene—survived and flourished while vast numbers of contemporary cults and mystery religions became extinct was that Christianity possessed a superior type of organization" (pp. 66–67). Nottingham cites La Piana, *Foreign Groups in Rome,* p. 370, for this observation.

[17] Rodney Stark, "Christianizing the Urban Empire: An Analysis Based on 22 Greco-Roman Cities," *Sociological Analysis* 52:1 (1991): 77. Similarly, Walter Burkert, *Greek Religion,* trans. John Raffan (Cambridge, Mass.: Harvard University Press, 1985), has stated in the concluding sentences of his book: "There was one ultimate point at which the polis religion was bound to collapse, the development of the very large and hence amorphous city. It was in the megalopolis of the ancient world that Christianity would most easily find a foothold" (p. 337).

[18] Stark, "Christianizing," p. 80. The source of this theory is Claude S. Fischer, "Toward a Subcultural Theory of Urbanism," *American Journal of Sociology* 80 (1975): 1319–41.

[19] Stark, "Christianizing," pp. 86–87. Stark indicates his intention to treat this topic in a future article. He does, however, provide the following explanation of the operation of urban social disorganization: "It is axiomatic that conformity to norms is the result of [interpersonal] attachments—to the extent that we value our relationships with others we will conform in order to retain their esteem. When people lack attachments, they have much greater freedom to

This view has also been expressed by Howard Clark Kee, who notes: "An important consequence of the breaking up of indigenous populations and cultures under the impact, first of Hellenization and then of extension of Roman imperial power and administration, was the rapid increase in the voluntaristic element in religion. With the hold of tradition and ethnic heritage broken by the new mobility, men and women felt free to choose new forms of religious identity that better served their needs."[20]

After nearly four centuries of urbanization, there probably existed a sizable number of residents in most Greek cities who could be classified as status-inconsistent. As already noted, it is from this group that Meeks believes the most prominent converts to Pauline Christianity originated. He provides possible examples of the psychosocial profiles of individuals within this group: "Independent women with moderate wealth, Jews with wealth in a pagan society, freedmen with skill and money but stigmatized by origin, and so on—brought with them not only anxiety but also loneliness, in a society in which social position was important and usually rigid."[21] Meeks then asks rhetorically: "Would, then, the intimacy of the Christian groups become a welcome refuge, the emotion-charged language of family and affection and the image of a caring, personal God powerful antidotes, while the master symbol of the crucified savior crystallized a believable picture of the way the world seemed really to work?"[22]

---

deviate from the norms. In modern studies, unconventional behavior is strongly correlated with various measures of population turnover and instability" (p. 86).

[20] *Miracle in the Early Christian World: A Study in Sociohistorical Method* (New Haven, Conn.: Yale University Press, 1983), p. 61.

[21] Meeks, *The First Urban Christians,* p. 191. One may conjecture that the feelings of anxiety, alienation, loneliness, and rootlessness experienced by many residents of ethnoculturally diverse urban areas may contribute to a condition of at least mild depression. According to the *Merck Manual of Diagnosis and Therapy,* ed. Robert Berkow, 13th ed. (Rahway, N.J.: Merck, Sharp & Dohme Research Laboratories, 1977), "depressed patients often see themselves as helpless or trapped in a hopeless situation, and empathy, support, and compassion are needed to help them find their way out" (p. 1495). The empathy, support, and compassion offered by the early Christian communities would certainly seem to appeal to the depressed individual. A recently reported epidemiological study of the increasing incidence of depression among young Americans has suggested environmental risk factors which correspond surprisingly well with the environment of early Christianity depicted thus far. According to Gerald L. Klerman and Myrna M. Weissman, "Increasing Rates of Depression," *Journal of the American Medical Association* 261:15 (1989): "The cohorts born since World War II have been among the healthiest physically and were raised during a period of economic prosperity in the United States and Western Europe. Nevertheless, they show high rates of alcoholism, substance abuse, depression, and suicide. The environmental risk factors for depression and other mental disorders for this cohort have not been established but probably include (a) demographic shifts, (b) changes in the ratio of males to females in the population, (c) increasing urbanization, (d) greater geographic mobility with resultant loss of attachments and face-to-face groups, (e) increasing social anomie, (f) changes in family structure, (g) alterations in the roles of women, especially the increased number of women in the work force, and (h) shifts in gender-related occupational patterns. . . . There are data that overall rates of depression are lower in rural as compared with urban areas" (p. 2234).

[22] Meeks, *The First Urban Christians,* p. 191.

Thus, from a sociopsychological perspective, the early Christian communities were not perceived as a means for social advancement, but rather as a social refuge and a center for egalitarian resocialization for those who experienced status inconsistency or cognitive dissonance. Observing that a theory of status inconsistency does not of itself explain why Christian converts "resolved the inconsistency by taking to Christianity rather than to any other cult,"[23] Robin Lane Fox suggests:

> We would do better to view its appeal not against inconsistency but against a growing social exclusivity. Christianity was least likely to attract the people who were most embedded in social tradition, the great families of Rome, the upper families who filled the civic priesthoods and competed in public generosity for the gods. There were exceptions, but it was also least likely to attract the teacher and antiquarian who were steeped in pagan learning. It could, however, offer an alternative community and range of values to those who were disenchanted by the display of riches, by the harshness of the exercise of power and the progressive hardening of the gradations of rank and degree. Only a simple view of human nature will expect such people to be none but the poor and the oppressed themselves. . . .
>
> On a longer view, the rise of Christianity owed much to a broader initial change, a loosening of the civic cohesion of the Greek city-state. Even in the classical city, the citizen had not been limited to his city's public cults, but as groups of non-citizens multiplied through migration from place to place and as tighter restrictions were placed on the holding of local citizenship, the general connection between a city's cults and its citizens had been greatly weakened.[24]

Another factor which often accompanies urbanization and ethnocultural destabilization and is related to the attractiveness of early Christianity, is the dissolution of the family unit. Meeks cites Franz Bömer to the effect that "the religious solidarity of the familia in old Roman agrarian society gave way under pressures of urbanization."[25] The destabilization of family life was reflected in the larger community of the town or city. As the levels of family and civic solidarity declined, the high level of group solidarity present within the local Christian communities became more apparent and attractive. The reputation of "brotherly love" among Christians would certainly have had some degree of appeal for spiritually and culturally alienated individuals. According to Fox, "this 'brotherly love' has been minimized as a reason for turning to the Church, as if only those who were members could know of it," whereas "in fact it was widely recognized" and "must have

[23] Fox, *Pagans and Christians*, p. 321.

[24] Ibid., pp. 321–22.

[25] Meeks, *The First Urban Christians*, p. 205 n. 139. The source cited here by Meeks is Franz Bömer, *Untersuchungen über die Religion der Sklaven in Griechenland und Rom*, vol. 1 (Mainz: Steiner, 1957), pp. 57–78. See also Keith R. Bradley, *Discovering the Roman Family: Studies in Roman Social History* (New York: Oxford University Press, 1991).

played its part in drawing outsiders to the faith."[26] John Ferguson, in his study *The Religions of the Roman Empire,* concurs:

> Wherein then lay the appeal of Christianity? It was first in the personality of the founder. . . . It was secondly in the way of love revealed, in the witness of community (*koinonia*), in a fellowship which took in Jew and Gentile, slave and free, men and women, and whose solid practicality in their care for the needy won the admiration even of Lucian. "How these Christians love one another!" was a respectful affirmation.[27]

The significance of early Christian social solidarity was noted earlier in this century by Pierre Batiffol, who wrote that "we must, indeed, attach a great importance to the social solidarity which it established among all its members," and claimed that "nothing in Christianity impressed the pagans more than the love of Christians for one another."[28] Although messianic hopes and apocalyptic fears had somewhat subsided by the middle of the second century, the fundamentally world-rejecting world-view expressed by these attitudes endured, albeit in a more secular form. Not only did Christianity offer its faithful the eternal benefits of redemptive salvation through Jesus Christ, but, as Fox has noted, "in cities of growing social divisions, Christianity offered unworldly equality."[29] A more detailed description of the effects of high population density[30] and of the high level of ethnocultural diversity found in the urban environment in which early Christianity appears to have flourished, is provided by Latourette in his discussion of the factors contributing toward the expansion of Christianity in the first five centuries:

> Another factor, and one which we have mentioned more than once, appears to have been the disintegration of society. From at least the time of Alexander the Mediterranean world had been in a state of flux. The passing of the old was hastened by the wars which culminated in the founding of the Roman Empire and was further accelerated by the Empire itself. The construction of a universal state could not but dissolve the barriers which divided people from people. In the consequent intermingling of individuals and ideas old cultures, with their religions, were weakened. In

---

[26] *Pagans and Christians,* p. 321.

[27] *The Religions of the Roman Empire* (Ithaca, N.Y.: Cornell University Press, 1970), p. 126.

[28] *Primitive Catholicism,* trans. from 5th ed. by Henri L. Brianceau (New York: Longmans, Green, 1911), p. 31. In support of this statement, Batiffol refers to Thessalonians 4:9–10 and Romans 12:10–13.

[29] Fox, *Pagans and Christians,* p. 335.

[30] Meeks, *The First Urban Christians*: "MacMullen estimates that the average population density in cities of the Roman Empire may have approached two hundred per acre—an equivalent found in Western cities only in industrial slums. Further, given that much of the space—one-fourth, by MacMullen's calculations—was devoted to public areas, 'the bulk of the population had typically to put up with most uncomfortable crowding at home, made tolerable by the attractive spaciousness of public facilities' " (pp. 28–29). Meeks is citing Ramsay MacMullen, *Roman Social Relations* (New Haven, Conn.: Yale University Press, 1974), p. 63.

the great cities especially were thousands of deracinated individuals, some of them slaves, some freedmen, and some merchants, who had been separated by force or voluntarily from their hereditary milieu. Often insecure, subject to oppression from the powerful, presumably many of them welcomed the fellowship afforded by the strong Christian organization and the security which the faith promised for the life to come. It is notable that Christianity had its first strongholds in the large cities, where these conditions were particularly prominent. . . . Had Christianity been born in a vigorous young culture whose adherents were confident of its virtues, it might have met a different fate.[31]

It becomes apparent that the intimacy, cohesion, and inclusiveness of early Christianity were prominent factors in attracting alienated individuals in the Roman Empire. This view is shared by Gilbert Murray:

It always appears to me that, historically speaking, the character of Christianity in these early centuries is to be sought not so much in the doctrines which it professed, nearly all of which had their roots and their close parallels in older Hellenistic or Hebrew thought, but in the organization on which it rested. . . . When I try to realize it as a sort of semi-secret society for mutual help with a mystical religious basis, resting first on the proletariats of Antioch and the great commercial and manufacturing towns of the Levant, then spreading by instinctive sympathy to similar classes in Rome and the West, and rising in influence, like certain other mystical cults, by the special appeal it made to women, the various historical puzzles begin to fall into place. . . . It explains its humanity, its intense feeling of brotherhood within its own bounds, its incessant care for the poor, and also its comparative indifference to the virtues which are especially incumbent on a governing class.[32]

In his *History of Religious Ideas,* Mircea Eliade also considers the factors which contributed toward the expansion of Christianity. His observations are remarkably similar to those of Meeks, Fox, Ferguson, Batiffol, Latourette, and Murray:

The causes of the final triumph of Christian preaching are many and various. First of all were the unshakable faith and moral strength of Christians, their courage in the face of torture and death—a courage admired even by their greatest enemies. . . . Furthermore, the solidarity of the Christians was unequaled; the community took care of widows, orphans, and the aged and ransomed those captured by pirates. During epidemics and sieges, only Christians tended the wounded and buried the dead. *For all the rootless multitudes of the Empire, for the many who suffered from loneliness, for the victims of cultural and social alienation, the Church was the only hope of obtaining an identity, of finding, or recovering, a meaning for life.* Since there were no barriers, either social, racial, or intellectual,

---

[31] *The Expansion of Christianity,* vol. 1: *The First Five Centuries* (New York: Harper, 1937), pp. 163–64.
[32] *Five Stages of Greek Religion,* 3rd ed. (Garden City, N.Y.: Doubleday, 1955), pp. 185–86.

anyone could become a member of this optimistic and paradoxical society in which a powerful citizen, the emperor's chamberlain, bowed before a bishop who had been his slave. In all probability, neither before nor afterward has any historical society experienced the equivalent of this equality, of the charity and brotherly love that were the life of the Christian communities of the first four centuries.[33]

Additionally, in his study *The Cult of the Saints,* Peter Brown has noted: "The church was an artificial kin group. Its members were expected to project onto the new community a fair measure of the sense of solidarity, of the loyalties, and of the obligations that had previously been directed to the physical family."[34] Although the sociopsychological appeal of early Christianity has been discussed in each of the works quoted above, the work which deals most exclusively with this subject is E. R. Dodds' *Pagan and Christian in an Age of Anxiety.*[35]

Dodds suggests that Christians in the period between 161 and 313 may have interpreted the prevalence of war, pestilence, and economic instability as an eschatological prelude to messianic and apocalyptic expectations.[36] The communal and transcendent aspects of early Christianity are likely to have been attractive to those urban inhabitants of the Roman Empire whose existence was fraught with loneliness, fear, and despair. Featuring greater organizational stability and solidarity than other religious or philosophical groups, Christianity offered the alienated individual, without regard to sex, ethnicity, or socioeconomic status, membership in a caring community, together with the hope of bodily resurrection. The high degree of Christian solidarity in the midst of widespread social anomie is thought by Dodds to constitute "a major cause, perhaps the strongest single cause, of the spread of Christianity."[37] His closing discussion which leads to this conclusion is worth reviewing, for it succinctly presents the classical socioreligious and sociopsychological environment of early Christianity—an environment with which the Germanic environment will later be compared and contrasted:

> The benefits of becoming a Christian were not confined to the next world. A Christian congregation was from the first a community in a much fuller sense than any corresponding group of Isiac or Mithraist devotees. . . . The Church provided the essentials of social security: it cared for widows

[33] *A History of Religious Ideas,* vol. 2, p. 413 (emphasis added).

[34] *The Cult of the Saints: Its Rise and Function in Latin Christianity* (Chicago: University of Chicago Press, 1981), p. 31.

[35] *Pagan and Christian in an Age of Anxiety: Some Aspects of Religious Experience from Marcus Aurelius to Constantine* (1965; reprint, New York: W. W. Norton, 1970). Scattered critical references to an "Age of Anxiety" are found in Fox, *Pagans and Christians,* chs. 3 and 4. Fox does not deny the presence of social anxiety in the period under discussion, but rather questions the "characterization of any one age in antiquity," since he feels that "anxiety was ever-present" and not the "distinctive tone of the Antonine age" (pp. 122–23). More critical of such a characterization is MacMullen, *Paganism,* pp. 122–25.

[36] Dodds, *Pagan and Christian,* p. 12.

[37] Ibid., p. 138.

and orphans, the old, the unemployed, and the disabled; it provided a burial fund for the poor and a nursing service in time of plague. But even more important, I suspect, than these material benefits was the sense of belonging which the Christian community could give. Modern social studies have brought home to us the universality of the "need to belong" and the unexpected ways in which it can influence human behaviour, particularly among the rootless inhabitants of great cities. I see no reason to think that it was otherwise in antiquity: Epictetus has described for us the dreadful loneliness that can beset a man in the midst of his fellows. Such loneliness must have been felt by millions—the urbanised tribesman, the peasant come to town in search of work, the demobilised soldier, the rentier ruined by inflation, and the manumitted slave. For people in that situation membership of a Christian community might be the only way of maintaining their self-respect and giving their life some semblance of meaning. Within the community there was human warmth: someone was interested in them, both here and hereafter. It is therefore not surprising that the earliest and the most striking advances of Christianity were made in the great cities—in Antioch, in Rome, in Alexandria.[38]

In his review of Dodds's work, Peter Brown concurs that "the 'Age of Anxiety' became, increasingly, the age of converts."[39] Brown also notes that "Professor Dodds has made us realize how much the social and religious historian, the psychologist and the sociologist must keep together, in order to understand the fateful ramifications of the increasing urge of so many members of the Roman Empire to become 'new' men."[40] From the pre-

---

[38] Ibid., pp. 136–38. One recent study which supports the significance of the "need to belong" in religious conversion is David G. Bromley and Anson D. Shupe, "Moonies," in *America: Cult Church and Crusade* (Beverly Hills, Calif.: Sage Publications, 1979), which found that "Unification Church conversion efforts became more successful when strong ties were established with prospective converts prior to revealing the movement's core beliefs" (pp. 39–40). The Unification Church's conversion methodology, including its technique of "love-bombing," has been examined in John Lofland, *Doomsday Cult*, enlarged ed. (New York: Irvington Press, 1977), and Eileen Barker, *The Making of a Moonie: Choice or Brainwashing?* (London: Basil Blackwell, 1984). Of related interest are John Lofland and Rodney Stark, "Becoming a World-Saver: A Theory of Conversion to a Deviant Perspective," *ASR* 30:6 (1965): 862–74; John Lofland, "Becoming a World-Saver Revisited," in James T. Richardson, ed., *Conversion Careers: In and Out of the New Religions* (Beverly Hills, Calif.: Sage Publications, 1978), pp. 10–23; and Eileen Barker, "Who'd Be a Moonie? A Comparative Study of Those Who Join the Unification Church in Britain," in *The Social Impact of New Religious Movements*, ed. Bryan Wilson (New York: Rose of Sharon Press, 1981). The recently published collection of essays presented at the fifth Phillips Symposium on "Jewish and Christian Traditions" at the University of Denver's Center for Judaic Studies, Martin E. Marty and Frederick E. Greenspahn, eds., *Pushing the Faith: Proselytism and Civility in a Pluralistic World* (New York: Crossroad, 1988), contains three particularly relevant works: John G. Gager, "Proselytism and Exclusivity in Early Christianity," pp. 67–77; H. Newton Malony, "The Psychology of Proselytism," pp. 125–42; and James T. Richardson, "Proselytizing Processes of the New Religions," pp. 143–54.

[39] Peter Brown, "Approaches to the Religious Crisis of the Third Century A.D.," in *Religion and Society in the Age of St. Augustine* (London: Faber & Faber, 1972), p. 80.

[40] Ibid. Also in substantial accord with Dodds, R. A. Markus, "The Problem of Self-

vious review of the opinions of Meeks, Fox, Ferguson, Batiffol, Latourette, Murray, Eliade, Brown, and Dodds it may be concluded that one of the most significant factors in the expansion of early Christianity appears to have been its appeal as an alternative community.

Despite the inherent dangers of comparing societies nearly two millennia apart, the contemporary urban social environment and that of the Hellenistic era seem at times to invite comparative analysis. Although a thorough analysis is beyond the scope of the current inquiry, one is tempted to at least tentatively apply to early Christianity some of the insights gained from the study of new religious developments. One of the more interesting new religions that seems to parallel the early Christian Church in many ways is the Unification Church. After noting difficulty in establishing a psychological profile of a typical potential Unification Church recruit, Eileen Barker considered the influence of contemporary social factors:

> In caricature, the potential recruit can see the non-Unification world as a divisive, turbulent, chaotic society, characterized by racial intolerance, injustice, cutthroat competition and lack of direction—a society which seems to be out of control and heading for imminent disaster. He can see an immoral (possibly amoral) society which no longer recognizes absolute values and standards; everything is relative to the utilitarian interests and desires of a pleasure-seeking, money-grubbing, power-hungry population. . . .
>
> It is a world in which the family is no longer a stable or a happy institution, and in which it is no longer the fundamental building block of a decent society. . . . It is a world in which there is no spirit of community; . . . It is a world of insecurity. . . .
>
> The Unification Church offers the potential recruit the chance to be a part of a family of like-minded people who care about the state of the world, who accept and live by high moral standards, who are dedicated to restoring God's Kingdom of Heaven on Earth. It offers him the opportunity to *belong;* it offers him the opportunity to *do* something that is of value and thus the opportunity to *be* of value.[41]

It appears then, that affiliation with the Unification Church may provide the individual with a means of resolving or adjusting to the anxiety generated by a discordant, meaningless, and anomic social environment.

Definition: From Sect to Church," in *The Shaping of Christianity in the Second and Third Centuries,* vol. 1 of *Jewish and Christian Self-Definition,* E. P. Sanders, ed. (Philadelphia: Fortress Press, 1980), observes of the third century: "The world around the Christians, Roman society from Gaul to Syria, was in the grip of a crisis of unprecedented depth. Not only its social fabric and political stability were in jeopardy; the essence of security of an ordered world was undermined and dissolving into a confusion of concepts, attitudes and feelings. Ancient traditions were losing their hold and Roman society had to rally all its conservatism to their defence. We have been reminded that the relationship between crisis and religious change is by no means a simple one; but I still find much force in Professor E. R. Dodds's suggestion that Christianity was the chief beneficiary of the urge which leads disoriented men to find a new hope in new groups and around new leaders" (pp. 11–12).

[41] Barker, *The Making of a Moonie,* pp. 240–44 passim.

The notion of religion as a mode of adjustment to stress is not new in the area of sociology.[42] However, the demonstration of a relationship between individual or social change and the inducement of stress, as well as the relationship of stress to disease, is relatively new. Recent medical research supports the notion that significant sociocultural transformations as well as personal life changes are "stressors" which not only may cause anxiety and depression, but also actually predispose individuals to physical illness.[43] Many nurses are currently taught that "adaptation to change, of whatever nature, requires expenditure of energy over and above that required for the maintenance of a 'steady state' of life," and that "therefore, if an individual is called upon to cope with many significant changes within a *short period of time,* it is likely that the person will be overextended and expend too much adaptive energy and, consequently, become ill."[44]

This sociopsychological and medical information is relevant to the present inquiry because it relates to the internal societal stress of urbanization, familial dissolution, immigration, and general anomie within the Roman Empire during the emergence of Christianity, stress factors which appear to have been substantially less evident in the more rural, internally cohesive, and stable Germanic societies at the time of their initial encounter with Christianity. The explanations of Meeks, Fox, Ferguson, Batiffol, Latourette, Murray, Eliade, Brown, and Dodds presented earlier regarding the expansion of Christianity in the classical world ascribe a significant role to Christianity's palliative effect on societal conditions of anomie, divisiveness, and anxiety. Current medical research seems to support the basic premise of this hypothesis, that is, that individuals who experience a confluence of stress factors, such as those present in the Roman Empire from the first

[42] See the chapter "Religion and Human Stress" in Nottingham, *Religion and Society;* and Talcott Parsons, *Religious Perspectives of College Teaching in Sociology and Social Psychology* (New Haven, Conn.: Edward W. Hazen Foundation, 1951), pp. 10–13.

[43] William W. Dressler, *Stress and Adaptation in the Context of Culture: Depression in a Southern Black Community* (Albany: State University of New York Press, 1991), in his first chapter, "Studies of Stress and Disease," states: "It is well-established that a portion of the risk associated with the development of diseases such as depression, hypertension, and coronary heart disease is due to the social and cultural circumstances in which a person lives, as well as the beliefs and attitudes held by that person. The research issue is not merely to demonstrate that this is so, but rather to work out in a refined and systematic way the processes involved" (p. 8).

[44] Joan Luckmann and Karen Creason Sorensen, *Medical-Surgical Nursing: A Psychophysiologic Approach,* 2nd ed. (Philadelphia: W. B. Saunders, 1980), p. 37. Studies in which, according to Luckmann and Sorensen, the link between life change and illness has been "systematically studied and irrevocably confirmed," include T. H. Holmes and R. H. Rahe, "The Social Readjustment Rating Scale," *Journal of Psychosomatic Research* 11 (1967): 213–18; J. S. Heisel et al., "The Significance of Life Events as Contributing Factors in the Diseases of Children," *The Journal of Pediatrics* 83 (1973): 119–23; R. H. Rahe, "Subjects' Recent Life Changes and Their Near-future Illness Reports," *Annals of Clinical Research* 4 (1972): 250–65; and E. S. Paykel, "Life Stress, Depression and Attempted Suicide," *Journal of Human Stress* 2 (1976): 3–12.

through third centuries A.D., would be prone to a significant increase in their level of anxiety.

It is likely that early Christianity functioned to some extent as a means of assisting alienated individuals to cope with social stress. Ari Kiev notes that "whether stress . . . leads to maladaptive responses depends on the individual's general vulnerability, as well as his ability to adapt to a particular kind of stress. Psychological defenses and/or cultural defenses—e.g. belief systems—may succeed in preventing the stress from impinging upon the individual's psychological or psychosomatic integrity."[45] He notes further that "the availability of beliefs and rituals for the reduction of tensions is an important factor in determining how stressful cultural pressures will be."[46]

The effect of communal religious experience has been studied by Kiev, who, in describing a West Indian Pentecostal service held in London, claims that it provides "a form of social integration for emotionally isolated immigrants, by supplying a structured world-view and methods of attaining grace that are independent of particular personal qualities and require only a willingness to have faith."[47] Kiev observes that "during the services, a reduction of self-identity and awareness, and a sense of merging with the group, are increased by the dogmatic preaching and the 'testimonies,' in an emotionally heightened atmosphere; this seems to contribute to an increase of positive good feeling, elation, and sometimes exaltation, such as may contribute to the therapeutic efficacy of the meetings."[48] Kiev believes that religious sects "can provide a sense of exclusiveness, together with a feeling of belonging to a true community, in which the individual remains all-important," and that "for many unhappy and dissatisfied individuals, who are socially isolated, membership in a religious sect fulfills a variety of needs."[49]

It may not be too tenuous a leap to consider the historical implications of research based on current social structures, if sufficient allowances for contemporary differences, such as the influence of industrialization, are made. This is particularly so if it is agreed that contemporary Western civilization has much in common with earlier civilizations when they underwent periods of post-expansion, urbanization, and destabilization.[50]

---

[45] *Transcultural Psychiatry* (New York: Free Press, 1972), p. 6.

[46] Ibid., p. 7.

[47] Ibid., pp. 127–28.

[48] Ibid., p. 129.

[49] Ibid., p. 35.

[50] An important discussion of "civilization dynamics" which may be helpful in comparing periods in different civilizations is contained in ch. 5, "Historical Change in Civilizations," in Carroll Quigley, *The Evolution of Civilizations: An Introduction to Historical Analysis,* 2nd ed. (Indianapolis, Ind.: Liberty Press, 1979). Following a period of expansion, Quigley posits an Age of Conflict which is characterized by "imperialist wars and of irrationality supported for reasons that are usually different in the different social classes. The masses of the people (who have no vested interest in the existing institution of expansion) engage in imperialist wars because it seems the only way to overcome the slowing down of expansion. Unable to get ahead by other

Therefore, it is believed that the current discussion of the relationship between sociocultural, psychological, and physiological factors will aid in elucidating certain principles of religious transformation, and particularly those operative in Christianization efforts among the Germanic peoples.

Some of the stress factors which may lead to anxiety,[51] and ultimately to disease, and which may also influence the development of individual and group religious attitudes, are rapidly changing cultural values, culture shock, migrations, and ecologic imbalance. Joan Luckmann and Karen Creason Sorensen discuss the operation of these factors in greater detail:

> *Rapidly changing cultural values* also can create a major source of anxiety. Old and traditional cultures appear to produce less stress and disease than newer, more radical societies. Values in traditional societies change little, and there are sanctioned ways for resolving anxiety and conflict. On the other hand, in societies where the "old ways" of life are breaking down and the "new ways" have not yet been fully established, stress and disease tend to become more prevalent. Indeed, disease can become a "way of life" in a society, like our own, which is rapidly changing, where nothing is defined and nothing is sacred, where everyone is potentially mobile, and where there is open choice and constant conflict.
>
> *Culture shock,* an upsetting psychologic phenomenon, can have a temporary but devastating effect upon the individual who moves into a new cultural environment. The disorientation and confusion that are characteristic of "culture shock" arise whenever a person leaves a familiar country, region, lifestyle, or occupation and enters an environment where dress, customs, beliefs, etc., are radically different. . . .
>
> One study of "social" coronary risk factors has demonstrated that migration, considered in the broad sense discussed above, plays an important role in the causation of heart disease. Some of the relevant factors named in the study are: (1) recent migration to an urban center, (2) high residential mobility, (3) high occupational mobility, (4) great discontinuity between childhood and adult environment and situation, (5) status incongruity (individuals high on one social status dimension and low on another), (6) residence in an area undergoing rapid increase in its degree of urbanization, (7) recent first entrance to an industrial occupation. . . .
>
> Ecologic balance is most easily maintained in environments that are stable and fairly settled, so that stresses and the need for change are at a minimum. However when people must exist under environmental condi-

---

means (such as economic means), they seek to get ahead by political action, above all by taking wealth from their political neighbors. At the same time they turn to irrationality to compensate for the growing insecurity of life, for the chronic economic depression, for the growing bitterness and dangers of class struggles, for the growing social disruption and insecurity from imperialist wars. This is generally a period of gambling, use of narcotics or intoxicants, obsession with sex (frequently as perversion), increasing crime, growing numbers of neurotics and psychotics, growing obsession with death and with the Hereafter" (pp. 151–52).

[51] "Anxiety is a normal reaction to many stresses of modern life," according to Neil R. Carlson, *Psychology: The Science of Behavior* (Boston: Allyn and Bacon, 1984), p. 664.

tions that are upset, unsettled, or highly complex, ecologic balance tends to break down and morbidity and mortality rates rise.[52]

It is significant that most of the stressors cited above were present in the Roman Empire during the pre-Constantinian expansion of Christianity. In a chapter about Rome in his recent study of anomie, Elwin H. Powell has noted: "Anomie is the touchstone of Roman history from Augustus onward."[53] Despite "a rising level of material comfort, and times of relative tranquility like the 2nd century A.D. . . . , beneath the splendor of imperial Rome was that 'profound malaise common to aging nations,' as Jacob Burckhardt said," and "by the third century A.D. anomie had become manifest everywhere; 'chaos and misery reigned through the empire,' writes Rostovzeff."[54] While the present focus is on the religious rather than the physiological effects of anxiety, the preceding discussion is important for its characterization of various social conditions as stress factors. The derivative relationship between social stress, anxiety, and the appeal of Christianity, as developed by Meeks, Fox, Ferguson, Batiffol, Latourette, Murray, Eliade, and Dodds, is further supported by sociological insights of Durkheim, Weber, and O'Dea which relate the attraction of the Christian promise of salvation to anomic social conditions.[55]

Latourette's speculation, cited earlier, that the expansion of Christianity would not have met with such success had it "been born in a vigorous

[52] Luckmann and Sorensen, *Medical-Surgical Nursing,* pp. 56–58. Of related interest are H. W. Gruchow, "Socialization and the Human Physiologic Response to Crowding," *American Journal of Public Health* 67 (1977): 455–59; J. J. Lynch, *The Broken Heart: The Medical Consequences of Loneliness* (New York: Basic Books, 1977); David Riesman, Nathan Glazer, and Reuel Denney, *The Lonely Crowd: A Study of the Changing American Character* (New Haven, Conn.: Yale University Press, 1950); and Rollo May, *Man's Search for Himself* (New York: W. W. Norton, 1953). The effects of migration are discussed in M. Micklin and C. A. Leon, "Life Change and Psychiatric Disturbance in a South American City: The Effects of Geographic and Social Mobility," *Journal of Health and Social Behavior* 19 (1978): 92–107. Also of interest is Paul Tillich, "The Meaning of Health," in D. Belgum, ed., *Religion and Medicine: Essays on Meanings, Values and Health* (Ames: Iowa State University Press, 1967).

[53] *The Design of Discord: Studies of Anomie,* 2nd ed. (New Brunswick, N.J.: Transaction Books, 1988), p. 225.

[54] Ibid., pp. 225–26. The quotation of Jacob Burckhardt is from *The Age of Constantine the Great,* trans. Moses Hadas (Garden City, N.Y.: Doubleday, 1956). The quotation of Mikhail Rostovzeff is from his *The Social and Economic History of the Roman Empire,* 2 vols., 2nd rev. ed., revised by P. M. Fraser (Oxford: Clarendon Press), pp. 491–492. Some "tangible measures of growing disorganization" noted by Powell are: "roads unsafe; public buildings deteriorating; population declining; banditry increasing; the disappearance of Latin as the official language and its replacement by native dialects; the final decay of art and high culture" (ibid.). An important survey of the sources of anomie in the Roman Empire is Ramsay MacMullen, *Enemies of the Roman Order: Treason, Unrest and Alienation in the Empire* (Cambridge, Mass.: Harvard University Press, 1966), particularly ch. 5, "Urban Unrest," and ch. 6, "The Outsiders."

[55] See above, pp. 20–21. In his study "Social Change as Stress," Ari Kiev, *Transcultural Psychiatry,* pp. 9–15, not only regards the "loss of old culture," "urbanization," and "change itself," as sources of stress which may contribute toward anxiety, depression, and physical illness, but also claims that "messianic religious cults . . . provide psychological support for oppressed peoples in disintegrating cultures" (p. 13).

young culture whose adherents were confident of its virtues,"[56] forms an appropriate introduction to a discussion of the early medieval encounter of Christianity with the Germanic peoples. For it may be from the perspective of a comparative history of civilizations that the distinctions between the Christianization process in the classical and Germanic worlds become most apparent. It is here that the study of what Carroll Quigley refers to as "civilizational dynamics,"[57] and others have referred to as the philosophy of history, may become a useful aid. In a previous reference to Quigley's schema,[58] the period of classical decline from which Christianity emerged was categorized as an Age of Conflict. Ramsay MacMullen, in the preface to his study *Enemies of the Roman Order,* piquantly describes the conflict-ridden sociopolitical environment of early Christianity:

> The Empire was "democratized," to use a greatly exaggerated term. The civilization called Roman, in the sense defined above, yields to another, compounded of heterogeneous elements formerly suppressed and latterly vital. Styles of art latent in the masses in Augustus' day, but excluded from the official monuments, emerged to full acceptance in the Arch of Constantine; beliefs about the supernatural, once illegal or contemptuously relegated to plowboys and servant girls, after the first century began to infect even the educated, and were ultimately embodied as a principal element in late antique philosophy. As a final illustration chosen from social and political history, the urban and rural poor began to be heard from, though not to control their own fates fully, through such forbidden activities as rioting and brigandage. In the end [the fourth century A.D.], the dichotomy on which this book rests [between Roman and un-Roman] breaks down. There was little "Roman" left in the Roman empire. Rather, the "un-Roman" elements had come to the fore, and now controlled the world in which they lived.[59]

To fully appreciate the very real disparity between the process of Christianization in classical and Germanic societies, one must recall that each was at a different stage of development when it encountered Christianity. The anomic, heterogeneous, urban stage of a senescent classical civilization must be contrasted with the more cohesive, homogeneous, pastoral-warrior stage of a nascent Germanic culture. Aspects of both which may be compared are their social structure, world-view, and religious attitudes. Throughout such a comparative effort, one should remain mindful of the relationship between classical and Germanic culture advanced by Georges Dumézil, that is, as successive manifestations of a common Proto-Indo-European language, mythology, ideology, and social organization.[60]

[56] *The Expansion of Christianity,* vol. 1, p. 163.
[57] *The Evolution of Civilizations,* p. 130.
[58] See above, p. 95 n. 50.
[59] MacMullen, *Enemies of the Roman Order,* pp. viii–ix.
[60] An introduction to Dumézil's theories may be found in his *L'Idéologie tripartie des Indo-Européens,* Collection Latomus, vol. 31 (Brussels: Latomus, 1958), in C. Scott Littleton, *The*

In a study entitled *Antike, Germanentum und Christentum,* Ildefons Herwegen compared the historical and cultural factors present in Christianity's successive encounters with Roman and Germanic societies.[61] Emphasizing that the Roman and Germanic characteristics under discussion should not be considered the exclusive domain of one group, but just more prevalent or *typisch* in one than the other, he described the predominant classical ethos as *sein* or "being-oriented," and the predominant Germanic ethos as *werden* or "becoming-oriented."[62] Accordingly, Herwegen considered the classical ethos to be primarily harmonious and objective, and the Germanic ethos to be primarily dynamic and subjective.[63] He elaborates:

> If Classical man found the meaning of life in the perfection of being, then Germanic man found it in the restlessness of becoming. Being is calmness, harmony, clarity; becoming is motion, change, uncertainty. The addition of rhythm as the movement of being may be contrasted with the multiplication of dynamics as the movement of becoming.
>
> It needn't be emphasized that no human life may be formed without both motives: being and becoming. However, it is a great difference whether Germanic man views becoming not only as the means, but also as his goal. . . . While Classical man experiences his feelings in the context of an objective ideal, Germanic man struggles to gain access to the infinite through the subjective perception of the concrete.
>
> This deep-rooted difference, which represents a real antithesis between Classical and Germanic psyches, leads one to expect that the reception, interpretation, and realization of Christianity by the Classical and Germanic worlds would be very different.
>
> In addition to this difference, derived from the blood and soil of the Classical and Germanic worlds, is the significance of the stage of development of each of these peoples with respect to Christianity. The Classical world was in its senescence, while the Germanic world was in its youth when it encountered Christ.[64]

While the present analysis is not in total agreement with Herwegen's speculation regarding distinctions between the classical and Germanic ethos—a subject which, by its very complexity, does not readily lend itself to consensus—his observations remain useful. The harmonious classical

---

New Comparative Mythology: An Anthropological Assessment of the Theories of Georges Dumézil, 3rd ed. (Berkeley: University of California Press, 1982), especially pp. 4–6, 130–32, and, more briefly, in the following chapter.

[61] *Antike, Christentum und Germanentum* (Salzburg: Verlag Anton Pustet, 1932).

[62] Ibid., p. 20.

[63] Ibid.

[64] Ibid., pp. 20–22 (my translation). If a detailed comparison were made of early Greek and Roman Indo-European societies, each might be found to have passed through a phase which could be described as "*werden*-oriented." Likewise, if the Renaissance were viewed as the more "mature" classical phase of Germano-European society, it might also be described as "*sein*-oriented." See also the discussion of the Germanic psyche in Stephen E. Flowers, "Toward an Archaic Germanic Psychology," *JIES* 11:1/2 (1983): 117–38.

ethos described by Herwegen may have prevailed among the Greeks until
the Peloponnesian Wars (431–404 B.C.), and among the Romans until the
Second Punic War (218–201 B.C.). However, these prolonged conflicts,
when combined with the conquests of Alexander (d. 323 B.C.), appear to
have irreversibly disrupted the harmonious ethos of the Classical world.
According to Eliade, when "the Second Punic War threatened the very existence of the Roman state, religion underwent a transformation in depth,"
during which "Rome appealed to all the gods, whatever their origin."[65] In
this period of Roman decline which preceded the emergence of Christianity, the stable, cohesive social structure which prevailed during the early
republic, and which is likely to have contributed substantially toward the
development of a harmonious, "being-oriented" Classical ethos, was rapidly
disintegrating.[66] An ethos of harmonious cohesion was gradually displaced
by an ethos of individual fulfillment, which in many instances became an
ethos of personal salvation. In his discussion "Specific Characteristics of
Roman Religiosity," Eliade succinctly describes this displacement process:

> The Roman genius is distinguished . . . above all, by the 'sacralization' of
> organic collectivities: family, *gens,* fatherland. The famous Roman disci-
> pline, their honoring of obligations (*fides*), their devotion to state, and the
> religious prestige they attributed to law are expressed by depreciation of
> the human person: the individual mattered only insofar as he belonged to
> his group. It was not until later, under the influence of Greek philosophy
> and the Oriental cults of salvation, that the Romans discovered the reli-
> gious importance of the person; but this discovery, which will have marked
> consequences, more especially affected the urban populations.[67]

As has been asserted earlier, the decline of the classical world, and
particularly the social destabilization of the urban centers of the Eastern
Empire, contributed to a social, psychological, and religious climate in which
alienated individuals sought refuge in socioreligious communities which
offered socialization in this world and salvation in the next. Given the general geographical area and sociocultural environment from which Christianity emerged, it is not very surprising that the strongest initial positive
response to the early Church came from Greco-Roman cities and towns in
Asia Minor that had substantial Jewish populations. As Christianity spread

---

[65] Eliade, *A History of Religious Ideas,* vol. 2, p. 133. Less religious significance is attributed to the Second Punic War by Alan Wardman, *Religion and Statecraft Among the Romans*
(London: Granada, 1982), pp. 33–41.

[66] Accounts of this process are provided by Arnold J. Toynbee, *Hannibal's Legacy: The
Hannibalic War's Effects on Roman Life,* 2 vols. (Oxford: Oxford University Press, 1965), and
H. E. L. Mellersh, *The Roman Soldier* (New York: Taplinger, 1964). While social conditions
may change rapidly as the result of wars and revolutions, the ethos of a society is usually molded
over a period of centuries. The inherent psychosocial depth of the ethos allows it to endure long
after the social order that engendered it has undergone substantial change. However, when
radical social change occurs, this "ethos lag," may contribute to ideological conflict.

[67] Mircea Eliade, *A History of Religious Ideas,* vol. 2, p. 115.

westward and northward, the degree of positive response appears to have diminished. Similarly, as the sociocultural environment changed from urban to rural, even among the Mediterranean inhabitants of the empire, the degree of acceptance of Christianity appears to have diminished. It seems that after Christianity moved beyond its original Judeo-Hellenistic socio-cultural environment, the primary factors contributing toward its acceptance in a given geographical area were the presence of a Jewish community, substantial exposure to Christianity, and an anomic urban social structure. While advocates of Christian expansion had some control over the amount of exposure Christianity received in a given community, there was little they could do to change a community's social structure.

In a community where the social structure diverged sharply from that of the Greek towns and cities in which early Christianity had first flourished, advocates of Christian expansion had two fundamental options: to candidly present Christianity with its Judeo-Hellenistic soteriology and be satisfied with minimal quantitative results, or to make substantial initial accommodations to the indigenous culture and hope to move the community gradually toward conformity with a more authentic Christianity.[68] The latter approach may yield a greater number of candidates for baptism, but it also includes a significant risk to the authenticity of their Christianization, given the potential for long-term religious syncretism. Furthermore, if those core elements of the Christian message which may conflict with an indigenous culture are deliberately or even unintentionally obscured or de-emphasized, while more compatible, though more peripheral aspects of Christianity are unduly emphasized, charges of misrepresentation may arise. Such has been a basic criticism of the contemporary "Jews for Jesus," who

---

[68] This latter approach appears to be endorsed for contemporary missionaries by Ary Roest Crollius, "What Is So New About Inculturation?" in idem, ed., *Inculturation: Working Papers on Living Faith and Cultures,* no. 5 (Rome: Centre "Cultures and Religions," Pontifical Gregorian University, 1984), pp. 1–20, who refers to the "dynamic relation between the Church and the variety of cultures" as "inculturation," or "insertion in a culture," preferring it to terms such as "adaptation," "accommodation," and "contextualisation," which he feels are more expressive of an "extrinsic contact" (pp. 3–4). He describes the initial stage of the process of inculturation as "that in which the Christian community has to assimilate the language and symbols of the local culture and to learn how to function according to the basic cultural patterns of the surrounding society. In this stage the local Church can be said to find itself in a 'conditioning process,' in which it cannot always exercise a perfect freedom of choice. *Certain elements may be assimilated, at least provisorily, which later prove to be conflictual with the core of its message and identity.* When, in a later stage, the local Church has effectively become present in its own culture and has learned to live with the language and values, the norms and expectations recognised by the surrounding society, then it is in a position to display a greater freedom in regard to the various alternatives in thought and conduct, in order to make choices which influence the local culture, reorienting it in accordance with the message of the Gospel" (p. 13; emphasis added). See also "Inculturation and the Early Missions" in Aylward Shorter, *Toward a Theology of Inculturation* (Maryknoll, N.Y.: Orbis Books, 1988); Louis J. Luzbetak, *The Church and Cultures: New Perspectives in Missiological Anthropology,* foreword by Eugene Nida (Maryknoll, N.Y.: Orbis Books, 1988); and Joseph P. Fitzpatrick, *One Church, Many Cultures: The Challenge of Diversity* (Kansas City, Mo.: Sheed and Ward, 1987).

were discussed earlier.[69] A correlate to the misrepresentation of an idea, even when unintentional, is the misunderstanding by the audience of the idea that is being presented.

As the end of Part I has now been reached, it is appropriate to provide an outline of the fundamental postulates of the general model of religious transformation that has been developed:

1. Social structure influences ideological structure and both contribute significantly to a society's general religious orientation.[70]

2. The appeal of the promise of salvation to a group is usually inversely related to the degree of solidarity among group members.[71]

3. Societies in which a desire for individual or group salvation exists, and which do not yet adhere to a universal religion, are usually predisposed toward accepting one.

4. Its association with a caring community, together with its promise of eternal salvation, constituted the fundamental appeal of early Christianity within the anomic urban centers of the Roman Empire.

5. In part because the development of early Christianity was organically related to, or "syngenic with," the decline of the Roman Empire, the social structure and ideological currents of the declining empire were in many ways inherently conducive to the promise of salvation offered by Christianity.

6. Societies in which a desire for individual or group salvation does not exist usually have little inherent interest in religions which promise salvation, particularly if they do not offer temporal benefits.

7. Whereas early Christianity was generally world-rejecting and universalist, with important universal ethical and doctrinal components, Indo-European religiosity was generally world-accepting and folk-centered, without formal ethical and doctrinal elements, and usually possessing heroic, religiopolitical, and magicoreligious characteristics.

8. Neither the cohesive social structure nor the Indo-European ideological heritage of the Germanic peoples predisposed them to desire salvation.

---

[69] See above, pp. 22–23.

[70] The observation of C. E. Stancliffe, "From Town to Country: The Christianisation of the Touraine, 370–600," in *The Church in Town and Countryside*, ed. Derek Baker, SCH, no. 16 (Oxford: Basil Blackwell, 1979), is worth noting in this regard: "I do not think that sociological analysis on its own can 'explain' religious conversion; but it can usefully throw light upon the sort of social conditions in which people are more likely to respond to the call of a prophetic religion. It can analyze the soil in which the word of God falls, and predict whether it has a high or low chance of taking" (p. 51 n. 43).

[71] "Group solidarity" or "cohesion" may be considered the antithesis of anomie. A recent work on the subject is Michael Hechter, *Principles of Group Solidarity* (Berkeley: University of California Press, 1987).

9. If a universal salvation religion is to succeed in making inroads in a folk-religious society which does not desire salvation, it must temporarily accommodate the predominantly world-accepting ethos and world-view of that society.

In Part II, this model of religious transformation will be applied to the encounter of the Germanic peoples with Christianity.

II
THE GERMANIC
TRANSFORMATION OF
CHRISTIANITY

5

Germanic Religiosity and Social Structure

The study of Germanic religiosity has always suffered from a paucity of reliable extant sources. However, the work of Georges Dumézil in the field of comparative mythology provides a framework through which this deficiency may be compensated in certain instances. Dumézil's comparative model of Indo-European societies posits the existence of a fundamental similarity in the ideological and sometimes the social structure among the ancient societies of India, Persia, Greece, Rome, and pre-Christian northern Europe. This association permits the careful application of evidence regarding a fundamental ideological concept or "mythologem"[1] found in one or more Indo-European societies to that mythologem as it exists in another Indo-European society. Through such a process of analogy, one may enhance the understanding of that mythologem in the latter society, for which the currently available documentation may be scanty or inconclusive. When Dumézil's model is applied to pre-Christian Germanic religiosity, various aspects of form and structure hitherto interpreted solely as local, Germanic phenomena, acquire a new dimension, derived from their association with the greater Indo-European family of peoples.

In this inquiry the term "Germanic" refers not only to the Gothic, Frankish, Saxon, Burgundian, Alamannic, Suevic, and Vandal peoples, but also to the Viking peoples of Scandinavia and the Anglo-Saxon peoples of Britain. In addition, the term "religiosity" is often used when referring to the

[1] Dumézil's notion of an antecedent mythologem, expressed somewhat differently in the myths of various Indo-European societies, may in some ways be said to parallel Karl Rahner's notion of a single dogma which may be expressed somewhat differently as "theologumena" by different Christian communities at different periods in history, as indicated in Rahner's discussion "What Is a Dogmatic Statement?" in *Theological Investigations,* trans. Karl Kruger, vol. 5 (Baltimore: Helicon, 1966), pp. 42–66; and *Sacramentum Mundi,* s.v. "Theologumenon." Both Dumézil's notion of mythologem and Rahner's of dogma seem to correspond to a primal, nonverbalized idea of a particular relationship between or among supernatural and human entities. An important difference is that a Christian dogma is implicitly held to be universally valid, while Dumézil's mythologem is exclusively Indo-European.

religious elements of Indo-European and particularly Germanic societies, while the term "religion" is usually reserved for Christianity and other universal religious movements. This is due to the organic relationship of the religious elements of folk-religious societies to other elements of those societies. Religious elements tend to be more extensively diffused throughout a folk-religious society, whereas, in a society where a universal religion such as Christianity predominates, religious elements tend to be more isolated in specific doctrines and practices.

The optimal sources that one could possess for reconstructing the pre-Christian religious attitudes of the Germanic peoples would be somewhat akin to the comprehensive exposition of early Christian religious beliefs and attitudes contained in the writings of the patristic authors. Unfortunately, there exist no extant sources written by members of pre-Christian Germanic societies. Since it is unlikely that such works exist, alternative sources must be carefully considered. These alternative sources may be generally categorized as written and archaeological. The written sources vary in their proximity to the conditions which they describe, while it is generally difficult to accurately derive religious attitudes from archaeological finds.[2] Early Roman accounts were essentially reports by visitors to Germanic lands which tended to focus on the material details of Germanic life. As may be expected, they failed to capture the inner spirit and structure of the Germanic ethos and world-view.

The earliest written record of Germanic religious attitudes is Julius Caesar's *De Bello Gallico.* He noted in book 6, written in 53 B.C.: "They have no Druids to control religious observances and are not much given to sacrifice. The only beings they recognize as gods are things that they can see, and by which they are obviously benefited, such as Sun, Moon, and Fire."[3] Over a century later, in A.D. 98, Cornelius Tacitus wrote in chapter 9 of his *Germania:*

> Above all other gods they worship Mercury, and count it no sin, on certain feast-days, to include human victims in the sacrifices offered to him. Hercules and Mars they appease by offerings of animals, in accordance with ordinary civilized custom. . . . The Germans do not think it in keeping with the divine majesty to confine gods within walls or to portray them in the

---

[2] Both the written and archaeological, as well as the linguistic sources of Germanic religiosity are considered in Edgar C. Polomé, "Germanic Religion: An Overview," in *Essays on Germanic Religion, JIES,* Monograph Series, no. 6 (Washington, D.C.: Institute for the Study of Man, 1989). See also "Die Quellen der germanischen Religion" and "Geschichte der Forschung," in Jan de Vries, *Altgermanische Religionsgeschichte,* 2nd ed., vol. 1 (Berlin: Walter de Gruyter, 1956–57).

[3] Gaius Julius Caesar, *The Conquest of Gaul,* trans. S. A. Handford (New York: Penguin Books, 1951), p. 35; original in C. Julius Caesar, *Libri VII De bello Gallico,* vol. 1 of *Commentarii,* ed. R. L. A. Du Pontet, Oxford Classical Texts (Oxford: Oxford University Press, 1900), par. 21: "Nam neque druides habent qui rebus divinis praesint neque sacrificiis student. Deorum numero eos solos ducunt quos cernunt et quorum aperte opibus iuvantur, Solem et Vulcanum et Lunam."

likeness of any human countenance. Their holy places are the woods and groves, and they apply the names of deities to that hidden presence which is seen only by the eye of reverence.[4]

Descriptions of Germanic religious practices may also be found in the collections of ordinances known as "capitularies" issued by the Frankish kings,[5] in the canons of the national Gallic Councils,[6] in the directives of local councils,[7] and in the biographies, sermons, and correspondence of Christian missionaries.[8] The description of Germanic religiosity contained in these documents reveals a widespread devotion to sacred trees, groves, springs, and stones, and an interest in prophecy and magic.[9] However, since the references to Germanic religiosity in these documents are made from an anti-pagan perspective and are often sketchy,[10] their contribution

[4] Cornelius Tacitus, *The Agricola and the Germania,* trans. with intro. by H. Mattingly, revised by S. A. Handford (New York: Penguin Books, 1970), pp. 108–9; original in Cornelius Tacitus, "De origine et situ Germanorum," ed. M. Winterbottom, in *Opera minora,* Oxford Classical Texts (Oxford: Oxford University Press, 1975), par. 9: "Deorum maxime Mercurium colunt, cui certis diebus humanis quoque hostiis litare fas habent. Herculem ac Martem concessis animalibus placant . . . ceterum nec cohibere parietibus deos neque in ullam humani oris speciem adsimulare ex magnitudine caelestium arbitrantur; lucos ac nemora consecrant, deorumque nominibus appellant secretum illud quod sola reverentia vident."

[5] The Frankish capitularies are arranged in the *Capitularia Regum Francorum, MGH Legum Sectio II* vol. 1, part 1, ed. Alfred Boretius (Hanover: Hahn Verlag, 1881).

[6] These records may be found in the *Concilia Galliae A. 511–A. 695,* ed. Carlo de Clercq, *Corpus Christianorum Series Latina,* 148A (Turnhout: Brepols, 1963).

[7] Documents issued by local councils are included in Carlo de Clercq, *La Législation religieuse franque de Clovis à Charlemagne: Etude sur les actes des conciles et des capitulaires, les statuts diocésains et les règles monastiques, 507–814,* 2nd series, no. 38 (Louvain: Bureaux du Receuil, Université de Louvain, 1938), and Odette Pontal, *Histoire des conciles mérovingiens,* (Paris: Cerf, 1989). Among the most interesting of the local councils, according to J. N. Hillgarth, *Christianity and Paganism, 350–750: The Conversion of Western Europe* (rev. ed. of *The Conversion of Western Europe, 350–750*) (Philadelphia: University of Pennsylvania Press, 1986), is the diocesan council of Auxerre, held in the latter half of the sixth century, which is "the only diocesan synod preserved from Merovingian Gaul" (p. 98). Hillgarth's translation of the canons of this council include those which condemn the following activities: participation in the festival of the Kalends of January, making vows "among woods or at sacred trees or at springs," and the consultation of "soothsayers or . . . augurs, or to those who pretend to know the future" (p. 103).

[8] A representative selection of these sources is translated in Hillgarth, *Christianity and Paganism.* See also Thomas Leslie Amos, "The Origin and Nature of the Carolingian Sermon," Ph.D. diss., Michigan State University, 1983.

[9] The most exhaustive compilation of such evidence remains Wilhelm Boudriot, *Die Altgermanische Religion in der amtlichen kirchlichen Literatur des Abendlandes vom 5. bis 11. Jahrhundert* (1928; reprint, Bonn: Ludwig Röhrscheid Verlag, 1964), while a recent interpretive analysis may be found in Valerie I. J. Flint, *The Rise of Magic in Early Medieval Europe* (Princeton, N.J.: Princeton University Press, 1991). See also "Seelen, Geister und Dämonen; Shicksalsmächte," in de Vries, *Altgermanische Religionsgeschichte,* vol. 1.

[10] An exception to the sketchy outline of Germanic religious practices contained in most Christian sources may have been a mid-eighth-century document which has come to be known as the *Indiculus Superstitionum et Paganiarum* (*Capitularia Regum Francorum,* pp. 222–23). Unfortunately, only the index to this document remains extant. It is discussed in Ruth Mazo Karras, "Pagan Survivals and Syncretism in the Conversion of Saxony," *Catholic Historical Review* 72 (1986): 561–66; and in Flint *The Rise of Magic,* pp. 41–44, 211–12.

to an understanding of Germanic religiosity and of the Germanic ethos and world-view is limited.

The Roman and Christian sources are complemented by a collection of Icelandic documents commonly referred to as the *Eddas*. They are usually divided into two collections: the *Elder* or *Poetic Edda,* the oldest of which may date back to A.D. 700, and the *Prose Edda,* written by the Christian Icelander Snorri Sturluson (d. 1241). Fortunately for the student of Germanic religiosity, Snorri's accounts of pre-Christian religious beliefs and practices do not follow the polemical style of his Latin Christian counterparts in their accounts of pre-Christian classical religion. This is all the more significant for the cause of Germanic religious studies, since Snorri's writings constitute the bulk of the contemporary documentation, while patristic apologetic documents do not constitute the sole source of classical paganism. In fact, Snorri's historical perspective transcends mere tolerance of the religion of his ancestors. Whereas many contemporary chroniclers were Icelandic monks whose major literary concern appears to have been the lionization of the missionary kings of Norway, Snorri's approach to his sources was more objective:

> Snorri's sagas are both more realistic and more entertaining. Snorri's ruthless handling of these earlier sagas, his sources, is, however, not due solely to his greater critical acumen and stricter regard for the truth. Rationalistic layman and chieftain as he was, he was repelled by the ecclesiastical spirit pervading the sagas in question—all the way from the legendary tales, sermons of edification, pious remarks and unctuous style, to the very delineation of character and interpretation of events themselves. In fact, behind all this is the political struggle between the old families of the aristocracy, who from the period of the conversion of Iceland had exercised complete authority over the church, and the bishops of the twelfth century and later, who were endeavouring to make the church as independent and powerful as it was in the rest of Europe—a state within a state.[11]

In spite of the Icelandic clergy's desire to eradicate pre-Christian religious beliefs and traditions, Snorri was able to avoid the suppression of his *Edda* by including a disclaimer, warning readers not to give them the assent of faith. For these reasons Sigurdur Nordal concludes that "the richest and purest source extant for the ideas and attitude to life of the early Germanic peoples is the literature of Iceland during the twelfth and thirteenth centuries."[12]

[11] Sigurdur Nordal, Introduction to *The Prose Edda of Snorri Sturluson,* ed. Jean I. Young (Berkeley: University of California Press, 1966), p. 9.

[12] Ibid., p. 8. Nordal's view is not, however, universally shared, as Edgar Polomé indicates in his discussion "Approaches to Germanic Mythology" in *Myth in Indo-European Antiquity,* ed. Gerald James Larson (Berkeley: University of California Press, 1974), pp. 51–66. Also of interest in the same volume is Udo Strutynski's article "History and Structure in Germanic Mythology: Some Thoughts on Einar Haugen's Critique of Dumézil," pp. 29–50.

Despite the quality of the Icelandic sources, there has always existed uncertainty regarding their expression of the cosmological and ideological perceptions of the early Germanic peoples. A critical area has been the interpretation of the two primary groups of Germanic deities: the Aesir, comprising the gods of sovereignty and battle, Odin and Thor; and the Vanir, comprising the gods of sustenance and reproduction, Njord, Frey, and Freya. The relationship between these two groups of deities is fundamental to an understanding of Germanic religiosity and provides an introduction to Dumézil's methodology.

Prior to Dumézil's studies, it had been common to "historicize" the battle between the Aesir and the Vanir as recounted in the *Poetic Edda*,[13] the *Prose Edda*[14] and the *Heimskringla*.[15] It had been thought, and it is still held by some today,[16] that the Vanir were the agrarian deities of an indigenous agricultural society which originally inhabited the lands later conquered by Indo-European invaders, while the warlike Aesir were the deities of the Indo-Europeans. Without denying the possible historical occurrence of these events in the evolution of Germanic society, Dumézil argued that "the duality of the Aesir and the Vanir is not a reflection of these events, nor an effect of evolution," but rather "it is a question . . . of two complementary terms in a unitary religious and ideological structure, one of which presupposes the other."[17] This religious and ideological structure did not develop as a response to conflicts which arose during Germanic conquests or migrations, but was "brought, fully articulated, by those Indo-European invaders who became the Germanic peoples,"[18] from

---

[13] "Voluspa," 21–24, in *The Poetic Edda*, 2nd ed., ed., trans., and intro. by Lee M. Hollander (1962; reprint, Austin: University of Texas Press, 1986), pp. 4–5. A primary source for the *Poetic Edda* in Old Norse is *Edda, die Lieder des Codex Regius*, 4th ed., ed. Gustav Neckel, rev. Hans Kuhn (Heidelberg: Winter Verlag, 1962).

[14] "Skaldskaparmal," ch. 5 of *Prose Edda*, ed. Young, p. 100.

[15] "Ynglingasaga," chs. 1–5 of *Heimskringla: History of the Kings of Norway*, 2nd rev. ed., trans. Lee M. Hollander (Austin: University of Texas Press, 1964), pp. 6–10.

[16] Foremost among the dwindling number of Dumézil's historicist critics is E. A. Philipson, author of *Die Genealogie der Götter in germanischer Religion: Mythologie und Theologie*, Illinois Studies in Language and Literature 37, no. 3 (Urbana: University of Illinois Press, 1953). It is significant to note the number of specialists in separate Indo-European disciplines who have come to endorse Dumézil's general Indo-European paradigm. Many, including specialists in the areas of Germanic religion, mythology, and philology, are noted in C. Scott Littleton, "The Disciples and the Critics," in *The New Comparative Mythology*, 3rd ed. (Berkeley: University of California Press, 1982). The most recent specialist in Germanic as well as Celtic and Scandinavian mythology to indicate her support for Dumézil is H. R. Ellis Davidson, *Myths and Symbols in Pagan Europe* (Syracuse, N.Y.: Syracuse University Press, 1988), pp. 220–28.

[17] Georges Dumézil, *Gods of the Ancient Northmen*, trans. Einar Haugen et al. (Berkeley: University of California Press, 1973), p. 12.

[18] Ibid. A recent examination of the route and chronology of the Germanic Indo-European migrations is contained in Edgar C. Polomé, "Who Are the Germanic People?" in Susan Nacev Skomal and Edgar C. Polomé, eds., *Proto-Indo-European: The Archaeology of a Linguistic Problem: Studies in Honor of Marija Gimbutas* (Washington, D.C.: Institute for the Study of Man, 1987), pp. 216–44.

their *Urheimat* on the steppes of the Urals.[19] The mythologem from which the Aesir-Vanir myth developed originated during the era of proto-Indo-European unity in the third millennium B.C. and "should be situated at that moment of mythological history when society is formed through reconciliation and the union of priests and warriors on the one hand [and] with farmers and all the powers of fecundity and nourishment on the other."[20] This foundational mythologem, as manifested in the Germanic Aesir-Vanir myth, is considered by Dumézil to support "the central motif of Indo-European ideology, the conception according to which the world and society can live only through the harmonious collaboration of the three stratified functions of sovereignty, force and fecundity."[21]

Dumézil did not arrive at this conclusion merely from a careful examination of the Germanic sources. Instead, in his derivation of this central mythologem, Dumézil drew upon his knowledge of the documents of other members of the Indo-European family of cultures:

> It is here that comparative considerations may [and must] intervene to assure us that our texts do in fact have meaning, and to determine what that meaning is. Let us be very precise: we are concerned here with comparative Indo-European considerations, implying a common genetic relation (filiation), not simply typological or universal considerations. . . . It is thus legitimate and even methodologically necessary, before denying significance or antiquity to a "theologeme" or myth among the Scandinavians, to ask if the religions of the most conservative Indo-European peoples, the

---

[19] The argument for locating the proto-Indo-European homeland in this area is cogently presented by Marija Gimbutas, "Proto-Indo-European Culture: The Kurgan Culture during the Fifth, Fourth, and Third Millennia B.C.," in George Cardona, Henry M. Hoenigswald, and Alfred Senn, eds., *Indo-European and Indo-Europeans: Papers Presented at the Third Indo-European Conference at the University of Pennsylvania* (Philadelphia: University of Pennsylvania Press, 1970), pp. 155–98. A recent linguistical challenge which locates the homeland in Anatolia has been presented by Thomas V. Gamkrelidze and V. V. Ivanov, *Indoevropejskij jazyk i Indoevropejcy*, 2 vols. (Tbilisi: Publishing House of the Tbilisi State University, 1984). An English version of this work is forthcoming from Mouton de Gruyter, while a summary is contained in idem, "The Early History of Indo-European Languages," *Scientific American* 262:3 (1990): 110–16. *JIES* 13:1/2 (1985) contains translations of three articles by Gamkrelidze and Ivanov, and is devoted to a discussion of their assertions. It also contains a response from Marija Gimbutas entitled "Primary and Secondary Homeland of the Indo-Europeans: Comments on the Gamkrelidze-Ivanov Articles." Also important is David W. Anthony, "The Archaeology of Indo-European Origins," *JIES* 19:3/4 (1991): 193–222. Related discussions of Indo-European topics are presented in J. P. Mallory, *In Search of the Indo-Europeans: Language, Archaeology and Myth* (London: Thames and Hudson, 1989); idem, "Human Populations and the Indo-European Problem," *Mankind Quarterly* 33:2 (1992): 131–54; T. L. Markey and John A. C. Greppin, eds., *When Worlds Collide: Indo-Europeans and Pre-Indo-Europeans* (Ann Arbor, Mich.: Karoma Publishers, 1990); and *Perspectives on Indo-European Language, Culture and Religion: Studies in Honor of Edgar C. Polomé*, 2 vols., *JIES* Monograph no. 7 (McLean, Va.: Institute for the Study of Man, 1991).

[20] Georges Dumézil, *Loki* (Paris: G.-P. Maisonneuve, 1948), p. 105; quoted in idem, *Gods of the Ancient Northmen*, p. 23.

[21] Georges Dumézil, *The Destiny of the Warrior*, trans. Alf Hiltebeitel (Chicago: University of Chicago Press, 1970), p. 4.

speakers of Sanskrit, Italic, and Celtic, do not present a similar belief or story. This is sometimes the case, and it happens that in the Indic version for example, which is attested earlier in books written directly by the keepers of divine knowledge, the structure of a formula or the meaning of a story appears more clearly, more obviously linked to religious and social life, than in the literary works of the Christian Snorri. . . . It happens that the problems of the Aesir and the Vanir are of the kind that lend themselves to such a method.[22]

Dumézil discovered parallels between Snorri's account of the Aesir and Vanir, and the Indian account of the conflict between Mitra, Varuna, and Indra, who collectively represented the functions of sovereignty and force, and the Nasatya, who represented the function of fecundity.[23] By carefully examining the details of each account, Dumézil discovered a pattern common to both, but nonexistent in the folklore of non-Indo-European peoples. This pattern is one in which a mythical character personifying intoxication appears "at the moment when divine society is with difficulty but definitely joined by the adjunction of the representatives of fecundity and prosperity to those of sovereignty and force, it is at the moment when the two hostile groups make their peace."[24] Dumézil has also noted a corresponding pattern in Roman epic history where the first three kings of Rome—Romulus, Numa, and Tullus Hostilius—collectively represented the functions of sovereignty and force, while the conquered Sabines represented the function of fecundity.[25]

In the above analysis a central assumption of Dumézil's system was introduced, that is, that the social structure and related ideology of proto-Indo-European society is reflected in the mythologies and epic histories of the various branches of the Indo-European family. Dumézil had originally hoped to substantiate both the retention of the original social structure of the proto-Indo-Europeans, *as well as* the expression of their ideology, as he had done in the case of India. However, he later conceded that because of organic developments that could take place in the life of an Indo-European society over a substantial period of time, it would be overly optimistic to hope to discover unmodified social structures in each of the

---

[22] Dumézil, *Gods of the Ancient Northmen*, p. 16.

[23] *Shriman Mahabharatam*, Ramachandra Kinjawadekar et al, eds., 6 vols. (Poona: Chitrashala Press, 1929–33), book 3, sect. 123–25.

[24] Dumézil, *Loki*, pp. 104–5, cited in *Gods of the Ancient Northmen*, p. 23. In the Germanic version of this mythologem the character personifying intoxication is named Kvasir, while in the Indian version he is named Mada (ibid., pp. 21–23).

[25] Dumézil, *Gods of the Ancient Northmen*, p. 24, and Littleton, *The New Comparative Mythology*, pp. 70–71. While the Germanic and Indo-Iranian branches of the Indo-European family tended to express Indo-European mythologems in the form of cosmic myths, the Roman branch tended to express these same mythologems as epic history, such as the events described by Livy in the first book of his *Histories*. A comprehensive discussion of the Roman mode of expressing Indo-European mythologems may be found in Georges Dumézil, *Archaic Roman Religion*, trans. Philip Krapp, with a foreword by Mircea Eliade, 2 vols. (Chicago: University of Chicago Press, 1970).

descendant Indo-European societies: "I recognized that, wherever one can establish its presence, the tripartite ideology is nothing (or is no longer, or perhaps never was) but an ideal and, at the same time, a method of analysis [*moyen d'analyser*], a method of interpreting the forces which assure the course of the world and the lives of men."[26] Dumézil has further delineated the limits of his comparative method in "what should be its Golden Rule, namely that it permits one to explore and clarify structures of thought but not to reconstruct events."[27]

Dumézil has characterized the fundamental social and ideological structure of proto-Indo-European society as one of "tripartition." Its foremost manifestation lies in the three major elements of the Indo-European social hierarchy: (1) chieftains and priests, constituting the "first function," that of sovereign and supernatural authority, with a considerable degree of bipolar tension between these elements; (2) warriors, constituting the second function of physical force; and (3) farmers and herders, constituting the third and last function of fecundity. Intrinsically associated with this tripartite social structure is a tripartite ideological structure, of which the characters and events contained in the writings of Snorri and in the *Mahabharata* are lasting manifestations. Beyond this direct relationship there existed in early Indo-European societies "a tendency to conceive of phenomena in general as divided into three interrelated categories, defined in terms of the three above-mentioned functions."[28] Julius Caesar's account of the Germanic worship of the Sun, the Moon, and Fire, referred to earlier, may have reflected this tendency.[29]

The present inquiry into the encounter of the Germanic peoples with Christianity stands to benefit from the application of Dumézil's comparative method to the religious development of the Greek, Roman, Celtic, and Germanic branches of the Indo-European family, both as individual societies and as interacting societies.[30] At this juncture it may be advantageous to examine those characteristics that have been generally attributed to Indo-European social structure and religion. In his recent article "Indo-European Culture, with Special Attention to Religion," Edgar Polomé discusses these characteristics:

[26] Translation from C. Scott Littleton, " 'Je ne suis pas ... structuraliste': Some Fundamental Differences Between Dumézil and Lévi-Strauss," *Journal of Asian Studies* 34 (1974): 154 n. 12; quoted in Udo Strutynski, introduction to Georges Dumézil, *Camillus* (Berkeley: University of California Press, 1980), p. 7.

[27] Dumézil, *Archaic Roman Religion*, p. xvi.

[28] Littleton, *The New Comparative Mythology*, p. 5. This work constitutes the most comprehensive and current introduction to Dumézil's system and method. The appendix to the third edition contains a guide to recent developments and applications.

[29] Dumézil, *Gods of the Ancient Northmen*, p. 19.

[30] Specific topics in this and other areas are suggested in Matthias Vereno, "On the Relations of Dumézilian Comparative Indo-European Mythology to the History of Religions in General," in Gerald James Larson, ed., *Myth in Indo-European Antiquity* (Berkeley: University of California Press, 1974), pp. 181–90.

Indo-European society, as far as we can judge, was agnatic and ethno-centric, its basic unit being the patriarchal, patrilinear, and essentially patrilocal extended family. Kindred was the foundation of its concentric structure, grouping the families in clans, claiming descent from a common ancestor, and the clans in tribes, presumably deriving their origin from some eponymous founder. Ethnic solidarity became especially manifest in contrast with outsiders. . . . Inside his group, with his kith and kin, the Indo-European is safe; outside lurk the dangers. Inside his family, his clan, his tribe, he enjoys all the rights and privileges that pertain to free members of the community. . . .

It has long been assumed that their oldest religious concepts were associated with nature and the cosmos—the supreme God being Father Sky (Vedic *Dyaus pita,* Gk. *Zeus pater,* Lat. *Juppiter,* etc.), whose main functions were sovereignty and creativity, the latter being manifested both in the cosmogony and his paternity in divine and human genealogies. . . .

The Indo-Europeans must have elaborated an extensive mythology; their tradition was transmitted orally, and after some of them acquired the skill of writing, a taboo was maintained against putting down in writing their religious lore. Their gods were close to them, though their attitude toward them was ambivalent, characterized by: 1) awe, and 2) trust, tinged with a certain familiarity. The religious fear was inspired by their holiness, and the reserved attitude of the Indo-Europeans was translated in their piety by a set of interdictions. As the gods were, however, accessible and interested in human affairs, the Indo-Europeans respected them for it, while giving them their full confidence, showing their feelings of trust and admiration for their deities in their prayers, their offerings and their entire cult.[31]

Beyond these fundamental observations, Polomé believes that "the most important problem in connection with Indo-European religion is, however, the validity of the Dumézilian hypothesis of the trifunctional religious ideology for the earliest period, as a reflex in the world of the divine of the fundamental structure of the nomadic pastoral society."[32] Acknowledging

---

[31] "Indo-European Culture, with Special Attention to Religion," in Edgar C. Polomé, ed., *The Indo-Europeans in the Fourth and Third Millennia* (Ann Arbor, Mich.: Karoma Publishers, 1982), pp. 161–67 passim. See also, idem, "The Indo-European Component in Germanic Religion," in Jaan Puhvel, ed., *Myth and Law Among the Indo-Europeans* (Berkeley: University of California Press, 1970), pp. 55–82.

[32] Ibid., p. 167. The sociological background of this hypothesis, ranging from Emile Durkheim and his colleague Antoine Meillet to Durkheim's disciples, his nephew Marcel Mauss and Marcel Granet, and then to Dumézil, is discussed by Littleton, *The New Comparative Mythology,* pp. 38–40. The key Durkheimian conclusion employed by Dumézil was that "religion is something eminently social," since "religious representations are collective representations which represent collective realities," which is developed in Durkheim, *The Elementary Forms of the Religious Life,* trans. Joseph Ward Swain (1915; reprint, New York: Free Press, 1965); the previous quote appears on p. 22. The first exposition of this notion appeared in Emile Durkheim and Marcel Mauss, "De quelques formes primitives de classification: contributions à l'étude des représentations collectives," *L'Année sociologique* 6 (1903): 1–72. Meillet, whose study of Indo-European linguistics and Iranian mythology influenced Durkheim, was Dumézil's doctoral mentor.

the complexity of substantiating such an inclusive hypothesis, Polomé nonetheless concludes:

> If we consider the fragmented and heterogeneous heritage of the Vedic Indians, of ancient Rome, and of medieval Scandinavia and Ireland, and the scattered elements provided by archaeology, votive inscriptions, runic formulae, onomastics, reports of ancient authors and early Christian missionaries, *capitularia* of Charlemagne, epic poetry and medieval historiography, and what not, it is undeniable that a set of striking correspondences emerges in which myths preserved in the Rigveda will find parallels in the legendary history of the kings of Rome as reported by Livy and in Scandinavian mythology in the collection compiled by Snorri Sturluson, as well as in some passages of the Irish epics. And, more important still, these traditions will be organized around a tripartite structure of the pantheon and of the corresponding society.[33]

One may question the uniqueness of Indo-European society and religion as just depicted. It may seem that the tripartite division of society is a natural or universal rather than a strictly Indo-European characteristic. In responding to such a criticism, C. Scott Littleton first cites Stuart Piggott's observation that "the tripartite arrangement is perhaps an obvious enough division of responsibilities within a community, but its formal recognition is characteristically Indo-European."[34] Noting also that "it was only among the Indo-Europeans" that the tripartite division of social functions "served, initially at least, as the basis for a societal stratification system,"[35] Littleton also provides examples of nontripartite divisions of social functions among non-Indo-European societies.[36]

But it is not only in societal tripartition that Indo-European socioreligious uniqueness may be located. The bipolar tension between the religious and political elements of the first function of sovereignty is an important, uniquely Indo-European characteristic, which is exemplified by the following pairs of divinities: the Vedic pair of Mitra and Varuna, the Germanic pair of Odin and Tyr, and the Roman pair of Jupiter and Dius Fidius.[37] Another "uniquely Indo-European phenomenon," which is more relevant to the subject at hand, was the existence of "a class of military specialists

---

[33] Polomé, "Indo-European Culture," pp. 167–68.

[34] *Prehistoric India* (Harmondsworth: Penguin Books, 1950), p. 260, cited in Littleton, *The New Comparative Mythology*, p. 221. The possibility of Indo-European influence in the development of the doctrine of the Trinity, suggested by Littleton (ibid., p. 231), is explored in Edward C. Hobbs and Andrew P. Porter, "The Trinity and the Indo-European Tripartite World-View," unpublished. I am grateful to Andrew P. Porter for providing me with a copy of this paper.

[35] Littleton, *The New Comparative Mythology*, p. 221.

[36] Ibid., p. 273.

[37] The bipolar tension between the political and religious elements of the first function of sovereignty as it has occurred in several Indo-European societies is discussed in detail in Georges Dumézil, *Mitra-Varuna: An Essay on Two Indo-European Representations of Sovereignty*, trans. Derek Coltman (New York: Zone Books, 1988), and idem, *Jupiter, Mars, Quirinus: essai sur la conception indo-européenne de la société et sur les origines de Rome*, Collection "La Montagne Sainte Geneviève," vol. 1 (Paris: Gallimard, 1941).

whose prime purpose was to exercise physical prowess, either in defense of the society or in order to conquer new territory."[38] Members of this class of military specialists usually organized themselves into a *comitatus* or *Männerbund,* "a band of young warriors led by a chief or king which was distinct from the other strata of society (i.e., the priests and the cultivators) and which exhibited in battle a remarkable recklessness and esprit de corps."[39] The *comitatus* figured "among the most prominent features of ancient Indo-European social organization."[40]

Continuing his study of the second Indo-European function of force as institutionalized in the *comitatus,* Dumézil discovered additional distinctive features. He noted the recurrence of specific themes concerning the behavior of the warrior in Indic, Greek, and Germanic mythology. This behavior, which has been summarized as "les trois péchés du guerrier,"[41] involves transgressions by a warrior hero against each of the three divisions of Indo-European society. These include regicide, a crime against the societal function of sovereignty; cowardice, a violation of the warrior ethic of the second function of force; and adultery, a violation of the third function of fecundity. Each of the warrior heroes, the Indic Indra, the Greek Heracles, and the Germanic Starkaðr, is punished after each transgression by losing some degree of his power, until he finally dies. The centrality of the warrior figure to the Indo-European and hence Germanic ethos has been summarized by Littleton:

> *Aspects de la fonction guerrière* must indeed be ranked among Dumézil's most significant publications, for in this delineation of the ambivalent position of the I-E warrior, an ambivalence clearly expressed in myth and saga, he touches upon what appears to have been a fundamental element of I-E ideology. More than any single military implement, the I-E warrior band, or *Männerbund,* organized around the person of a fearless leader (cf. Finn and the *fianna,* Indra and the *Maruts*), seems to have been the "secret weapon" that facilitated the I-E expansion. The warrior was thus the prop and, in many respects, the pivot of the social system.[42]

Given this pivotal role, it is understandable that, despite the pacifying effects of Christianity, the ethos of the warrior band or *comitatus* endured through the Middle Ages and remained at the center of the medieval epic, testifying to the vitality of the Indo-European ideological heritage.[43] Also,

[38] *Encyclopedia of Religion,* s.v. "War and Warriors: Indo-European Beliefs and Practices," by C. Scott Littleton.

[39] Littleton, *The New Comparative Mythology,* p. 156.

[40] *Encyclopedia of Religion,* s.v. "Indo-European Religions: History of Study," by C. Scott Littleton.

[41] This is the title given by Dumézil to the second essay in his *Aspects de la fonction guerrière chez les Indo-Européens,* Bibliothèque de l'Ecole des Hautes Etudes, Section Religieuse, vol. 68 (Paris: Presses Universitaire de France, 1956).

[42] Littleton, *The New Comparative Mythology,* p. 127.

[43] See John Simpson, "Comparative Structural Analysis of Three Ethical Questions in *Beowulf,* the *Nibelungenlied* and the *Chanson de Roland,*" *JIES* 3 (1975): 239–54. Simpson

since the Germanic peoples constitute the last wave of Indo-European expansion, and since, prior to their encounter with Christianity, they had minimal interaction with non-Indo-European peoples, it is likely that at the time of their encounter with Christianity they embodied Indo-European social and ideological traditions somewhat more authentically than the older and more socioculturally heterogeneous Greek and Roman branches of the Indo-European family. For these reasons, as well as the immediate sociopolitical reality of intertribal competition and military conflict with Rome, the Indo-European warrior ethos, with its emphasis on high group solidarity and individual courage, was preserved by the Germanic peoples throughout the periods of contact with Christianity in late antiquity and the early Middle Ages and perhaps beyond. Littleton has noted that "European society of the eleventh and twelfth centuries, though professing belief in a religious system having its roots in the Semitic tradition, was nevertheless an I-E speaking one and, as such, heir to the common I-E ideology."[44]

The prominence of the *comitatus* and its warrior ethic as a distinguishing feature of early medieval Germanic society has lead Mary Crawford Clawsey to assign it a Germanic origin.[45] Although she does not employ an Indo-European comparativist approach to the *comitatus,* Clawsey argues that "this institution, wherein a noble served his lord in return for material rewards and the opportunity to win glory, and in fear of shame if he failed to live up to his oath, persisted among the Germanic peoples, though not necessarily in the same precise form in every tribe, long after they had given up their pagan religion and in many cases their language."[46] Not only did the institution of the *comitatus* persist among the Germanic peoples, according to Clawsey, but also, "there is little evidence of its independent existence elsewhere."[47] The primary description of the *comitatus* may be found in Tacitus's *Germania:*

> Both prestige and power depend on being continually attended by a large train of picked young warriors, which is a distinction in peace and a protection in war. And it is not only in a chief's own nation that the superior number and quality of his retainers bring him glory and renown. Neighbouring states honor them also, courting them with embassies and complimenting them with presents. Very often the mere reputation of such men will virtually decide the issue of a war.

---

utilizes a Dumézilian approach to establish that the ethical behavior of the hero of each of these epics conforms to the Indo-European warrior code.

[44] Ibid., p. 122, n. 13. The developmental course of the Germanic ethos and world-view and their interaction with Christianity, from the Middle Ages through the Reformation to the present, may be studied in subsequent inquiries.

[45] "The *Comitatus* and the Lord-Vassal Relationship in the Medieval Epic" (Ph.D. diss., University of Maryland, 1982), p. 24.

[46] Ibid., p. 2.

[47] Ibid., p. 24.

On the field of battle it is a disgrace to a chief to be surpassed in courage by his followers, and to the followers not to be equal to the courage of
their chief. And to leave a battle alive after their chief has fallen means
lifelong infamy and shame. To defend him and protect him, and to let him
get the credit for their own acts of heroism, are the most solemn obligations of their allegiance. The chiefs fight for victory, the followers for their
chief.[48]

The main "distinguishing characteristic of the *comitatus*," which Clawsey
finds lacking in classical and non-Western analogues, is "its reciprocity—
more precisely, its being at once vertical and reciprocal," that is, "only the
comitatus combined both qualities and made the assumption that the
leader in a vertical relationship had obligations as much as did the follower
and that therefore a voluntary element existed on both sides."[49] This simultaneous verticality and reciprocity would seem to contribute to a high degree
of group solidarity, which is why it is especially relevant to this study. Not
only the generally heroic nature of the age during which the Germanic peoples initially encountered Christianity (376–754),[50] but also the particular
cohesiveness engendered by the *comitatus* relationship, denote a fundamental social departure from the anomic environment of the urban centers
of the declining Roman Empire which were so conducive to the expansion
of early Christianity.

At the heart of the *comitatus* relationship lay the Germanic notion of
honor or *êre*. However, as George Fenwick Jones advises, one must be
careful that contemporary connotations of honor do not obscure its Old
High German (OHG) meaning: "Above all, *êre* should not be rendered as
Ehre, except in certain specific contexts, such as in 'show honor to' or 'in
honor of.' "[51] Jones refers to the *Mittelhochdeutsches Wörterbuch* for "the

---

[48] Tacitus, *The Agricola and the Germania*, pp. 112–13; original in Cornelius Tacitus, "De
origine et situ Germanorum," pars. 13–14: "haec dignitas, hae vires magno semper electorum
iuvenum globo circumdari, in pace decus, in bello praesidium. nec solum in sua gente cuique sed
apud finitimas quoque civitates id nomen, ea gloria est, si numero ac virtute comitatus eminaet;
expetuntur enim legationibus et muneribus ornantur et ipsa plerumque fama bella profligant.
Cum ventum in aciem, turpe principi virtute vinci, turpe comitatui virtutem principis non
adaequare. iam vero infame in omnem vitam ac probrosum superstitem principi suo ex acie
recessisse; illum defendere tueri, sua quoque fortia facta gloriae eius adsignare praecipuum
sacramentum est: principes pro victoria pugnant, comites pro principe."

[49] Ibid., p. 32. Clawsey refers to D. H. Green, *The Carolingian Lord: Semantic Studies on
Four Old High German Words: Balder, Frô, Truhtin, Hêrro* (Cambridge: Cambridge University
Press, 1965), pp. 115, 156.

[50] A concise study of this factor and its role in Christianization efforts is found in Clinton
Albertson's introduction to his *Anglo-Saxon Saints and Heroes* (New York: Fordham University
Press, 1967). Also significant are Henry Munro Chadwick, *The Heroic Age* (Cambridge: Cambridge
University Press, 1912); and Jan de Vries, *Heroic Song and Heroic Legend*, trans. B. J. Timmer
(1963; reprint, Salem, N.H.: Ayer, 1988).

[51] George Fenwick Jones, *Honor in German Literature*, Studies in the Germanic
Languages and Literatures, no. 25 (Chapel Hill: University of North Carolina Press, 1959), p. 4.
Jones, who was Clawsey's doctoral mentor, discusses this semantic problem in greater detail in
pp. 5–7.

true meaning of the word *êre*," which is defined there as "splendor, glory, the higher standing, partly that which arises from power and wealth (high position, superior feudal rank), partly that which arises from courage and bravery."[52] The notion of honor in the Germanic Early Middle Ages was focused upon the external approval which one usually merited by courageous acts performed on behalf of one's kin or one's lord. The predominantly external focus of OHG honor, which stemmed from a desire to avoid being publicly shamed, may be contrasted with the predominantly internal focus of the Christian notion of honor as a moral quality stemming primarily from a desire to avoid the feelings of guilt and the fear of punishment associated with sinfulness.

Since the early Germans could not rely upon the protection and assistance of a bureaucratic empire when they were threatened with attack or famine, it was incumbent upon each man and woman of the community to adhere to the fundamental sociobiological principle of group survival embodied in the bonds of familial and communal solidarity. One's status in society depended upon how closely one adhered to this fundamental principle. Those who behaved honorably, thereby contributing toward the advancement of their community, were materially rewarded and thus increased their wealth, power, and influence. It is likely that the coalescence of honor, wealth, influence, and power within Germanic society inhibited the spread of status inconsistency and its potentially anomic effects, and served to further reinforce Germanic group solidarity.

To better illustrate the disparity between Germanic and Christian values, it may be helpful to read Jones's Germanic parody of the Beatitudes from the Sermon on the Mount in Matthew 5:3–12:

> Blessed are the rich, for they possess the earth and its glory.
> Blessed are the strong, for they can conquer kingdoms.
> Blessed are they with strong kinsmen, for they shall find help.
> Blessed are the warlike, for they shall win wealth and renown.
> Blessed are they who keep their faith, for they shall be honored.
> Blessed are they who are open handed, for they shall have friends and fame.
> Blessed are they who wreak vengeance, for they shall be offended no more, and they shall have honor and glory all the days of their life and eternal fame in ages to come.[53]

---

[52] Adolf Ziemann, ed., *Mittelhochdeutsches Wörterbuch* (Leipzig, 1838), p. 78, cited ibid.

[53] Jones, *Honor in German Literature,* pp. 40–41. The appropriateness of using the Sermon on the Mount to establish a comparison of Germanic and Christian values is reinforced by Hans Dieter Betz, "Cosmogony and Ethics in the Sermon on the Mount," in Robin W. Lovin and Frank E. Reynolds, eds., *Cosmogony and Ethical Order: New Studies in Comparative Ethics* (Chicago: University of Chicago Press, 1985), who claims: "The author or authors of the Sermon were very close in time and religious and cultural environment to the historical Jesus. If they determined that this teaching was the essence of Jesus' teaching, they had a greater chance with it than with any other text in the New Testament of being right" (p. 158).

Excerpts from an early Norse-Germanic source which succinctly expresses the Germanic attitude toward posthumous rewards, and which may be contrasted with the world-rejecting Christian aspirations of individual salvation and eternal bliss, are found in strophes 69 and 76 of the "Havamal" ("Sayings of the High One"), which are rendered from the Old Norse in Lee M. Hollander's translation of the *Poetic Edda:*

> All undone is no one though at death's door he lie:
>   some with good sons are blessed,
> and some with kinsmen, or with coffers full,
>   and some with deeds well-done.
>
> Cattle die and kinsmen die,
>   thyself eke soon wilt die;
> but fair fame will fade never,
>   I ween, for him who wins it.[54]

Given the disparity between Germanic and Christian values, Jones concludes that there was not much to which the missionaries could appeal."[55] Instead of directly confronting this opposing value system and attempting to radically transform it—an approach which almost certainly would have resulted in an immediate rejection of Christianity—the missionaries apparently sought to redefine the Germanic virtues of strength, courage, and loyalty in such a manner that would reduce their incompatibility with Christian values, while at the same time "inculturating" Christian values as far as possible to accommodate the Germanic ethos and world-view.

However, it was inevitable that some degree of conflict would arise from such a strategy. The notion of Christian honor, with its goal of individual salvation, directly opposed the supremacy of the Germanic concept of the *vridu,* the bond of kinship which could be extended to others through an oath of loyalty, as in the *comitatus.* This bond included the duty to avenge a kinsman or lord's death, as well as the obligation to follow one's lord into a battle, even if death was imminent. To survive one's lord in battle was cause for disgrace, exceeded in shamefulness only by acts of cowardice and outright betrayal. In fact, the intensity of the *comitatus* bond seems to exceed even that of kinship. The force of the societal pressure behind the *vridu* of the *comitatus* was so strong that, in those instances where a conflict between one's personal salvation and loyalty to one's lord arose, the latter tended to prevail. Based upon her survey of medieval epic literature, Clawsey concludes that "in the epics, men generally choose, however sorrowfully or reluctantly, to fight for their lords against those who personally mean more to them—their friends, their own flesh and blood, even their own salvation."[56]

---

[54] *The Poetic Edda,* pp. 17, 25.

[55] Jones, *Honor in German Literature,* p. 41.

[56] Clawsey, "The *Comitatus,*" p. 146. On p. 144 she also cites George Fenwick Jones, *The*

An example of the persisting primacy of the pre-Christian Germanic institution of the blood feud over concern for individual salvation is dramatized in *Njal's Saga,* when Njal and his sons are surrounded in their home by Flossi, who is seeking to avenge the murder of his son-in-law by Njal's sons. Aware of the superior warrior skills of Njal's sons over his own men, Flossi concludes: "There are only two courses open to us, neither of them good: we must either abandon the attack, which would cost us our own lives, or we must set fire to the house and burn them to death, which is a grave responsibility before God, since we are Christian men ourselves. But that is what we must do."[57]

Jones and Clawsey are not alone in documenting the vitality of the Germanic ethos and world-view well beyond the eighth-century Christianization efforts of Boniface and other missionaries. One may recall the popular admonition in the Sermon on the Mount "not to resist the evildoer; on the contrary, if someone strike thee on the right cheek, turn to him the other also,"[58] and contrast it with the Germanic duty of vengeance within the *comitatus* and kin group. This notion of vengeance received literary endorsement long after Boniface's death, albeit in a somewhat compromised form. In his review of recent research, "Moral Values in the Icelandic Sagas," Claiborne W. Thompson cites "the thirteenth century Norwegian

---

Ethos of the Song of Roland (Baltimore: Johns Hopkins Press, 1969): "When vassals had to choose between feudal loyalty and excommunication, they usually placed their worldly honor above their immortal soul" (p. 179). For a further analysis of the tension between the obligations a vassal owed to his biological kinfolk and to his lord, see George Fenwick Jones, "Rüdeger's Dilemma," *Studies in Philology* 57 (1960): 7–21. Also of interest is John Lindow, *Comitatus, Individual and Honor: Studies in North Germanic Institutional Vocabulary,* University of California Publications in Linguistics, vol. 83 (Berkeley: University of California Press, 1975).

[57] *Njal's Saga,* trans. and intro. Magnus Magnusson and Hermann Palsson (Harmondsworth: Penguin Books, 1960), p. 265. Despite the earlier historical and mythological references contained in the Icelandic sagas, which had previously led students of the sagas to ascribe their origins to an ancient oral tradition, Claiborne W. Thompson, "Moral Values in the Icelandic Sagas: Recent Re-evaluations," in Harald Scholler, ed., *The Epic in Medieval Society* (Tübingen: Max Niemeyer Verlag, 1977), reminds the reader that a current consensus holds the sagas to be "products of thirteenth century literary consciousness" (p. 349). Furthermore, Thompson notes that "the effect of this re-thinking on a study of moral values is to remind us that what we encounter in an Icelandic Saga is more likely to be a reflection of thirteenth century concerns than of pagan Germanic culture, for in the thirteenth century Iceland was a part of the Christian community of Western Europe and shared in the learning of the time" (ibid.). Therefore the persistence of Germanic values in the sagas may be interpreted as a more reliable indicator of the persistence of these values throughout Western Europe in the thirteenth century. This opinion should not in any way affect the credibility of the earlier *Poetic Edda,* parts of which may date back to A.D. 700, and which is generally viewed as being representative of a more thoroughly pagan era of Germanic religiosity. The dating of the *Poetic Edda* is discussed in greater detail in Lee M. Hollander's general introduction to his translation, pp. xxvii–xxix. See also, "The Bloodfeud of the Franks," in J. M. Wallace-Hadrill, *The Long-Haired Kings,* Medieval Academy Reprints for Teaching, no. 11 (1962; reprint, Toronto: University of Toronto Press, 1982).

[58] Matthew 5:39.

didactic treatise called the *King's Mirror,*"[59] in which Lars Lönnroth "finds not only an attitude sympathetic to worldly honor, but also a reserved approval of the revenge principle," as expressed in the following excerpt: "Keep your temper calm though not to the point of suffering abuse or bringing upon yourself the reproach of cowardice. Though necessity may force you into strife, be not in a hurry to take revenge; first make sure that your effort will succeed and strike where it ought."[60]

Although Lönnroth is not comparing Germanic and Christian values from the perspective of the transformation of religious attitudes, as does the current inquiry, his observations of the status of thirteenth-century Icelandic and, mutatis mutandis, Germanic Christianity may be interpreted as a testimony to the Germanization of Christianity which accompanied the attempted Christianization of the Germanic peoples. Thompson summarizes Lönnroth's position:

> Arguing against the prevalent notion that the Christian and pagan moral codes stood in stark contrast to one another, Lönnroth sees much overlapping. Whereas previous scholars tend to associate the virtues of humility, forgiveness, compassion, and obedience to the Church with the Christian "system," and worldly honor, the duty of revenge, and loyalty to the family with the pagan "system," Lönnroth believes that given a certain leniency on the part of thirteenth century Icelanders, most of the heroic pagan ideals would be found acceptable to a Christian audience. There are, to be sure, certain aspects of paganism, such as heathen sacrifice and worship, the exposure of children, the practice of sorcery and witchcraft, which are completely unacceptable in Christian eyes (and condemned in the sagas), but otherwise most of the so-called heathen values can be found to be supported in Christian documents of the thirteenth century.[61]

[59] "Moral Values in the Icelandic Sagas," p. 350.

[60] Ibid. The translation of the *King's Mirror* cited by Lönnroth and Thompson is by L. M. Larsen (New York: American-Scandinavian Society, 1917), p. 6, while the original Norwegian version may be found in L. Holm-Olsen, *Konungs skuggsja* (Oslo: Norske historiske kildeskriftfond, 1945), p. 85. Of related interest is John Simpson, "Comparative Structural Analysis of Three Ethical Questions in *Beowulf,* the *Nibelungenlied* and the *Chanson de Roland.*"

[61] "Moral Values in the Icelandic Sagas," pp. 349–50. A transformational development from a more strictly Germanic ethic to a moderation of the heroic pagan ideal in some of the Icelandic sagas has also given rise to an explanation by T. M. Andersson, "The Displacement of the Heroic Ideal in the Family Sagas," *Speculum* 45 (1970): 575–93 which, according to Thompson, tends to "minimize the debt to Christianity, viewing the emphasis on moderation as evidence of a new social consciousness analogous to the Greek notion of sophrosyne" (p. 351). He cites Andersson, p. 592: "What we probably have in the sagas is not so much the replacement of a pagan ideal with a Christian ideal as the replacement of a warrior ideal with a social ideal." In his conclusion, Thompson, advocates a paradigm of social pragmatism which seems to favor Andersson's approach: "I think, too, that there is an aspect of the pragmatic also lying behind the sagas' criticism of violence and the feud mentality. As was the case with the Icelanders' conversion from paganism to Christianity, the institution of blood revenge was examined in its pragmatic implications as well as its moral ones. Just as Thorgeir goði found it politically unwise for Iceland to risk civil war by attempting to resist the new faith, so some saga characters realize

That pre-Christian Germanic values, particularly those relating to the Germanic code of honor, retained acceptance in Western European Christian circles in the thirteenth century seems to indicate that, as Christianity expanded to include the Germanic peoples, some of its core values, such as its world-rejecting notion of honor, its pacifism, and its focus on individual posthumous salvation, were substantially transformed in a process of Germanization. With the additional impetus of an "Ottonian Captivity of the Church," these Germanized ethics, along with Germanic liturgical and spiritual developments, eventually became normative throughout European Christendom.[62]

Medieval hagiography provides further evidence of the ongoing influence of the Germanic ethos and value system. In discussing the *Vita Sancti Geraldi,* written by Cluny's second abbot, St. Odo (d. 944), Barbara H. Rosenwein notes that while generally adhering to the "well-worn genre of Saints' Lives," Odo "saw some things differently from his predecessors."[63] Since he lived at a time during which hagiographers were attempting "to formulate a new model combining piety with coercive power,"[64] Odo sought to sublimate the Germanic warrior ethos into the service of the Church:

> The potentate was to assist with temporal force when the church's spiritual sanctions proved ineffective. There was no question that violence was involved. . . . In the *Vita Geraldi,* the ideal was realized. Gerald was explicitly set forth as a model for the *potentiores.* . . . Gerald was rich (*dives*) and powerful (*potens*) and a warrior (*pugnator*). Gerald wanted to be a monk, and indeed he became one, but he hid his tonsure under his cap and continued to function as a *potens. This was a radical redefinition of the virtuous life.* According to Odo, it was the best way to perform the work of God.[65]

In apparent anticipation of those who might question any degree of acceptance of the Germanic warrior ethos, even in a sublimated form, Odo states: "Truly, no one ought to be worried because a just man sometimes makes use of fighting, which seems incompatible with religion."[66]

---

that a social system based on inflexible honor and vengeance is out-of-date, self-defeating, and foolish" (p. 359). See also, Richard North, *Pagan Words and Christian Meanings, Costerus,* n.s., vol. 81 (Amsterdam: Rodopi, 1991).

[62] Josef A. Jungmann, "The Sacraments and the Mass," in *The Church in the Age of Feudalism,* vol. 3, in Hubert Jedin and John Dolan, eds., *History of the Church,* trans. Anselm Biggs (New York: Crossroad, 1987), notes that "a double stream of powerful intellectual and institutional influence moved from the north toward Italy and the centre of Christianity in the tenth and eleventh centuries. The one was constituted by the Italian expedition of the German emperors from Otto the Great; in their retinue many clerics came south. The other proceeded from Cluny" (p. 307).

[63] Barbara H. Rosenwein, "Looking Out: The Cluniac Perception of the World," in *Rhinoceros Bound: Cluny in the Tenth Century* (Philadelphia: University of Pennsylvania Press, 1982), pp. 57–58.

[64] Ibid., p. 71.

[65] Ibid., pp. 73–75 (emphasis added).

[66] Ibid., p. 76. The quote from the *Vita Geraldi,* 1.8, may be located in *PL* 133: col. 647:

In his study "Greek Influence on the Eleventh-Century Western Revival of Hermitism," John McDonald Howe also discusses the emergence of a sublimated warrior ethos in the hagiographies of the tenth and eleventh centuries:

> Christianity in northern Europe replaced cults that had emphasized the religious functions of war and had stressed heroic morality. How much they affected northern hagiographical ideals has been debated. It does seem safe, however, to postulate the influence of non-Classical non-Christian heroic traditions on particular hagiographic works such as the first Anglo-Saxon *life* of Guthlac, where a Latin original based on Classical models suddenly is put into an even more heroic mode when it is recast in the vernacular. In the later Middle Ages, hagiography and secular romance literature merge frequently.
>
> Hagiographers writing between 970 and 1070 had an abundance of heroic models available. Whatever attitudes Christians may have had towards actual physical violence, they found the images of the Christian moral struggle in the heroic life. Stock phrases describe combat with the world, the flesh, and the devil. Military terms designate the saintly hero. Thus even though military imagery may serve to evoke specific images such as the victory of the good angels over the demons, or Christ's resistance to temptation, its non-Christian and pre-Christian prototypes show that the heroic image had its own coherence, independent of the Christian glosses that were put on it.[67]

The impact of the Germanic warrior ethos on the *Lives* of early medieval hermits was not, however, relegated to the realm of metaphor. In a regional comparison of hermits' *Lives,* Howe concludes: "Hermits who are literal soldiers are a northern theme. Northern 'servant of God' phrases too show a *'vir Dei'* who is more often an *'athleta,'* a *'miles,'* a member of the heavenly *'militia'* than are his Mediterranean counterparts. Overall these combatants are in somewhat different fields—the Mediterranean hermits fight more interior battles against their flesh, against demons who attack their perceptions, and they are 'slaves of God' in undertaking these combats; while the northern hermits, on the other hand, fight more concrete external opponents, are more literal soldiers, and are hailed as 'men of God.' "[68]

One reason for the formidable impact of pre-Christian Germanic values on medieval religious culture was the substantial Germanic contribution to the development of the feudal system, through which the essence of the *comitatus* relationship seems to have been preserved. According to Mircea Eliade:

"Nemo sane moveatur, quod homo justus usum praeliandi, qui incongruus religioni videtur, aliquando habuerit."

[67] "The Christian Spiritual Warrior," section in the chapter "The Hermit as Warrior," in "Greek Influence on the Eleventh-Century Western Revival of Hermitism" (Ph.D. diss., University of California, Los Angeles, 1979), p. 68.

[68] Ibid., p. 104.

After the conversion of the Germanic tribes to Christianity, this institution [the *comitatus*] was preserved. It is found at the base of feudalism and chivalry. . . . The institution briefly described by Tacitus had, to be sure, a religious dimension: the promotion of the young man announced the completion of his military initiation; absolute loyalty to the chief constituted, in fact, a religious mode of being. Conversion to Christianity gave rise to many reinterpretations and revalorizations of such ancestral traditions. But it never succeeded in effacing the pagan heritage.[69]

The *comitatus* relationship is not the only social example of Germanic group solidarity. The entire Germanic kinship structure is such that group solidarity is reinforced at every level of the family and community. This is quite the opposite of the situation that existed in the urban centers of the Roman Empire when Christianity was taking root and expanding. One explanation of the conditions which contributed toward a decline in family solidarity in the Roman Empire at this stage may be derived from Michael Hechter's observation of "the massive changes in family structure that have occurred in the course of industrialization,"[70] changes which, allowing for the obvious differences between the Roman and modern eras, are also likely to have occurred in third- and fourth-century Rome, commensurate with increased urbanization, bureaucratization, and taxation:

[69] "The Assimilation and Reinterpretation of Pre-Christian Traditions: Sacred Kingship and Chivalry," sect. 267 of *A History of Religious Ideas,* vol. 3, *From Muhammed to the Age of Reforms,* trans. Alf Hiltebeitel and Diane Apostolos-Cappadona (Chicago: University of Chicago Press, 1985), pp. 91–92. Eliade also notes in sect. 266 that "the feudal system and its ideology are of Germanic origin" (p. 87), while Albertson, *Anglo-Saxon Saints and Heroes,* comments that "it was no little achievement of later medieval society to have Christianized this Germanic warrior-ethos into chivalry" (p. 17 n. 42). Taking a mediating position between those who reject any continuity between the *comitatus* and feudalism, and those who, like Eliade, argue for a direct influence, D. H. Green, *The Carolingian Lord,* posits that "if it is possible to show, as I believe the linguistic evidence permits, that Frankish feudalism shares a number of peculiar characteristics with the *comitatus* which it cannot have derived from the Gallo-Roman *clientela* or from any other institution about which we have historical evidence, then this surely argues in favor of the Germanic institution having survived actively at least long enough to pass on some of its most characteristic features to the form of society which replaced it in medieval Europe" (p. 63). Further discussions of Germanic influence are contained in Carl Stephenson, *Medieval Feudalism* (Ithaca, N. Y.: Cornell University Press, 1942); and Marc Bloch, *Feudal Society,* trans. L. A. Mayon, with a foreword by M. M. Postan (Chicago: University of Chicago Press, 1961). For valuable archaeological and literary insights, see A. Margaret Arent, "The Heroic Pattern: Old German Helmets, *Beowulf* and *Grettis saga,*" in Edgar C. Polomé, ed., *Old Norse Literature and Mythology: A Symposium* (Austin: University of Texas Press, 1969), pp. 130–99.

[70] *Principles of Group Solidarity* (Berkeley: University of California Press, 1987), p. 57. The decline in family solidarity has been cited above (p. 88), while the composition and structure of the Roman household is discussed in Marleen B. Flory, "Family and 'Familia': A Study of Social Relations in Slavery" (Ph.D. diss., Yale University, 1975), pp. 17–55; B. M. Rawson, "Family Life Among the Lower Classes at Rome in the First Two Centuries of the Empire," *Classical Philology* 61 (1966): 71–83; idem, ed., *The Family in Ancient Rome: New Perspectives* (Ithaca, N.Y.: Cornell University Press, 1986); Keith R. Bradley, *Discovering the Roman Family: Studies in Roman Social History* (New York: Oxford University Press, 1991), and Suzanne Dixon, *The Roman Family* (Baltimore, Md.: Johns Hopkins University Press, 1991).

One way to read the history of the family in western societies is as the story of the erosion of family members' dependence on the head of the household. The preindustrial family was the sole source not only of shelter, sustenance, and emotional support for most wives and children, but also of education, occupational training, employment and, most generally, welfare. Women and children were extremely dependent on the heads of households. . . . Since the members of such households worked at home, these families had a high control capacity. As a result, the solidarity of families was at a peak. Today, much has changed. In the first place, many of these functions have been taken over by the welfare state, making women and children much less dependent on men. In the second place, the separation of workplace and residence, coupled with high levels of female labor force participation, have sharply reduced the family's control capacity. In consequence, family solidarity has reached a nadir: high rates of divorce are one of these changes, runaway children another.[71]

Not only was Roman family solidarity in a state of decline during the expansion of Christianity in the third and fourth centuries, but national solidarity was also waning, as evidenced by the increasing need to employ Germanic mercenaries to protect a Roman populace which lacked the will to defend itself. Examining the military organization of the Western Empire from the reign of Diocletian (284–305) to the end of the empire in 476, J. B. Bury observes:

The army of this age had a large admixture of men of foreign birth, and for the historian this perhaps is its most important feature. In the early Empire the foreigner was excluded from military service; the legions were composed of Roman citizens, the *auxilia* of Roman subjects. Every able-bodied citizen and subject was liable to serve. Under the autocracy both these principles were reversed. The *auxilia* were largely recruited from the barbarians outside the Roman borders; new troops were formed, designated by foreign names; and the less civilised these soldiers were the more they were prized. . . . The fact that most of the soldiers whom we know to have held the highest posts of command in the last quarter of the fourth century were of German origin speaks for itself.[72]

The Germanization of the Roman army was further accelerated as a result of the allotment of imperial provincial territory to armed bands of Goths

[71] Hechter, *Principles of Group Solidarity*, pp. 57–58.

[72] *History of the Later Roman Empire*, vol. 1, p. 38. Bury later (p. 99) attributes a significant rise in German military influence to the attitude of Constantine. Citing Julius Caesar's *De bello Gallico*, 4.12, and Tacitus's *Histories*, 4.20, E. A. Thompson, *The Early Germans* (Oxford: Clarendon Press, 1965), notes that "from Caesar's day onwards German horsemen were frequently used in the Roman army. But their number was severely limited, for only a few Germans could afford to keep a horse" (p. 116). Further analysis of the Germanic role in the post-Diocletian Roman army may be found in A. H. M. Jones, *The Later Roman Empire, 284–602: A Social, Economic, and Administrative Survey*, 2 vols. (Oxford: Oxford University Press, 1964), pp. 199–200, 619–23; and Manfred Waas, *Germanen im römischen Dienst im 4. Jahrhundert nach Christus* (Bonn: Habelts Dissertationsdrucke, 1965).

and Burgundians.[73] Finally, Valentinian "expressly enacted that 'no Roman citizen should be compelled to serve,' except for the defence of his town in case of danger."[74] In the previously cited words of Robert M. Adams: "This indeed is the simplest definition of decadence; it is not failure, misfortune, or weakness, but deliberate neglect of the essentials of self-preservation—incapacity or unwillingness to face a clear and present danger."[75] It may be speculated that as a nation expands into a vast empire, incorporating diverse nationalities, the extent to which individual citizens identify with the state, and hence the extent to which they feel obligated to support the state, may tend to diminish, particularly if the general citizenry has not materially benefited from imperial exploits.

The decline in familial and national solidarity in the Roman Empire may be contrasted with the high sense of familial, communal, and tribal solidarity among the Germanic peoples. These kinship ties originated in fundamental interlocking sociobiological relationships, and were supplemented by the more elective *comitatus* relationship discussed earlier. When it is recalled that one of the greatest appeals of the Christian Church in a socially disintegrating Roman Empire was its role as an alternative community, it becomes apparent that in a closely knit social system with strong bonds of kinship and vassalage, the social appeal of the Christian Church may be substantially diminished.[76]

At this point it may be useful to recall Walter Ullmann's axiom that "the history of jurisprudence is the history of civilization," and his formulation of Henry Charles Lea's approach: "In order to see and explain and understand an institution or the actuality of living in an historical period or in a particular country, there is no better guide and no more reliable mirror than the law enacted and practised."[77] In her comprehensive studies of the law codes of the Burgundians, Lombards, Visigoths, Franks, and Anglo-Saxons, Katherine Fischer Drew has corroborated the existence of a high level of group solidarity among the Germanic peoples.[78] Her impressions are summarized in a recent article:

---

[73] A new interpretation of this development is presented in Walter Goffart, *Barbarians and Romans: A.D. 418–584: The Techniques of Accommodation* (Princeton, N.J.: Princeton University Press, 1980).

[74] Bury, *History of the Later Roman Empire*, vol. 1, p. 39.

[75] *Decadent Societies* (San Francisco: North Point Press, 1983), p. 36, cited above, p. 73 n. 98.

[76] The social appeal of early Christianity is discussed in greater detail in the preceding chapter.

[77] "Historical Introduction" to Henry Charles Lea, *The Inquisition of the Middle Ages*, abridged by Margaret Nicholson (New York: Macmillan, 1963), p.12, cited by Edward Peters, in an introduction to his edition of Henry Charles Lea, *The Duel and the Oath* (1866; reprint, Philadelphia: University of Pennsylvania Press, 1974), pp. 6, 9.

[78] A number of her articles have recently been collected and republished as Katherine Fischer Drew, *Law and Society in Early Medieval Europe: Studies in Early Medieval History* (London: Variorum Reprints, 1988). These include "Legal Materials as a Source for Early Medieval Social History," "The Germanic Family of the Leges Burgundionum," and "The Law

Although these codes vary greatly—from those reflecting strong Roman influence (the Burgundian, Lombard and Visigothic) to those reflecting little if any Roman influence (the Frankish and Anglo-Saxon)—all have certain features in common, and I would like to point out and emphasize one of them here.

This common feature is the development of a concept of collective security. This was closely related to two Germanic institutions: the family and kin group on the one hand and personal lordship on the other. . . .

. . . I think that the Germanic concept of the role of the family and kin group came to dominate in all parts of the early-medieval population, whether descended from Roman or German. . . . The underlying concept was the assurance that each individual knew at all times whom he could call upon to support him in getting offenders against his peace into the courts or in providing proof or in supporting his oath in the courts, and in some cases (certainly among the Franks and Anglo-Saxons) helping him pay compositions assessed against him. In return for this real or merely moral support, the kin group had an established place in the inheritance patterns of all the Germanic kingdoms. . . .

The Germanic inheritance laws provide some of our best evidence for the importance of the kin group. . . . Even among the Visigoths, whose laws specifically covered Romans as well as Visigoths and where the influence of Roman law was greater than among the other Germanic peoples, the Visigothic holder of family land could not alienate all of that land if he or she had direct descendants—it must pass to the heirs.

So membership in a family and kin group was one means of guaranteeing peace and security to the individual during the period when the state was weak. The other means was for a man to be under the legal protection of someone stronger than he who was not a member of his family or kin group.[79]

Whereas the *comitatus* institution, as discussed earlier, existed primarily among members of the military aristocracy, Drew believes that a more common "lord-man relationship existed throughout almost all levels of society."[80] The social bonds established through kinship and the lord-man relationship, later referred to as "vassalage," protected the individual not only

---

of the Family in the Germanic Barbarian Kingdoms: A Synthesis." Included ibid. is the first publication of "The Family in Frankish Law" and "The Family in Visigothic Law." Of related interest are *The Burgundian Code: Book of Constitutions or Law of Gundobad and Additional Enactments,* trans. idem, with a foreword by Edward Peters (Philadelphia: University of Pennsylvania Press, 1972); *The Lombard Laws,* trans. idem (Philadelphia: University of Pennsylvania Press, 1973); and *The Laws of the Salian Franks,* trans. and intro. idem (Philadelphia: University of Pennsylvania Press, 1991).

[79] Katherine Fischer Drew, "Another Look at the Origins of the Middle Ages: A Reassessment of the Role of the Germanic Kingdoms," *Speculum* 62:4 (1987): 804, 807–8. See also, "Family, Kin and Law," in Edward James, *The Origins of France: From Clovis to the Capetians, 500–1000,* New Studies in Medieval History (London: Macmillan Press, 1982), who observes that "the study of the way in which a society organises its structures of kinship and marriage, out of the immense variety of possibilities, is fundamental for an understanding of how the whole society works" (p. 73).

[80] Drew, "Another Look," p. 808.

from the threats of physical attack and exploitation, but the equally real threat of social alienation. As Marc Bloch comments, "in the eyes of tenth-century Anglo-Saxon law, the lordless man is an outlaw unless his relatives are prepared to assume responsibility for him."[81] These bonds of kinship and vassalage were supplemented by the bonds of tribe, nobility, and kingship.[82]

Together, these social bonds served to forge a strong sense of group solidarity within the Germanic peoples. When complemented by the rigorous tribal selection process which occurred during the *Völkerwanderungszeit* (A.D. 375–568), the result was "a social structure of unprecedented solidarity and firmness"[83] in the emerging Germanic kingdoms. Regarding the role of the nobility and king in achieving "internal solidarity," Josef Fleckenstein notes that "all the tribes had a similar nucleus of noblemen who flourished whether under a monarchy or dukedom and who constituted the decisive element in the tribe's success and survival, encouraging it to take root in the countryside so thoroughly that later, after they had become incapable of carrying out their former functions, the countryside proved to be the bond which ensured the tribe's cohesion."[84]

---

[81] Bloch, *Feudal Society*, p. 224. In this important section "Vassalage as a Substitute for the Kinship Tie," Bloch describes the emergence of vassalage as "a sort of substitute for, or complement to, the solidarity of the family, which had ceased to be fully effective" (ibid.). He attributes this decline in effectiveness to the persistence of matrilineal kinship bonds, along with the more common patrilineal bonds which had enjoyed exclusivity in Roman society. However, the occasional conflict between matrilineal and patrilineal bonds need not necessarily imply a decline in overall kinship-based solidarity, since such a "bilateral" or "cognatic" kinship structure also increases the number of kin who would be bound to defend the individual. Supporting the notion of a bilateral kinship structure, Alexander Callander Murray, *Germanic Kinship Structure: Studies in Law and Society in Antiquity and the Early Middle Ages* (Toronto: Pontifical Institute of Medieval Studies, 1983), suggests that social stability may actually have been enhanced by additional kinship bonds, since "most feud was undoubtedly local feud and the more kindreds remained in the same localities, the more complex and interlocking became the kinship network; consequently the more likely reconciliation became, as kinsmen and affines with divided loyalties would be less inclined to take sides. For some time now it has been recognized that the interlocking network of relationship was an important factor conducive to compensation and reconciliation. The same factor would also tend to limit the size of the vengeance group when violence broke out" (pp. 136–37). Murray cites J. M. Wallace-Hadrill, *Early Germanic Kingship in England and on the Continent* (Oxford: Clarendon Press, 1971), pp. 41–43, in support of this contention.

[82] Tribal bonds are discussed in ch. 1, "The Social Basis," while the bonds uniting a king, nobility and people are discussed in ch. 2, "Political Forces and Institutions," in Josef Fleckenstein, *Early Medieval Germany*, trans. Bernard S. Smith, Europe in the Middle Ages: Selected Studies, vol. 16 (Amsterdam: North-Holland, 1978).

[83] Ibid., p. 13. A challenge to traditional assumptions about the significance of the *Völkerwanderungen* is made in "The Barbarians in Late Antiquity and How They Were Accommodated in the West," in Goffart, *Barbarians and Romans;* and idem, "The Theme of 'The Barbarian Invasions' in Late Antique and Modern Historiography," in idem, *Rome's Fall and After* (London: Hambledon Press, 1989), pp. 111–32.

[84] *Early Medieval Germany*, pp. 13–14. A discussion of the development of kingship from an Indo-European perspective is presented in Roger Pearson, "Chieftainship as an Evolutionary

Thus far, the high group solidarity of Germanic society and the anomic social environment of early Christianity have been established and contrasted. Durkheim's association of religious development with social conditions, together with O'Dea's synthesis of Durkheim's concept of anomie with Weber's association of salvation religions with deprivation,[85] have been applied to the disparate social environments of early Christianity and early medieval Germanic society. It is believed that these disparate social environments contributed significantly to the development of disparate world-views, value systems, and religious attitudes. Consequently, it has been argued that the low level of anomie within Germanic society, at least prior to the ninth century, substantially diminished the social appeal of Christianity as an alternative community.[86]

It has further been proposed that the disparity in world-views was the primary obstacle to the Christianization of the Germanic peoples and that the primary missiological response to this obstacle was a methodology of initial accommodation to a pre-Christian Germanic world-view. This methodology presumed an ongoing program of catechetical instruction, which would facilitate the gradual acceptance of Christian beliefs, attitudes, values, and behavior, and ultimately a Christian world-view. However, the catechetical expectations were never fully realized, and thus, simultaneous with an attempted Christianization of the Germanic peoples, there occurred a substantial Germanization of Christianity and Christian religious culture. The resulting Germanic Christianity eventually became normative throughout most of medieval Europe.[87] Thus when Clawsey concludes that

---

Stage in the Transition from Tribal to Feudal Society," *Mankind Quarterly* 28:2 (1987): 139–50, who proposes that "with the concentration of authority in the hands of a central chief, the IE [Indo-European] chief represents a 'proto-feudal' situation. . . . The chiefdom is a stage or form of social evolution in the transition from gemeinschaft to gesellschaft, from folk to mass society. It marks an early stage in the decline of ascription in favor of achievement; it marks (at least in IE society) the widespread acceptance of 'clientship' as a significant and acceptable social relationship quite distinct from and eventually in replacement of kinship. . . . IE chiefdoms were proto-feudal, heroic societies that in successful cases blossomed into the full complexity of European feudalism" (p. 147). Also relevant is the discussion of Germanic kingship in Henry A. Myers and Herwig Wolfram, *Medieval Kingship* (Chicago: Nelson-Hall, 1982), pp. 2–6, as well as ch. 4, "Carolingian Kingship: Problems of *Regna* and the *Imperium.*"

[85] See above, pp. 20–21.

[86] "The quest for community is a way of circumventing the alienation engendered by anomie: it leads to subsocieties in which the anomie of the larger community is rendered less acute by the solidarity of the smaller," states Barbara H. Rosenwein in the concluding chapter, "Looking at Cluny in Context," of *Rhinoceros Bound: Cluny in the Tenth Century*, p. 106. Rosenwein views the Cluniac ideal as a stabilizing response to social disruption caused by contention between the expansion of Carolingian state institutions and "first, the warrior tradition, which tied success and leadership to conquest," and second, "the family tradition, which demanded the expansion of the patrimony" (p. 105).

[87] Although this conclusion is similar to that of Josef A. Jungmann, "The Defeat of Teutonic Arianism and the Revolution in Religious Culture in the Early Middle Ages," in *Pastoral*

the pre-Christian Germanic *comitatus* ethos "pervaded heroic literature for well over a thousand years after Tacitus first observed it,"[88] it is an indication that neither the Christianization efforts of Boniface, nor those of his immediate successors achieved the level of societal religious transformation which could be considered Christianization in accordance with the objectivist definition of Christianity adopted for this inquiry.[89]

Implicit in this discussion is the anthropological premise that the world-view of a society comprises that society's most fundamental assumptions about reality and as such directly influences that society's religious attitudes, customs, and beliefs. Such deeply held assumptions, some of which may be held implicitly, are unlikely to be rapidly transformed by an encounter with Christian missionaries. In his guide for contemporary missionaries, Paul G. Hiebert further discusses the dynamics of world-view transformation:

> Our world view *monitors culture change*. We are constantly confronted with new ideas, behavior, and products that come from within our society or from without. These may introduce assumptions that undermine our cognitive order. Our world view helps us to select those that fit our culture and reject those that do not. It also helps us reinterpret those we adopt so that they fit our overall cultural pattern. For example, villagers in South America began to boil their drinking water, not to kill germs, but (as they saw it) to drive out evil spirits. World views, therefore, tend to conserve old ways and provide stability in cultures over long periods of time. Conversely, they are resistant to change.
>
> But world views themselves do change, since none of them are fully integrated, and there are always internal contradictions. Moreover, when we adopt new ideas they may challenge our fundamental assumptions. Although we all live with cultural inconsistencies, when the internal contradictions become too great, we seek ways to reduce the tension. Normally, we change or let go of some of our assumptions. The result is a gradual world-view transformation of which we ourselves may not even be aware.
>
> Sometimes, however, our old world view no longer meets our basic needs. If another and more adequate one is presented to us, we may reject the old and adopt the new. For example, some Muslims and Hindus may decide that Christianity offers better answers to their questions than their old religions. *Such world view shifts are at the heart of what we call conversion.*[90]

The resistance to change of the Germanic world-view, even under external pressure, has been noted by Georges Duby. In assessing the progress of Christianization among the Germanic peoples, he concludes:

Liturgy (New York: Herder and Herder, 1962), it is here attributed to the persistence of the Germanic ethos and world-view, rather than to doctrinal dialectics.

[88] Clawsey, "The *Comitatus*," p. 204.

[89] See above, p. 35.

[90] *Anthropological Insights for Missionaries* (Grand Rapids, Mich.: Baker Book House, 1985), pp. 48–49 (emphasis added). This subject is treated in greater detail in "World Views," ch. 18 of Hiebert's *Cultural Anthropology,* 2nd ed. (Grand Rapids, Mich.: Baker Book House, 1983).

> Very striking, for example, is the slow progress made by Christianity . . . in the tribes which the great migrations of the early middle ages brought into close contact with less rudimentary civilizations. Archaeology has revealed that Christian symbols were only very gradually insinuated into the graves of Germanic burial grounds, and that pagan beliefs for long persisted under the superficial guise of rites, tales and formulae imposed by force on the rest of the tribe by the converted chiefs. Eleventh century prelates were still eager to extirpate them, and they had not wholly disappeared, at the very end of the middle ages, even in those provinces of Christianity most securely appropriated by the church.[91]

As suggested in chapter 3, the world-view of early Christianity was organically related to the world-rejecting world-view of the Judeo-Hellenistic environment in which it initially expanded. Notwithstanding this primary influence on the formation of early Christianity, some elements of the earlier Indo-European Greek tradition of Hellenic rationalism were incorporated into an emerging Christian philosophy via patristic writings such as the *Stromata* of Clement of Alexandria.[92] Additionally, the legal and organizational structure of the Church was substantially derived from Roman models, to the extent that the distinction between *Romanitas* and *Christianitas* may have eventually become blurred to some who stood outside the empire.[93] Both Greek and Roman influences contributed toward some degree of an Indo-Europeanization of Christianity, not by actively seeking to do so, but as the passive result of the rapid expansion of Christianity to include people in whom the traditional world-accepting Indo-European world-view remained alive and meaningful.

This prior Indo-Europeanization of Christianity may have eased its acceptance within a Germanic society which retained the traditional Indo-European world-view long after it was supplanted in the classical world. The vitality of the Indo-European Germanic world-view in its encounter with Christianity, is attested to by the accommodation of the Germanic ethos in medieval hagiographic literature and liturgical developments, as well as by the religiopolitical and magicoreligious reinterpretation of Christianity which will be discussed in the following chapters.

---

[91] *The Chivalrous Society,* trans. Cynthia Postan (Berkeley: University of California Press, 1977), p. 216.

[92] English translations of the *Stromata* and other works of Clement of Alexandria may be found in Alexander Roberts and James Donaldson, eds., *The Ante-Nicene Fathers,* vol. 2 (1925; reprint, Grand Rapids, Mich.: Eerdmans, 1983). See also the discussion of Indo-European influence on early Christianity above on pp. 59–62.

[93] Walter Ullmann, *The Growth of Papal Government in the Middle Ages: A Study in the Ideological Relation of Clerical to Lay Power,* 3rd ed. (London: Methuen, 1970), has concluded that, by 754, "the Romans, in a word, are synonymous with Latin Christians. This is indeed the fruit of St. Boniface's work and in a wider sense of Gregory I: it is the ideological conflation of *Romanitas* and *Christianitas*" (p. 61).

6

Germanization and Christianization: 376–678

The purpose of this chapter is not to provide a comprehensive historico-religious survey of the Germanic peoples from their initial entrance into the Roman Empire in 376 until the Anglo-Saxon mission inaugurated by Bishop Wilfrid of York's visit to Frisia in 678. It is rather to examine those developments during this period that seem to most clearly reveal the operation of the processes of Germanization and Christianization. This examination will be conducted in light of the sociohistorical and socio-psychological observations of the preceding chapters. The developments which will be examined include the expansion of Germanic Arianism, the affiliation of the Merovingians with the Catholic Church, the development of the *Eigenkirche* and *Eigenkloster* institutions and the *Adelsheilige* hagiographies, the unification of socio-politico-religious attributes in Germanic kingship, the influence of the Irish mission, and the metaphysical conflict between Germanic and Christian concepts of time.

This religiohistorical period may be approached through its division into two prominent themes: Germanic Arianism and Frankish Catholicism. The first major contact between Christianity and a Germanic society[1] occurred in A.D. 376 when the Visigoths, who had occupied the former Roman province of Dacia (modern Romania) in the previous century, crossed the Danube into the Imperial Roman province of Moesia, seeking refuge from the onslaught of the Huns.[2] It is likely that the leadership of

[1] Employing a philological as well as historical approach, Knut Schäferdieck, "Zur Frage früher christlicher Einwirkungen auf den westgermanischen Raum," *ZKG* 98:2 (1987): 149–66, has sought evidence for earlier contact.

[2] The migrations of the Germanic peoples in the *Völkerwanderungszeit* are discussed in Lucien Musset, *The Germanic Invasions: The Making of Europe, A.D. 400–600,* trans. Edward and Columba James (University Park: Pennsylvania State University Press, 1975); and J. B. Bury, *The Invasion of Europe by the Barbarians* (1928; reprint, New York: W. W. Norton, 1967). "The Barbarians in Late Antiquity and How They Were Accommodated in the West," in Walter Goffart, *Barbarians and Romans A.D. 418–584: The Techniques of Accommodation* (Princeton, N.J.: Princeton University Press, 1980), provides an overview of recent scholarship and reevaluates the role of the *Völkerwanderungen* in Germanic-Roman relations, while idem,

the Tervingi, one of the larger Gothic confederations, negotiated with Valens, the Arian Christian emperor of the Eastern Empire, to adopt his religion in return for asylum.

In this initial encounter of the Germanic peoples with Christianity may be found elements which were to pervade their relationship for at least the next four centuries. Chief among these elements was the importance of political considerations. The mass mode of Christianization in which political leaders vouched for their subjects is established at this time.[3] Also important here is the association of Christianity with Roman culture and Roman polity, the absence of adequate religious instruction before and after baptism,[4] and the emergence of a Germanic folk-religious reinterpretation of Christianity. Additionally, "the total absence of Visigothic documents"[5] which might provide a Germanic perspective on their attempted Christianization is a problem that persists through the mission of St. Boniface. Finally, the inadequacy of the term "conversion," except when employed qualifiedly, as Heather does below, also becomes evident at this time. In considering these issues it may be useful to recall the historiographical advice of J. B. Bury: "There are two ways in which the subject may be treated, two points of view from which the sequence of changes which broke up the Roman Empire may be regarded. We may look at the process, in the earliest and most important stage, from the point of view of the Empire which was being dismembered or from that of the barbarians who were dismembering it. . . . We must, however, try to see things from both points of view."[6]

The personality most frequently associated with the Visigothic encounter with Christianity is the Arian Gothic bishop Ulfila. Although he is sometimes referred to as the "Apostle to the Goths," it should be recalled that the actual purpose of his consecration in 341 was not the initiation of a Gothic mission, but rather "to serve as bishop of those Christians who were already living in Gothia in 341 and who were, we may suppose, not Visigoths at all but Roman prisoners or their descendants."[7] While pursuing this task, Ulfila apparently attracted a number of native Visigothic

---

"The Theme of '*The* Barbarian Invasions' in Late Antique and Modern Historiography," in idem, *Rome's Fall and After* (London: Hambledon Press, 1989), pp. 111–32, reevaluates their overall significance.

[3] Peter Heather, "The Crossing of the Danube and the Gothic Conversion," *Greek, Roman and Byzantine Studies* 27:3 (1986), concludes that "the link between conversion and the legal crossing of the Danube made by the Tervingi carries with it the implication that religion was a political issue to Roman and Goth" (p. 316).

[4] See *New Catholic Encyclopedia*, s.v. "Catechumenate," by J. A. Jungmann.

[5] E. A. Thompson, *The Visigoths in the Time of Ulfila* (Oxford: Clarendon Press, 1966), p. 109.

[6] *Invasion*, p. 3.

[7] E. A. Thompson, "Christianity and the Northern Barbarians," in Arnaldo Momigliano, ed., *The Conflict Between Paganism and Christianity in the Fourth Century* (Oxford: Clarendon Press, 1963), p. 63. The basic reference for this period remains Thompson, *The Visigoths in the Time of Ulfila*.

converts. In 348 an anti-Christian persecution arose, causing Ulfila and his followers to flee to an area near Nicopolis in the Roman province of Moesia, where Constantius II, the Arian eastern Roman emperor, granted them territory. While there, Ulfila and a circle of associates devised a Gothic alphabet into which they translated the Bible. It is likely that they also contributed toward the development of a Gothic liturgy and liturgical calendar. A subsequent persecution of Visigothic Christians, conducted by Athanaric from 369 to 372, probably added to the number of Gothic Christian refugees in the area of Nicopolis. Athanaric appears to have been motivated by a desire to preserve the ancestral religion of the Goths, as well as to check any religiocultural inroads made by the traditional Roman enemy.[8]

Debate continues over the time and circumstances of the "mass conversion" of the Visigoths. In a recent article Peter Heather provides a concise background of the dispute and qualifies the concept of conversion as it is usually applied to the Visigoths.

> The date of the conversion has great historical importance, for it establishes the circumstances of the mass penetration of the Danube frontier by the Goths in 376. . . . On one level a single date for the conversion of a people does not make sense. *Conversion is a process, not an event, and takes time to come to fruition.* . . . A single date can have meaning, however, where it marks an intention, often on the part of the leadership of a group, to advance the process of conversion consistently. *Such a date refers not to a group adherence body and soul to a new set of beliefs, but marks rather a determination to change public practice.*[9]

This is considered the "traditional view" by Eugen Ewig.[10] However, claiming that fourth-century authorities do not refer to "a spectacular conversion in 376 or at any other time,"[11] E. A. Thompson has postulated that "the bulk of the Visigoths . . . became a Christian people in the years 382–395," after Ulfila's death in about 383.[12] His explanation appears to be based upon notions of social adaptation and assimilation:

> The conversion took place when the Visigoths were living in close association with the Roman inhabitants of Moesia. Since the optimates were now becoming landowners, their social interests were approximating more and more closely to the interests of the Roman landowners around them. The tribal religion had decayed with the decay of the tribes themselves; and

---

[8] Athanaric's motivation is discussed further in Thompson, *Visigoths,* pp. 98–102, where Thompson also suggests that the Visigothic council or "megistanes" used the Christians as a scapegoat for their own military failures.

[9] "Crossing," pp. 292–93 (emphases added).

[10] "The First Contacts of Christianity with the Germans and the Conversion of the Goths," in Hubert Jedin and John Dolan, eds., *History of the Church,* vol. 2, trans. Anselm Biggs (New York: Crossroad, 1980), p. 227.

[11] *Visigoths,* p. 90.

[12] Ibid., p. 106.

hence, living as they were in a Roman environment, the Visigothic leaders were accepting the outlook of the Roman propertied classes whose social position they hoped to reproduce in their own society.[13]

Even if 376 is accepted as the year of a negotiated acceptance of Arian Christianity, Thompson's dates of 382–395 may yet be valid as the time when proselytization actually got under way. Although Ulfila is not considered by Thompson to have personally effected the conversion of the Goths, he "must have left behind him an active and able school of clerics" who, utilizing Ulfila's Gothic translation of the Bible, "must have gone among the optimates [tribal chiefs] in Moesia in 382–395 so as to explain the tenets of Arian Christianity and to instruct them in the faith."[14]

The Arian form of Christianity, which was to some extent accepted by many Visigoths residing within the Roman province of Moesia, was subsequently transmitted to other Germanic peoples.[15] Departing from Moesia in 395, the vast majority of the Visigoths embarked on a westward expedition under the kingship of Alaric and Athaulf through the Balkan and Peloponnesian provinces to northern Italy, Rome, Gaul, and Spain, where Athaulf's brother Wallia founded the Toulousian Visigothic kingdom in

[13] Ibid., p. 107. Elsewhere Thompson speculates further on the relationship between the decay of the tribe and the decay of the tribal religion: "I would suggest as an hypothesis that the decay of the tribal religion and the spread of Roman influence were both alike merely symptoms of the collapse of tribalism. If tribal life had still been in a healthy condition, its religion would not be disintegrating and spiritual influences from the Roman Empire would not have been making much headway in Gothia. Tribal religion was an integral part of the tribal system itself: neither could exist in its old form without the other. But now the accumulation of privately owned wealth and the concentration of political power into comparatively few hands were putting an end to the significance of the tribes and hence to the religion of the tribes. That, we may think, is why paganism declined and Christianity triumphed in the last quarter of the century rather than sooner or later" (p. 101). While it is likely that the internal disruption of a social system may predispose it to the acceptance of new religious forms, as was likely the case in the later Roman Empire, it remains unclear whether a comparable degree of internal social disruption was experienced by the Visigoths.

[14] Ibid., p. 118. Unfortunately, more specific information on the strategy of these first missionaries to the Germanic peoples does not appear to be available. Nor does there appear to exist documentation on the pagan response to their proselytizing.

[15] The process by which the majority of the Germanic peoples became affiliated with a form of Arian Christianity remains an enigma. The most comprehensive treatment of this topic, and of the attempted Christianization of the various Germanic peoples in general, is found in Kurt Dietrich Schmidt, *Die Bekehrung der Germanen zum Christentum,* 2 vols. (Göttingen: Vandenhoeck & Ruprecht, 1939–42). Most relevant to the expansion of Germanic Arianism is vol. 1, *Die Bekehrung der Ostgermanen zum Christentum (Der ostgermanische Arianismus)*, particularly ch. 22, "Die Gotenmission unter den 'deutschen' Stämmen," and ch. 23, "Die Bedeutung des germanischen Arianismus." More recent discussions of the topic include Knut Schäferdiek, "Die geschichtliche Stellung des sogenannten germanischen Arianismus," in idem ed., *Die Kirche des früheren Mittelalters,* first half of vol. 2 of *Kirchengeschichte als Missionsgeschichte* (Munich: Chr. Kaiser Verlag, 1978), pp. 79–90; idem, "Gab es eine gotisch arianisch-christliche Mission im südwestdeutschen Raum?" *Zeitschrift für bayerische Landesgeschichte* 45 (1982): 239–57; and idem, "Zur Frage früher christlicher Einwirkungen auf den westgermanischen Raum."

419. However, the first group of Ulfila's disciples who accompanied him to Nicopolis following the initial anti-Christian persecution of 348, together with their descendants, apparently refused to accompany their kinfolk in their westward expedition. It is this Gothic remnant mentioned briefly by Jordanes and sometimes referred to as the *"Kleingoten,"*[16] that is thought to have been responsible for missionary efforts among the Ostrogoths while the latter were living in the Roman province of Pannonia (Hungary) in 456–472, after the disintegration of the Hunnic empire, or at an earlier date.[17] These Gothic missionaries are also believed to have been responsible for missionary efforts among the Gepids toward the end of the fifth century, when the Gepids migrated southward from Transylvania to Dacia.[18] The Suevi and the Vandals, who had migrated to Spain together by 409, were probably proselytized by Arian Visigothic missionaries who arrived several years later with Athaulf and his followers. A political alliance of the Burgundians with the Visigoths against the Huns in 451 may have contributed to sympathy among the Burgundians for Arianism, and an alliance of the Visigoths with the Suevi in 464 may have functioned similarly.[19] By the middle of the sixth century, the Rugi, Heruli, Alans, Bavarians, Thuringians, and Lombards are also believed to have accepted Arianism to some degree, whereas the Franks, Alamanni, Frisians, and Saxons seem to have remained unaffected.

More relevant to the current inquiry than the expansion of Germanic Arianism is the elusive question of the nature of its appeal among the Germanic peoples. Thompson has sought to explain the distribution of Arianism among the various Germanic peoples by hypothesizing generally that "the act of crossing the imperial frontiers and settling down as landlords or the like on Roman soil necessarily and inevitably entailed the abandonment of paganism and conversion to the Roman religion," since "neither phenomenon is found except in company with the other."[20] His conclusion that "the religious history of the Germans in the Roman period

[16] Jordanes, *Getica* 51.267, cited by Thompson, *Visigoths,* p. 103. The historiography of this period is discussed in Walter Goffart, "Jordanes and His Three Histories," in *The Narrators of Barbarian History (A.D. 550–800): Jordanes, Gregory of Tours, Bede, and Paul the Deacon* (Princeton, N.J.: Princeton University Press, 1988).

[17] Thompson, "Christianity," p. 73. Thompson believes that while the Ostrogoths were living under the domination of the Huns (375–455), Christianization efforts among them would have proven unfruitful because of Hunnic opposition. However, Thomas Burns, *A History of the Ostrogoths* (Bloomington: Indiana University Press, 1984), believes that "there is no doubt that the Ostrogothic leaders were Arian Christians before they crossed into Pannonia in 455" (p. 150), and suggests that some of the Ostrogothic nobility may have come into contact with the Kleingoten c. 420–427. Ewig, "First Contacts," concurs with Burns that "the Ostrogoths probably accepted Ulfila's Christianity even before their migration to Pannonia in 455" (pp. 29–30).

[18] Thompson, "Christianity," p. 75.

[19] Ewig, "First Contacts," p. 230.

[20] "Christianity," p. 78.

cannot be divorced from their political history" is undeniable,[21] whereas his assertion that "the move into a new economic and social world was necessarily followed by a move into a new spiritual world,"[22] while likely, requires further socioreligious validation.

The question naturally arises: Why did the leaders of most of the Germanic peoples accept the Arian form of Christianity, just as this heresy was in the process of being extirpated throughout the Roman empire? Observing the lack of documentation relating to the question, Thompson notes that some have postulated the existence of an inherent conceptual correlation between Germanic social structure and the hierarchical structure of the Arian divinity, according to which the Son is subordinate to the Father.[23] Thompson himself favors an explanation based upon the sociopolitical notion of group identity:

> By accepting Catholicism they [the Visigothic leaders] could scarcely have failed before very long to have been absorbed into the organization of the Universal Church, which in Theodosius' reign they would not all have cared to do, nor, if they had, would their followers have been likely to acquiesce in their action. As Catholics they would unquestionably have lost something of their freedom of organization. Their priests would have been liable to take their instructions from an authority outside the people, who at this date would scarcely have submitted to any form of government which was directed by Romans. Now, Arianism was not a centralized or inter-provincial organization; it remained a number of essentially separate, local, and independent churches and hence was more suited organizationally to

[21] Ibid. Heather, who disagrees with Thompson regarding the time of Visigothic "conversion," states in "The Crossing": "It would seem that the Tervingi were afraid that Christianity would undermine that aspect of Gothic identity which was derived from a common inherited religion, and that Christianity was associated with an empire whose influence they attempted to resist. That religion was a political issue to Gothic leaders is confirmed by the way in which persecution followed important events in Gothic-Roman relations" (p. 316). While assertions of political motivation may sometimes appear to express a form of political reductionism or a diminishment of religious influence, it should be recalled that pre-Christian Germanic religion, like most folk religions, was essentially bound up with the political life of the community. Contemporary notions of the "separation of church and state" were unknown and would have seemed preposterous to a folk-religious mentality.

[22] Thompson, "Christianity," p. 78.

[23] Thompson, *Visigoths,* p. 109. Thompson cites Jacques Zeiller, *Les Origines chrétiennes dans les provinces danubiennes* (Paris: E. de Boccard, 1918), p. 517; C. A. A. Scott, *Ulfilas, Apostle of the Goths* (Cambridge: Cambridge University Press, 1885), p. 78; and Helmut Lother, *Die Christusauffassung der Germanen* (Gütersloh: Verlag C. Bertelsmann, 1937), pp. 17ff. Also sharing this opinion is Schmidt, *Die Bekehrung der Germanen zum Christentum,* vol. 1, p. 275; and Heinz-Eberhard Giesecke, *Die Ostgermanen und der Arianismus* (Leipzig: Teubner, 1939), pp. 57–61. Rejecting it are Ewig, "First Contacts," p. 228, who attributes the association of Arianism with the Germanic peoples to coincidental factors; Schäferdiek, "Die geschichtliche Stellung des sogenannten germanischen Arianismus," p. 88; and Walter Baetke, *Die Aufnahme des Christentums durch die Germanen: Ein Beitrag zur Frage der Germanisierung des Christentums,* special ed. (Darmstadt: Wissenschaftliche Buchgesellschaft, 1962), pp. 14–19.

a people who wished to preserve their social identity inside the Roman Empire.[24]

Heather makes a similar observation regarding the concerns of the Tervingi Visigoths, claiming that "they were afraid that Christianity would undermine that aspect of Gothic identity which was derived from a common inherited religion, and that Christianity was associated with an empire whose influence they attempted to resist."[25] Herwig Wolfram also believes that the function of "a 'Gothic' faith as a means of preserving ethnic identity" might have been "responsible for the conversion of the overwhelming majority of the Goths who had penetrated the empire, even though, or precisely because, their Roman environment became more and more radically Catholic."[26]

As a result of economic exploitation by Roman merchants, the relationship between the Visigoths and their Roman hosts became embittered.[27] The hostility between the Visigothic immigrants and the Romans erupted in the battle of Adrianople (378), in which the Visigoths under Fritigern were victorious, and in which the Roman emperor Valens, an Arian, was killed. After the renewed condemnation of Arianism at the Council of Constantinople (381), summoned by Valens' Catholic successor Theodosius the Great, the popularity of Arianism generally declined throughout the empire.[28] This disassociation of Arianism from the empire may have served to make it more acceptable to the Visigoths and other Germanic peoples, for eventually Arianism became nearly the exclusive religious domain of the non-Frankish Germanic kingdoms.

The significance of religion as an important factor in forming the identity of groups as well as individuals has been recognized by anthropologists.

---

[24] Thompson, *Visigoths,* p. 110. Zeev Rubin disagrees with Thompson's dating scheme, but agrees with his view toward the "decay of the tribal religion," and the sociological implications of conversion to Arian Christianity. In "The Conversion of the Visigoths to Christianity," *Museum Helveticum* 38 (1981), Rubin concludes: "The Visigothic enclave within the Empire found itself separated from its environment by a barrier of religious creed. In the long run this barrier helped it to retain its special identity and its internal cohesion, whereas both adherence to paganism and conversion to Catholicism would have ended in complete assimilation. This lesson was very soon learned by the leaders of other barbarian nations who sought settlement in Roman territories" (p. 54).

[25] Heather, "Crossing," p. 316. He surmises that "these fears on the part of the Gothic leadership had some basis in reality, for the Empire had a manifest interest in the spread of Christianity. . . . It may be that the idea was already current that Christianity could help to pacify dangerous peoples. . . . Religion seems therefore to have been a political issue to both Empire and Goths in the fourth century" (pp. 316–317).

[26] *History of the Goths,* Thomas J. Dunlap, trans., rev. from 2nd German ed. (Berkeley: University of California Press, 1988), p. 85.

[27] E. A. Thompson, *Romans and Barbarians: The Decline of the Western Empire* (Madison: University of Wisconsin Press, 1982), p. 39.

[28] The conciliar canons condemning Arianism were amplified by subsequent Theodosian legislation.

In a recent study of the interaction of Christianity with indigenous cultures, George R. Saunders provides a modern example remarkably similar in structure to the subject at hand:

> In local-level religious politics, schisms often develop around differing interpretations of issues in the "core reference system," the group's conceptualization of the definitive and essential features of Christianity. For example, two Jamaican Pentecostal sects are distinguished primarily by the fact that one baptizes in the name of Jesus alone, while the other baptizes in the name of the entire Trinity. The difference may appear trivial to outsiders, but is extremely important to members of the two sects. The distinctions provide each group with important criteria for differentiating themselves, and encourage group solidarity and identity. The differences are symbolic, and the symbols selected for the definition of group boundaries may to some degree be arbitrary, as long as they serve to distinguish the two groups.[29]

Focusing on the Ostrogoths rather than the Visigoths, Thomas Burns's evaluation of Arianism reflects the centrality of sociopolitical concerns of group identity and solidarity :

> Theology, specifically the Arian denial of the Trinity, mattered little to most Goths. . . . Theodoric and the nobility essentially viewed religion as a part of politics. . . .
>
> The Ostrogoths as a people clung to Arianism for political and social, not theological, reasons. Theodoric championed Arianism in the Eastern Empire as an extension of his role in Italy, where he set about to control the process of assimilation. He envisioned distinct spheres for the Ostrogoth and the Roman, despite the fact that government and settlement increasingly threw them together. One viable center of Ostrogothic society was their Arian faith, which set them apart from the Orthodox majority. . . .
>
> Arianism was their national religion, and as such it was an institutional force acting in concert with the monarchy to preserve a special and distinctive place for the Ostrogoths in Italy. . . . Once the political and social reasons for group solidarity and exclusivity had lessened, there would undoubtedly have been little resistance to conversion. . . .
>
> Arianism was understandably slow to penetrate the elemental world of pagan cult practice, long so much a part of agrarian life. . . . Ostrogothic Arianism allowed them to be Christians and hence part of the larger world

---

[29] "Transformations of Christianity," in George R. Saunders, ed., *Culture and Christianity: The Dialectics of Transformation,* Contributions to the Study of Anthropology, no. 2 (Westport, Conn.: Greenwood Press, 1988), p. 186. Hans Mol, *Identity and the Sacred* (New York: Free Press, 1976), suggests that a similar utilization of religious distinction to reinforce group identity was functional in the *filioque* question: "Organizational exclusion reinforced group identity, but often some latent reasons for schisms were hidden behind manifest doctrinal controversies. A good example was the ideological disputes about the addition of *filioque* (the Holy Spirit also proceeding 'from the Son') to the Creed, which was the ostensible source of schism between the Eastern and Roman Church. Many scholars are convinced that the cultural differences between Hellenic East and Roman West was the more authentic reason" (p. 74). As representative of this opinion, Mol cites Richard H. Niebuhr, *The Social Sources of Denominationalism* (New York: Meridian Press, 1957), p. 114.

of *Christianitas* and *Romanitas* without asking them to forsake either Gothic pride or their ancestors. That is why it is necessary to understand their Arianism as a tribal religion and not as some lingering form of an Alexandrian heresy.[30]

Some indication of the moderate degree of the process of Christianization that was inspired by Germanic Arianism may be gleaned from the contents of Martin of Braga's catechetical guide, *De correctione rusticorum* (c. 574), which reveals ecclesiastical concerns regarding a considerable pagan survival and recidivism among the indigenous rural population of the Suevic Germanic kingdom.[31] In the terms of universal and folk religions discussed earlier, one may consider Germanic Arianism to constitute a thoroughly indigenous reinterpretation of a universal religion, a "Germanization of Arian Christianity."[32] The general opposition to Romanization that propelled Germanic Arianism, was also expressed in political, cultural, and educational affairs, and may have contributed toward the emergence of the proprietary church, or *Eigenkirche*.[33] Pierre Riché attributes a general

[30] *A History of the Ostrogoths*, pp. 158–61. Burns also suggests that the initial conversions of some of the Ostrogothic elite to Arian Christianity while they lived under Hunnic domination may have been "a statement of political independence" directed toward the pagan Huns (p. 150). His view that Ostrogothic Arianism permitted the maintenance of Gothic tradition is amplified by Hermann Josef Vogt, "Theological Discussions," in Jedin and Dolan, eds., *History of the Church*, vol. 2, who concludes that "Catholic Christianity developed an individual denominational moral sense among the newly converted German peoples, whereas Arian Christianity continued to be determined by the principles of the German *comitatus*" (p. 714). However, Kurt Aland, "Christianity Among the Germans at the Time of the Migrations," in *A History of Christianity*, vol. 1, trans. James L. Schaaf (Philadelphia: Fortress Press, 1985) generally attributes Germanic affiliation with both Arian and Roman Christianity to genuine religious commitment.

[31] C. W. Barlow, ed., *Martini episcopi Bracarensis Opera Omnia*, Papers and Monographs of the American Academy in Rome, no. 12 (New Haven, Conn.: Yale University Press, 1950), pp. 183–203; English translation in J. N. Hillgarth, ed., *Christianity and Paganism, 350–750: The Conversion of Western Europe*, (rev. ed. of *The Conversion of Western Europe, 350–750*) (Philadelphia: University of Pennsylvania Press, 1986), pp. 57–64. Judith Herrin, *The Formation of Christendom* (Princeton, N.J.: Princeton University Press, 1987), notes that "subsequent records suggest that Christianity was not deeply rooted" in the Suevic kingdom (p. 222).

[32] Piergiuseppe Scardigli, "La conversione dei Goti al Cristianesimo," *Settimane* 14 (1967): 47–86, has argued for the existence of a conscious intention on the part of Ulfila to develop an indigenous Germanic scripture and liturgy to advance Gothic cultural independence from Rome, while P. D. King, *Law and Society in the Visigothic Kingdom* (Cambridge: Cambridge University Press, 1972), views Arianism as contributing to a "national character of credal cleavage" (p. 4).

[33] Ewig, "First Contacts," p. 229. In his inaugural lecture delivered in 1894, Ulrich Stutz, "The Proprietary Church as an Element of Medieval Germanic Ecclesiastical Law," in *Medieval Germany (911–1250): Essays by German Historians*, trans. Geoffrey Barraclough, Studies in Mediaeval History, vol. 11 (Oxford: Basil Blackwell, 1961), noted that "the private church was an institution common to all Germanic peoples," and that it "must have permeated and outlived the ecclesiastical régime of the Arian period" (p. 44). Additional discussion of this topic may be found in "Arianismus und Germanismus," in Ulrich Stutz, *Geschichte des kirchlichen Benefizialwesens* (Berlin: H. W. Müller, 1895); and Hans von Schubert, *Staat und Kirche in den arianischen Königreichen und im Reiche Chlodwigs* (Munich: R. Oldenbourg, 1912). William A. Chaney, *The*

"rejection of classical culture"[34] by the Arian Germanic peoples primarily to demographic factors:

> The Barbarian aristocracy possessed its own culture, a culture to which it remained faithful. The Barbarian people formed a minority in the West which, in order to preserve its strength, refused to integrate with the Roman population. The aristocracy worked to preserve its originality and to give its children an education that conformed to Germanic tradition.[35]

An insight into Germanic attitudes toward *Romanitas* may be provided by an examination, following Riché's exposition, of the attitude of the Ostrogothic king Theodoric, who was educated in Byzantium and ruled the Western Roman Empire from 493 until his death in 526.

As previously noted, it is likely that their status as an alien ruling minority within the borders of the empire contributed more to the isolationist attitude of the Goths, Burgundians, and Vandals than did their religious dissimilarity. Indeed, the contemporary consensus appears to be that their social status and the distinctiveness of their religion were mutually reinforcing. In appraising the nature of the relationship between the Arian Germanic aristocracy and Roman culture, Riché advises: "We must insist on the distinction between the protection which the princes were able to provide scholars and the princes' personal intellectual formation. Were they simply, in short, adopting the role of a Maecenas, or were they themselves men of letters? Had the Barbarian aristocracy been won over to classical culture?"[36] In Riché's view, the Ostrogothic king Theodoric was "a genuine Maecenas."[37] Despite a personal concern for the maintenance of classical culture which was encouraged by Cassiodorus, Theodoric "never permitted Goths to place their children in Roman schools" as a part of "the general policy of a Barbarian king who, as king of Italy, accepted Roman culture for himself and for his family but refused it to his people in order to preserve their identity."[38]

In summary, according to Riché: "Barbarian and Gothic aristocrats imitated the Roman way of life, but as we have seen, they were not won over to classical culture. Their own culture and the Arian religion they

---

Cult of Kingship in Anglo-Saxon England: The Transition from Paganism to Christianity (Berkeley: University of California Press, 1970), tracing the origins of the *Eigenkirche* into the pre-Christian era, claims that "the Germanic *Eigentempel* provides part of the politico-religious background—in parallel, if not origin—for the *Eigenkirche* of the Christian Middle Ages, with churches 'owned' by the secular nobility, and temporal power and control closely associated with ecclesiastical foundations" (pp. 73–74).

[34] Pierre Riché, *Education and Culture in the Barbarian West: From the Sixth Through the Eighth Century,* trans. John J. Contreni, with a foreword by Richard E. Sullivan (Columbia: University of South Carolina Press, 1976), p. 64.

[35] Ibid.

[36] Riché, *Education and Culture,* pp. 52–53.

[37] Ibid., p. 56.

[38] Ibid., pp. 63–64.

professed help to explain their indifference."[39] While it has been asserted that the Arianism of the Goths, Burgundians, and Vandals was primarily "a way of emphasizing their independence and sense of identity, and a safeguard against too rapid assimilation,"[40] it appears that it was not only successful in this regard, but that, somewhat ironically, it also may have contributed toward a degree of political weakness, since "their Arian faith . . . deprived them of the support of the Church."[41]

An Arian episcopacy existed among the Visigoths until the Third Council of Toledo in 589. This council was convoked by King Recared two years after his own conversion to Catholicism from Arianism.[42] Following a declaration of faith by Recared, "eight bishops recanted their Arian belief."[43] Riché has commented:

> The Arian heresy, however, was a live issue in Spain. The kings wanted to complement the political unity of the kingdom with religious unity and hoped that Catholic clerics would abjure. In 580, Leovigild called a conference at Toledo, where Catholic and Arian bishops opposed each other, but he was not able to impose the heresy on the entire realm. Central Spain seems to have been the bastion of Arianism. Unfortunately, even though we can discern the activities of Arian bishops and the culture of Visigothic laymen, we cannot pursue our research much farther, since all the texts concerning Arianism have been destroyed.[44]

Leovigild's desire to complement political unity with religious unity at this time may have been provoked by concerns of sympathy among the Catholic hierarchy and populace for the Byzantine Catholic invaders of southern Spain.

Hillgarth has noted that Recared's conversion in 587 occurred after a more successful attempt to impose Catholicism by Byzantium.[45] His conversion may therefore have been derived from a desire to reap the sociopolitical benefits of a single national religion, whether Arian or Catholic.[46] One may recall Procopius's report in his *Bellum Gothicum* that the Italian

---

[39] Ibid., pp. 218–19.

[40] Musset, *The Germanic Invasions,* p. 184.

[41] J. B. Bury, *History of the Later Roman Empire,* vol. 1 (1923; reprint, New York: Dover, 1958), p. 347.

[42] The conciliar texts have been published in *Concilios Visigóticos e Hispano-Romanos,* ed. José Vives (Barcelona: Instituto Enrique Florez, 1963), pp. 107–45.

[43] Herrin, *The Formation of Christendom,* pp. 228–29, referring to *Concilios,* ed. Vives, p. 123.

[44] Riché, *Education and Culture,* pp. 274–75.

[45] Hillgarth, *Christianity and Paganism,* has concluded that: "The Vandal and Ostrogothic kingdoms perished, at least in part, because of the religious division between the Arian barbarians and their Roman subjects. The Visigoths barely saved themselves from the same danger. It was after the Byzantines had occupied the Southeast of Spain (552) and exploited a Catholic pretender to the throne (580–84) that King Recared became a Catholic in 587. In 507 the Visigoths had already lost almost all Gaul to the Franks, led by Clovis, a convert from paganism to Catholicism" (p. 73).

[46] Musset, *The Germanic Invasions,* p. 43.

cities of Narnia, Spoletium, Perugia, and others, as well as the region of Rimini, voluntarily had allied themselves earlier with the Byzantine general Belisarius against the Arian Goths.[47] Furthermore, "in 538 the archbishop of Milan and some other notables of that city begged Belisarius to send them a small force with which they undertook to deliver Milan and the whole of Liguria into his hands."[48] While religious affiliation alone cannot have accounted for such actions,[49] it seems likely that, in fulfilling its function of preserving the cultural identity of its adherents, the Arianism of the Ostrogoths and Visigoths also served to decrease the level of allegiance felt toward them by their native Roman subjects.

Not all of the Germanic peoples became affiliated with Arian Christianity and not all rejected classical culture. Given their relative geographical isolation in northern Germania during the fifth-century expansion of Gothic Arianism, the Franks, Frisians, Saxons, and the majority of the Thuringians remained pagan. The most significant developments for the study of the attempted Christianization of the Germanic peoples occurred among the Franks, "a political amalgamation of many small tribes which took place in the first and second centuries A.D. in the lands between the Weser and the Rhine."[50] This Frankish confederation then migrated westward over the

[47] See "The Byzantine Conquest of Italy: Public Opinion," in Thompson, *Romans and Barbarians*, p. 103, referring to Procopius, *Bellum Gothicum*, 5.10.5 and 5.16.3.

[48] Ibid., referring to Procopius, *Bellum Gothicum*, 6.7.38.

[49] However Bury, *Invasion*, claims that "although the Ostrogoths did not persecute, their rule could never establish itself on a popular basis because they were Arians; and it was the difference in faith, keeping the Goths and the Italians apart, and the rallying of the Italians to the side of an orthodox conqueror, that conduced above all to the success of the imperialist armies which reconquered Italy under Justinian" (p. 215). Emphasizing instead the underlying cultural disparity which Ostrogothic Arianism exemplified, Thompson, *Romans and Barbarians*, claims that: "It is hardly a problem to see why educated Italians rejected Ostrogothic rule in spite of all the generosity of Theodoric and his successors. The war was fought between barbarians on the one side and civilized men on the other. The Italians chose civilization, and no one followed them more heartily than some sections of the Ostrogothic nobility" (pp. 108–9).

[50] Peter Lasko, *The Kingdom of the Franks: North-West Europe Before Charlemagne* (New York: McGraw-Hill, 1971), p. 14. According to Hermann Kinder and Werner Hilgemann, *Anchor Atlas of World History*, vol. 1, trans. Ernest A. Menze (Garden City, N.Y.: Doubleday, 1974), pp. 109, 111, and especially 120–21, the four major tribes at this time were known as the Usipetes, Tencteri, Sicambri, and Buctri. In the third century the main groupings became known as the Salians, Ripuarians, Moselle and Main Franks, and Chatti. The ethnogenesis of the Franks as well as other Germanic peoples is treated in detail in Bruno Krüger, ed., *Von den Anfängen bis zum 2. Jahrhundert unserer Zeitrechnung*, vol. 1 of *Die Germanen: Geschichte und Kultur der germanischen Stämme in Mitteleuropa* (Berlin: Akademie-Verlag, 1983). Sources for the religious history of the Franks include Kurt Dietrich Schmidt, "Die Franken," in *Die katholische Mission unter den Westgermanen*, vol. 2 of *Die Bekehrung der Germanen zum Christentum;* Albert Hauck, "Die fränkische Landeskirche," book 2 of vol. 1 of *Kirchengeschichte Deutschlands*, 4th ed. (1904; reprint, Berlin: Akademie Verlag, 1954); Hans von Schubert, "Die Anfänge eines neuen germanisch-römischen Katholizismus," and "Die Blütezeit der merowingischen Reichskirche bis Dagobert,"in *Geschichte der christlichen Kirche im Frühmittelalter* (Tübingen: J. C. B. Mohr (Paul Siebeck), 1921); Edouard Salin, *Les Croyances*, vol. 4 of *La Civilisation mérovingienne d'après les sépultures et le laboratoire* (Paris: Picard, 1959); J. M.

Rhine to become *foederati* in northern Brabant (Belgium) in 358. In the fifth century, led by the Salian Franks, they expanded further westward into Gaul, conquering the city of Tournai in 446. Their first recorded chieftain was Childeric (d. 482), whose tomb was discovered in 1653. It contained artifacts which reflect the "orientalizing tastes that can be traced in upper layers of Late Roman society," and indicate that Childeric "saw himself as a successor to the Roman rulers of Gaul, ready to absorb their cultural aspirations," according to Peter Lasko.[51] However, Lasko may be extrapolating a bit too far. The apparent appeal of the prestige of the Roman emperor to Childeric and later to his son, Clovis,[52] should be qualified, lest it be considered evidence of a more general desire for the assimilation of Roman culture. A more precise understanding of the attitude of the Arian Germanic peoples and of the Franks toward *Romanitas* is thus desirable,[53] especially since it has recently been asserted by John Moorhead that "conversion was a *rite de passage* for barbarians on the way to becoming civilized, which meant that for barbarians anxious to become and be seen as civilized it was a desirable thing."[54]

The concept of Romanization, like that of Christianization, requires specificity when applied to the Germanic peoples, their culture, and their

---

Wallace-Hadrill, *The Long-Haired Kings*, Medieval Academy Reprints for Teaching, no. 11 (1962; reprint, Toronto: University of Toronto Press, 1982); and idem, *The Frankish Church* (Oxford: Clarendon Press, 1983). Important sociopolitical background information is contained in André Joris, "On the Edge of Two Worlds in the Heart of the New Empire: The Romance Regions of Northern Gaul During the Merovingian Period," in *Studies in Medieval and Renaissance History*, vol. 3, ed. William Bowsky (Lincoln: University of Nebraska, 1966), pp. 3–52, while the interaction between Celtic, Greek, Roman, and Germanic influences in pre-Merovingian Gaul is discussed in Anthony King, *Roman Gaul and Germany*, Exploring the Roman World, no. 3 (Berkeley: University of California Press, 1990). See also, John Drinkwater and Hugh Elton, eds., *Fifth Century Gaul: A Crisis of Identity?* (Cambridge: Cambridge University Press, 1992).

[51] *Kingdom of the Franks*, p. 26.

[52] Gregory of Tours, *Libri historiarum*, MGH SRM, ed. Bruno Krusch and Wilhelm Levison, vol. 1, 2nd ed. (1937–51; reprint, Hanover: Hahn Verlag, 1961), 2.38, p. 89; translated in Gregory of Tours, *The History of the Franks*, trans. and intro. by Lewis Thorpe (Harmondsworth: Penguin Books, 1974), p. 154. The authenticity of Gregory's depiction of Clovis dressing and behaving like a Roman ruler following his victory over the Visigoths at Vouillé in 506, as well his reception of the title of consul from the Eastern Emperor Anastasius, is maintained by Riché, *Education and Culture*, p. 220 n. 271. Clovis's transferral of the Frankish court from Tournai to the traditional residence of Roman governors of Gaul in Paris may also be considered consistent with his desire to symbolically participate in Roman grandeur.

[53] While studies of Roman pagan and Christian attitudes toward the Germanic peoples exist, Riché's discussion of Germanic attitudes toward Roman civilization, interspersed throughout *Education and Culture in the Barbarian West*, appears to be unique. A thorough treatment of the former topic is contained in Gerhart B. Ladner, "On Roman Attitudes Toward Barbarians in Late Antiquity," *Viator* 7 (1976): 2–26.

[54] "Clovis' Motives for Becoming a Catholic Christian," *Journal of Religious History* 13:4 (1985): 339. Moorhead contends that "Clovis' conversion was not prompted by a politically motivated desire to look well in the eyes of the Gallo-Romans, but rather by a culturally motivated desire to be like the Gallo-Romans" (pp. 338–39).

religion. As in the case of Theodoric, a distinction between the self-identification of some Frankish leaders with Roman imperial traditions and the
actual assimilation of Roman culture by Frankish society should be made.
It may be helpful to circumscribe the concept of Romanization somewhat
by applying Riché's rigorous definition of Roman culture in the fifth century as primarily literary and, as such, requiring the existence of an appropriate educational system in which the essentials of grammar, rhetoric, and
dialectic could be transmitted.[55]

Employing such a precise description, Riché has noted that the Franks
initially had little interest in assimilating Roman culture.

> What we can gather from the texts and from archaeology does in fact
> seem to indicate that the western Germans were much more attached to
> their primitive way of life than the eastern Germans. Arriving much later
> on the borders of the Roman empire, still living as pagans, the Franks
> were much less interested in preserving antique civilization than were the
> Goths and the Burgundians. A comparison between Salic law and the laws
> of the Burgundians and Visigoths is quite instructive: Salic law reflects a
> society of warriors and herdsmen little interested in Roman culture. Only
> Frankish chiefs, leaders who had for a long time served the Empire faith-
> fully, could perhaps comprehend the value of Roman culture. Childeric, a
> federate and Clovis' father, had himself portrayed on the setting of his
> ring dressed as a Roman. Clovis followed his example.[56]

Recalling Riché's conclusion that the Visigothic, Ostrogothic, and Burgundian aristocracy held a generally isolationist attitude toward classical
culture,[57] it may appear confusing that Riché now implies that they were
more interested than the Franks in "preserving antique civilization." Also,
if the Visigoths and the Burgundians appear to have been more favorably
disposed toward Roman culture than the Franks, one may wonder why
they were not also more likely to accept the Roman Catholic religion. First
of all, one should bear in mind the distinction between the "preservation"
and the "adoption" of a foreign culture. Secondly, it should be recalled
that Riché is referring here to Frankish attitudes in the late fifth and early
sixth centuries. He subsequently comments that "Frankish aristocrats and
kings of the second half of the sixth century were more open to Roman
literature than the Goths, Burgundians, or even their Merovingian predecessors."[58]

[55] Riché, *Education and Culture*, pp. 4–7. By the last centuries of the empire, Roman
culture had become more exclusively literary. When, following the Germanic invasions, the political rationale for the retention of Roman culture subsided, "the lettered gave themselves up to
intellectual pastimes and forgot the misfortunes of the times. . . . [w]hile their studies have the
air of decadence, they bear witness to an astonishing fidelity to what had been the glory of Rome"
(p. 13). Riché later characterizes antiquity as "the civilization of the written word" (p. 21). A
more extensive discussion of the Roman educational system is Henri I. Marrou, *A History of
Education in Antiquity,* trans. George Lamb (New York: Sheed and Ward, 1956).

[56] Riché, *Education and Culture*, p. 211.

[57] See above, pp. 142–144.

[58] Riché, *Education and Culture*, pp. 225–26.

Although some degree of affinity for Roman grandeur undoubtedly existed among the Frankish elite, and although it may be heuristically appealing to attribute the Roman Catholic affiliation of the Franks, as Moorhead does, to a desire to embrace Roman culture, such a proposition is not substantially supported by extant sources. Rather, it appears that Frankish Roman Catholic affiliation may be more properly derived from the coincidence of a threatened Catholic Gallo-Roman episcopacy in the midst of Arian Germanic kingdoms,[59] and an adventuresome yet astute young king in search of the means to effectively consolidate his dominion. A study of the correspondence of St. Remigius, bishop of Reims, the evidence contained in the *Libri historiarum* of Gregory of Tours, and an analysis of the Arian threat to the Gallo-Roman episcopacy suggest that, from the time of his accession in 481 as king of the Franks of the Tournai region, Clovis was recruited for the role of a champion of Roman Catholicism.[60]

It seems reasonable to assume that, at the time of Clovis's accession in 481, Remigius and his fellow Gallo-Roman bishops were aware of the expansion of the Toulousian Visigothic kingdom of King Euric into Aquitaine up to the southwestern border of the Roman kingdom of Syagrius. The conditions of the Catholic episcopacy under Euric's rule are not reported to have been good. Despite his general tendency to exaggerate anti-Catholic actions taken by Arian Germanic leaders,[61] Gregory of Tours's

---

[59] Albert Hauck, "Die fränkische Landeskirche," book 2 of vol. 1 of *Kirchengeschichte Deutschlands,* states: "Vergegenwärtigt man sich den Zustand des Abendlandes in der Zeit, als Chlodowech zu regieren begann, so schien der Arianismus, nachdem er im römischen Reich der katholischen Kirche unterlegen war, noch einmal eine große Zukunft vor sich zu haben. Fast in allen abendlichen Provinzen herrschten arianische Fürsten: in Italien, dem größten Teile von Gallien, in Spanien und Afrika; die katholische Kirche war die Kirche der Unterworfenen" (p. 109).

[60] Summarizing the career of St. Remigius as presented in Hincmar of Reims, *Vita S. Remigii,* Samuel Dill, *Roman Society in Gaul in the Merovingian Age* (London: Macmillan, 1926), states: "We shall see a Catholic bishop, with no material force at his command, by strength of will and sense of a lofty mission, mastering the young impetuous chief of the pagan Franks, and, with the gentle aid of the pious Queen, along with the glamor of miracles, winning him from paganism to be the champion of the Church" (p. 32). The authenticity of the contents of Hincmar's biography is defended in part 2 of "Archbishop Hincmar and the Authorship of Lex Salica," in Wallace-Hadrill, *The Long-Haired Kings.* The disappearance of an earlier *Life of Remigius* which was a source for Gregory of Tours is most unfortunate, as it may have provided additional details regarding Remigius's relationship with Clovis.

[61] Goffart, *Narrators of Barbarian History,* comments on the religiopolitical circumstances at the time Gregory wrote his *History of the Franks* (573–594): "For more than a half-century, Arian kings had been cleared from all but a small part of Gaul and, for good measure, from Italy and Africa as well. Gregory had resided since birth in a land safe for Catholicism, in which even a memory of persecution at the hands of heretics would not easily have been come by, except in written form. . . . Arianism occasions what may be Gregory's most credulous statement: the Ostrogothic princess Amalansuntha, to avenge her slave-lover, murdered her mother by pouring poison into the communion chalice. . . . Gregory's forgetful audience was reminded that the Catholic Church of Gaul had been fiercely assailed by Arian attacks and had been saved by the pagan convert Clovis. Whatever other virtues the Merovingians lacked, they had gotten where they had by God's nurturing, to preserve His Church from enduring foes" (pp. 213–16).

depiction of Euric's reign suggests that the Gallo-Roman episcopacy felt threatened: "Euric, King of the Goths, crossed the Spanish frontier and began a terrible persecution of the Christians in Gaul. Without more ado he cut off the heads of all who would not subscribe to his heretical opinions, he imprisoned the priests, and the bishops he either drove into exile or had executed."[62] At the time of Clovis's accession in 481, Euric's dominion was "at the height of its territorial power, and it seemed in these years, from 480 onwards, far the greatest and most promising state of western Europe,"[63] and as such, "the Goths seemed almost certain to be the ultimate inheritors of all Gaul."[64] Also, a distinct possibility existed that the new Frankish king Clovis himself might convert to Arianism since "one of his sisters, Lenteildis, had received arian baptism, although she apparently lived among the Franks."[65]

The potential for Arian domination in Gaul and subsequent Gallo-Roman episcopal displacement thus arose from two sources: the possible affiliation of Clovis with Arianism, and the possible conquest of Gaul by the Arian Visigoths. Although Moorhead argues that the Gallo-Roman aristocracy was not particularly concerned about the religious affiliation of their ruler,[66] given the social proximity of the secular aristocracy and the episcopacy, it seems unlikely that either would remain aloof to this issue. Patrick J. Geary has succinctly presented the relationship between the Gallo-Roman episcopacy and aristocracy in a recent study of Merovingian society:

> The first church in Gaul had been the episcopal church, and its traditions stretched back into the most distant memory of the senatorial aristocracy.

[62] Gregory of Tours, *Libri historiarum,* 2.25, Thorpe, p. 138.

[63] Bury, *Invasion,* pp. 212–13.

[64] Ibid., p. 214.

[65] Ian N. Wood, "Gregory of Tours and Clovis," *RBPH* 63 (1985): 267, citing Avitus, *hom.* 31, in *MGH AA,* ed. Rudolph Peiper, vol. 6, part 2 (Berlin: Weidmannsche Buchhandlung, 1883). The Arianism of Lenteildis is also acknowledged by Gregory of Tours, *Libri historiarum,* 2.31, Thorpe, p. 145, according to whom she was "converted at the same time" as her brother. In his revisionist account, Wood contends that Clovis was originally converted to Arianism.

[66] Moorhead, "Clovis' Motives for Becoming a Catholic Christian," in seeking to attribute Clovis' baptism "to a genuine commitment to a new faith which he perceived as something culturally desirable" (p. 330), attempts to minimize the political concerns of the Gallo-Roman episcopacy and aristocracy by asserting that Gregory of Tours's account of Euric's persecution of Catholic priests and bishops "was based on a misreading of a passage of Sidonius Apollinaris, in which we are simply told that numerous bishops had been deprived of their sees, which remained vacant and suffered decay" (p. 331). Particularly when one considers the observation of Patrick J. Geary, *Before France and Germany: The Creation and Transformation of the Merovingian World* (New York: Oxford University Press, 1988), that "from the fourth century on, enormous amounts of land had been passing into the hands of the church, and all this was controlled by the bishop," and his comment that "the continued prosperity of the family demanded that it control bishopric wealth, and after generations of such donations it is little wonder that families came to view episcopal succession as a hereditary right worth killing to defend" (p. 126), attempts to trivialize the potential threat that an Arian ruler might pose to the Gallo-Roman episcopacy and aristocracy seem less reasonable.

In fact, its period of establishment, the late third century, corresponded to the period of the provincial aristocracy; thus both were born together and formed an inseparable institution.

The great majority of early Merovingian bishops were of aristocratic Gallo-Roman background. This was only to be expected given the role the episcopacy played in late Roman Gaul. . . .

. . . one can speak of "episcopal families" that controlled sees for generations. The most famous is that of the historian Gregory of Tours. . . .

Such complex family rivalries focused on the office of bishop because it was a prize worth fighting for. Control of major bishoprics was the key to the continued regional power of the kindred. It also provided great wealth.[67]

It is against such a background that Remigius of Reims, who was the metropolitan of the region which included Tournai, wrote encouragingly to the fifteen-year-old Clovis upon his accession in 481: "You should defer to your bishops and always have recourse to their advice. If you are on good terms with them your province will be better able to stand firm."[68] It appears that throughout his career Clovis generally abided by Remigius's counsel. Since the Gallo-Roman episcopacy was the last operative administrative remnant of Roman dominion in Gaul, one may assume that Clovis benefited from an amicable relationship with it, particularly following his conquest of the Gallic kingdom of Syagrius in 486.

Clovis's relationship with the Gallo-Roman episcopacy was not the first cooperative venture between Romans and Franks. Geary has demonstrated the existence of a long tradition of Frankish exposure to Roman material culture and Roman military tradition.[69] If the Franks were more predisposed to become affiliated with Roman Christianity than other Germanic peoples, it may be due in some degree to a more gradual and less antagonistic relationship with the Romans, unlike that of the Visigoths

[67] *Before France and Germany*, pp. 123–26. The social status and background of the Gallo-Roman episcopacy is studied in Martin Heinzelmann, "L'Aristocratie et les évêchés entre Loire et Rhin jusqu'à la fin du VIIe siècle," *Revue d'histoire de l'église de France* 62 (1975): 75–90. A more general study of the Gallo-Roman episcopacy may be found in idem, *Bischofsherrschaft in Gallien: Zur Kontinuität römischer Führungsschichten vom 4. bis zum 7. Jahrhundert. Soziale, prosopographische und bildungsgeschichtliche Aspekte*, Beihefte der Francia, vol. 5 (Munich: Artemis Verlag, 1976).

[68] *Ep. 3, Epistolae Austrasicae, MGH Epistolae*, ed. Wilhelm Gundlach, vol. 3 (Berlin: Weidmannsche Buchhandlung, 1892): "Et sacerdotibus tuis debebis deferre et ad eorum consilia semper recurre; quodsi tibi bene cum illis convenerit, provincia tua melius potest constare" (p. 113). Translation from Hillgarth, *Christianity and Paganism*, p. 76. Wallace-Hadrill, *The Long-Haired Kings*, comments: "The tone of the letter is patronizing: the pagan barbarian will wish to reflect on the advantage of having the Gallo-Roman Church on his side. It is not, in so many words, a warning against the Arianism of the neighbouring Visigoths and Burgundians, nor a direct appeal for conversion to Catholicism. It is rather a statement of fact: Belgica is Roman and is run by Roman bishops; and a prudent rex will wish to take note of this, since most of his subjects will be Romans. Clovis has crossed the frontier and is welcomed in, on terms" (p. 166).

[69] Geary, *Before France and Germany*, pp. 5–8, 20–23, 93.

and Ostrogoths who established their kingdoms quite suddenly within the borders of the empire. Instead of being a conquering minority without a native homeland, anxious to maintain cultural and political integrity in a society with an attractive, sophisticated culture, as were the Arian Goths, the Franks retained a native homeland region known as Toxandria on the northwestern bank of the Rhine, and gradually, and for the most part peacefully, expanded into areas in northern Gaul which Gallo-Roman landlords had abandoned. This abandonment appears to have been related to a decline in the degree of military protection which could be afforded to frontier regions of the empire while the city of Rome itself was threatened with invasion. In return for the territory on which they settled, the Franks provided military assistance to the Romans in the defense of Gaul. Such a symbiotic relationship must have had religious implications.

Here, as in the case of the Visigoths vis-à-vis the Romans, the concept of group identity may provide an insight into religious orientation and transformation. Whereas the Visigoths had been treated oppressively by the Eastern Romans prior to their initial encounter with Christianity, the overall relationship between Franks and Romans in the century preceding the baptism of Clovis in 496[70] was one of relative harmony. Contributing to this relationship was the military alignment of the Salian Franks with the Romans in several conflicts. These included joint opposition to the Hunnic invasion of Gaul in 451 and allegiance as *foederati* under Childeric in the battle of Orléans against the Visigoths in 464. Within this context, Clovis's victory at Soissons in 486 over Syagrius, the Roman ruler of much of northern Gaul, should not be viewed as a hostile exception, inasmuch as "Syagrius ruled independently of the Empire."[71] In fact, it may be argued that the Franks perceived their greatest potential military threat as coming from neighboring Germanic peoples, rather than from the Romans. Consequently, the relative harmony between the Franks and the Roman Empire, as compared with the intermittent hostilities between the Franks and neighboring Arian Germanic peoples,[72] may have contributed to the affiliation of Clovis and his retinue with Catholic Christianity.

Also contributing to this affiliation may have been Clovis's perception of the authority of the Catholic episcopate among the Gallo-Romans at a time when the imperial administrative system within Gaul was deteriorating. Essentially by secular default, Catholic bishops, most of whom were

---

[70] The date of Clovis's baptism has been contested for the past century, and has been placed by some as late as 506. Discussions are found in Hauck, "Ort und Zeit der Taufe Chlodowechs," appendix 1, *Kirchengeschichte Deutschlands,* pp. 595–99; Wilhelm Levison, *Aus rheinischer und fränkischer Frühzeit* (Düsseldorf: Verlag L Schwann, 1948), pp. 202–28; and more recently in Georges Tessier, "La Conversion de Clovis et la christianisation des Francs," in *Settimane* 14 (1967): 149–89; and Knut Schäferdiek, "Ein neues Bild der Geschichte Chlodwigs?" *ZKG* 84 (1973): 270–77.

[71] Wallace-Hadrill, *The Long-Haired Kings,* p. 160.

[72] These included the Thuringians, Alamanni, and Visigoths.

descended from aristocratic Gallo-Roman families, emerged as the pre-eminent local administrators. However, historians differ widely on the degree to which Clovis's baptism may be ascribed to political motivation. Emphasizing religiocultural factors, Moorhead has minimized both the opposition of the Gallo-Roman episcopacy toward Arian rulers and consequently their desire for a non-Arian champion,[73] whereas Bury had suggested that Clovis deliberately sought a Catholic wife so as to ingratiate himself with an anti-Arian episcopate which might provide future support.[74]

It may be surmised that the Gallo-Roman episcopacy was a pastoral and administrative network in search of a champion, while Clovis was, as already stated, an adventuresome yet astute young king in search of the means of effectively expanding his dominion. That the episcopacy was attuned to Clovis's political ambitions is indicated in a letter written to him on the occasion of his baptism by Bishop Avitus, the metropolitan of Vienne, who reassured Clovis that the military effectiveness of the Christian baptismal charism would exceed that associated with the charism or *Heil* of his royal lineage.[75] The far-reaching significance of Clovis's affiliation with Roman Catholicism has been noted by Hillgarth:

> The conversion of Clovis is a great turning point. It made possible the shift from a Mediterranean-centered Christianity to one whose capital was situated by 800 at Aachen and whose spiritual centers were in England, North France (as Gaul was becoming), and Germany. This shift greatly accentuated the cultural—as yet not formal ecclesiastical—break with the Byzantine East, still centered at Constantinople.[76]

However, the religious and metaphysical aspects of this major shift in the history of Christianity remain difficult to isolate. It is generally agreed that the circumstances surrounding Christianization efforts among the Germanic peoples in the fifth through seventh centuries could result only in a superficial or nominal Christianity in which elements of pre-Christian Germanic religiosity persisted. Although these pagan survivals indicate a

---

[73] "Clovis' Motives for Becoming a Catholic Christian."

[74] *Invasion,* p. 241. Bury elaborates: "If I am right in this conjecture the policy and conversion of Clovis appear in a new light. He still hesitated to become a Christian himself, but appreciating the power of the Church, he saw what an enormous help it would be to have a Catholic wife; he saw of what use she could be in negotiations with the ecclesiastics. . . . It [his marriage to a Catholic] was deliberately intended as a substitute for becoming a Christian himself, and it made clear what form of Christianity he would embrace, if he ever embraced any. But why did he hesitate? Here is the point where there comes in another influence, which has so often prevailed over statesmanship—the influence of superstition. Clovis had not the smallest doubt of the God of the Christians, but, believing in the existence of his own gods too, the question was, which was the most powerful?" (pp. 241–42).

[75] *Ep. 46, Alcimi Ecdicii Aviti, MGH AA,* ed. Rudolf Peiper, vol. 6, part 2 (Berlin: Weidmannsche Buchhandlung, 1883): "Faciet, sicut creditis, regum florentissime, faciet inquam indumentorum ista mollities, ut vobis deinceps plus valeat rigor armorum; et quicquid felicitas usque hic praestiterat, addet hic sanctitas" (pp. 75–76).

[76] "Christianity in a Non-Roman World," part 2 of Hillgarth, *Christianity and Paganism, 350–750: The Conversion of Western Europe,* p. 85.

resistance of the Germanic ethos and world-view to Christianity, they do not of themselves substantiate a thoroughgoing Germanization of Christianity.[77] A summary evaluation of the religious status of Clovis and the Merovingians has been provided by David Harry Miller:

> Baptism aside, Clovis was almost certainly not a Christian in any significant sense. That his act nonetheless committed the Merovingians to the church cannot be doubted. . . . The conversion of the Merovingians, however, did not entail the conversion of the Frankish people, whether Clovis' immediate retinue followed his example or not. Court schools appear to have promoted the spread of Christianity among the younger nobility. Decrees were issued condemning pagan practices among the people; similar conciliar decrees were given the status of public law; and an occasional temple was destroyed. Some missionary enterprises were given at least a modicum of royal support, primarily in the Rhineland where ecclesiastical leaders were anxious to regain once-Christian territories lost during the chaos of the fifth century. But the Merovingians did not really enforce their laws in respect of the matter of paganism, even at court, and the behavior of the dynasty, as opposed to its rhetoric, was plainly tolerant of continuing paganism. As a consequence, the Franks, as well as elements of the Gallo-Roman population, remained largely pagan.[78]

Hillgarth has observed that the Frankish support which the Church gained as a result of Clovis's baptism was accompanied by a relationship in which the Merovingian ruler "was liable to interfere in its internal affairs"[79] and, as exemplified by the precedent of Clovis's convocation of the Council of Orléans in 511, by a relationship in which the bishops became increasingly dependent upon the Merovingian ruler for the implementation of their objectives. This reliance was eventually to prove disastrous for the Christianization process as the initially Gallo-Roman episcopacy became increasingly

---

[77] Hans Kuhn, "Das Fortleben des germanischen Heidentums nach der Christianisierung," *Settimane* 14 (1967): 743–57, minimizes the extent of pre-Christian Germanic religious survival, conceding only a short-lived pagan-Christian syncretism, and rejecting the notion of a Germanization of Christianity. This view, which presumes the exclusion of ethical and popular religious elements from consideration, has been termed "minimalist" by Robert A. Markus, *The End of Ancient Christianity* (Cambridge: Cambridge University Press, 1990), since "the implicit assumption on which it is based minimises what is included in the scope of conversion: baptism, certainly, renunciation of overt idol-worship, and very little else" (pp. 9–10).

[78] "Sacral Kingship, Biblical Kingship, and the Elevation of Pepin the Short," in Thomas F. X. Noble and John J. Contreni, ed., *Religion, Culture, and Society in the Early Middle Ages: Studies in Honor of Richard E. Sullivan,* Studies in Medieval Culture, no. 23 (Kalamazoo, Mich.: Medieval Institute Publications [Western Michigan University], 1987), pp. 135–36. A discussion of Merovingian and Carolingian antipagan legislation may be found in Jean Imbert, "L'influence du christianisme sur la législation des peuples francs et germains," *Settimane* 14 (1967): 365–96, while a comprehensive survey of the Merovingian councils, with valuable religiopolitical analysis, has recently been published in Odette Pontal, *Histoire des conciles mérovingiens* (Paris: Cerf, 1989), where, in a section entitled "La Survivance du paganisme," pp. 292–95, it is asserted: "Les chrétiens qui abandonnent les rites païens trouvent un succédané dans le culte des saints et le culte des reliques. Les saints se substituent aux divinités de la mythologie" (p. 294).

[79] Hillgarth, *Christianity and Paganism,* p. 75.

populated with Merovingian political appointees, and as the Merovingian monarchy declined in strength and respectability.[80] From the death of Clovis in 511 until the arrival of the Irish missionary monk Columbanus in Gaul about 590, the progress of Christianization among the Germanic peoples, aside from the Merovingian court, was negligible.[81] As Georges Tessier has remarked, "La conversion de Clovis est une chose, la christianisation des Francs en est une autre."[82] Ewig has observed that "there was no compulsory conversion of pagans; only the sanctification of Sundays and holy days was imposed under penalty at the end of the sixth century—a sign of the cultic and ritual view of Christianity."[83] There were, however, two important religiopolitical developments which spread in this era: the *Eigenkirchensystem*, or "proprietary church system,"[84] and the *Eigenklostersystem*, or "proprietary monastery system."[85] Of these developments, Ewig has concluded: "Like the proprietary church system, the monastic system of the new kind could not but lead, in the chaos of the late Merovingian epoch, to a far-reaching dissolution of the ecclesiastical organization."[86]

With the exception of Dagobert I (d. 639), and, to a lesser extent, Guntram (d. 593), the Merovingian kings appear to have expressed little interest in sponsoring religious education and reform among those already baptized. Neither does the Merovingian aristocracy in general appear to

---

[80] Thomas Leslie Amos, "The Origin and Nature of the Carolingian Sermon," (Ph.D. diss., Michigan State University, 1983), pp. 58–59.

[81] Kurt Aland, "The Church in the Kingdom of the Franks after Clovis," section in *History of Christianity*, vol. 1, trans. James L. Schaaf (Philadelphia: Fortress Press, 1985), p. 237.

[82] "La Conversion de Clovis et la christianisation des Francs," *Settimane* 14 (1967): 169.

[83] Eugen Ewig, "The Conversion of the Franks and the Burgundians: Origin and Organization of the Merovingian National Church," in Jedin and Dolan, eds., *History of the Church*, vol. 2, p. 538.

[84] Ibid., p. 533. Ewig ponders: "Whether this process must be understood as a germanization of the ecclesiastical constitution is uncertain. It is certainly not to be evaluated only negatively, since the many proprietary churches, despite their defects, also promoted the christianization of the rural areas" (ibid.). Uta-Renate Blumenthal, *The Investiture Controversy: Church and Monarchy from the Ninth to the Twelfth Century* (Philadelphia: University of Pennsylvania Press, 1988), notes: "We now know that this form of ownership also existed in non-Germanic areas of the former Roman Empire and in similar guise among the Slavs and the Irish" (pp. 4–5). This does not weaken the association of the *Eigenkirchensystem* and the *Eigenklostersystem* with the Germanization of Christianity. Indeed, Friedrich Kempf, "Constitution of the Church: 700 to 1050," in Jedin, ed., *History of the Church*, vol. 3, states that in the West "the Germanic peoples were undoubtedly the propelling element" in the development of the *Eigenkirche* (p. 259). The Indo-European origins of the *Eigenkirche* are considered in Robert Höslinger, "Die 'alt-arische' Wurzel des Eigenkirchenrechts in ethnologischer Sicht," *Österreichisches Archiv für Kirchenrecht* 3 (1952): 267–73.

[85] The first major *Eigenkloster* may be attributed to St. Radegunde, wife of Clovis's son Chlotar I, who founded the Convent of the Holy Cross at Poitiers in 547. Her biography, which includes a description of her convent, has recently been translated in Jo Ann McNamara and John E. Halborg, with E. Gordon Whatley, *Sainted Women of the Dark Ages* (Durham, N.C.: Duke University Press, 1992).

[86] Eugen Ewig, "The Conversion of the Franks and the Burgundians: Origin and Organization of the Merovingian National Church," in Jedin and Dolan, eds., *History of the Church*, vol. 2, p. 535.

have been overly concerned with the religious beliefs of their subjects. The Merovingians did, however, perceive the potential for sociopolitical cohesion which could be achieved through Christianization efforts and thus sought to reestablish bishoprics in the north-east Rhineland area which had been won from the Alamanni by Clovis.[87] To a significant degree, the aristocracy appears to have viewed ecclesiastical offices, churches, and monastic foundations from a pre-Christian Germanic perspective, as sources of sacral charism and legitimation. Instead of attempting to impose doctrinal orthodoxy, they appear, in keeping with the religious culture of their milieu, to have been more concerned about "orthopraxy,"[88] that is, adherence to the cultic and ritual observances of Christianity.

In a chapter on "Castes, Estates, Classes and Religion," Max Weber briefly compares the development of early and medieval Christianity, and provides insights which may contribute to an understanding of the Merovingian aristocracy's attitude toward Christianity:

> Actually, early Christianity was an urban religion, and as Harnack decisively demonstrated, its importance in any particular city was in direct proportion to the size of the urban community. In the Middle Ages too, fidelity to the church, as well as sectarian movements in religion, characteristically developed in the cities. It is highly unlikely that an organized congregational religion, such as early Christianity became, could have developed as it did apart from the community life of a city. . . . The specific qualities of Christianity as an ethical religion of salvation and as personal piety found their real nature in the urban environment; and it is there that they constantly set in motion new stimuli in contrast to the ritualistic, magical or formalistic re-interpretation favored by the dominant feudal powers.
>
> As a rule, the class of warrior nobles, and indeed feudal powers generally, have not readily become the carriers of a rationalistic religious ethic. The life pattern of a warrior has very little affinity with the notion of a beneficent providence, or with the systematic ethical demands of a transcendental god. Concepts like sin, salvation, and religious humility have not only seemed remote from all elite political classes, particularly the warrior nobles, but have indeed appeared reprehensible to its sense of honor. To accept a religion that works with such conceptions and to genuflect before the prophet or priest would appear plebian and dishonorable to any martial hero or noble person, e.g., the Roman nobility of the age of Tacitus, or the Confucian mandarins. It is an everyday psychological event for the warrior to face death and the irrationalities of human destiny. Indeed, the chances and adventures of mundane existence fill his life to such an extent that he does not require of his religion (and accepts only reluctantly) anything beyond protection against evil magic or such ceremonial rites as

[87] Amos, "The Origin and Nature of the Carolingian Sermon," pp. 64–65.

[88] The distinction between orthodoxy and orthopraxy has been advanced by Janet Nelson, "Society, Theodicy and the Origins of Heresy: Towards a Reassessment of the Medieval Evidence," in Derek J. Baker, ed., *Schism, Heresy and Religious Protest,* SCH, vol. 9 (Cambridge: Cambridge University Press, 1972), pp. 65–77.

are congruent with his caste, such as priestly prayers for victory or for a blissful death leading directly into the hero's heaven.[89]

In addition to a possible inherent attraction toward itinerant Irish monks by the rural Celtic remnant in Gaul,[90] the heroic self-discipline and asceticism of Irish monasticism may have appealed to the Germanic warrior spirit, and perhaps the structure of the Irish penitentials may have corresponded with that of the system of *wergild* embodied in the Germanic law codes.[91] Whatever the sources of attraction were, Columbanus and his followers succeeded in establishing a network of monasteries, free from local episcopal control, on the property of the northern Frankish aristocrats. In fact, all the leading Frankish families "had one or more members who were strongly attracted to this new monasticism and either visited or entered Luxeuil as monks."[92] Friedrich Prinz has proposed that these monasteries, which became associated with aristocratic families, together

---

[89] *The Sociology of Religion,* pp. 84–85.

[90] A precise demographic view of Celtic Gaul in the sixth through eight century is difficult to establish. Owing to their common Indo-European heritage, pre-Christian Celtic and Germanic religiosities are generally considered quite similar. Wallace-Hadrill, *The Frankish Church,* conjectures: "It is just possible, . . . that some Franks had found the Romano-Celtic gods so like their own that they had accepted Roman-Celtic names for their own gods while keeping their attributes. It could have been as easy for the Franks to absorb Celtic gods as it had undoubtedly been for the Celts to absorb Roman gods. . . . This coming together of Celt and German would explain much, as, for instance, why a huge statue of Diana should have been worshipped by the Franks on the hills of Yvois" (pp. 17–19). Discussing the resemblance between the religiosities of the Germanic and Celtic peoples from the perspective of their common Indo-European heritage, H. R. Ellis Davidson, *Myths and Symbols in Pagan Europe* (Syracuse, N.Y.: Syracuse University Press, 1988), concludes: "It might be argued that such parallels are simply due to a similar way of life, a constant background of warrior activity continuing alongside farming and herding at home, so that heroic traditions and close links with the natural world influenced the rites and imagery of religion. But much of the resemblance seems to go deeper than this; it indicates an accepted framework, with an emphasis on certain symbols and motifs which may be traced beyond Ireland and Iceland to what we know of the Celtic and Germanic peoples in earlier times. . . . It is accepted that Celts and Germans were once closely associated, hard to distinguish from one another in the Roman period except by their difference in language, and at an earlier period still having one language in common. The idea of their common ancestry is strengthened by the type of parallels found in their religious symbols and practices" (pp. 218–19).

[91] C. H. Lawrence, *Medieval Monasticism: Forms of Religious Life in Western Europe in the Middle Ages* (New York: Longman, 1984), notes that "for Columbanus, the life of the monk was a heroic and unremitting warfare to conquer his own self-will and sensuality" (pp. 40–41), and cites his statement taken from the *Sancti Columbani Opera,* ed. G. S. M. Walker (Dublin: Institute for Advanced Studies, 1957), "if you remove the battle, you remove the crown as well" (p. 142). Implicitly applying a comparative Indo-European approach, D. A. Binchy, "A Pre-Christian Survival in Medieval Irish Hagiography," in Dorothy Whitelock, Rosamond McKitterick, and David Dumville, eds., *Ireland in Early Medieval Europe: Studies in Memory of Kathleen Hughes* (Cambridge: Cambridge University Press, 1982), pp. 165–78, makes the following observation: "In form—and to a large degree in substance—the Irish *Heiligensage* is based on the Irish *Heldensage.* Each saint is depicted as a conquering hero who never loses a battle but triumphs over all his enemies, especially the druids who oppose his mission" (p. 167).

[92] Binchy, "A Pre-Christian Survival," p. 172.

with the eventual hagiographical commemoration of family members, may have fulfilled a desire among the Frankish nobility for the sacral reinforcement and legitimation of their social status, analogous to that which had been imparted to Clovis through his baptism.[93] Prinz relates the aristocratic desire for Christian religiopolitical legitimation to the decline of the pre-Christian Germanic notion of inherited sacral character, or *Geblütsheiligkeit,* among the Franks.[94]

According to the Weberian interpretation which Prinz applies, "groups in a position of political responsibility are peculiarly sensitive, not only to the amount of power they command, in the strictly 'realistic' sense of this term, but to the basis of *legitimation* of the use of this power, which is in the longer run a primary factor in the extent of power itself."[95] Herein is located a major source of the "political religiosity" that was to permeate medieval Christianity. An additional "key factor in Merovingian religious

[93] "Die 'Selbstheiligung' des fränkischen Adels in der Hagiographie," section in the chapter "Der geistige und gesellschaftliche Wandel des Mönchtums zwischen Spätantike und Mittelalter," in *Frühes Mönchtum im Frankenreich: Kultur und Gesellschaft in Gallen, den Rheinlanden und Bayern am Beispiel der monastischen Entwicklung (4. bis 8. Jahrhundert)* (Munich: R. Oldenbourg Verlag, 1965), pp. 489–93. A second edition was published in 1988 by the Wissenschaftliche Buchgesellschaft in Darmstadt. Of related interest is Jacques Fontaine, "King Sisebut's *Vita Desiderii* and the Political Function of Visigothic Hagiography," in Edward James, ed., *Visigothic Spain: New Approaches* (Oxford: Clarendon Press, 1980), pp. 93–129.

[94] Prinz, *Frühes Mönchtum,* notes: "Die germanische Adelsherrschaft, einst religiös in ihrer politisch-charismatischen Funktion sanktioniert, durch ihre 'Geblütsheiligkeit' herausgehoben aus der Gesellschaftspyramide, verlor ja mit der Christianisierung einen Gutteil der religiösen Sanktion ihres Herrschaftsanspruches. . . . Im 7. Jahrhundert, entsteht dem Adel durch die Heiligen aus seinen Reihen eine neue, jetzt jedoch christliche Sanktionierung seiner Herrschaft, die zahlreichen Klostergründungen dieser Epoche sind Ausdruck und zugleich Festigung der inneren Verbindung des Adels mit dem neuen Gott und daher die Heiligen aus den Reihen dieses Adels zugleich die neuen christlichen Garanten der alten Adelherrschaft. Hier kann man gleichsam in statu nascendi beobachten, was man die 'politische Religiosität' des Mittelalters genannt hat, und zwar in einem sehr konkreten Sinn: als neue religiöse Legitimierung der Herrschaft" (p. 492). For a further discussion of this Germanic notion, Prinz refers to Karl Hauck, "Geblütsheiligkeit," in Bernhard Bischoff, ed., *Liber Floridus: Mittellateinische Studien (Paul Lehmann zum 65. Geburtstag am 13. Juli 1949 gewidmet)* (St. Ottilien: Eos Verlag der Erzabtei St. Ottilien, 1950), pp. 187–240, especially pp. 194–95. Generally speaking, just as the development of the *Eigenkloster* and the *Adelsheilige* hagiographies functioned to legitimate the social status of the Merovingian nobility, so did association with the Anglo-Saxon missionaries and the papal authority which they represented, function to legitimate the rising status of the Carolingians, whose role in Germanization and Christianization will be studied in the following chapter.

[95] Talcott Parsons, introduction to Max Weber, *The Sociology of Religion,* trans. Ephraim Fischoff (Boston: Beacon Press, 1963), pp. 84–85. Regarding the legitimation of Frankish power, Prinz, *Frühes Mönchtum,* p. 493, n. 126, refers to "Domestikation der Beherrschten," a section in Max Weber, *Wirtschaft und Gesellschaft: Grundriss der verstehenden Soziologie,* ed. Johannes Winckelmann (Tübingen: J. C. B. Mohr (Paul Siebeck), 1956); and Karl Bosl, "Die germanische Kontinuität im deutschen Mittelalter: Adel, König, Kirche," in *Antike und Orient im Mittelalter,* vol. 1 of *Miscellanea Mediaevalia: Veröffentlichungen des Thomas-Instituts an der Universität Köln,* Paul Wilpert and Willehad Paul Eckert, eds. (Berlin: Walter de Gruyter, 1962), pp. 1–25.

life" which may have been associated with the establishment of religiopolitical legitimacy was the construction of monasteries, shrines, and churches over the tombs of deceased nobles by their families.[96] Paul Fouracre regards these constructions as "cult-centres" and views Merovingian Christianity itself as a " 'cult' religion,"[97] while Geary has concluded that "the family tomb was also a center of spiritual power and prestige for its members."[98]

A further examination of the structure of Irish monasticism and the missionaries it inspired should contribute to an appreciation of their influence among the Germanic peoples. In Ireland the government of a monastery was closely associated with that of the kingdom in which it existed. Geary has succinctly described the folk-centered structure of Irish monasticism: "Lacking the tradition of Roman cities and provincial organization, Ireland was hardly an ideal area for the development of an episcopal church, and in the sixth century the Irish church became a federation of monastic communities, each corresponding roughly to a tribe and each under the jurisdiction of the 'heir' of the founding saint of the region."[99] Given the rural Irish environment, the prestige and authority of the bishop was subordinated to that of the abbot. This non-Roman Celtic structure was a good model for a similarly rural Germanic society. However, the prior existence of a Gallic episcopal structure, coupled with the disregard expressed by Columbanus and his Iro-Frankish followers for its authority, often resulted in antagonisms which diminished the effectiveness of their Christianization efforts. Also, upon the death of their typically charismatic founding abbots, the Iro-Frankish monasteries usually declined in significance as foci for Christianization in the regions where they were located.[100]

Despite the generally apolitical attitude of the Iro-Frankish missionaries themselves, their potential for advancing social cohesion and political jurisdiction through Christianization was not lost on Merovingian rulers. Thomas Leslie Amos has noted that Dagobert I, "the last Merovingian king to exercise direct rule over the entire Frankish realm (629–39) . . . took a strong interest in the Christianization of the lands on his borders, and offered the district of Utrecht to the bishop of Cologne if he would evangelize it."[101] Members of Dagobert's court who became itinerant missionary bishops in northern Gaul included Eligius of Noyon and Audoenus of Rouen. Remarking on the Merovingian encouragement of Iro-Frankish Christianization activities, Geary has stated:

---

[96] Paul Fouracre, "The Work of Audoenus of Rouen and Eligius of Noyon in Extending Episcopal Influence from the Town to the Country in Seventh-Century Neustria," in *The Church in Town and Countryside,* ed. Derek Baker, SCH, no. 16 (Oxford: Blackwell, 1979), p. 81.

[97] Ibid.

[98] Geary, *Before France and Germany,* p. 174.

[99] Ibid., p. 169.

[100] Hauck, *Kirchengeschichte Deutschlands,* vol. 1, p. 347.

[101] Amos, "The Origin and Nature of the Carolingian Sermon," pp. 68–69.

The more active involvement of the northern Frankish aristocracy as well as that of wandering Irish monks such as Columbanus began to introduce Christian observance and cult into the countryside. Religious cult and political power were understood as inseparable, whether at the level of Dagobert or at the local level of Frankish aristocrats who sought to introduce uniformity in cult in their areas of power. Thus it was in the interest of aristocracy to assist in the implantation of Christianity.[102]

The growth of commercial activity in Frisia during this period provided an additional impetus for Christianization efforts along the northern border of Gaul and in areas east of the Rhine. It is from a predominantly pagan village in the vicinity of Noyon that one of the few Germanic responses to Christianization efforts has been preserved. While preaching against pagan celebrations, Eligius was interrupted by community leaders who angrily exclaimed: "Roman that you are, although you are always bothering us, you will never uproot our customs, but we will go on with our rites as we have always done, and we will go on doing so always and forever. There will never exist the man who will be able to stop us holding our time-honoured and most dear games."[103]

In a structural sense, Columbanus may be viewed as a catalyst for the Germanization of Merovingian monastic organization, since he introduced monastic concepts which contributed to the development of the *Eigenklostersystem*.[104] In a religious sense, however, Columbanus may be viewed as a genuinely Christianizing force in whose *instructiones* one encounters a prototype of the Carolingian reform of the ninth century which, in the following chapter, is described as the "second phase" of Christianization. By this it is meant that, instead of having focused on the power of the Christian God to fulfill the worldly concerns of the Germanic peoples, as did Remigius and Avitus in their communications with Clovis, Columbanus appears to have focused more upon the attainment of "moral perfection."[105] J. M. Wallace-Hadrill describes the novel ethical orientation of Columbanus as follows:

> It is in his sermons and letters rather than in the better-known penitentials and Rules that he can best be seen. What immediately strikes the reader is the gulf between the piety of the Frankish Church, centred upon relics and the patronage of local holy men, and the piety of Columbanus, focused upon God and the relationship of God with man. It was indeed a gust of fresh air. Columbanus' influence was personal, not institutional. His sermons or *instructiones* are about God, not about saints. The first in the

---

[102] Geary, *Before France and Germany*, p. 177.

[103] *Vita Eligii episcopi Noviomagensis, MGH SRM*, ed. Bruno Krusch, vol. 4, book 2, ch. 20, pp. 711–12; translated in Fouracre, "The Work of Audoenus," p. 82.

[104] J. M. Wallace-Hadrill, *The Frankish Church* (Oxford: Clarendon Press, 1983), notes that "as much as any Frank or Burgundian, he propagated the idea of monasteries as local centres of aristocratic cultus, such as he had known in Ireland" (p. 65).

[105] Ibid., p. 64.

dossier of thirteen is about faith. . . . He does not deny that the inter-
cession of the saints will help; for like all great spiritual teachers he is
haunted by the problem of access to God. . . . The seventh sermon is on
poverty; not on the need to give as the Frankish Church taught it, but on
the need to have nothing to give. . . . The eleventh sermon, on remorse,
ends with a magnificent meditation on love. There is a sharp contrast here
with contemporary Frankish thinking, in so far as we know it.[106]

Despite the zeal of Columbanus and the Iro-Frankish missionaries, as
Merovingian strength and prestige declined after the death of Dagobert I
in 639,[107] the progress of Christianization efforts likewise declined.[108] That
this decline was not a steady one, however, is attested to by the activities
of Queen Balthildis, the wife of Dagobert's son Clovis II (d. 657), who
after her husband's death founded the monastery of Corbie and the nun-
nery of Chelles.

In pondering the effects of Columbanus's mission, Wallace-Hadrill
queries: "What could survive of a mission so immensely personal?"[109]
Although private penance may have existed on the continent before Columbanus, his work and the popularization of his ethical teachings among
his Iro-Frankish successors certainly contributed to the development of a
mentality according to which frequent private confession provided a means
of assuaging feelings of guilt.[110] It also may be noted that the types of sin
which were emphasized in Columbanus's *Penitentials* differed from those
most commonly associated with Merovingian Gaul. For example, whereas
Columbanus emphasizes personal, internal sins such as the *desire* "to kill
a man, or to commit fornication, or to steal, or to feast in secret and be

---

[106] Ibid., pp. 63–64.

[107] Geary, "Merovingian Obsolescence," in *Before France and Germany,* explains that the re-
peated failure of Merovingian kings to leave adult heirs contributed to destabilizing aristocratic
in-fighting. "However," he notes, "it is insufficient to explain completely what happened. . . . The
loss of Merovingian power was part of a much more complex transformation of the Frankish
world in the seventh and early eighth centuries. While these transformations grew out of the
political, social, economic, and religious traditions already forming in the reign of Chlotar II and
Dagobert, they were not such as to inevitably lead to the obsolescence of Merovingian kingship,
but combined with the series of minorities, they proved fatal" (p. 181).

[108] Gustav Schnürer, "The Activity of the Irish Missionaries—Decline of the Frankish
Church," in *Church and Culture in the Middle Ages,* vol. 1, trans. George J. Undreiner (Paterson,
N.J.: St. Anthony Guild Press, 1956), pp. 325–35.

[109] Wallace-Hadrill, *The Frankish Church,* p. 67.

[110] Regarding Frankish society, Wallace-Hadrill, *The Frankish Church,* speculates in a
psychohistorical vein: "A society burdened with a sense of guilt required the remedy of readily
accessible reassurance; and not only accessible but repeatable. Confession and penance became
a part of daily life, because the sense of sin was" (p. 65). But from where did this internal sense
of sin and guilt arise in a shame-oriented society, if Columbanus was the first major advocate of
the concepts of sin and repentance? Perhaps these concepts did not become widespread until
the second phase of Christianization efforts in the ninth century. See also Heinz Rupp, "Leid
und Sunde im *Heliand* und in Otfrids *Evangelienbuch,*" *Beiträge zur Geschichte der deutschen
Sprache und Literatur,* part 1: 78 (1956): 421–69; and part 2: 79 (1957): 336–79.

drunken, or indeed to strike someone,"[111] the sins which appear to have been most common prior to his arrival are those which involved offenses against cult and ritual, such as the observance of Sunday and holy days and disrespect for the cults of various saints, particularly St. Martin.[112]

It is difficult to gauge the effect of the Christianization efforts of Columbanus and his Iro-Frankish followers on their audience, which represented all walks of Frankish life. Unfortunately, there appears to exist no adequate analysis of the evolution of the concepts of sin, repentance, and salvation in Frankish society in the early Middle Ages. Jacques Le Goff does, however, urge that "it should be stressed that it was the monasteries which made Christianity and the values it conveyed penetrate slowly into the countryside, which hitherto had been little affected by the new religion."[113] In his study *The Birth of Purgatory,* Le Goff has provided an excerpt from Columbanus's ninth *Instructio,* which appears to place him within an Augustinian eschatological tradition which includes Gregory the Great and Caesarius of Arles:

> Here is the way the human being's miserable life runs: from the earth, on the earth, in the earth, from the earth into the fire, from the fire to judgement, from judgement either to Gehenna or to life (everlasting). You have been created from the earth, you tread the earth, you will be laid to rest in the earth, you will rise in the earth, you will be tried in fire, you will await the judgement, and then either torture or the kingdom of heaven will be yours forever.[114]

Le Goff also cites a sermon of Eligius of Noyon, whose eschatological and soteriological orientation appears to parallel that of Columbanus.[115] Acknowledging "the difficulty of identifying the true 'barbarian' legacy,"[116] Le Goff proffers a brief explanation of the Celto-Germanic influence in the development of the idea of Purgatory:

> Even more, perhaps, than the Celtic, the Germanic imagination of the hereafter, by the time it becomes accessible to us, already seems to have been subjected to strong influence from the high culture of Latin Christianity....
>
> Doubtless the most important change was that the rather cheerful other worlds of primitive Celtic and German mythology turned somber, subterranean, and infernal under Christian influence. At the moment of Purgatory's

---

[111] "The Penitential of St. Columbanus," par. 2, in Hillgarth, *Christianity and Paganism, 350–750: The Conversion of Western Europe,* p. 131.

[112] Raymond Van Dam, *Leadership and Community in Late Antique Gaul* (Berkeley: University of California Press, 1985), pp. 260–69, provides several examples complemented by a socioreligious analysis.

[113] *Medieval Civilization: 400–1500,* trans. Julia Barrow (Oxford: Basil Blackwell, 1988), p. 120.

[114] *The Birth of Purgatory,* trans. Arthur Goldhammer (Chicago: University of Chicago Press, 1984), p. 101. The original quotation may be found in *PL,* vol. 80, col. 246–47.

[115] Ibid., p. 101.

[116] Ibid., p. 109.

inception, we shall see how the optimistic Celtic (and perhaps Germanic) conception of a place of waiting and purification gave way to the image of Purgatory as cruel, for a time, as Hell, an image that came from oriental apocalyptic sources and from official Christian tradition. The old conception did not disappear completely but was rather absorbed into visions of Paradise. These ambivalent other worlds of "folklore" were forced to gravitate toward either the positive or the negative pole, while Purgatory lingered for a time, occupying the middle ground.[117]

As the Middle Ages progressed, the Celto-Germanic attitude toward death and an afterlife was increasingly replaced by a Christian one, causing Le Goff to remark elsewhere that "if we do not keep the obsession with salvation and the fear of hell which inspired medieval men in the forefront of our minds we shall never understand their outlook on life."[118] Perhaps equally significant to an understanding of the medieval world-view, but more elusive, is the process by which the Christian ideological matrix of sin-repentance-salvation gained ascendancy over Celto-Germanic notions of fate and destiny, a process which may be identified with Christianization. However, the ideological movement toward Christianization was one which regularly encountered unyielding elements of pre-Christian Germanic ideology. To the extent that the Christian ideological matrix of sin-repentance-salvation advanced among the Germanic peoples in the early Middle Ages, it may be said that they were Christianized, while to the extent that Christianity accommodated the religiopolitical and magicoreligious orientation of pre-Christian Germanic religiosity during this period, it may be said to have been Germanized.

Discussing analogous developments in the Celtic world, Joseph Campbell has commented:

> A culture historian today surely has the right to ask the meaning of such a mass conversion as takes place when a pagan king submits to baptism and all his people follow. . . .
>
> Surely it is permissible to ask: How, exactly, was this Levantine institution with its supporting myth received and understood by the recently pagan, hyperborean population, to whose well-being in the yonder world

---

[117] Ibid., p. 110. The Germanic perception of an afterlife is discussed in detail by Hilda Roderick Ellis, *The Road to Hel: A Study of the Conception of the Dead in Old Norse Literature* (1943; reprint, New York: Greenwood Press, 1968), who concludes that "the Norse mind, in the literature as we have it, does not readily turn to develop imaginative and spiritual conceptions of life after death. Perhaps it is the reality of the present life, and its importance in the eyes of the creators of that literature which served to keep them from indulging in elaborate and enthusiastic speculation about the future one" (p. 147). E. O. G. Turville-Petre, *Myth and Religion of the North: The Religion of Ancient Scandinavia* (1964; reprint, Westport, Conn.: Greenwood Press, 1975), has concluded that, according to Norse sources, "death is the greatest evil known to man, but yet it can be overcome. Live well and die bravely and your repute will live after you. Fate will decide the moment and manner of your death, but fate will not decide how you will face it. A brave death will be rewarded, not with pork and mead as in Valhöll, but with the esteem of your friends, kinsmen and even your enemies. They will tell how you lived and how you died. Your story will live, as has that of many a northern hero" (p. 274).

[118] *Medieval Civilization*, p. 187.

its magic now was to be applied.

One important clue may be seen in the heresy of two Irishmen, contemporaries of Patrick, Pelagius and his chief disciple Caelestius. In their essentially Stoic doctrine of free will and the innate goodness of nature, which is not corrupted but only modified by sin, they opposed diametrically their great antagonist Augustine, for whom (as for the Church), nature, though created good, was so corrupted by the sin of Adam that virtue is impossible without grace....

A second clue to the temper of the north may be seen in the Irish Neoplatonic philosopher ... Johannes Scotus Erigena (c. 815–c. 877 A.D.) ... [according to whom] sin is the misdirected will and is punished by the finding that its misjudgements are vain. Hell is but the inner state of a sinning will.[119]

One manner in which a Christian consciousness of sin and a consequent desire for salvation was advanced in Germanic society was through the Anglo-Saxon missionary policy of accommodation. An example of the manner in which this policy was implemented may be found in the deliberate semantic transformation of the Old English root *hailagaz* from connoting societal prosperity, to connoting individual holiness and salvation.[120] Although semantic transformation will be discussed in greater detail in the following chapter, it may be noted here that "in the Germanic languages, the term *salvation* very explicitly connotes not only a healing of man's soul but a more general healing (*heilen, helen*)."[121]

[119] *Occidental Mythology,* vol. 3 of *The Masks of God* (Harmondsworth: Penguin Books, 1964), pp. 464–66. Philosophical resistance to the Christian notion of eternal damnation, perhaps grounded in a more monistic, immanent, and pantheistic Celto-Germanic world-view, may have played a role in the eschatological speculation of Erigena, *De divisione naturae, PL,* vol. 122, col. 441–1022, which has been summarized by Etienne Gilson, *History of Christian Philosophy in the Middle Ages* (New York: Random House, 1955): "In a universe where matter shall be dissolved into its intelligible elements, there is no place for a material hell. Like Origen, Erigena considers the notion of a material Gehenna to be a remnant of pagan superstition that the real Christians should get rid of" (p. 127). That proto-Pelagian notions, particularly with regard to the monastic life, may have been transmitted to Ireland via the monastic community at Lérins, which later became associated with semi-Pelagianism, is possible, if one traces the path of the Eastern monastic tradition to Ireland through Lérins, as does Geary, *Before France and Germany,* p. 169. Contrary to Campbell's assumption of Pelagius's Irish origin, a recent reappraisal by B. R. Rees, *Pelagius: A Reluctant Heretic* (Woodbridge: Boydell & Brewer, 1988), asserts that "Britain is by far the strongest candidate for the honor, if such it be, of providing him with a birthplace, even if all efforts to pinpoint its precise location have been characterised by ingenuity rather than conviction" (p. xiii). Rees also notes "evidence of the existence of the Pelagian commentary in three libraries on the continent, all of them connected with the Irish mission and one of them being St. Gallen," and concludes that "the later [late eighth- and early ninth-century] Irish Church certainly reveals a considerable respect for the Pelagian commentary" (p. 122). N. P. Williams, *The Grace of God* (1930; reprint, Hodder & Stoughton, 1966), pp. 77–83, traces adherence to semi-Pelagianism from Cassian through Peter Lombard, the medieval Franciscan schoolmen Alexander of Hales and Bonaventure, and the later nominalists Duns Scotus, William of Occam, and Gabriel Biel to the sixteenth- and seventeenth-century Jesuit schools of Molina and Suarez.

[120] Baetke, *Aufnahme,* p. 52.

[121] Antoine Vergote, "The Consciousness of Evil and the Labyrinth of Culpability," part 2 of *Guilt and Desire: Religious Attitudes and Their Pathological Derivatives,* trans. M. H. Wood

Of Columbanus and his Iro-Frankish successors, it may be observed that those who were encouraged in their missionary endeavors by Dagobert I appear to have diverged in the degree to which they emphasized various aspects of Christianity. When they addressed audiences in southern, western, or central Gaul that had already been baptized, a moderate, moralizing, "secondary-phase" approach appears to have been preferred. However, on those occasions when Columbanus or Amand approached Germanic peoples along the northern and eastern borders of Gaul, such as the Alamanni, whose previous exposure to Christianity had been minimal, these Iro-Frankish missionaries usually relied on "primary phase" dramatic magicoreligious confrontations with pagan cult objects and practices in order to convince their audiences of the superior power of the Christian God. For example, while preaching in the northern county of Beauvais, Amand instructed a blind woman who had venerated a tree dedicated to an idol to "take an axe and cut down this abominable tree by which you have lost your bodily sight and your soul's salvation," after which her sight was restored.[122]

In comparing the Christianization efforts of the Iro-Frankish and Anglo-Saxon missionaries, one apparent distinction is the emphasis among the latter upon imposing a Rome-oriented *canonica rectitudo* in ecclesiastical discipline, custom, and organization.[123] A less obvious distinction lies in the

---

(New Haven, Conn.: Yale University Press, 1988), p. 43. Vergote notes further: "It is the paradox of Christianity that in proclaiming freedom from sin and deliverance from the law it accentuates the demands of the law and sharpens the sense of sin. Thus the call to salvation also invokes a call to conversion" (ibid.). Of related interest is the hypothesis of Elaine Pagels, *Adam and Eve and the Serpent* (New York: Random House, 1988): "Many people need to find reasons for their sufferings. Had Augustine's theory not met such a need—were it not that people often *would rather feel guilty than helpless*—I suspect that the idea of original sin would not have survived the fifth century, much less become the basis of Christian doctrine for 1600 years" (p. 146). For a historical discussion of the notions of sin and salvation in various religious cultures, see *Dictionary of the History of Ideas*, s.v. "Sin and Salvation," by S. G. F. Brandon. See also Frederick S. Paxton, *Christianizaing Death: The Creation of a Ritual Process in Early Medieval Europe* (Ithaca, N.Y.: Cornell University Press, 1990); and Jean Delumeau, *Sin and Fear: The Emergence of a Western Guilt Culture, 13th–18th Centuries*, trans. Eric Nicholson (New York: St. Martin's Press, 1990).

[122] *Vita S. Amandi, episcopi et confessoris, MGH SRM*, ed. Bruno Krusch, vol. 5 (Hanover: Hahn Verlag, 1910), pp. 447–48; translated in Hillgarth, *Christianity and Paganism*, pp. 147–48. Additional examples of Iro-Frankish intolerance for pagan rites include the destruction by Columbanus of a cask of beer which was being offered to Wotan by the Swabians, reported in Jonas, *Vitae Colombani abbatis discipulorumque eius libri duo, MGH SRM*, ed. Ernst Dümmler, vol. 4, (Hanover: Hahn Verlag, 1902), *Vita I*, p. 102, translated in Edward Peters, ed., *Monks, Bishops and Pagans: Christian Culture in Gaul and Italy, 500–700*, with an introduction by Edward Peters (Philadelphia: University of Pennsylvania Press, 1975), p. 108; and the destruction of metal idols belonging to the Alamanni by SS. Columbanus and Gall, reported in Walafrid Strabo, *Vita Galli, MGH SRM*, ed. Bruno Krusch, vol. 4, pp. 290–91.

[123] Timothy Reuter, "Saint Boniface and Europe," in idem, ed., *The Greatest Englishman: Essays on St. Boniface and the Church at Crediton* (Exeter: Paternoster Press, 1980), p. 80. Paul Willem Finsterwalder, "Wege und Ziele der irischen und angelsächsischen Mission im fränkischen Reich," *ZKG* 47 (1928): 203–26, introduces an internal-external dichotomy in discussing

relatively personal, straightforward, and apolitical approach of the Iro-Frankish missionaries as compared with that of their Anglo-Saxon successors. An example which illustrates this straightforward and apolitical Iro-Frankish approach may be found in Columbanus's response to the appeal of a companion who suggested that he pray for the victory of Theudebert II of Austrasia over Theuderic II of Burgundy. The latter king had offended Columbanus more grievously than the former. Whereas Remigius and Avitus, Gallo-Roman bishops in search of a champion against Arianism, associated military victory with Christian affiliation in their correspondence with Clovis, Columbanus responded to his companion in an apolitical, world-rejecting, and eschatological manner. According to Columbanus's *Vita:* "His attendant said with rash presumption: 'My father, aid Theudebert with your prayers, so that he may defeat the common enemy, Theuderich.' Columban answered: 'Your advice is foolish and irreligious, for God, who commanded us to pray for our enemies, has not so willed. The just Judge has already determined what He wills concerning them.' "[124]

The extent to which the influence of the Iro-Frankish mission diminished as the Merovingian dynasty declined is difficult to determine. In the introduction to his translation of the correspondence of St. Boniface, C. H. Talbot makes the following observation:

> The missionary efforts of the Frankish Church were small, unsustained, and too fitful to cope with the enormous difficulties to be faced. The Irish, under Columbanus, were earlier in the field and at first enjoyed unprecedented success. From Luxeuil, where their monastery was situated, they spread their influence far and wide, but their singular views on the observance of Easter and the form of the tonsure, their independence of local bishops and Columbanus's outspoken denunciations of the morals at court, made their position untenable and they were forced to depart. Round the lake of Constance, where the Abbey of St. Gall still stands as a reminder of their activities, and at Bobbio, in northern Italy, where their learning shone with

the spiritual and moral concerns of the Irish missionaries and the organizational and disciplinary concerns of the Anglo-Saxon missionaries. From a Protestant perspective, Otto Wissig, *Iro-schotten und Bonifatius in Deutschland: Eine kirchengeschichtlich-urkundliche Untersuchung* (Gütersloh: C. Bertelsmann, 1932), argues that the Scotts-Irish mission had performed the actual work of Christianization in Germany, and that Boniface's role had primarily been that of a "Romanizer." A thorough presentation of both missions is contained in Heinrich Timerding, ed., *Die christliche Frühzeit Deutschlands in der Berichten über die Bekehrer* (Jena: Eugen Diederichs Verlag, 1929), vol. 1, "Die irisch-fränkische Mission," and vol. 2, "Die angelsächsische Mission." See also Friedrich Prinz, "Peregrinatio, Mönchtum und Mission," in *Kirchengeschichte als Missionsgeschichte,* first half of vol. 2 of *Die Kirche des früheren Mittelalters,* pp. 445–65; H. B. Clarke and M. Brennan, eds., *Columbanus and Merovingian Monasticism,* British Archaeological Reports, series 113 (Oxford: British Archaeological Reports, 1981); and Proinseas Ni Chathain and Michael Richter, *Irland und Europa: Die Kirche im Frühmittelalter* (Stuttgart: Klett-Cotta, 1984).

[124] Jonas, *Vitae Columbani abbatis discipulorumque eius libri duo, MGH SRM,* ed. Ernst Dümmler, vol. 4, *Vita Columbani I,* ch. 57; translated in Peters, ed., *Monks, Bishops and Pagans,* p. 111.

undimmed lustre throughout the Middle Ages, their labours were of a more enduring character; but, on the whole, their practice of consecrating bishops with no fixed responsibilities, no jurisdiction, no ties and no superiors, except the abbot of the monastery to which they were attached, was not conducive to the establishment of Christianity on a lasting basis among the pagan population. Lofty ascetic ideals and burning missionary zeal were not enough. Too much depended upon the personal character of the preacher, so that when the first enthusiasm had spent its force the itinerant missionary too often left his converts to fend for themselves. . . . Thus by the time the Anglo-Saxon missionaries arrived on the scene the work of conversion in most parts had to be begun afresh. The memory of the early Irish saints was still alive, but the fruits of their labours had either disappeared or been interwoven with pagan practices and superstitions.[125]

According to Talbot and Derek Baker, it was the establishment of a Rome-directed episcopal organization by Boniface in the latter half of his career that provided the foundation for sustained Christianization activities.[126]

To the extent that Christianity did spread among the Germanic peoples, one is led, in the tradition of Latourette, to question: "What was the form of the Christianity which spread?"[127] From the perspective of the current inquiry, this question may be focused more sharply by asking: "Was the form of Christianity which spread a Germanized one, and if so, how did it become Germanized?" To answer this question, it may be helpful to recall that in previous chapters it has been asserted that pre-Christian Germanic religiosity and social structure were fundamentally interrelated, and that pre-Christian Germanic religiosity and social structure tended to exhibit the basic characteristics of Indo-European societies in their early, more authentic stages. These characteristics consisted of a social structure with high group solidarity, an associated world-accepting

[125] *The Anglo-Saxon Missionaries in Germany* (New York: Sheed and Ward, 1954), pp. viii–ix.

[126] Ibid., pp. ix, xiv–xv. Derek Baker, "Sowing the Seeds of Faith: Theory and Practice in the Mission Field," in idem, ed., *Miscellanea Historiae Ecclesiasticae,* vol. 3 (Louvain: Publications Universitaires de Louvain, 1970), states: "However the missionary enterprise might begin, whether in the planned expedition of a Gregory the Great or the individual initiative of a Nikon [apostle of Crete, d. 998], it had to progress quickly from the confused compromise of the early stages of conversion towards the 'greater perfection' which all the missionaries desired. The alternative was that Christian paganism which Boniface encountered in Germany and noted in Rome, and which was to be found throughout Christendom. Its eradication, and the establishment of a genuinely Christian practice and belief, was the life's work of men like Columbanus and Cuthbert, but there was more to Christianization than individual labour and personal example. . . . A stable ecclesiastical order had to be created to give permanence to these personal achievements. Initially this meant the establishment of monastic centres of teaching and example . . . but in time these centres had to be incorporated in the diocesan organization particularly associated with the names of Theodore of Tarsus and Boniface" (p. 105). For a recent discussion of the Frankish episcopacy prior to and during Boniface's reform, see Wilfried Hartmann, "Die Synoden des Bonifatius," in *Die Synoden der Karolingerzeit im Frankenreich und in Italien* (Paderborn: Ferdinand Schöningh, 1989).

[127] See Latourette's first question, above, p. 15.

folk religion which was predominantly religiopolitical and magicoreligious, as opposed to being pre-dominantly doctrinal and ethical, and a prominent warrior-band or *comitatus* institution. Another important Germanic socio-religious characteristic which has been associated with Indo-European societies is that of "sacral kingship."[128] Insofar as these and other characteristics of pre-Christian Germanic religiosity were inculturated by early medieval Christianity, it may be considered to have been Germanized.

Three caveats should be borne in mind during this discussion. First, the effects on various aspects of Christianity as a result of its encounter with the Germanic peoples are not claimed to be unique; they may have also occurred in other circumstances throughout the history of Christianity. For example, devotion to the saints and their relics existed prior to the Germanic encounter with Christianity, but it was as a result of this encounter that this devotion rose to a level of prominence in early medieval Western Christianity. Second, those aspects of Christianity which are asserted to have been Germanized are not asserted to have endured in their Germanized form until the present era. Third, since world-view transformation is a slow process, some effects of Germanization did not fully materialize until centuries following the initial encounter of Christianity with the Germanic peoples. An important instance of this form of gradual world-view transformation may be found in Carl Erdmann's explanation of the development of the Crusade ideology:

> The entrance of the Germans into Christian history had created an entirely new situation. War was the life-style of the Germanic peoples who increasingly formed the most important element in the church's constituency. The moral precepts that accompanied them from their pagan past were completely oriented to war, focusing on heroism, famous deeds on the part of the leader, loyalty on the part of the followers, revenge for those killed, courage unto death, contempt for a comfortable life at home. For them, war as such was a form of moral action, a higher type of life than peace. All this stood at the opposite pole from Christian morality, which is based on love and readiness for peace and can discuss war only with reference to aims and duties. The acceptance of Christianity could not possibly cause the old Germanic mode of thinking to lose its power overnight. This mentality took centuries to overcome, and still has some appeal today. Characteristically, the stories of the conversion of the Frank Clovis and of the Lombard Romuald represent God's guidance of the fortunes of battle as the decisive element in the turning to Christianity. Moreover ethics and religion were separate in Germanic paganism, so that the supplanting of the pagan by the Christian cult did not simultaneously imply a change in the realm of ethics.
>
> The church was therefore confronted with a massive barrier of pagan ways, which for centuries were beyond its power to master. . . .

[128] Jan de Vries, *Altgermanische Religionsgeschichte*, vol. 1 (Berlin: Walter de Gruyter, 1956), p. 397.

Nevertheless, the German mentality also exercised a positive influence upon the development of the ecclesiastical morality of war. *When the church encountered pagan elements that it could not suppress, it tended to give them a Christian dimension, thereby assimilating them.* This happened to the ethics of heroism. The whole crusading movement may justifiably be seen from this perspective; Christian knighthood cannot otherwise be understood. This evolution began in earnest only around the year 1000, . . . but prefigurations of it do, of course, appear earlier. To some extent, the development of the Christian cult of the archangel Michael symbolizes the process.[129]

Another example of the developmental process associated with the Germanization of Christianity may be found in the increasing attribution of military virtues and noble origins to saints, known as *Adelsheilige,* whose *Lives* were written in the seventh and eighth centuries.[130] Franz Irsigler's

---

[129] Carl Erdmann, *The Origin of the Idea of Crusade,* trans. Marshall W. Baldwin and Walter Goffart, with a foreword by Marshall W. Baldwin (Princeton, N.J.: Princeton University Press, 1977), pp. 19–20 (emphasis added). John Gilchrist, "The Erdmann Thesis and the Canon Law, 1083–1141," in Peter W. Edbury, ed., *Crusade and Settlement* (Cardiff: University College Cardiff Press, 1985), pp. 37–45, has questioned Erdmann's assertion that the canonists of the Crusade period approved of the Crusade ideology, and suggests that they expressed an older and more temperate Augustinian doctrine of the *bellum justum;* but Gilchrist has not sought to refute Erdmann's attribution of the Crusade ideology to Germanic influences. In fact, after stating that "the essence of [Erdmann's] thesis was that, in the eleventh century, the Church turned warfare on its behalf into an ethical activity," Gilchrist acknowledges that "in recent years Erdmann's thesis has been highly praised" (p. 37). Additional contributions to the study of the evolution of Christian attitudes toward warfare may be found in R. A. Markus, "Saint Augustine's Views on the 'Just War,' " in W. J. Sheils, ed., *The Church and War,* SCH, no. 20 (Oxford: Basil Blackwell, 1983), pp. 1–14, who notes that "Augustine's thought on the 'just war' has suffered more perhaps than any other idea from the uprooting to which it has been subjected by medieval lawyers and theologians in search of *auctoritates* and by historians in search of a homogeneous doctrinal tradition" (p. 11). Another relevant article in this volume is Janet L. Nelson, "The Church's Military Service in the Ninth Century: A Contemporary Comparative View?" pp. 31–46, who, suggesting that this service might constitute a phase in the evolution of the Crusade ideology, concludes that by the ninth century "war had become a fact of ecclesiastical life" and that "the institutionalized warfare of the Church was not just permissible but necessary: in practical terms because it sustained the Carolingian state, in ideological terms because it transcended the opposition between apostolicity and landed wealth. The solution was *zeitbedingt* in both senses of that useful word: it was needed by churchmen at a particular time and it required the conditions of that time. . . . The liturgy of knighthood has ninth-century West Frankish roots (I am thinking of the benediction super militantes in the Leofric Missal), and the earliest dubbing rituals should be linked with the warrior-households of particular bishops, that is, with the *familiae* of particular saints. Can we believe that any wide gulf separates these *milites* from, on the one hand, those warriors of Carolingian bishops and abbots and abbesses who went to war behind their banners and kept their mail-shirts in holy places, and on the other, the *militia sancti Petri* and the soldiers of Christ?" (pp. 28–29). See also, E. O. Blake, "The Formation of the 'Crusade Idea,' " *JEH* 21 (1970): 11–31; and Ovido Capitani, "Sondaggio sulla terminologia militare in Urbano II," *Studi Medievali,* 3rd ser., 31 (1990): 1–25.

[130] In the previous chapter, pp. 124–25, military motifs in tenth- and eleventh-century hagiographies were discussed. According to Wallace-Hadrill, *The Frankish Church,* the *Adelsheilige* included Arnulf of Metz, Eligius of Noyon, Audoenus of Rouen, and Wandrille of Fontenelle, as well as "a separate but related group, stretching farther back, of those of royal blood," which

article, "On the Aristocratic Character of Early Frankish Society," documents this adaptation, and also affirms the usefulness of the study of hagiographical literature for the analysis of world-view transformation:

> The new works by Graus and Prinz have shown what value hagiographic sources have, once one penetrates beyond the mere establishing of the presence of topoi [standard themes] and looks at changes in their use and the occurrence of individual traits, which can themselves become commonplaces. Such changes are without a doubt to be ascribed to the influence of social structure and society's scale of values. *We must also remember that in view of the conservative nature of hagiographic sources, new characteristics, especially in the description of the qualities and the way of life of a saint, would only become established after a certain time lag.*
>
> The basic change in the ideal of sanctity and the hagiographic surround [*sic*] of the saint in the course of the seventh and eighth centuries and its extraordinary importance for the understanding of social changes in the early middle ages has already been intensively studied in recent research. What Graus calls, from a Marxist historian's standpoint, a "feudalization of hagiography" in the Carolingian period has been described by Prinz as a development from the strictly ascetic and monastic ideal of late Roman Gaul to the type of the "noble saint" of the seventh and eighth centuries, a man who generally comes from the highest stratum of society, and, however much he may observe the traditional ideal of asceticism, remains a saintly abbot or bishop tied to his own class and to its scale of values.
>
> Particularly illuminating is the judgement of Merovingian hagiographers on the various signs of a noble life-style, since these were most typically elements of the *vita secularis* and thus stood in sharp contrast to true asceticism. Just how highly skill in handling weapons, courage, and sheer machismo were valued in the sources of the Merovingian period can clearly be seen from many of the quotations in the course of this study.[131]

---

included Sigismund, Radegunde, and Dagobert II and III (p. 89). See also Karl Bosl, "Der 'Adelsheilige': Idealtypus und Wirklichkeit, Gesellschaft und Kultur im merowingerzeitlichen Bayern des 7. und 8. Jahrhunderts," in *Speculum Historiale: Geschichte im Spiegel von Geschichtsschreibung und Geschichtsdeutung. Festschrift für Johannes Spörl aus Anlass seines 60. Geburtstages,* ed. Clemens Bauer, Laetitia Boehm, and Max Müller (Munich: Verlag Karl Alber, 1965), pp. 167–87.

[131] "On the Aristocratic Character of Early Frankish Society," trans. Timothy Reuter, in idem, ed., *The Medieval Nobility: Studies on the Ruling Classes of France and Germany from the Sixth to the Twelfth Century,* Europe in the Middle Ages, vol. 14 (Amsterdam: North-Holland, 1978), pp. 118–19 (emphasis added). It may be recalled from chapter 3 above, pp. 58–59, that the Indo-Europeans tended to impose an aristocratic feudal-like social structure in the territories which they conquered. The references made by Irsigler are to František Graus, "Die Gewalt bei den Anfängen des Feudalismus und die 'Gefangenenbefreiungen' der merowingischen Hagiographie," *Jahrbuch für Wirtschaftsgeschichte* 1 (1961): 64; idem, *Volk, Herrscher und Heiliger im Reich der Merowinger: Studien zur Hagiographie der Merowingerzeit* (Prague: Nakladatelství Ceskoslovenské Akádemie Ved, 1965), pp. 206–7; and Friedrich Prinz, "Heiligenkult und Adelsherrschaft im Spiegel merowingischer Hagiographie," *Historische Zeitschrift* 204 (1967): 530–31; idem, "Zur geistigen Kultur des Mönchtums im spätantiken Gallien und im Merowingerreich," *Zeitschrift für bayerische Landesgeschichte* 26 (1963): 76ff. I am indebted to Patrick J.

It may be worthwhile to note here that not only did saints' *Lives* reflect social and ideological developments, but as Jaroslav Pelikan has observed, "in [Albert] Schweitzer's words, it has been characteristic of each age of history to depict Jesus in accordance with its own character."[132] While Pelikan does not treat the Germanic "Jesus as Hero" theme extensively, he does mention that "one of the greatest early poems in the English language, *The Dream of the Rood,* has the tree of the cross describe the 'young Hero' who would ascend it for his combat with death and, succumbing in the combat, would nevertheless prevail." He also mentions the medieval fondness for the metaphors of "the victory-granting cross" and "the wondrous battle," and the popularity of the theme of *Christus Victor,* exemplified in the *Pange lingua* of Venantius Fortunatus.[133]

Geary for providing an advance copy of "Saints, Scholars, and Society: The Elusive Goal," which is to appear in a collection of his essays entitled *Living with the Dead* (Ithaca, N.Y.: Cornell University Press, forthcoming). Geary cautions against generalized assumptions when seeking to derive social values from hagiographies, stressing that "hagiographical manuscripts were created through a wide variety of manners that suggest a spectrum of uses and purposes as well as modes of production." In *Before France and Germany,* Geary observes that "the author of the life of Arnulf of Metz even praises Arnulf's extraordinary skill with arms," and asserts that Merovingian hagiography was "essentially a form of propaganda, and these accounts of noble saints were part of a program, developing both at court, and, increasingly, in the power centers of the northern aristocracy, to celebrate, justify, and promote the formation of a self-conscious Christian Frankish elite" (p. 176). Raymond Van Dam, "Images of Saint Martin in Late Roman and Early Merovingian Gaul," *Viator* 19 (1988), has noted that, "although Sulpicius and later writers had once tried to make Martin into a civilian saint by deemphasizing his long military service, the early Cluniacs regarded Saint Martin as the forerunner of the chivalrous knight, and by the time of the Crusades Saint Martin had reemerged as one prototype of the Christian soldier" (p. 26). See also Barbara Rosenwein, "St. Odo's St. Martin: The Uses of a Model," *Journal of Medieval History* 4 (1978): 317–31. Recent discussions of the sociohistorical significance of medieval hagiographical literature may be found in "The Sources," in Susan J. Ridyard, *The Royal Saints of Anglo-Saxon England: A Study of West Saxon and East Anglian Cults* (Cambridge: Cambridge University Press, 1988); Thomas J. Heffernan, *Sacred Biography: Saints and Their Biographers in the Middle Ages* (New York: Oxford University Press, 1988); Thomas Head, *Hagiography and the Cult of the Saints: The Diocese of Orléans, 800–1200,* Cambridge Studies in Medieval Life and Thought, no. 4 (Cambridge: Cambridge University Press, 1990); McNamara and Halborg, with Whatley, *Sainted Women of the Dark Ages;* and Julia M. H. Smith, "Early Medieval Hagiography in the Late Twentieth Century," *Early Medieval Europe* 1:1 (1992): 69–76.

[132] *Jesus Through the Centuries: His Place in the History of Culture* (New York: Harper & Row, 1985), p. 2. Just prior to this quotation, Pelikan provides a more complete reference to Schweitzer's position: "Would we not find it more accurate to substitute for the first century formula 'the same yesterday and today and forever' the twentieth-century words of Albert Schweitzer? 'Each successive epoch,' Schweitzer said, 'found its own thoughts in Jesus, which was, indeed, the only way in which it could make him live'; for typically, one 'created him in accordance with one's own character.' 'There is,' he concluded, 'no historical task which so reveals someone's true self as the writing of a Life of Jesus.' " Pelikan is providing here his own revised translation of Albert Schweitzer, *The Quest of the Historical Jesus,* trans. William Montgomery (New York: Macmillan, 1961), p. 4.

[133] Pelikan, *Jesus,* pp. 99–102. The complete text is: "Pange, lingua, gloriosi proelium certaminis et super crucis tropaeo dic triumphum nobilem, qualiter redemptor orbis immolatus vincerit." Of related interest is a suggestion of Pelikan's: "The ecclesiastical system of satisfac-

Having thus documented hagiographical and Christological examples of the Germanization process, and having previously attributed the development of the *Eigenkirchensystem* and *Eigenklostersystem* to the process of Germanization, this inquiry will now focus on the less obvious ideological dialectics which contributed toward this process. One may begin with the fundamental socio-politico-religious synergy that characterizes pre-Christian Germanic religiosity, and which may be a function of the high level of group solidarity present in early medieval Germanic society. In this society, religious cults and rituals expressed and advanced sociopolitical cohesion.

Walter Baetke has stressed the prevailing sociopolitical character of Indo-European religiosity in general:

> For the Indogermanic [Indo-European] peoples, the fundamental alliance between state and religion is attested to by history. . . . The oldest political order of Rome is grounded entirely in a sacred context. The cult of the gods was bound to the community. Similarly, we also find with the Germans that political unity is founded upon the cult of a particular deity. For the Greeks, Romans, and the Germanic peoples, the veneration of the gods was an absolute duty, the neglect of which constituted a crime against the state. This association between state and religion is considered to be normal and organic.[134]

---

tion, moreover, may have contained echoes of civil law as well, in which, according to the ancient Germanic requirement of *wergild,* one was obliged to make good for a crime in accordance with the standing of the injured party in society. Since in this case God was the injured party, only a *wergild* paid by one who was both God and man would have been adequate" (p. 108). The heroic Christ is discussed in greater detail in G. Ronald Murphy, *The Saxon Savior: The Germanic Transformation of the Gospel in the Ninth-Century Heliand* (New York: Oxford University Press, 1989), who concludes that the author of the *Heliand* "remained faithful to the orthodox Christian teaching of the Gospel, and yet in his contemplation of that Gospel imagined an almost unthinkably new and different form of Christianity, thereby transforming the Gospel into the traditional religious imagery and values of his people" (ibid., p. ix). The extent to which the *Heliand,* despite its Germanized setting, expresses the world-rejecting ethos of early Christianity, particularly in its treatment of the Beatitudes, has led Baetke, *Aufnahme,* pp. 27–36, and J. Knight Bostock, *Handbook on Old High German Literature,* 2nd ed., rev. by K. C. King and D. R. McLintock (Oxford: Clarendon Press, 1976), pp. 148–52, to reject it as an example of the Germanization of Christianity. However, despite its author's scrupulous attention to doctrinal and ethical orthodoxy, it is likely that to a doctrinally unsophisticated audience, the *Heliand's* thoroughly Germanized form and setting spoke louder than its orthodox content. If such were the case, the net effect may have been an assumption by its audience that Christian and Germanic world-views and value systems were compatible, if not identical.

[134] "Der Gemeinschaftcharakter der Religion," sect. 8 of "Das Phänomen des Heiligen: Eine religionswissenschaftliche Grundlegung," part 1 of *Das Heilige im Germanischen* (Tübingen: J. C. B. Mohr (Paul Siebeck), 1942), pp. 32–33 (my translation). Baetke also acknowledges a close relationship between the religious and political spheres of the ancient Egyptian and Babylonian cultures. Such a relationship in Hellenic Greece has been discussed by H. D. F. Kitto, *The Greeks* (Harmondsworth: Penguin Books, 1957), pp. 75–79, who remarks: "How intimately religious and 'political' thinking were connected we can best see from the *Oresteia* of Aeschylus. . . . It is the concern of the Olympian gods to defend Order; they are particularly the gods of the Polis" (p. 76). See also, Angela Della Volpe, "On Indo-European Ceremonial and

The reception of Christianity in the Mediterranean world might have been much the same as in the Germanic world, had it not been for the anomic, folk-dissolving effects of the Hellenistic transformation, which disrupted the intimate and stabilizing relationship between sociopolitical and religious spheres that had existed in the Greek polis and the Roman gens.[135] The consequential social destabilization and alienation enhanced the appeal of an alternative Christian community in which the criteria for membership were belief and behavior, rather than ethnocultural identity. Baetke has contrasted the Hellenistic and Germanic religiosities which Christianity encountered:

> It is not generally understood that Germanic religion had a totally different nature and structure than the Hellenistic gnosis. It was not a philosophical religion, but a national cult-religion, and as such, was what Augustine in his *City of God* termed a "political" religion, with a national way of life belonging to it, in contrast to a "mythical" or "natural" (or "philosophical") religion. . . . The Germanic gods were neither nature deities nor ethical ideals, but national gods like those of the Romans and the gods of the Greek polis. Germanic religion was a concern of the political community and was intimately associated with the legal, political, and social life. . . . It was from this religious perspective that the Germanic peoples came to terms with Christianity.[136]

The socio-politico-religious synergy within Germanic societies at the time of their encounter with Christianity, as just described by Baetke, is epitomized by the king's role in pre-Christian Germanic society.[137] Emphasizing this unity, William A. Chaney introduces a survey of Germanic kingship by stating that "the most fundamental concept in Germanic kingship is the indissolubility of its religious and political functions."[138] An

---

Socio-Political Elements Underlying the Origin of Formal Boundaries," *JIES* 20:1/2 (1992): 71–122.

[135] Baetke, *Aufnahme*, clarifies this: "Dort [among the Greeks] hatten die Mysterienkulte und die hellenistische Philosophie dem Christentum den Weg bereitet. Etwas Entsprechendes gab es in der germanischen Welt nicht" (p. 24).

[136] Baetke, *Aufnahme*, pp. 41–42 (my translation). Baetke further asserts: "The political perception of Christianity has been the primary reason for the alliance of the state with the Church. There exists a continuum from the Arian national churches and the Frankish imperial church, through the Christian Empire of the Middle Ages, to the Lutheran national, state, and regional churches. That is the Germanic constant in church history" (p. 51, my translation).

[137] Introductions to this subject include J. M. Wallace-Hadrill, *Early Germanic Kingship in England and on the Continent* (Oxford: Oxford University Press, 1971); and Henry A. Myers and Herwig Wolfram, *Medieval Kingship* (Chicago: Nelson-Hall, 1982).

[138] *The Cult of Kingship in Anglo-Saxon England: The Transition from Paganism to Christianity* (Berkeley: University of California Press, 1970), p. 11. The charismatic, sacral dimensions of Germanic kingship are the focus of Otto Höfler, "Der Sakralcharacter des germanischen Königtums," in *The Sacral Kingship: Contributions to the Central Theme of the VIIIth International Congress for the History of Religions (Rome, 1955),* Studies in the History of Religions, no. 4 (Leiden: E. J. Brill, 1959), pp. 664–701; Jan de Vries, "Das Königtum bei den Germanen," *Saeculum* 7 (1956): 289–309; Peter H. Sawyer and Ian N. Wood, eds., *Early Medie-*

appreciation of the nature and development of the institution of Germanic kingship is critical for an understanding of the reciprocal processes of Germanization and Christianization which occurred between 376 and 754, especially given the centrality of the Frankish kings in these processes.

Prior to the *Völkerwanderungszeit* (A.D. 375–568), it appears that the "Germanic peoples had two sorts of kings, one essentially religious, the other military."[139] Writing in A.D. 98, Tacitus wrote in chapter 7 of his *Germania:* "They choose their kings [*reges*] for their noble birth, their commanders [*duces*] for their valor."[140] This distinction, reminiscent of the bipolar tension attributed by Dumézil to the religious and political elements of the first function of Indo-European sovereignty,[141] has contributed to the hypothesis advanced by Jan de Vries and generally accepted by others that the sacral qualities of the *reges*—or in Gothic, the *thiudans*—were assimilated by the *duces*—or in Celto-Germanic, the *reiks*—because of the need for highly organized war confederations during the *Völkerwanderungszeit.*[142]

This social development was accompanied by a religious one. The *thiudans,* who "was apparently chosen from a royal family, that is a family with which the ethnic, historical, and cultural traditions of the tribe were most closely identified, . . . was closely associated to the Germanic (in fact, Indo-European) god Tiwaz, who was the protector of a stable social order and guarantor of laws, fertility, and peace."[143] Henry A. Myers and Herwig

---

val *Kingship* (Leeds: The School of History, University of Leeds, 1977); and recently and most relevant to the current inquiry, Miller, "Sacral Kingship, Biblical Kingship, and the Elevation of Pepin the Short." Appreciation is extended to David Harry Miller for providing a copy of the lecture notes for his course on the Franks, as well as an extensive current bibliography. One of the earliest records alluding to sacral leadership among the Germanic peoples is found in a description of the Gothic victory over the Romans during the reign of Domitian (A.D. 81–96), recorded in Jordanes, *Getica,* 78: "tum Gothi . . . magnaque potiti per loca victoria iam proceres suos, quorum quasi fortuna vincebant, non puros homines, sed semideos id est Ansis vocaverunt." This passage is reproduced in Goffart, "Jordanes and His Three Histories," in *Narrators of Barbarian History,* p. 76 n. 273, and is discussed there on pp. 76–79.

[139] Geary, *Before France and Germany,* p. 55.

[140] Cornelius Tacitus, *The Agricola and the Germania,* trans. with intro. by H. Mattingly, rev. by S. A. Handford (New York: Penguin Books, 1970), p. 107; original in Cornelius Tacitus, "De origine et situ Germanorum," ed. M. Winterbottom, in *Opera minora,* Oxford Classical Texts (Oxford: Oxford University Press, 1975), par. 7: "Reges ex nobilitate, duces ex virtute sumunt."

[141] See above, pp. 114, 116.

[142] Jan de Vries, "Das Königtum bei den Germanen," pp. 296–300, whose view is generally accepted by Chaney, *The Cult of Kingship in Anglo-Saxon England,* who notes: "However close to historical reality this ingenious hypothesis may be, it must lie indeed in the realm of prehistorical conjecture; nonetheless, when the light of history and tradition falls on Germanic kingship of the age of migrations, the king is leader of the war-hosts but also the charismatic mediator with the divine, the sacral holder of the tribal 'luck' " (p. 14). Meyers and Wolfram, *Medieval Kingship,* pp. 2–6, and Geary, *Before France and Germany,* pp. 55–56, 61–62, also appear in general agreement with de Vries's hypothesis.

[143] Geary, *Before France and Germany,* p. 55. The association of Tiwaz with fertility appears somewhat tenuous, at least from a Dumézilian perspective, according to which Tiwaz, or Tyr in Old Norse (not to be confused with the warrior-god Thor), and Odin were respectively

Wolfram have further described the socio-politico-religious function of the *thiudans:*

> The early Germanic *thiudans* personified the tribe in a very real way. His tribe saw in him the best man to please the gods of war and nature because of his *Heil,* that certain something about him the ancient deities liked. His tribe entrusted him with their very identity: the divine liking for him meant a greater probability of victory or survival in the face of calamity than tribesmen could hope for on their merits. . . . The immersion of tribal identity in such a man resulted in assurance that these virtues permeated the total tribal personality. In his possession of *Heil,* the *thiudans* swayed fate on the tribe's behalf, and as the living embodiment of the tribe in a single royal personage, he gave his people an enduring unity which was, of course, transmitted by blood through a royal house or dynasty.
>
> The royal role of personifier did not disappear when tribes became Christian, much larger, or both.[144]

The *reiks,* or "military king," in turn became a devotee of Odin, who in one of his aspects was the god of war.[145] The military kings and their tribes looked to Odin "as the giver of victory, and through victory, a new sort of religious justification for their position."[146] During the *Völkerwanderungszeit,* as the *reiks* type of kingship eclipsed the *thiudans* type, the former apparently incorporated the hereditary and charismatic qualities of the latter.[147] An individual example of this development may be found in the Visigothic king Alaric (d. 410), who seems to have begun his career "as a *reiks,* or as an elected warrior king by one name or the other," but "developed his position into that of a *thiudans,* or permanent tribal king, before his career was over."[148]

Regarding the amalgamation of the two forms of Germanic kingship, Meyers and Wolfram have commented on the "auspiciousness" of the Ostrogothic king Theodoric's name: " 'Theodoric' was only what Greeks and Romans made out of *Thiuda-reiks,* thus 'nation-king' and 'warrior-chief' in one person. The all-around luster of his name and descent [supposedly the sixteenth king of the Amal dynasty] was enough to attract a substantial Germanic following, not originally limited to Ostrogoths, who soon took

---

divine representatives of the juridical and magicoreligious aspects of the function of sovereignty (Georges Dumézil, *Mitra-Varuna,* trans. Derek Coltman [New York: Zone Books, 1988], pp. 113–28). Edgar C. Polomé, *Encyclopedia of Religions,* s.v. "Germanic Religion," has proposed that during the migration and postmigration periods, the fertility function was represented by Freyja and forms of *Ingw[az].

[144] *Medieval Kingship,* pp. 348–49.

[145] This and other aspects of Odin's complex character are discussed in de Vries, *Altgermanische Religionsgeschichte,* vol. 2, pp. 27–107; and E. O. G. Turville-Petre, *Myth and Religion of the North* (1964; reprint, Westport, Conn.: Greenwood Press, 1975), pp. 35–74.

[146] Geary, *Before France and Germany,* p. 61.

[147] Meyers and Wolfram, *Medieval Kingship,* pp. 5–6.

[148] Ibid., p. 66.

on an Ostrogothic identity."[149] Also contributing to the religious prestige
of the Germanic king may have been the apparent absence of an organized
priesthood.[150] A confluence of ascribed sacral attributes and achieved
military attributes occurred not only within the Arian Germanic kingdoms,
but also with the pagan Frankish kings, who considered themselves to be
Wotanic war-kings of divine descent.[151] The pre-Christian religious symbolism surrounding Clovis, Theodoric's Merovingian counterpart, has been
discussed by Miller:

> The Frankish Merovingian kings were Wotanic kings. The tomb of the
> Frankish king Childerich, at Tournai, contained a relic of surpassing inter-
> est, a large sculptured bull's head, covered in gold, and bearing between
> its horns a golden solar disk. The obvious implication is that Childerich
> was a devotee of a solar deity who had some cultic associations with the
> bull as a prime religious symbol. Wotan was, among other things, the All-
> Father figure in Germanic mythology, which means that he was the solar
> deity as well. . . . Thus, when Bishop Avitus of Vienne wrote to Clovis
> upon his baptism, congratulating him for having abandoned a claim to a
> false divine descent for a simple nobility, he was not merely engaging in
> rhetoric.[152]

The religiopolitical complementarity within Germanic societies, as expressed in the kingship function, endured throughout the Middle Ages.[153]
It may be considered the most significant long-term factor in the Germanization of early medieval Christianity.[154]

[149] Ibid., p. 70.

[150] After discussing the role of druids in Celtic society, Davidson, *Myths and Symbols in
Pagan Europe,* notes: "Much less is known about the Germanic and Scandinavian priesthood,
which seems never to have been as efficiently organised as were the druids. Julius Caesar em-
phasises this difference, and indicated that the priests and seers among the Germans had less
political influence. . . . In Iceland the chiefs undertook certain priestly duties, organising the
religious feasts and sometimes taking responsibility for shrines of the gods, although these
might be under the guardianship of particular families. The term *goði* used for a chief in Iceland
who represented his district at the Thing seems likely originally to have been a priestly title"
(pp. 157–58). See also the discussion of the existence of a priestly class in Germanic and Indo-
European societies in de Vries, *Altgermanische Religionsgeschichte,* vol. 1, pp. 397–400.

[151] Miller, "Sacral Kingship," pp. 133–34.

[152] Ibid.

[153] The ideological transformation of the kingship function into that of emperor is discussed in David Harry Miller, "The Roman Revolution of the Eighth Century," *Mediaeval
Studies* 36 (1974): 79–133. See especially the conclusion, pp. 132–33.

[154] Meyers and Wolfram, *Medieval Kingship,* note: "The conversion of Clovis to Trinitarian
Christianity proved historically to be of tremendous influence in making the Franks preeminent
in western Europe for centuries to come. Gregory's story of the event underscores at once a
variety of notions concerning kingship. On one hand, it sanctions the idea that the faith of the
king decides the faith of the people, a principle which was to live on after many transformations
into the seventeenth century as *Cuius regio eius religio.* Simultaneously it affirms the Old Testament and early Christian idea that the faith of the king determines how God is going to treat the
people. In the Middle Ages it became more nearly axiomatic than ever that a king strong in the
right faith meant victory and prosperity, while a religiously deviant king meant disaster" (p. 83).
For a further discussion of the complementarity of religious and political elements as they

In a metaphysical sense, the predominantly world-accepting, folk-centered world-view of the Germanic peoples may be viewed as antithetical to the predominantly world-rejecting, individualist, and soteriological world-view of early Christianity. It is not surprising to discover that the religiosity of a rural, agricultural-pastoral, world-accepting folk society was deeply attuned to the cycles of nature. In the resistance of such a society to the linear Christian temporality that is integral to salvation history, the deeper metaphysical disparity between the world-view of early Christianity and that of the Germanic peoples becomes apparent. Carol J. Greenhouse has summarized the views of Oscar Cullmann and Jacques Le Goff on this subject:

> The expansion of Christianity into Europe brought with it two ideas about time that had long roots in Jewish and autochthonous Christian tradition: first, the origin of time in Creation, and second, the end of time in a Day of Judgement. The linearity of time derives simply from the geometric connection between these two endpoints. These arrived as new ideas to Europe, and it is difficult to know how they affected ordinary people as they encountered them in the long process of Europe's conversion to Christianity.[155]

Appraising the impact of these new Christian temporal ideas on indigenous pre-Christian temporal ideas, Le Goff has suggested that throughout the Middle Ages the Christian sense of time remained subordinate to the cyclical rhythm of "natural time." He notes that "not only did most of the great religious feasts succeed to pagan feasts which themselves were in direct relation to the natural cycle of the year, but more especially the liturgical year was in agreement with the natural rhythm of agricultural tasks."[156]

An even greater pre-Christian impact is perceived by Peter Brown, who has noted that, in areas of Gaul, "the process of Christianization was brought to a standstill by the silent determination of human groups who would not alter the immemorial patterns of their working life to pay reverence to the saints, or to bend their habits to please yet another class of *domini*."[157] Brown concludes his study of the cult of the saints in late

---

developed in medieval kingship, see Ernst H. Kantorowicz, *The King's Two Bodies: A Study in Mediaeval Political Theology* (Princeton, N.J.: Princeton University Press, 1957).

[155] "Just in Time: Temporality and the Cultural Legitimation of Law," *Yale Law Journal* 98 (March 1989): 1634. See also Augustine, *De civitate Dei*, 12.14; Jacques Le Goff, "Merchant's Time and Church's Time in the Middle Ages," in *Time, Work and Culture in the Middle Ages*, trans. Arthur Goldhammer (Chicago: University of Chicago Press, 1980), pp. 29–42; Oscar Cullmann, *Christ and Time: The Primitive Christian Conception of Time and History*, trans. F. V. Filson (London: SCM Press, 1951); Gerhart B. Ladner, *The Idea of Reform: Its Impact on Christian Thought and Action in the Age of the Fathers* (New York: Harper & Row, 1967), pp. 10–16, 203–12, 222–38, 451–54; and idem, "The Impact of Christianity," in Lynn White, ed., *The Transformation of the Roman World: Gibbon's Problem after Two Centuries* (Berkeley: University of California Press, 1966), pp. 88–90.

[156] Le Goff, *Medieval Civilization*, p. 181.

[157] *The Cult of the Saints: Its Rise and Function in Latin Christianity* (Chicago: University of Chicago Press, 1981), p. 122.

antiquity by remarking upon the fundamental disparity between pre-Christian and Christian world-views:

> It seems to me that the most marked feature of the rise of the Christian church in western Europe was the imposition of human administrative structures and of an ideal *potentia* linked to invisible human beings and to their visible human representatives, the bishops of the towns, at the expense of the landscape itself. Saint Martin attacked those points at which the natural and the divine were held to meet: he cut down the sacred trees, and he broke up the processions that followed the immemorial lines between the arable and the nonarable. His successors fulminated against trees and fountains, and against forms of divination that gained access to the future through the close observation of the vagaries of animal and vegetable life. They imposed rhythms of work and leisure that ignored the slow turning of the sun, the moon, and the planets through the heavens, and that reflected, instead a purely human time, linked to the deaths of outstanding individuals. What is at stake behind the tired repetitions of antipagan polemic and the admonitions of the councils in sixth-century Gaul and Spain is nothing less than a conflict of views on the relation between man and nature.[158]

Although phrased in terms differing from the world-rejecting versus world-accepting paradigm of Robert Bellah, Brown's analysis of the effect of Christianization efforts illustrates the same fundamental distinction, that is, that "the most marked feature of the rise of the Christian church in western Europe" is essentially its world-rejecting world-view which interrupts the natural cyclic continuum with the notion of God acting in human history through prophets, in revelation, and in sending his Son as a redeemer to effect the salvation of the faithful before Judgement Day. This "salvation history" mentality runs directly counter to the traditional Indo-European and Germanic world-accepting, folk-centered world-view.

The disparity between Germanic and early Christian conceptions of time has been discussed in detail by Paul Bauschatz, whose central thesis is that "Germanic culture was dominated by its conception of its own past."[159] When representatives from an eschatological, otherworldly, future-oriented, Christian society confronted members of a past-oriented, this-worldly Germanic society, offering salvation from a world from which the Germanic peoples did not desire to be saved, fundamental problems were inevitable. Bauschatz has considered the substantial conceptual difficulties which may have arisen from the attempt by the Germanic peoples to resolve the novelty and disparity of Christian temporality with the traditional Germanic temporality:

> The temporal reorientation toward the future, which the Christian conception stresses so strongly, involved a 180-degree wrench away from the past toward a future that did not even exist prior to Christianization. The doctrine

---

[158] Ibid., pp. 124–25.

[159] *The Well and the Tree: World and Time in Early Germanic Culture* (Amherst: University of Massachusetts Press, 1982), p. ix.

of salvation and the idea of a closed, fixed eternity must also have been difficult. Sin, repentance, and absolution must have seemed very strange at first. Repentance and absolution involve a moment in which the sins of the past are confronted, repented of, and, in effect, washed away. The absolved individual at this moment enters a state of grace; the past disappears, and he is born anew. How the Germanic peoples must have struggled with the idea that the past could ever disappear! . . . Finally, *wyrd*, the term for the power of the past upon the present, lingers on long after Christianization. It alone of early Germanic concepts seems to have been so firmly rooted in the consciousness and language of the people that the religious and temporal reorientation did not supplant it quickly or easily.[160]

Bauschatz thus makes clear the existence of deep-rooted and complex problems associated with the attempted Christianization of the Germanic peoples.

The disparity between Germanic and early Christian world-views is also reflected in their conceptions of history. This may be observed more clearly if one momentarily moves beyond the *Merowingerzeit* to the thirteenth century to compare the allegorical and moralistic orientation of Augustinian salvation history as epitomized by *De civitate Dei*, with the far more objective Germanic depiction of historical events in the *Nibelungenlied* and the Icelandic sagas. In these latter works, which represent the epic literature of societies in which Christianity appears to have been Germanized, it seems that neither the Christian historical vision of the Creation and Last Judgment as historical endpoints bisected by the Resurrection, nor the notion of a providential force acting in secular history, was substantially incorporated. As Frederick P. Pickering has observed: "These 13th cent. works recognize no pattern of history other than that inherent in the events they treat. . . . No City ('civitas') of this world or the next arises from the devastation, there is no promise of a better future. . . . The sagas reflect a conception of history in which a fall, original sin or guilt, redemption and salvation play no role."[161] Similarly, of *Beowulf,* the *Nibelungenlied,* and the *Chanson de Roland,* John Simpson has concluded that "the actions of the warriors in the poems, of those of them with ethical integrity, are predicated upon the ethical commitments of the Indo-European, and more specifically, Germanic heroic warrior. . . . [T]he ethic of the heroic warrior is the fundamental and pervasive motif and the most vital unifying

---

[160] Ibid., p. 154. Bauschatz's criteria for Christianization are evidently less rigorous than those applied herein.

[161] "Historical Thought and Moral Codes in Medieval Epic," in Harald Scholler, ed., *The Epic in Medieval Society,* pp. 8–9. Pickering locates the reemergence of salvation history in the High Middle Ages, with one of its first exponents being Joachim of Fiore (d. 1202), whose millenarist and reformist writings gained widespread popularity and ignited substantial controversy in the thirteenth century, particularly in relation to their adaptation by elements of the Spiritual Franciscans. Additional information on the Joachimite phenomenon and associated forms of salvation history may be found in Bernard McGinn, "Apocalypticism in the Middle Ages: An Historiographical Approach," *Mediaeval Studies* 37 (1975): 252–86.

theme."[162] Just as the Christian Church was a novelty in the classical and Germanic worlds, and not a replacement for an indigenous institution, so the Christian world-view of sin, redemption, and salvation history was not merely a slight modification of an existing belief system, but a totally new way of perceiving reality from an otherworldly perspective.[163]

Because of the complexity of the Christianization process, references to Christianization within this inquiry will continue to be qualified as "attempted." To use the word "Christianization" unqualifiedly would imply that the substantial conceptual problems discussed above were resolved by the time a people was described as Christianized, but this was usually not the case. A more rigorist usage of the words "Christianization" and "Christian" in historical studies is not common, although it might be helpful in delineating more precisely the nature of the religious transformation which occurred as a result of the encounter of non-Christian peoples with Christianity. Part of the complexity is due to the fact that Christianity was more than just a new cult. If it had been merely a new cult, Christianization would have involved only the transferral of allegiance and devotion to a new deity. Indeed this is what is likely to have been the initial response of those among the Germanic peoples who viewed Christ as a powerful new god to be incorporated into their pantheon. But this cannot be considered Christianization in the proper sense. Instead, it constitutes a fundamental folk-religious reinterpretation of Christianity, and may more properly be described as a syncretic development.[164]

As noted in chapter 3, our own locus within a Christian religious milieu may cause us to wrongly assume that "all forms of religion have one common structure; so a person's shift of allegiance toward Christianity need

[162] John Simpson, "Comparative Structural Analysis of Three Ethical Questions in *Beowulf,* the *Nibelungenlied,* and the *Chanson de Roland," JIES* 3 (1975): 253.

[163] Gerhart B. Ladner, "The Impact of Christianity," asserts that Gibbon, "great historian though he was, did not fully understand the new dimensions that the concepts of time and history had received in Christian thought through the coming of Christ and the phenomenon of the Church," (p. 67), and states that "the Christian view of time . . . was not only a *novum* in the world into which Christianity entered, but also continued to be of great importance for the civilization shaped by the Christian religion, and quite especially for western civilization" (p. 88). A detailed discussion of the notions of time and history in non-Christian and pre-Christian societies may be found in Mircea Eliade, *The Myth of the Eternal Return or, Cosmos and History,* trans. Willard R. Trask (Princeton, N.J.: Princeton University Press, 1954), who notes that "Christianity translates the periodic regeneration of the world into a regeneration of the human individual" (p. 129). One area in which cyclical time may have retained an influence is the liturgical year, as is indicated ibid., p. 130, and as implied in ch. 1, "Cosmic Time and Human Life," in Adolf Adam, *The Liturgical Year: Its History and Its Meaning after the Reform of the Liturgy,* trans. Matthew J. O'Connell (New York: Pueblo, 1981).

[164] Given the imprecision and disparaging connotation associated with the term, the exercise of some caution is appropriate when describing a religious development as "syncretic." *The Encyclopedia of Religion,* s.v. "Syncretism," by Carsten Colpe, trans. Matthew J. O'Connell, provides an important detailed analysis of the many uses of the term and describes it as "always a transitional phase." Further discussion of the nature of the transformation of Christianity which occurred as a result of its encounter with the Germanic peoples will follow in the Conclusion.

have involved only the exchange of one theology or theodicy or liturgy or system of morals for some other that was seen as preferable," or we may just as wrongly assume that "religion means doctrine."[165] However, as a universal, prophetic religion, Christianity requires more from its converts than intercessory appeals for solutions to worldly problems. It demands ethical conformity and doctrinal belief, two dimensions which are largely absent from most folk religions. In his discussion of Karl Kerényi's approach to Greek and Roman religion, Johannes Kleinstück observes that:

> Religion [in the Roman sense] is first and foremost a set of rules observed by human beings when dealing with the divine; it implies activity, a way to behave—cult. . . . It is probably due to a long tradition of Christian thinking that some people assume belief to be the essence of all religions, including the pagan ones. This, however, is a mistake, and again philology comes in to correct it. Christian belief is *pistis* or *fides,* "faith," implying trust; it consists in the soul's trustful surrender to the will of God who is true and therefore trustworthy, who is indeed, truth's very self. Both faith and trust are continually exposed to the danger of being undermined by doubt, and doubt may slip off into despair, which can only be overcome by the grace of God. No pagan Greek or Roman ever held that kind of blind belief.[166]

Neither did the pre-Christian Germanic peoples.

The initial result of attracting members of a folk religion to Christianity is often the reinterpretation of Christianity as a folk religion which focuses on the same worldly needs and desires which had previously been addressed by the supernatural forces associated with the pre-Christian folk religion. A liturgical example of such a Germanic folk-religious reinterpretation of Christianity was the popularization of supplementary Masses offered for personal intentions, known as "private" or "votive" Masses. Architectural evidence of their growth in popularity may be derived from the increase in the number of "side altars" which were constructed in churches as the Middle Ages progressed. Commenting upon the views of Cyrille Vogel toward the medieval popularity of the private Mass, William G. Storey and Niels Krogh Rasmussen have noted: "For Vogel in particular, this 'sacerdotalization' of the entire mass is due to a basic changeover in religious and liturgical psychology—radically different from that of the early church. The mass has become a good work, 'which takes its place among the other ascetical exercises through which the religious sanctify themselves.' "[167] Storey and Rasmussen note further: "It is undeniable that there is a difference in the theology of Church, Orders, and Eucharist

---

[165] See above, p. 48, citing MacMullen, *Christianizing the Roman Empire,* p. 8.

[166] "Kerényi's Humanistic Approach to Ancient Religion," in Edgar C. Polomé, *Essays in Memory of Karl Kerényi, JIES* Monograph Series, no. 4 (Washington, D.C.: Institute for the Study of Man, 1984), pp. 70–71.

[167] *Medieval Liturgy: An Introduction to the Sources,* trans. and rev. William Storey and Niels Rasmussen (Washington, D. C.: Pastoral Press, 1986), p. 156.

between that of the early Church and that of the medieval Church. . . . Without such a change in Eucharistic understanding the actual practice of the early Middle Ages would be unthinkable—the piling up of masses and the 'offering of the sacrifice for' so many reasons."[168]

A conjectural account of the reinterpretive process by which Christianity acquired folk-religious characteristics has been proposed by C. E. Stancliffe in an article on the Christianization of the Touraine during the fifth through seventh centuries. After discussing the fundamental differences between natural and prophetic religions generally, and between "indigenous Gallic paganism" and Christianity particularly, Stancliffe succinctly describes the choices which confronted Christian missionaries:

> To a farmer who was accustomed, for instance, to carrying images of the gods around his very own fields in order to ensure the success of his crops, Christianity could all too easily have appeared distant and irrelevant. One might characterize the situation by saying there was, at best, a certain lack of coincidence between a pagan peasant's expectations of religion on the one hand, and Christianity on the other.
>
> Given this situation, there seem to me to be theoretically two approaches to the task of converting the countryside. One option would be to continue to preach the gospel as a prophetic religion; to insist that Christianity is essentially about entering into a relationship with God, and that becoming a Christian necessitates making an absolute break with one's pagan past. . . . The alternative to this forthright proclamation of the gospel would be to try and build a bridge between religion as a pagan understood it, and Christianity. Here the Christian God would be presented as the true source of the health and prosperity for which the peasant had formerly looked to pagan deities. In such ways one would try and widen the church's reach to embrace everyone, on the grounds that once they had become members of the church, there would be greater opportunities for educating them gradually in the true nature of Christianity.[169]

It appears that from the "lack of coincidence" between the this-worldly concerns of the pagans and the otherworldly Christian promise of salvation, there emerged a Christianization methodology of accommodation and gradualism. This methodology is exemplified in the miracle stories about St. Martin of Tours, written or edited by Gregory of Tours, which address the most common pagan concerns: the restoration of personal health and the avoidance of adverse weather conditions.[170] In short, "the church tried

---

[168] Ibid., p. 158.

[169] "From Town to Country: The Christianisation of the Touraine, 370–600," in *The Church in Town and Countryside,* ed. Derek Baker, SCH, no. 16 (Oxford: Blackwell, 1979), pp. 54–55. Of related interest in the same volume is I. N. Wood, "Early Merovingian Devotion in Town and Country," pp. 61–76.

[170] These stories are collected in Gregory's *Libri de virtutibus S. Martini episcopi,* ed. Wilhelm Arndt and Bruno Krusch, *MGH SRM,* vol. 1, part 2 (Hanover: Hahn Verlag, 1885). An important comparative study of the varying images of St. Martin from the fourth through sixth

to fit Christianity to the sort of religious demands which peasants would make on it: it stressed the efficacy of Christian saints and their relics to achieve those results for which peasants had formerly looked to their pagan gods."[171] The results of this policy were "far from ideal."[172] As Stancliffe concludes: "The point is, that if one seeks to embrace everyone within the church, and does not demand too great a reorientation of life and attitudes of those who come seeking baptism, then one must attempt to teach them gradually the true meaning of the religious commitment they have taken upon themselves; otherwise, there is little point in pretending they are Christians. It was here that the Merovingian church failed so dismally. One searches through the sixth-century synods in vain for demands that priests should teach the people about Christianity."[173] Unfortunately, from the perspective of establishing a doctrinally and ethically orthodox Christianity, the catechumenate system of religious instruction, which might have facilitated a gradual reorientation of the Germanic world-view toward a Christian world-view, no longer functioned in the *Merowingerzeit*. Even if it had, one wonders how successful it would have been, given the vitality of the Germanic world-view.

---

centuries, as portrayed in the successive works of Sulpicius Severus, Paulinus of Périgueux, Fortunatus, and Gregory of Tours, is Raymond Van Dam, "Images of Saint Martin in Late Roman and Early Merovingian Gaul." Additional recent research on St. Martin includes idem, *Leadership and Community in Late Antique Gaul* (Berkeley: University of California Press, 1985), and C. E. Stancliffe, *St. Martin and His Hagiographer: History and Miracle in Sulpicius Severus* (Oxford: Oxford University Press, 1983).

[171] Stancliffe, "From Town to Country," p. 58.
[172] Ibid.
[173] Ibid., pp. 58–59.

7

Germanization and Christianization: 678–754

As in the preceding chapter, the purpose here is to examine those develop-ments which seem to most clearly reveal the operation of the processes of Germanization and Christianization. It is during this period of the Anglo-Saxon missions, from St. Wilfrid's visit to Frisia in 678 through St. Boniface's martyrdom there in 754, that the conversion of the Germanic peoples is often thought to have been completed. However, it will be shown that the form of Christianity which emerges from this period is a substantially Germanized one. Some of the factors which contributed to this result were the development of a missionary policy of accommodation and gradualism, the decline of the catechumenate system of religious formation, the vitality of pre-Christian Germanic religiosity, and the papacy's growing depend-ence upon Frankish military power.

The Anglo-Saxon missionary "school," of which St. Boniface is the most prominent member, may trace its origins to Pope Gregory the Great. It was he who initiated Anglo-Saxon Christianization efforts when he sent St. Augustine of Canterbury, the abbot of St. Andrew's monastery in Rome, and several fellow monks[1] to Britain in 596. In fact, the notion of "mission," as currently understood, is primarily derived from its "Gregorian" imple-mentation. Prior to Gregory, Christianity expanded primarily by a gradual process of diffusion throughout the Roman Empire. This diffusion occurred

---

[1] St. Andrew's monastery had formerly been Gregory's family mansion. He himself had been a monk there for several years. Although it was asserted by Alfons M. Zimmermann, *Kalendarium Benedictum*, vol. 1 (Metten: Verlag der Abtei Metten, 1933), 53ff., cited in Gerhart B. Ladner, *The Idea of Reform: Its Impact on Christian Thought and Action in the Age of the Fathers* (New York: Harper & Row, 1959), p. 400 n. 60, that Augustine of Canterbury was a Benedictine monk, Ladner suggests that "it is at least equally probable" that the way of life at St. Andrew's was that of the Roman basilicas." It is significant that Gregory chose monks for this endeavor, since they were to predominate in the missionary efforts of the next two centuries. Augustine's mission was not, however, the first instance of monks pursuing missionary activities. St. Columbanus founded the monasteries of Luxeuil in Gall and Bobbio in Italy, and was active in evangelization efforts in Gall in 591.

through Jewish and Hellenistic communities, through public attention to the acts of the martyrs, through merchants and travelers, and through the "underprivileged of the Greco-Roman world to whom the Christian message of salvation for all without distinction of race, condition, or sex would carry conviction."[2]

A primary reason that no missionary efforts had been made to the northern provinces of the empire prior to Gregory was the generally negative attitude of the Romans toward the Germanic peoples. This attitude prevailed even among Roman Christian apologists until the pontificate of Gregory the Great, who was probably "the first among great Roman leaders who greatly appreciated barbarians as human beings."[3] It is likely that Gregory's missionary initiative was also at least partially motivated by an apocalyptic vision of his era. Gregory appears to have perceived the political calamities of his age as eschatological indicators. Time was running out for people to be saved, and thus a rationale for administering baptism without prior catechetical formation may have been implicitly established. In a letter to King Æthelbert of Kent, Gregory writes: "We would also have Your Majesty know what we have learned from the words of Almighty God in holy Scripture, that the end of this present world is at hand and the everlasting kingdom of the Saints is approaching. When the end of the world is near, unprecedented things occur. . . . Not all these things will happen during our own lifetimes, but will ensue in due course. . . . I have mentioned these matters in this short letter, my illustrious son, in the hope that as the Christian faith grows more strong in your kingdom, our correspondence with you may become more frequent. So my pleasure in addressing you will keep pace with the joy in my heart at the glad news of the complete conversion of your people."[4]

---

[2] W. H. C. Frend, "The Missions of the Early Church: 180–700 A.D.," in Derek Baker, ed., *Miscellanea Historiae Ecclesiasticae,* vol. 3 (Louvain: Publications Universitaires de Louvain, 1970), p. 6. Frend notes (p. 3) that Karl Holl felt that "the early Church lacked a specific calling of missionary," and that Holl, in his *Gesammelte Aufsätze zur Kirchengeschichte,* vol. 3 (1928; reprint, Darmstadt: Wissenschaftliche Buchgesellschaft, 1965), pp. 121–22, had concluded that "the early Church conducted no obvious or planned propagation of the word." A more extensive analysis of Christian expansion until the death of Gregory the Great is contained in Frend, *The Rise of Christianity* (London: Darton, Longman and Todd, 1984).

[3] Gerhart B. Ladner, "On Roman Attitudes Toward Barbarians in Late Antiquity," *Viator* 7 (1976): 25. Ladner notes that Gregory was "the most effective transmitter to the new peoples of the West of the theological heritage of the Fathers and of the monastic tradition, in the forms which they had received from Saint Augustine and Saint Benedict" (ibid.). The Augustinian notion of predestination, with its corollary that the "elect" may include Anglo-Saxons among their numbers, may have contributed toward Gregory's missionary plans.

[4] Beda Venerabilis, *Historia Ecclesiastica, PL,* vol. 95, book 1, ch. 32, subsequently referred to as Bede, *HE;* the English translation is taken from Bede, *A History of the English Church and People,* trans. and intro. Leo Sherley-Price, rev. R. E. Latham (1955; Harmondsworth: Penguin Books Ltd., 1968), p. 90, subsequently referred to as Sherley-Price. While Sherley-Price believes that this eschatological comment refers to "the current expectation that the end of the world would come in the year A.D. 1000" (p. 340), G. R. Evans, *The Thought of*

Since Boniface shared in the Gregorian missionary tradition, it is valuable to note Gregory's own thoughts on the methodology of Christianization. Fortunately, the contents of Gregory's letters of advice to Augustine and his associate, Abbot Mellitus, as well as to King Æthelbert, have been preserved by Bede in his *History of the English Church and People.*[5] An apparent contradiction exists between the Christianization methodology contained in Gregory's letter to Æthelbert[6] and that in his letter to Mellitus.[7] In his letter to Æthelbert, Gregory urges him to "press on with the task of extending the Christian Faith among the people committed to your charge," and to "make their conversion your first concern; suppress the worship of idols, and *destroy their shrines [fanorum aedificia everta]*."[8] In an apparently subsequent letter to Mellitus, who was in Gaul en route to Britain, Gregory requested:

> When by God's help you reach our most reverend brother, Bishop Augustine, we wish you to inform him that *we have been giving careful thought to the affairs of the English,* and have come to the conclusion that *the temples of the idols among the people should on no account be destroyed [fana idolorum destrui in eadem gente minime debeant].* The idols are to be destroyed, but the temples themselves are to be aspersed with holy water, altars set up in them, and relics deposited there. For if these temples are well-built, they must be purified from the worship of demons and dedicated to the service of the true God. In this way, we hope that the people, seeing that their temples are not destroyed, may abandon their error and, flocking more readily to their accustomed resorts, may come to know and adore the true God. And since they have a custom of sacrificing many oxen to demons, let some other solemnity be substituted in its place, such

---

Gregory the Great (Cambridge: Cambridge University Press, 1986), in her discussion of Gregory's attitude toward prophecy, has stated: "When Gregory became Pope he expected the end of the world to come at any time. When he answered letters or gave advice, he did so on that assumption. . . . The imminence of the end seemed to him a reason, not to relax, but to strive harder on behalf of the Church in her hour of glory. . . . The world is in crisis, but the Church, paradoxically, is coming to her highest triumph in the Last Judgement. . . . This new strong sense of an end to all things coming close governs his thinking in all his work for church and state" (p. 43).

[5] A more complete version of Gregory's correspondence than that contained in *HE,* may be found in *Gregorii I papae Registrum Epistolarum,* 11.9, ed. Paul Ewald and Ludwig M. Hartmann, *MGH Epistolae,* vols. 1 and 2 (Berlin: Weidmannsche Buchhandlung, 1899), hereinafter referred to as Gregory, *Epistolae.* Discussions of the authenticity of the Anglo-Saxon correspondence, particularly Gregory's detailed reply to Augustine's inquiries contained in *HE,* 1.27 (*Epistolae,* 11.56ª) are found in Suso Brechter, *Die Quellen zur Angelsachsenmission Gregors des Großen* (Münster: Aschendorff, 1941), who rejects its authenticity, and in Paul Grosjean and Margaret Deanesley, "The Canterbury Edition of the Answers of Pope Gregory I to St. Augustine," *JEH* 10 (1959): 1–49, R. A. Markus, "The Chronology of the Gregorian Mission to England: Bede's Narrative and Gregory's Correspondence," *JEH* 14 (1963): 16–30, and J. M. Wallace-Hadrill, "Rome and the Early English Church: Some Questions of Transmission," in *Early Medieval History* (Oxford: Basil Blackwell, 1975), who generally affirm its authenticity.

[6] Bede, *HE,* 1. 30.

[7] Bede, *HE,* 1. 32.

[8] Bede, *HE,* 1. 32; Sherley-Price, p. 89 (emphasis added).

as a day of Dedication or the Festivals of the holy martyrs whose relics are enshrined there. They are no longer to sacrifice beasts to the Devil, but they may kill them for food to the praise of God, and give thanks to the Giver of all gifts for the worldly plenty they enjoy. If the people are allowed some worldly pleasures in this way, they will more readily come to desire the joys of the spirit. For it is certainly impossible to eradicate all errors from obstinate minds at one stroke, and *whoever wishes to climb to a mountain top climbs gradually step by step, and not in one leap.* It was in this way that the Lord revealed Himself to the Israelite people in Egypt, permitting the sacrifices formerly offered to the Devil to be offered thenceforward to Himself instead. So He bade them sacrifice beasts to Him, so that, *once they became enlightened, they might abandon one element of sacrifice and retain another.* For, while they were to offer the same beasts as before, they were to offer them to God instead of to idols, so that they would no longer be offering the same sacrifices. Of your kindness, you are to inform our brother Augustine of this policy, so that he may consider how he may best implement it on the spot.[9]

From a recent comparative examination of these letters, R. A. Markus has determined that, although Gregory's letter to Mellitus (urging temple preservation) precedes his letter to King Æthelbert (urging temple destruction) in Bede's *History,* "it [the letter to Mellitus] was written almost exactly a month after the letter to the king."[10] In his earlier June letter to Æthelbert, Gregory is probably responding to initial reports of Augustine's success in Britain and is seeking to encourage greater support from Æthelbert for missionary activities. Gregory's advocacy of the destruction of pagan

---

[9] Bede, *HE,* 1. 30; Sherley-Price, pp. 86–87 (emphases added). The interpolated Latin text is taken from Bertram Colgrave and R. A. B. Mynors, eds., *Bede's Ecclesiastical History of the English People* (Oxford: Clarendon Press, 1969), p. 106. As to the implementation of this policy, Gale R. Owen, *Rites and Religions of the Anglo-Saxons* (New York: Dorset Press, 1985), p. 131, has suggested that the church of St. Pancras in Canterbury was built on the site of a pagan temple belonging to Æthelbert and that this site was rededicated by Augustine. While noting that "the ritual sacrifice of oxen is a feature of Anglo-Saxon paganism evidenced repeatedly by archaeology," she mentions that "in the early fourteenth century ox-heads were found at the south side of St. Paul's Cathedral in London" (p. 45). The general reluctance of Christians in pre-Gregorian times to transform pagan temples into Christian churches is discussed in Richard P. C. Hanson, "The Transformation of Pagan Temples into Christian Churches in the Early Christian Centuries," in idem, ed., *Studies in Christian Antiquity* (Edinburgh: T. & T. Clark, 1985), pp. 347–58, where he states: "It is *a priori* unlikely that in the first flush of their triumph over paganism the Christians should have taken over and merely reconsecrated with few alterations pagan temples wholesale, for they regarded these temples as the abodes of filthy devils, inveterate enemies of Christianity. Christians would naturally avoid such places. . . . That the first impulse of Christians was to pull down and destroy pagan temples, and that this was the earliest policy followed toward them, there can be no doubt" (pp. 347–48). However, Hanson acknowledges that "the original *temenos* area might be preserved" (ibid.). See also F. W. Deichmann, "Frühchristliche Kirchen in antiken Heiligtümern," *Jahrbuch des Deutschen Archäologischen Instituts* 54 (1939): 105–36.

[10] R. A. Markus, "Gregory the Great and a Papal Missionary Strategy," in G. J. Cuming, ed., *The Mission of the Church and the Propagation of the Faith,* SCH, vol. 6 (Cambridge: Cambridge University Press, 1970), p. 35.

temples is consistent with his general policy toward pagans elsewhere—a policy according to which "coercion by the available authorities was an unquestioned prop of the Gospel, and the prototype was ready to hand in the image of Constantine and the establishment of the Christian Roman Empire."[11] Markus conjectures that during the next few weeks Gregory became more aware of the "entrenched strength of English paganism" and began to empathize with Æthelbert's reluctance to proceed too quickly.[12] The results of this reflection are noted in the more conciliatory tone and contents of Gregory's later July letter to Mellitus, asking him to tell Augustine not to destroy the pagan temples but to adapt them to Christian worship.

Gregory's letter to Mellitus marks "a real turning point in the development of papal missionary strategy."[13] Whereas there had previously been an "almost unquestioned policy of reliance on coercion by the secular authorities,"[14] there now existed a policy of accommodation, backed up by less overt political pressure. Although Markus views this as a strategy replacing coercion, it might also be viewed as an additional tactic in an overall missionary strategy which did not exclude coercion in circumstances where it was deemed appropriate.[15] The general missionary policy of Gregory, and later Boniface, may be summarized as "that which cannot be supplanted by preaching or coercion, may be accommodated."[16]

[11] Ibid., p. 34.

[12] Ibid., p. 36.

[13] Ibid., p. 37. J. N. Hillgarth, *Christianity and Paganism, 350–750: The Conversion of Western Europe* (rev. ed. of *The Conversion of Western Europe, 350–750*) (Philadelphia: University of Pennsylvania Press, 1986), notes: "Gregory's advice that pagan temples should be turned into churches—though not always followed in England, where many temples were destroyed—canonized general practice. But the way Gregory in Rome could envisage conditions in England is remarkable" (p. 150).

[14] Markus, "Gregory the Great and a Papal Missionary Strategy," p. 37.

[15] It would be difficult to document papal displeasure at the implementation of coercive Christianization tactics toward pagans by Christian secular leaders. Christian missionaries often viewed Frankish military victories as opportunities for evangelization. Conversely, victims of Frankish expansionism, particularly the Saxons, often associated Christianity with Frankish political domination. An extreme example of papal approval for Frankish expansion is cited by J. M. Wallace-Hadrill, *The Barbarian West, 400–1000: The Early Middle Ages* (New York: Harper & Row, 1962), where he recalls that following Charlemagne's victory over the Saxons at Verden in 782 and his massacre of 4500 pagan Saxon prisoners, he received a letter from Pope Hadrian I announcing "three days of thanksgiving for this great Christian victory" (p. 103).

[16] This is suggested by the observation of David Keep, "Cultural Conflicts in the Missions of St. Boniface," in Stuart Mews, ed., *Religion and National Identity,* SCH, no. 18 (Oxford: Basil Blackwell, 1982): "Many of our modern christmas customs have their origin in local pre-christian midwinter festivities. The church was unable to suppress them, so found it more expedient to blend them subtly into its cult" (p. 50). The same observation was made by Carl Erdmann, *The Origin of the Idea of Crusade,* and is cited in the previous chapter, pp. 167–68, regarding the Church's view of the morality of war: "The German mentality also exercised a positive influence upon the development of the ecclesiastical morality of war. When the church encountered pagan elements that it could not suppress, it tended to give them a Christian dimension, thereby assimilating them. This happened to the ethics of heroism."

As Gregory indicated, concessions toward pagan practice were intended to be only of a temporary nature, so that "once they [the newly baptized Anglo-Saxons] became enlightened, they might abandon one element of sacrifice and retain another."[17] Commenting on this stipulation, D. H. Green notes: "Such an attitude of prudent accommodation is of course far removed from actual approval. When Gregory advises Mellitus not to forbid outright the pagan practice of sacrificing oxen and of ritual feasting, this is clearly not because he has any respect for the ceremony in which the pagan celebrants offered their cattle as sacrifice to the gods, but simply because he hopes to convert this old-established practice to new ends (i.e. a feast in praise of God as the giver of all gifts) and even eventually to abandon it altogether."[18] However, with such a strategy of temporary accommodation there is always a danger of long-term syncretism. This is particularly likely in cases such as that of the Germanic peoples in the seventh and eighth centuries, where a thorough and ongoing catechetical corrective to the accommodated form of Christianity was not provided.[19] As stated at the close of the previous chapter, given the vitality of Germanic religiosity at this time, one may only speculate whether post-baptismal catechesis would have produced significant results—or might even have proved counterproductive by alienating those who had no interest in the soteriological-eschatological core of Christianity. Instead, a Germanic interpretation of Christianity was gradually syncretized with Christian concepts of sin and salvation over the succeeding centuries. The gradual nature of this process contributed toward its general imperceptibility within early medieval society.

Gregory's letter to Mellitus is also significant in its Old Testament analogy. The redirection of sacrifice from idols to God is descriptive of the effect that Gregory's missionary policy had upon the Anglo-Saxons and upon their continental Germanic brethren. The worldly, magicoreligious, heroic, folk religiosity of the pre-Christian Germanic peoples was transferred from Odin, Tiwaz, Thor, and Freyja, and the shrines and amulets dedicated to them, to Christus Victor, his loyal saints, and their shrines and relics. Whether Gregory intended this transferral of devotion as a first step toward a fuller ethical and doctrinal acceptance of Christianity in its traditional soteriological form, or whether he felt that this transferral of devotion was all that could reasonably be hoped for given the circumstances,

---

[17] Bede, *HE,* 1.30; Sherley-Price, p. 87.

[18] *The Carolingian Lord: Semantic Studies on Four Old High German Words: Balder, Frô, Truhtin, Hêrro* (Cambridge: Cambridge University Press, 1965), p. 320.

[19] After claiming that the medieval era "contented itself too easily with religious usage and paid too little attention to the religious formation of the mind, knowledge and the understanding," and hence contributed to the success of the Reformation, Josef A. Jungmann, *Handing on the Faith: A Manual of Catechetics,* trans. A. N. Fuerst (Freiburg: Herder and Herder, 1959), p. 19, suggests that the real catechetical instruction of the European populace came about as a result of the Reformation and Counter-Reformation.

is not explicitly stated in this letter or in his other correspondence. However, given the depth to which a worldly, heroic, magicoreligious religiosity was rooted within the world-accepting, folk-centered Germanic worldview, the general result of this policy of accommodation or "inculturation," whether intended or not,[20] was the emergence of a worldly, heroic, magicoreligious, folk-centered Christianity. The magicoreligious reinterpretation of Christianity may be considered the most immediate and salient effect of its Germanization,[21] while the folk-centered religiopolitical reinterpretation of Christianity may be considered its most enduring effect.[22] This

[20] In her comprehensive study *The Rise of Magic in Early Medieval Europe* (Princeton, N.J.: Princeton University Press, 1991), Valerie I. J. Flint argues that "some, at least, of the wiser spirits within the early medieval Christian Church were alerted to the benefits of the emotional charge certain sorts of magic offered and tried hard to nourish and encourage this form of energy; and they were alerted (again perhaps to a greater degree than some of their successors) to the advantages the accommodation of non-Christian magical practices afforded in the matter of the peaceful penetration of societies very different than their own" (p. 4). See also Pamela Berger, *The Goddess Obscured: Transformation of the Grain Protectress from Goddess to Saint* (Boston: Beacon Press, 1985), which discusses the transferral of magicoreligious attributes to Saints Radegunde, Macrina, Walpurga, Milburga, and Brigid.

[21] This is not a claim of exclusivity. Christian missionary efforts among non-Germanic peoples have also resulted in local magicoreligious and religiopolitical reinterpretations of Christianity. However, Germanic religiopolitical influence in Rome in the tenth and eleventh centuries contributed significantly toward causing this and other aspects of Germanization to eventually spread throughout the Western Church.

[22] The religiopolitical reinterpretation of Christianity has been discussed by Henry A. Myers and Herwig Wolfram, *Medieval Kingship* (Chicago: Nelson-Hall, 1982), who state that: "The Franks were given their first official designation as the people of God (*populus Dei*) in a document of Pippin the Short's brother, Karlomann, in 742. The phrase stuck: its meaning was to become that of a people who had replaced the Hebrews as the chosen people" (p. 124). The document referred to by Myers and Wolfram is the "Karlmanni Principis Capitulare, 742. April. 21," issued at the conclusion of the *Concilium Germanicum,* which was presided over by Boniface. It may found in the *Capitularia Regum Francorum, MGH Legum Sectio II* vol. 1, part 1, ed. Alfred Boretius (Hanover: Hahn Verlag, 1881), pp. 24–26: the phrase *populus Dei* is used in the fifth decree, while the phrase *populus Christianus* is used in the preface. Walter Ullmann discusses the development and significance of this concept in *The Carolingian Renaissance and the Idea of Kingship* (London: Methuen, 1969), pp. 17–25, where he states that "there was no conceptual distinction between a Carolingian State and a Carolingian Church, nor anything approaching a pluralistic society" (p. 17). In "The Frankish Ethos After Charlemagne," in *The Growth of Papal Government in the Middle Ages: A Study in the Ideological Relation of Clerical to Lay Power,* 3rd ed. (London: Methuen, 1970), Ullmann refers to the second *Prologue* to the *Lex Salica* (*Lex Salica, 100 Titel-Text,* Germanenrechte N.F., ed. Karl August Eckhardt [Weimar: Hermann Böhlaus, 1953], p. 88), which is believed to have been composed in the mid-eighth century, and according to which "the Franks alone were the chosen Christian people: 'Vivat qui Francos diligit Christus' " (p. 62). This affirmation is translated in Hillgarth, *Christianity and Paganism,* as "Long live Christ who loves the Franks," while the *Prologue* as a whole, according to Hillgarth, portrays Christ as "almost a national God" (p. 90). Hillgarth also documents the Visigothic contribution to what he terms "the beginning of the long growth of the great myths of religious nationalism" (p. 90), with English translations of King Recared's condemnation of Arianism before the Third Council of Toledo in 589 (pp. 90–93; original in *PL* 84, col. 342–45), and of excerpts from the *Ordo quando rex cum exercitu ad prelium egreditur,* a seventh-century rite of blessing the weapons of a king before battle (pp. 93–95; original in *Le "Liber Ordinum,"* ed. M. Férotin, *Monumenta Ecclesiae Liturgica,* vol. 5 [Paris: Firmin-Didot, 1904], col. 149–53).

religiopolitical reinterpretation is significant for its contribution to the development of the Crusade ideology as well as to a Eurocentric particularization of Christianity epitomized by the concept of Christendom.[23]

The form and function of pagan temples in pre-Christian Germanic and Celtic society is relevant not only from the perspective of the implementation of Gregory's missionary policy, but also from the perspective of the insights which may be provided regarding the nature of pre-Christian Germanic religious devotion and its impact on Christian worship and piety. In her discussion "Holy Places," H. R. Ellis Davidson remarks:

> While so far there is little definite evidence for early shrines among the Germanic peoples, the wooden stave churches built in Norway between the eleventh and thirteenth centuries may provide a possible clue as to what kind of sacred buildings were set up there in pre-Christian times. . . .
>
> It is clear that sacred buildings in various parts of Celtic and Germanic territory developed in different ways according to outside influences and the building materials and skills available. They were raised to house figures of the gods and cult objects, for the making of private offerings and consultation of the supernatural powers, not for congregational services and large assemblies. They would be visited by the faithful, and the processional way round the building would make it possible for visitors to view sacred objects without entering the sanctuary. The treasures stored in the temple sometimes necessitated a wall or a fence to enclose it, and this also served to mark off sacred space. Communal feasts and rituals in which the neighbourhood took part, however, would normally be held out of doors or in suitably large buildings where feasts could be prepared, as in the hall of the king or local landowner. In spite of occasional encircling walls, it is essential to see the sacred place as something not set apart from the ordinary secular world, but rather as providing a vital centre for the needs of the community and for the maintenance of a kingdom. It offered a means of communication with the Other World, and was regarded as a source of power, inspiration, healing and hidden knowledge.[24]

Hillgarth believes Visigothic Spain played a "mediating role . . . in the introduction of the idea of the Divine Christian ruler into barbarian Western Europe," as it was transmitted from Byzantium to the Visigothic rulers, and through Spain to Charlemagne and his Ottonian successors (p. 89). See also J. M. Wallace-Hadrill, *The Frankish Church* (Oxford: Clarendon Press, 1983), pp. 186–87, for a discussion of the notions of *populus christianus* and *imperium christianum*.

[23] Paul Johnson, *A History of Christianity* (New York: Atheneum, 1979), has remarked that "there was a price to be paid for the Frankish experiment in creating a Christian social structure and culture. It gave to the western Church a wonderful sense of unity and coherence; it gave to western society great dynamism, which lies at the source of the European impact on the world. But it involved a degree of doctrinal, liturgical and at bottom, cultural and racial intolerance, which made an ecumenical Church impossible. Unity in depth was bought at the expense of unity in breadth" (p. 185).

[24] "The Enclosed Sanctuary," section in the chapter "Holy Places," in H. R. Ellis Davidson, *Myths and Symbols in Pagan Europe: Early Scandinavian and Celtic Religions* (Syracuse, N.Y.: Syracuse University Press), pp. 34–35.

This description evokes consideration of the Germanic impact on early medieval Christian liturgical developments as described by Josef A. Jungmann and others,[25] such as the greater physical and spiritual distance between the celebrant and a less participatory faithful, the increased focus of attention on sacred objects such as shrines and relics, which were accompanied by processions and feasts when they were transferred, and the generally magicoreligious character of the relationship between the Germanic peoples and Christ and his saints. According to this "magicoreligious character" it was expected that Christ and his saints would intervene in the affairs of individuals and groups in direct response to specific prayers or rituals.[26]

A magicoreligious acceptance of Christianity by a society may not be as permanent as a soteriological acceptance, and, from the perspective of an early Christian model of Christianity, neither is it a full and authentic

[25] The major features of the Germanized liturgy were its allegorical, dramatic, and historical orientation, which deviated from the predominantly soteriological focus of the apostolic and patristic eras—a focus which Jungmann sought to restore. This contrast is discussed in detail in Josef Jungmann, *The Mass of the Roman Rite: Its Origin and Development* (*Missarum Sollemnia*), trans. Francis A. Brunner, vol. 1 (New York: Benziger Brothers, 1951), pp. 74–103. Further background on the Germanization of liturgical forms in general may be found in Theodor Klauser, "Die liturgischen Austauschbeziehungen zwischen der römischen und der fränkisch-deutschen Kirche vom 8. bis zum 11. Jahrhunderts," *Historisches Jahrbuch der Görresgesellschaft* 53 (1933): 169–89, as well as in Anton L. Mayer, "Altchristliche Liturgie und Germanentum," *JL* 5 (1925): 80–96; idem, "Die Liturgie und der Geist der Gotik," *JL* 6 (1926): 68–97; and Odo Casel, "Das Mysteriengedächtnis der Meßliturgie im Lichte der Tradition," *JL* 6 (1926): 113–204, especially 185–93. The critical role of Alcuin of York and his votive Masses is presented by Gerard Ellard, *Master Alcuin, Liturgist* (Chicago: Loyola University Press, 1956), while an important analysis of liturgical dramatization is contained in Christine Catharina Schnusenberg, *The Relationship Between the Church and the Theatre: Exemplified by Selected Writings of the Church Fathers and by Liturgical Texts Until Amalarius of Metz: 775–852 A.D.* (Lanham, Md.: University Press of America, 1988). A valuable ethnocultural approach to the general development of early medieval religious culture is advanced by Ildefons Herwegen, *Kirche und Seele* (Münster: Aschendorff, 1926); and idem, *Antike, Germanentum und Christentum* (Salzburg: Verlag Anton Pustet, 1932). See also, Theodor Klauser, *A Short History of the Western Liturgy*, 2nd ed., trans. John Halliburton (New York: Oxford University Press, 1979).

[26] In his discussion "Christianity and Folk Religions," Mennonite missionary and anthropologist Paul G. Hiebert, *Anthropological Insights for Missionaries* (Grand Rapids, Mich.: Baker Book House, 1985), notes: "Folk religions deal with the problems of everyday life, not with ultimate realities. . . . Christians have given many answers for everyday problems. Roman Catholics have often turned to the doctrine of saints as intermediaries between God and humans. . . . It is no coincidence that many of the most successful missions have provided some form of Christian answer to these questions. In dealing with Christian responses to problems of everyday life, however, we must guard against syncretism. One danger is to make Christianity a new kind of magic in which we seek to use formulas to manipulate God into doing our will. . . . The difference between magic and worship is not in form, but in attitude. . . . The gospel does deal with God's care and provision in the everyday lives of people, but its central focus is on their salvation and eternal destiny" (pp. 222–24). For the medieval scenario, see Flint, *The Rise of Magic in Early Medieval Europe*; G. Ronald Murphy, "Magic in the Heliand," *Monatshefte* 83:4 (1991): 386–97; and the illustrated studies of Teresa Pàroli, "Santi e demoni nelle letterature germaniche nell'alto Medievo," *Settimane* 36 (1989): 411–90, with subsequent discussion, 491–98; and Victor H. Elbern, "Heilige, Dämonen und Magie an Reliquiaren des frühen Mittelalters," *Settimane* 36 (1989): 951–80.

acceptance of Christianity. When devotion to Christ, a saint, or a relic does not produce the desired result, the magicoreligious basis for Christian affiliation may be weakened. Also, as scientific explanations for natural phenomena become more widely accepted, they may undermine religious affiliation that is based primarily on magicoreligious grounds. Conversely, affiliation based primarily on soteriological, ethical, and doctrinal premises may not be challenged as much by advances in science and medicine, and hence may prove to be more permanent. However, adherents of folk religions are likely to consider such premises as alien to their world-view, and may thus be prone to reject the new religion altogether. Herein lies a large part of the problem of historical Christianization efforts among the Germanic peoples, as well as contemporary efforts among other folk-religious peoples. As Paul G. Hiebert notes, "young Christians may turn to traditional folk religions if they are given no Christian answers for their everyday problems."[27]

It may be of interest to note that, at least in the liturgical realm, Germanization was the unintentional result of Germanic leaders who sought to accomplish the exact opposite. Discussing the desire of Pepin the Short and Charlemagne to Romanize the Frankish liturgy, Cyrille Vogel has commented that "even St. Boniface, *missus sancti Petri,* apostle of Germany and reformer of the Frankish church, did not seem anxious to impose the Roman liturgy north of the Alps, despite his insistence on total *subjectio* to the Apostolic See." However, Pepin and Charlemagne were highly motivated to impose liturgical uniformity, since "besides the real veneration felt by Pepin and Charlemagne for all things Roman, there were excellent political reasons in favor of Romanization. Liturgical unification would both foster unity within the kingdom and help consolidate the alliance between the Holy See and the Frankish monarchy, the protector of the *iustitia sancti Petri.*"[28]

In reviewing St. Boniface's missionary career, one may wonder how directly his methodology had been influenced by Gregory the Great. Evidence of a conscious desire by St. Boniface to be appraised of Gregory's missionary strategy may be found in his letter to Nothelm, the bishop of Canterbury, in 735, requesting a copy of Gregory's response[29] to questions of Church custom and discipline which had been raised by Augustine of Canterbury.[30] Whether or not Boniface ever received a copy of this document

[27] Hiebert, *Anthropological Insights,* p. 223 fig. 29.

[28] *Medieval Liturgy: An Introduction to the Sources,* trans. and rev. William Storey and Niels Rasmussen (Washington, D. C.: Pastoral Press, 1986), pp. 148–50.

[29] *HE,* I. 27; Gregory, *Epistolae,* XI. 56ᵃ.

[30] *S. Bonifatii et Lulli epistolae,* ed. Michael Tangl, *Die Briefe des Heiligen Bonifatius und Lullus, MGH Ep. sel.* (Berlin: Weidmannsche Buchhandlung, 1916), *Ep.* 33, pp. 56–58, hereinafter referred to as Boniface, *Epistolae.* English translations are taken from *The Letters of Saint Boniface,* trans. and intro. Ephraim Emerton (New York: Columbia University Press, 1940), hereinafter referred to as Emerton, *LSB;* this excerpt is found on pp. 62–63.

is not known. From the contents of a letter from Cardinal Gemmulus in 743,[31] it appears that Boniface had requested copies of some of Gregory's letters which had not yet been sent to him. However, in a subsequent letter to Archbishop Egbert of York in 746 or 747, Boniface indicated that he had received copies of many of Gregory's letters, which were "obtained from the archives of the Roman Church."[32] Unfortunately, the dates of Boniface's letters are too late to substantiate his familiarity with Gregory's letters during the height of his missionary activity, that is, between 719 and 732. However, it is safe to conclude that, given Boniface's thorough intellectual and ecclesiastical formation,[33] he was generally aware of Gregory's missionary policy by this time.[34] Furthermore, in a letter from Bishop Daniel of Winchester, which Boniface is likely to have received in 723,[35] he was advised to utilize techniques of accommodation. Daniel urges Boniface to adopt a moderate and somewhat captious approach when discussing the superiority of Christianity with pagans:

> These and many similar things which it would take long to enumerate you ought to put before them, *not offensively or so as to anger them, but calmly and with great moderation.* At intervals you should compare their superstitions with our Christian doctrines, touching upon them from the flank, as it were, so that the pagans, thrown into confusion rather than angered, may be ashamed of their absurd ideas and may understand that their infamous ceremonies and fables are well known to us.
>
> This point is also to be made: *if the gods are all-powerful,* beneficent,

[31] Boniface, *Epistolae,* 54, pp. 96–97; Emerton, *LSB,* pp. 90–91.

[32] Boniface, *Epistolae,* 91, pp. 206–8; Emerton, *LSB,* pp. 167–69.

[33] Chs. 2 and 3 of *Vita Bonifatii auctore Willibaldo,* in *Vitae Sancti Bonifatii MGH SSrG,* ed. Wilhelm Levison (Hanover: Hahn Verlag, 1905), attest to Boniface's intellectual prowess. Future references to this work will be to *Vita Bonifatii.* English translations are taken from Willibald, *The Life of Saint Boniface,* trans. George W. Robinson (Cambridge: Harvard University Press, 1916), hereinafter referred to as Robinson, *Life.* George Greenway, "Saint Boniface as a Man of Letters," in Timothy Reuter, *The Greatest Englishman: Essays on St. Boniface and the Church at Crediton* (Exeter: Paternoster Press, 1980), notes: "A closer and more potent stimulus [than that of the Northumbrian religious culture of Bede] during his cloister life at Nursling was provided by Aldhelm, abbot of Malmesbury and later bishop of Sherborne, the presiding genius of West-Saxon learning, and indeed the most learned man of his age, next after Bede" (p. 34).

[34] After concluding that Boniface had not personally seen Bede's *HE,* or any other form of Gregory's letters before the conclusion of the central missionary phase of his career in 735, Suso Brechter, "Das Apostolat des heiligen Bonifatius und Gregors des Grossen Missions-Instruktionen für England," in *Sankt Bonifatius: Gedenkausgabe zum zwölfhundertsten Todestag* (Fulda: Parzeller, 1954), nonetheless concludes: "Die Wirksamkeit der Sendungstat Gregors war so stark, daß die ganze missionarische Tradition der englischen Kirche von ihr geprägt wurde. Romgedanke und Heimatliebe sind die beiden verpflichtenden Bindungen und tragenden Säulen, auf denen das Missionswerk des hl. Bonifatius aufruht. Daraus erwuchs seine Berufung, das bestimmte auch seine Methode, und so wurde Bonifatius, ohne die römischen Instruktionen für die Angelsachsenbekehrung zu kennen, auf dem Kontinent ein getreuer Vollstrecker der dynamischen Missionsgedanken Papst Gregors des Großen" (p. 33).

[35] In an article devoted to a discussion of Daniel's letter, Derek Baker, "Sowing the Seeds of Faith: Theory and Practice in the Mission Field," in Baker, ed., *Miscellanea Historiae Ecclesiasticae,* vol. 3, pp. 92–106, this date is proposed on p. 92 n. 4.

and just, they not only reward their worshipers but punish those who reject them. If, then, they do this in temporal matters, how is it that they spare us Christians who are turning almost the whole earth away from their worship and overthrowing their idols? And while these, that is, the Christians, possess lands rich in oil and wine and abounding in other resources, they have left to those, that is, the pagans, lands stiff with cold where their gods, driven out of the world, are falsely supposed to rule.[36]

Markus views this as an indication that Gregory's policy of accommodation was transmitted to Boniface via Daniel.[37] It is at least clear here that Daniel is urging Boniface to present Christianity in terms familiar to his Germanic audience, appealing to their temporal concerns.

Assuming that he generally followed the suggestions of his mentor,[38] it

---

[36] Emerton, *LSB,* pp. 49–50 (emphases added); Boniface, *Epistolae,* 23, p. 40: "Haec et his similia multa alia, quae nunc enumerare longum est, *non quasi insultando vel inritando eos, sed placide ac magna obicere moderatione debes.* Et per intervalla nostris, id est christianis, huiuscemodi conparandae [*sic*] sunt dogmatibus superstitiones et quasi e latere tangende, quatenus magis confuse quam exasperate pagani erubescant pro tam absurdis opinionibus et ne nos latere ipsorum nefarios ritus ac fabulas estimant. Hoc quoque inferendum: *Si omnipotentes sunt dii* et benefici et iusti, non solum suos remunerant cultores, verum etiam puniunt contemptores. Et si hec utraque temporaliter faciunt, cur ergo parcunt christianis totum pene orbem ab eorum cultura avertentibus idolaque evertentibus? Et cum ipsi, id est christiani, fertiles terras vinique et olei feraces ceterisque opibus habundantes possident provincias, ipsis autem, id est paganis, frigore semper rigentes terras cum eorum diis reliquerunt, in quibis iam tamen toto orbe pulsi falso regnare putatur" (emphases added).

[37] Markus, "Gregory the Great and a Papal Missionary Strategy," p. 37. For a general historical survey of the implementation of missionary policies of accommodation, see Alfons Väth, *Das Bild der Weltkirche: Akkomodation und Europäismus im Wandel der Jahrhunderte und in der neuen Zeit* (Hanover: Verlag Joseph Giesel, 1932). A discussion of Gregory and Boniface's Christianization methodologies within this context may be found in ch. 3, "Christliche Antike und Germanentum im Frühmittelalter," pp. 26–29.

[38] Richard E. Sullivan, "Carolingian Missionary Theories," *Catholic Historical Review* 42:3 (1956): 273–95, has described Daniel's letter as "the most explicit example of the thinking on the problem of persuading a pagan to surrender to Christianity" (p. 276). But Theodor Schieffer, *Winfrid-Bonifatius und die Christliche Grundlegung Europas* (1954; reprint with updated bibliography, Darmstadt: Wissenschaftliches Buchgesellschaft, 1972; reprint with corrections, 1980), pp. 147–48, and John Cyril Sladden, *Boniface of Devon: Apostle of Germany* (Exeter: Paternoster Press, 1980), pp. 69–70, suggest that Boniface rejected Daniel's advice as too academic and thus impractical for his audience. Instead, Schieffer and Sladden believe that Boniface followed his instincts and decided that a dramatization of the power of the Christian God would be a more effective stimulus than dialectical discussions. The apotheosis of such a dramatization occurred when Boniface fell the Sacred Oak of Geismar, which had been dedicated to Thor, and used the fallen timber to construct a church dedicated to St. Peter on the same location where the oak had stood (*Vita Bonifatii,* ch. 6, p. 31; Robinson, *Life,* pp. 63–64). However, if one defines accommodation more broadly, Schieffer and Sladden's interpretation need not significantly detract from the assertion that Boniface advanced Gregory's policy of accommodation. It may be argued that in his actions at Geismar, Boniface accommodated a fundamental premise of Germanic religion, that is, that the most powerful god should be worshiped. The act of constructing a church at the site of the Thor Oak, and using its very timber as construction material, further supports the assertion that Boniface pursued a Gregorian missionary policy according to which accommodation, when likely to succeed, was readily employed. While Boniface may have avoided the details of Daniel's dialectical suggestions, he did not fail

is likely that Boniface emphasized the temporal as well as eternal rewards which might accrue to those who were baptized. Among the temporal rewards, the one which was likely to have been prized most highly by his audience was victory in battle. In his letter of October 745 to the Frankish clergy, nobility, and laity, urging them to support the reforms of Boniface, Pope Zachary himself enunciates both temporal and eternal rewards, probably in the order of their presumed appeal to the secular elements of his audience: "If your priests are pure and clean of all unchastity and blood-guiltiness, as the sacred canons teach and as our brother Boniface preaches in our stead, and if you are in all things obedient to him, no people can stand before you, but all pagans shall fall before your face and you shall remain victors. And more, for your well-doing you shall inherit eternal life."[39]

Unfortunately there appears to exist no extant record of the actual contents of Boniface's sermons. A recent attempt to reconstruct their contents has been made by Thomas Leslie Amos in his study "The Origin and Nature of the Carolingian Sermon." Noting the failure of the Frankish missionary Wulframm to convert the Frisian duke Radbod after straightforwardly telling him that his pagan ancestors were damned,[40] Amos discerns a difference in the "Anglo-Saxon approach to missionary preaching," which "concentrated on stressing the power of the Christian divinity and the positive virtues of Christianity."[41] He then proceeds to compare the approach of Willibrord and other Anglo-Saxon missionaries with that of Wulframm:

> Although their sermons refuted pagan ideas and practices with verbal confrontations based on scriptural knowledge, they were sufficiently flexible to avoid such problems as Wulframm fell into with Radbod. Alcuin inserted a

---

to abide by Daniel's general theme of accommodating, at least temporarily, the Germanic worldview. Further discussion of Daniel's advice to Boniface may be found in Franz Flaskamp, *Die Missionsmethode des hl. Bonifatius* (Hildesheim: Franz Borgmeyer, 1929), pp. 37–38; Josef Lortz, "Untersuchungen zur Missionsmethode und zur Frömmigkeit des hl. Bonifatius nach seinem Briefen," in Nikolaus Goetzinger, ed., *Willibrordus: Echternacher Festschrift zur XII. Jahrhundertfeier des Todes des heiligen Willibrord* (Luxembourg: Verlag der St. Paulus-Druckerei, 1940), pp. 257–58; and Heinz Löwe, "Missionsmethode," sect. 3 in "Pirmin, Willibrord und Bonifatius: Ihre Bedeutung für die Missionsgeschichte ihrer Zeit," in Knut Schäferdiek, ed., *Die Kirche des früheren Mittelalters*, first half of vol. 2 of *Kirchengeschichte als Missionsgeschichte* (Munich: Chr. Kaiser Verlag, 1978), pp. 219–20.

[39] Emerton, *LSB*, p. 112; Boniface, *Epistolae*, 61, p. 126: "Nam si mundos et castos ab omni fornicatione et homocidio liberos habueritis sacerdotes, ut sacri precipiunt canones et nostra vice predicat prefatus Bonifatius frater noster, et ei in omninus oboedientes exstiteritis, nulla gens ante vestrum conspectum stabit, sed correunt ante faciem vestram omnes pagane gentes et ertis victores; insuper et bene agentes vitam possidebitis aeternam."

[40] *Vita Vulframni episcopi Senonici, MGH SRM*, ed. Wilhelm Levison, vol. 5, p. 668. Radbod expressed the Germanic ideal of group solidarity in his response to Wulframm by stating his preference for the company of his ancestors in hell over eternal life in heaven without them (ibid.).

[41] "The Origin and Nature of the Carolingian Sermon" (Ph.D. diss., Michigan State University, 1983), p. 109.

sermon in the *Vita Willibrordi* which, if not actually spoken by Willibrord, reflected the style of preaching he used.

In this sermon purportedly given to Duke Radbod, Willibrord told the Duke that he must give up worshipping idols, believe in Christ and accept baptism which would wash away his sins and allow him to possess eternal glory at the end of his life on earth. In this particular instance Willibrord avoided any discussion of Radbod's ancestors, the topic which had caused such difficulty for Wulframm. The Anglo-Saxon missionary preachers always accentuated the positive, emphasizing the power of God and Christ to do things for the faithful in this life and to reward them in the next.[42]

Despite Boniface's skill in preaching, it is clear from his correspondence that he considered secular support to be an essential component of his Christianization strategy. After an unsuccessful missionary campaign to the Frisians in 716, during which he appears to have relied primarily on the efficacy of his preaching, Boniface realized the need for papal endorsement which could assist in obtaining local protection and coercive authority. In a letter to Daniel of Winchester, dated between 742 and 746, he concedes that "without the support of the Frankish prince [Charles Martel] I can neither govern the members of the Church nor defend the priests, clerks, monks and maids of God; nor can I, without orders from him and the fear inspired by him, prevent the pagan rites and the sacrilegious worship of idols in Germany."[43]

The relationship between Boniface and Charles Martel was a mutually beneficial one. Geary has concluded that "through their support of the missionary bishop, the Carolingians had gained control of a well-disciplined, effective instrument of central control."[44] As challengers of the Merovingian sacral kingship, the emergent Carolingians also viewed the Church as an alternative source of sacral legitimation since, despite their decline in actual political authority, the Merovingians retained their claim to the *stirps regia* and its associated sacral aspects. In order for the Carolingians to overcome this obstacle, they needed to realign the sacral prestige and power traditionally associated with the Merovingian line. As Boniface was in search of a protector and the Church was in search of a defender against the Lombards,[45] the relationship between the emergent Carolingian dynasty

---

[42] Ibid. Further discussion of Willibrord's career may be found in Henry C. Hoeben, "Frisia and the Frisians at the Time of St. Willibrord" (Ph.D. diss., Fordham University, 1967).

[43] Emerton, *LSB*, pp. 115–16; Boniface, *Epistolae*, 63, p. 130: "Sine patrocinio principis Francorum nec populum ecclesiae regere nec presbiteros vel clericos, monachos vel ancillas Dei defendere possum nec ipsos paganorum ritus est sacrilegia idolorum in Germania sine illius mandato et timore prohibere valeo."

[44] Patrick Geary, *Before France and Germany: The Creation and Transformation of the Merovingian World* (New York: Oxford University Press, 1988), p. 217.

[45] The papacy's political realignment from Byzantium to the Franks and its significance for Christianization efforts is discussed in Thomas F. X. Noble, *The Republic of St. Peter: The Birth of the Papal State, 680–825* (Philadelphia: University of Pennsylvania Press, 1984), pp. 15–98; and David Harry Miller, "The Roman Revolution of the Eighth Century: A Study of the Ideo-

and the Church had important political as well as religious ramifications.[46]
This relationship reached a climax in 751 with the recognition of Pepin the
Short by Pope Zachary as the king of the Franks. In July of 754—one
month after Boniface's death, and three months after Pepin promised to
defend the Church, the pope, and the papal territories—he was anointed
and consecrated by Pope Stephen II, who also "invested Pepin and his
sons with the title *Patricius Romanorum."*[47]

Thus the Anglo-Saxon missionary campaign among the Germanic peoples relied upon papal endorsement as well as local political support, and
upon dramatic acts of confrontation with pagan icons as well as preaching.
Richard E. Sullivan has summarized early medieval missionary methodologies in the West as follows:

> The western missionary made very little attempt to instruct his pagan audi-
> ence in Christian dogma. Western missionary sources contain very little evi-
> dence bearing on matters of theology and its presentation to pagans. . . .
>
> The technique most commonly used in the West was one of offering the
> pagans dramatic proof of the superiority of Christianity, such demonstra-
> tions often being staged so as to have the maximum emotional effect on the
> pagans. . . .
>
> Behind this picture of western missionaries seeking to shock the pagan
> world into acceptance of Christianity lies the key to the western method of
> presenting Christianity. The missionaries bent every effort to fit their religion
> to the pattern of religious behavior and thinking which was already familiar
> to the pagans. . . .
>
> It is this aspect of western missionary method that savors so strongly of
> the barbarization of Christianity. The western missionary would have denied
> such an accusation. His immediate goal was to convince the pagan to accept a
> new deity on the pagan's own grounds, which end was achieved when the
> pagan was baptized. The corrective for the new convert's ignorance of Chris-
> tianity had still to be applied. Western missionary method envisaged a long
> period of education for the convert during which there was to be imposed on
> him a complete change of conduct designed to please the new God.[48]

---

logical Background of the Papal Separation from Byzantium and Alliance with the Franks,"
Mediaeval Studies 36 (1974): 79–133.

[46] Patrick Geary, *Before France and Germany,* summarizes this relationship: "Boniface's
genuine concern for his mission and his tremendous organizational skills proved fruitful. He
established Benedictine monasteries as points of acculturation and bishoprics as centers of
ecclesiastical control in Hesse, Thuringia, and Franconia. . . . The extent to which this organizational activity benefited Charles and his successors was considerable. By 742 it was possible to
call a council of all the bishops of the Austrasian regions under the authority of Charles's son
Carlomann. This council, which met to establish a strict hierarchical order within the church, set
the style for future church assemblies" (pp. 216–17).

[47] Noble, *The Republic of St. Peter,* p. 87. See also pp. 71–86 for the immediate background
of these events, as well as chs. 8 and 9 for an analysis of their significance.

[48] "Early Medieval Missionary Activity: A Comparative Study of Eastern and Western
Methods," *Church History* 23 (1954): 28–30. Compared with western missionary methods,
Sullivan notes that eastern missionary methods benefited from the active involvement of the

However, a comprehensive program of postbaptismal religious education never materialized. The catechumenate had declined and Christian formation did not usually extend beyond a superficial level. Jungmann has summarized the status of the preparation for Christian initiation in the Middle Ages: "After the 6th century, because adult baptism had become a rarity, the traditional rites of the catechumenate were used for infants with only superficial adjustment. The scrutinies, now transferred to weekdays, served as a substitute for catechesis, which was no longer possible. . . . There was no longer a catechumenate in the Middle Ages. The traditional forms were no longer used either upon the conversion of the Germans or when the Slavs entered the Church."[49] Given these circumstances, it is not surprising that the Germanic perception of Christianity as primarily a magicoreligious cult of a powerful deity[50] endured at least through the eighth century.[51]

---

whole spectrum of Byzantine society: "Lay society, and especially the imperial government, accepted this duty, calling upon the Greek church only to complete the formal process of conversion" (p. 18). However, such a degree of official support did not exist for the western missionary, "who did not have his prospective converts prepared for him by other agencies of society. Such political aid as he might receive and the impression which the heathen might gain of western culture were both the results of the missionary himself. For that reason neither was likely to be as decisive as was the case in the East" (p. 20).

[49] *New Catholic Encyclopedia*, s.v. "Catechumenate." Jungmann also notes that "although Gregory the Great still demanded a preparation of 40 days, the Apostle of the Suevians, Martin of Braga, insisted on only 20 days; however even this policy was often not followed in the case of mass baptism" (ibid.). A further discussion of the decline of the catechumenate may be found in "Christian Initiation in Gaul and Germany from the Seventh to the Twelfth Century," in J. D. C. Fisher, *Christian Initiation: Baptism in the Medieval West: A Study in the Disintegration of the Primitive Rite of Initiation,* Alcuin Club Collections, no. 47 (London: S.P.C.K., 1965); L. Kilger, "Zur Entwicklung der Katechumenatspraxis vom 5. bis 18. Jahrhundert," *Zeitschrift für Missionswissenschaft* 15 (1925): 166–82; and A. Dondeyne, "La Discipline des scrutins dans l'église latine avant Charlemagne," *Revue d'histoire ecclésiastique* 28 (1932): 533, 751–87.

[50] Schieffer, *Winfrid-Bonifatius und die Christliche Grundlegung Europas,* states: "Die Annahme des Christentums vollzog sich demnach als ein Wechsel des offiziellen Stammeskultes und war insofern auch eine politische Entscheidung, zu der in manchen Fällen—von den Angelsachsen haben wir solche Nachrichten—die Könige mit Zustimmung ihrer Großen das Signal gaben. Sie entsprang nicht etwa der Einsicht, daß der Glaube an den bisherigen Gott eine irreale Vorstellung sei, sondern der Überzeugung, daß sich Christus als der stärkere Gott erwiesen habe" (p. 39). Hanns Rückert, *Die Christianisierung der Germanen: Ein Beitrag zu ihrem Verständnis und ihrer Beurteilung,* 2nd rev. ed. (Tübingen: J. C. B. Mohr (Paul Siebeck), 1934), concludes: "Die vorherrschende Stimmung, aus der heraus der Germane den Übertritt vollzog, kleidet sich in unseren Quellen immer wieder in den ganz einfachen Satz: Der Gott des Christentums ist mächtiger als die alten Götter" (p. 16). Despite the preeminence of Christ as the most powerful god, that he did not always completely supplant the traditional pagan deities is indicated in *HE*, 2.13; Sherley-Price, p. 130, where Bede notes that King Redwald of the East Angles "had in the same temple an altar for the holy Sacrifice of Christ side by side with an altar on which victims were offered to devils."

[51] "Tacit complicity with pagan survivals is noted for a much later period in France," observes J. N. Hillgarth, "Popular Religion in Visigothic Spain," in Edward James, ed., *Visigothic Spain: New Approaches* (Oxford: Clarendon Press, 1980), p. 55 n. 1, referring to M. Vovelle, "Le Monde alpin et rhodanien," *Revue régionale d'ethnologie* 5 (1977): 7–32. Hillgarth continues: "In this valuable article Vovelle sees the vital change in popular religion in the fourteenth–sixteenth

The observations of Gregory Dix on this situation are instructive: "The barbarians followed their chiefs submissively into the fold of the church, . . . [b]ut that did not in fact make them responsible Christians. Their mass-movements into christianity or from Arianism to orthodoxy did not betoken any sort of change of heart. . . . But again one must remember that the church's own resources for giving instruction had been immensely decreased."[52] Contemporaneous with the decline of the catechumenate was a decline in general familiarity with Scripture. Robert E. McNally has noted that "Holy Scripture . . . as a direct, vital force in the spiritual life of the faithful gradually fell into deep shadow as new religious forms, less biblical but more popular, arose to take its place. . . . The Bible could not, therefore, have played a direct and immediate role in the formation of Christian piety."[53]

This does not mean that there was no ideological movement toward a Christian world-view among the Germanic peoples. However, since no official system of postbaptismal instruction had been devised, the newly baptized individual's religious training depended largely on the level of interest of the local prince, bishop, or abbot, and the likelihood that a missionary preacher might pass by. One such preacher was the Visigothic Benedictine abbot and bishop Pirmin (d. 753), whose extant sermon *De singulis libris canonicis scarapsus*[54] was addressed to the recently baptized. It is considered by Amos to have had "a wide influence for both the eighth-century missionaries and the Carolingian reformers."[55] Sullivan provides a detailed analysis of this significant document:

> Pirmin devoted the first section . . . to a summary of the history of mankind with special emphasis on man's fall and God's provision for his salvation. . . .
> Post-baptismal instruction ought to begin by a thorough review of the material that should have been learned before baptism.
>   Pirmin then came to the real point of his tract. "A Christian who has

---

centuries, when there is perceptible the first real attempt to Christianize the rural world, largely with fear of damnation, and to combat the existing mélange of Christian and pagan customs." This is consonant with the views of Delumeau, Thomas, Ginzburg, and Strauss, as noted above, p. 37.

[52] *The Shape of the Liturgy,* additional notes by Paul V. Marshall (1945; reprint, New York: Seabury Press, 1982), pp. 595–96.

[53] *The Unreformed Church* (New York: Sheed and Ward, 1965), p. 70. See also Robert E. McNally, *The Bible in the Early Middle Ages,* Woodstock Papers, no. 4 (1959; reprint, Atlanta: Scholars Press, 1986); and Beryl Smalley, *The Bible in the Early Middle Ages* (Oxford: Oxford University Press, 1952).

[54] *De singulis libris canonicis scarapsus, PL,* vol. 89, col. 1029–50. After noting that "a lack of valid sources complicates any attempt to discuss the content of missionary preaching designed to win converts," Sullivan, "The Carolingian Missionary and the Pagan," *Speculum* 28 (1953), describes this document as "perhaps the best example of the content of . . . an explanation of the Christian version of history," and a tract "compiled as a kind of handbook to be used by priests to instruct Alamannians whose faith was shaky and whose knowledge of Christianity was extremely vague and confused" (pp. 715–16).

[55] "The Origin and Nature of the Carolingian Sermon," p. 112.

the name but does not do the deeds will not be glorified by Christ. He is a Christian who imitates and follows Christ in all things. . . ." The author listed and explained in detail the chief sins through which Christians transgress God's commands, and attempted to elucidate the nature of certain general and abstract sins, like cupidity, vainglory, and pride. . . . He placed an unusually heavy emphasis on the sinfulness of engaging in pagan practices. This preoccupation with sin suggests that the Carolingian missionary theorists felt that an explanation of the nature of sin must be given an important place in the education of new converts.

. . . Pirmin closed with a discourse on the glories of the celestial kingdom and the terrors of hell. . . . *Here, as throughout the tract, Pirmin revealed an undercurrent of anxiety that his audience had not yet fully grasped the otherworldly point of view which he considered vital to Christian life. He wanted to make certain that this concept be made part of the outlook of his charges.*[56]

The contents of the *Scarapsus* are valuable because they document both the predominantly "this-worldly" view of its audience, and what may be described as the second phase of the Christianization process. Rosamond McKitterick has similarly observed that "the encouragement to come to be baptized, the swearing of the baptismal vows and the firm establishment of the church in every part of the Frankish lands, both in the missionary areas to the east and the regions where churches had long existed, were all really the first stage in the process of conversion, while it is the teaching of a Christian way of life and thought which constitutes the second stage."[57] After pagan audiences were convinced of the greater power of the Christian God and baptized, depending on their location, some were urged to modify their behavior, attitudes, and values, and to accept a rudimentary Christian belief system.

Herein lies a fundamental problem. For the Christianization of a folk-religious people to occur in accordance with the terms of the current inquiry, it is necessary that their ethos and world-view be directed away from a world-accepting, folk-centered, magicoreligious orientation toward a world-rejecting, individual-centered, soteriological orientation. However, the prebaptismal accommodations of Christianity to a Germanic world-view were likely to have obscured the inherent disparity between Germanic and Christian world-views. Since the missionaries do not appear to have elicited an informed assent to their contrary world-view before they

---

[56] "Carolingian Missionary Theories," pp. 287–88 (emphases added).

[57] *The Frankish Church and the Carolingian Reforms, 789–895* (London: Royal Historical Society, 1977), p. 156. Commenting on the degree of "conversion" among the Germanic peoples from the reign of Clovis until the mission of Boniface, Wilhelm Levison, *England and the Continent in the Eighth Century* (Oxford: Clarendon Press, 1946), notes: "The conversion of a chieftain or king in these centuries, as often today in primitive tribes, meant the 'conversion' of many of his followers also, superficial as the simultaneous baptism of hundreds or thousands must have been; the real religious education remained to be given after the acceptance of the Christian belief. . . . Pagan practice was mixed up with Christian custom everywhere" (pp. 47–48).

baptized people,[58] it is not surprising that their postbaptismal efforts to impose Christian ethics and doctrines met with resistance, and that significant compromises with Germanic religiosity occurred. Amos has described the response of ninth-century Carolingian sermon authors to this situation:

> Authors of Carolingian sermons showed a close familiarity with the surviving forms of pagan religious practices, and they worked constantly to root out such practices among their parishioners. Sermons forbade such things as worship of or at the sacred springs, stones and trees which had been holy sites in both classical and Germanic religions. The preachers also attacked pagan magicians and magical practices, from divination to healing the sick with charms and incantations. Most of these pagan practices were only survivals of what had once been organized religions with temples, priests and priestesses. They survived in part because they met certain spiritual and practical needs which Christianity either could not answer or had not yet begun to answer. . . .
>
> Where sermon authors did not or could not supply rational explanations of natural events in terms of God's laws, they still stressed that such events were caused by God, and that if people propitiated Him, the events could have fortunate outcomes. . . . The sermon authors helped to desacralize the natural world which had played such a large part in the *Weltanschauung* of pagan religions. This desacralization helped to open the forest areas for exploitation and helped put an end to the surviving pagan cults.
>
> Just as Martin of Braga advised the members of his flock to use the sign of the Cross to protect themselves against the host of demons facing them, so too the Carolingian preachers told their flocks to take advantage of Christian magic. If sickness struck a household, its members should avoid pagan magicians and diviners and go instead to the church where the sick

[58] Practically speaking, it is quite understandable that they did not seek such an assent, since, as in the case of Radbod, the more the disparity of Christian and Germanic world-views became apparent to potential converts, the less likely it appears that they were willing to be baptized. Without attempting to impose contemporary standards of freedom of religion on early medieval society, it may be of interest to consider the prerequisites for adult baptism in mission countries as presented in Bernard Leeming, *Principles of Sacramental Theology* (Westminster, Md.: Newman Press, 1956): "The catechumenate in mission countries lasts sometimes for several years. Does the Church, therefore, believe that the catechumens must remain without remission of original, and perhaps actual, sin for all that time? Surely not, for the catechumens are taught how to make an act of contrition, so that they may attain the state of grace even before Baptism. The practice of the long catechumenate looks to making a member of the Church, as well as to the conferring of invisible grace; and looks to stability in Christianity after baptism. A similar principle holds in baptizing infants; unless there is reasonable prospect of a Christian education and life, the Church does not confer the sacrament, except in danger of death. The very significance of the sacrament demands postponement, or even refusal of Baptism, in cases where a Christian life may not follow reception of the sacrament; for one fundamental symbolism is that of death to the old life and rebirth into a new, which does, normally, remit sin and confer grace, but which looks first to living in the Christian society. Thus, there is ample theological justification for the practice of a long catechumenate in mission countries, and for refusal of Baptism without security of a Christian education; hasty Baptisms are not justified by theological reasons" (pp. 357–58).

person could be anointed with holy oil which would not only cure the sickness but remit sins.[59]

Appraising the methods employed by the Frankish Church to advance a Christian ethical system, McKitterick describes the fundamental problem of Germanic unawareness of the scope of world-view transformation which the Church associated with the reception of baptism: "The essential point is that with the acceptance of Christianity and the new god in the whole of the Frankish lands, East and West, the 'newly born' Christian had to recognize, learn, and attempt to live by a whole new code of moral values. How aware were the Franks that this was incumbent upon them?"[60] Given the absence of an ethical dimension in Germanic religiosity,[61] as is generally the case with Indo-European and other folk religiosities, and given a missionary policy which accommodated the pre-Christian Germanic religiosity to a significant degree, it is likely that the Franks and other Germanic peoples were generally unaware that the acceptance of Christian baptism implicitly committed them to the transformation of their traditional value systems.

This lack of awareness has led Walter Baetke to conclude that, while kings and nobles may have been attracted to Christianity for political or cultural reasons, for many of their subjects the reception of baptism was not the result of a conscious decision to reject their Germanic religiosity, but rather the result of a misunderstanding of the extent to which Christianity represented a radical break with their traditional thinking, feelings, and ethical behavior.[62] Since Christianity was not initially presented to the Germanic peoples as requiring a radical break with their traditional ethos and world-view, it is not surprising that, for them, baptism did not imply such a transformation. Robert A. Markus has observed:

> The early history of Germanic Christianity is dominated by the paradox that mass conversion required some considerable continuity. The new religion had to be seen to meet existing needs, and not to overtax the courage its converts would need to break with the religion of their ancestors. But, once converted, they needed to define their new identity: they had to create discontinuities which would draw a line between their Christian present and their pagan past. The realignment of these societies was necessarily slow, their central value-systems resistant to change. Gregory of Tours and Bede

---

[59] "The Origin and Nature of the Carolingian Sermon," pp. 323–28 passim. On the general problem of the encounter of Christianity with folk religions, see above, pp. 191–92, 191 n. 26. See also "The Magic That Was Needed: Rescued Means of Magical Intervention" and "Encouraged Magic: The Process of Rehabilitation" in Flint, *The Rise of Magic*.

[60] *Frankish Church*, p. 156.

[61] As Green, *The Carolingian Lord*, p. 302, has observed, Germanic ethical ideals were derived from *comitatus* and kinship relationships. These ideals were discussed in the previous two chapters.

[62] Walter Baetke, *Die Aufnahme des Christentums durch die Germanen: Ein Beitrag zur Frage der Germanisierung des Christentums*, special ed. (Darmstadt: Wissenschaftliche Buchgesellschaft, 1962), p. 8.

both knew that the conversion of their peoples to Christianity had done something to the religion to which they were converted. . . . They were also aware of an even deeper change in the texture of Christianity: it had become the religion of a warrior nobility whose values and culture it had necessarily to absorb in the process of Christianizing them.[63]

The extent to which Anglo-Saxon Christianization efforts among the Germanic peoples in the first half of the eighth century succeeded is difficult, if not impossible, to assess. What can be said is that these efforts provided a basis for the "second-phase" work of the Frankish Church through the ninth century, which focused on ethical modification. As McKitterick concludes regarding the content of contemporary ethical treatises, or *florilegia,* "it is above all a consciousness of sin that is to be inculcated, the acknowledgement of the comparatively miserable and short nature of human life and the possibility of greater meaning being lent it by Christianity and faith."[64] This inculcation of "a consciousness of sin" and the consequent desire for salvation has led Hans-Joachim Schoeps to remark:

> Originally the Teutonic tribes scarcely manifested any profound grasp of the doctrines of the new religion. They misunderstood a great deal. Apparently, very few among them noticed that they were expected to shift to a new concept of reality. Walter Baetke has rightly observed: "It is perverting the relationship of Christianity to the Teutonic religion to regard it as a consummation or perfecting of elements already present in the pagan faith. *Christianity did not answer questions that the early Teutons had already posed. . . . Rather, Christianity had first to make them desire salvation in order to bring salvation to them.* The Teutonic religion provided no base on which Christian missionaries could build this aspect of their doctrine."
>
> It might be said that, on the contrary, a certain Teutonization of Christianity took place, for Teutonic thought, forms of public worship and ways of life influenced Christian liturgy, art, ecclesiastical customs and even canon law.[65]

---

[63] "From Rome to the Barbarian Kingdoms (330–700)," in John McManners, ed., *The Oxford Illustrated History of Christianity* (Oxford: Oxford University Press, 1990), p. 89. Attention is also called to the facing illustration on p. 88 of "Christ as the Divinity of a Germanic Warrior Aristocracy." A similar view regarding the tenacity of pre-Christian values and attitudes among the Anglo-Saxons is expressed by Patrick Wormald, "Bede, Beowulf, and the Conversion of the Anglo-Saxon Aristocracy," in Robert T. Farrell, ed., *Bede and Anglo-Saxon England,* British Archaeological Reports, no. 46 (Oxford: British Archaeological Reports, 1978), pp. 65–69, who notes that "although the Anglo-Saxon aristocracy was willing to accept a new God, it was *not* prepared to jettison the memory or the example of those who had worshipped the old. Aristocracies in these circumstances very rarely are. As anthropological study of societies not dissimilar from the Anglo-Saxons has shown, memories of the past and cultural values are often inseparable" (p. 67).

[64] *Frankish Church,* p. 183. See also p. 202: "The sinfulness of man and the necessity for his redemption, were the most constant themes of the Carolingian instruction of the people. The emphasis on sin is also evident."

[65] *The Religions of Mankind: Their Origin and Development,* trans. Richard and Clara

As is customary in homogeneous, folk-religious societies, especially during a heroic age, the standards of ethical conduct among the Germanic peoples appear to have been ultimately derived from a sociobiological drive for group survival through in-group altruism. Ethical misconduct thus consisted primarily in violating the code of honor of one's kindred or one's *comitatus.* Punishment for these violations included execution, banishment, or the payment of a fine or *wergild.* It was the responsibility of one's kin, or the fellow members of one's *comitatus,* to assist in avenging dishonorable behavior. The motivation which compelled compliance with these codes of honor was derived from the desire to avoid shame to oneself and to one's kin or *comitatus.* Similarly, the motivation for exemplary heroic behavior stemmed from the foreknowledge that such behavior would bring glory to oneself during one's lifetime and would be shared by one's kin and descendants. If one's deeds were truly extraordinary and benefited one's entire people, they might be memorialized forever in heroic legends. As Jan de Vries has surmised: "The hero, then, lives in order to win eternal fame. . . . In those days people were very sensitive to fame and blame. The former enhanced the value of life, the latter destroyed it."[66]

How then could missionaries instill a desire for salvation from sin in a society where Christian concepts of sin and guilt were alien? The high degree of disparity between Christian and Germanic world-views and ethics appears to have prompted the Anglo-Saxon Church and its missionaries to pursue a course of world-view and ethical reorientation through semantic transformation. An appreciation for the problem of translating the fundamental concepts of Christianity from the Latin language of Roman culture into the languages of the Germanic peoples contributes to an understanding of how this process of semantic transformation unfolded.[67]

Winston (Garden City, N.Y.: Doubleday, 1968), pp. 113–14 (emphasis added). Schoeps's translation of Baetke is from *Aufnahme,* p. 39. Schoeps excludes by ellipses from this quotation the following excerpt, which is relevant to the current discussion: "Questions regarding the meaning of death, the hereafter, the fate of the soul after death, and notions of sin, redemption, and judgement—all of this was alien to their religion and was introduced to them through Christianity. Therefore, not only in the answers, but in the questions as well, lay the novelty of Christianity" (my translation).

[66] "The Hero and the Heroic Age," in *Heroic Song and Heroic Legend,* trans. B. J. Timmer (1963; reprint, Salem, N.H.: Ayer, 1988), p. 183. de Vries elaborates: "Honour and fame were the pivots of man's life—of the hero's life first and foremost; through these he could be hurt most severely. . . . Man was not yet the individual then that he became later. He was a member of the family, the temporary link in an eternal chain. Fame and blame were transmitted to children and grandchildren, or reached back to the ancestors. The man who failed in his honor was a weak link in the chain; it could snap. . . . The worst horror was that the man who did not behave in accordance with the code of honour which his lineage demanded of him cast a blemish on his family, a blemish that could not be erased" (pp. 186–87).

[67] That an analogous problem has confronted Christian missionaries in Africa is attested to by Matthew Schoffeleers, "Folk Christology in Africa: The Dialectics of the Nganga Paradigm,"

Heinz Rupp has proposed that German literature originated as an interim learning aid for young German monks studying Christian Latin texts. Explanations of foreign concepts were written in the margins of these texts using familiar German terms, with the reciprocal result that eventually "the content of native expressions was reshaped."[68] At the same time, spoken German was the object of "an attempt . . . to embed these new concepts to be expressed with *old* words in a context from which their new sense would only slowly become apparent."[69] One of the primary concepts which was "contextualized" in this fashion was that of sin.[70] Other related concepts which were treated similarly were those of salvation, holiness, and lord.

In the previous chapter the religiopolitical significance of the Germanic concept of sacral kingship was discussed. The importance of the sacral king's *Heil* or charisma was noted. As a result of the Christianization efforts of the Anglo-Saxon missionaries and their German compatriots, however, the noun *Heil* and its associated adjective *heilig* became imbued with Christian connotations of salvation and holiness. Baetke has summarized this critical semantic transformation as follows: "The real Christian turning-point in the conversion process was achieved in the concept of salvation. It is the transformation of the connotation of *Heil* from political well-being, the soundness of the kingdom and the nation, to the salvation of the individual soul."[71] While Christianity was perceived by Clovis and his warriors as a source of political and military salvation, the second phase of Christianization sought to introduce and advance Christian ethical values and a world-view centered about individual salvation. This was to be accomplished through the semantic transformation of Germanic concepts, the incorporation of Germanic imagery, and the metaphorical interpretation of those Germanic elements which were deemed beyond the pale of

---

Journal of Religion in Africa 19:2 (1989): 157–83. Further comparisons may be found in Peter Munz, "Early European History and African Anthropology," *New Zealand Journal of History* 10 (1976): 37–50.

[68] Heinz Rupp, "The Adoption of Christian Ideas into German, with Reference to the *Heliand* and to Otfrid's *Evangelienbuch*," *Parergon* 21 (1978): 33–41. This process is discussed further in Werner Betz, "Lehnwörter and Lehnprägungen im Vor- und Frühdeutschen," in vol. 1 of *Deutsche Wortgeschichte*, 3rd rev. ed., ed. Friedrich Maurer and Heinz Rupp, rev. Heinz Rupp (Berlin: Walter de Gruyter, 1974), pp. 135–60. See also Heinz Rupp, "Leid und Sünde im Heliand und in Otfrids Evangelienbuch," *Beiträge zur Geschichte der deutschen Sprache und Literatur*, part 1: 78 (1956): 421–69; and part 2: 79 (1957): 336–79.

[69] Rupp, "The Adoption of Christian Ideas into German," p. 36. See also Stephen E. Flowers, "Toward an Archaic Germanic Psychology," in *JIES* 11:1/2 (1983): 117–37, and especially pp. 124–25 for a discussion of the semantic transformation of the ancient Germanic **gaist* from denoting inner emotional arousal to the OHG *geist* denoting spirit in a Christian context.

[70] For a discussion of the optimal missionary approach to indigenous cultures, see "Critical Contextualization," in Hiebert, *Anthropological Insights*, pp. 171–92.

[71] *Aufnahme*, p. 52 (my translation).

accommodation. Old High German literary examples of this approach may be found in the early ninth-century *Heliand* epic and especially in the *Liber Evangeliorum,* composed by Otfrid of Weissenburg between 860 and 870.[72]

These semantic transformations were consonant with the general Anglo-Saxon missionary strategy of implementing a policy of accommodation where pre-Christian ideals or practices were too deeply ingrained to be modified by a straightforward exposition of Christianity or by coercion.[73] In discussing why the Anglo-Saxon missionaries did not choose the more numinous Old English (OE) root **wihaz* over the more political **hailagaz* to connote salvation and holiness, as Ulfila had done in his translation of the Bible, Baetke argues that while Ulfila deliberately sought to avoid the strong pagan connotations of **hailagaz,* the Anglo-Saxon missionaries deliberately translated *sanctus* as *hailag* so as to exploit, accommodate, and eventually transform the strong inherent Germanic association of *Heil* with magical, charismatic power.[74]

Hailag was not the only OE word to have undergone such a transformation. More recently, D. H. Green has applied Baetke's methodology to the OE term for the leader of the *comitatus, dryhten,* selected by the Anglo-Saxons to represent the Latin term for Christ, *dominus.*[75] Green suspects that "the christianisation of this word and of the other terms from the sphere of the *comitatus* was no more than a tactical move by the Anglo-Saxon church, the result of a realistic assessment of long-term advantages

---

[72] Primary sources for these works are Otto Behaghel, ed., *Heliand und Genesis,* 9th ed., rev. Burkhard Taeger (Tübingen: Max Niemeyer Verlag, 1984); and Oskar Erdmann, ed., *Otfrids Evangelienbuch* (Tübingen: Max Niemeyer Verlag, 1973). The *Heliand* and particularly the *Liber Evangeliorum* are discussed from the perspective of religious and ethical education by McKitterick, *Frankish Church,* pp. 196–204. See also Rupp, "The Adoption of Christian Ideas into German"; idem, "Leid und Sünde"; and Hulda Göhler, "Das Christusbild in Otfrids *Evangelienbuch* und im *Heliand,*" *Zeitschrift für deutsche Philologie* 59 (1935): 1–52. An annotated English translation of the *Heliand* has recently been completed by G. Ronald Murphy, *The Heliand: The Saxon Gospel: A Translation and Commentary* (New York: Oxford University Press, 1992).

[73] For contemporary linguistical insights into the modification of such deeply ingrained ideals and practices, see "The Primacy of Deep Structure," in the chapter "Theological and Religious Pluralism," in Irene Lawrence, *Linguistics and Theology: The Significance of Noam Chomsky for Theological Construction,* American Theological Library Association Monograph Series, no. 16 (Metuchen, N.J.: American Theological Library Association, 1980), pp. 109–17. Also of interest is Rudolf Bultmann, *Faith and Understanding,* ed. Robert W. Funk (New York: Harper & Row, 1966), who states: "Every theological exposition of the saving event and of the Christian's existence is constructed with contemporary conceptions" (p. 279).

[74] *Das Heilige im Germanischen* (Tübingen: J. C. B. Mohr (Paul Siebeck), 1942), pp. 220–26. Baetke specifically relates this process of deliberate semantic accommodation to Gregory's missionary policy, a policy which differed from that of Ulfila, whose more direct, less accommodating—and ultimately less effective policy—may have caused him to exclude the Book of Kings from his translation of the Bible lest it reinforce the warrior ethic of the Goths.

[75] See "The Military Origins of *Truhtin,*" and "The Dissociation of *Truhtin* from the Sphere of Warfare," chs. 9 and 10 in Green, *The Carolingian Lord.*

and of possible disadvantages."[76] An obvious benefit from the utilization of the *comitatus* terminology lies in the fact that it already had an established base of positive connotation within Germanic society. Also, since the *comitatus* was a primary source of ethical values, Green feels that by utilizing its terminology the Church might "bridge the gap" between cultic religious observations and ethical obligations that had existed in Germanic religion.[77] The less obvious danger lay in the possibility that, after Germanic terms were semantically associated with Christian concepts, the missionaries' efforts to Christianize them might not be sufficiently intensive or sustained to prevent a reciprocal Germanization of the Christian concepts themselves.

While it is clear that a Germanic terminology was utilized, the extent to which this process of accommodation resulted in a general semantic transformation and a genuine Christianization of the Germanic world-view and value system is more difficult to determine. From the persistence of Germanic attitudes and values in secular Germanic literature, and the Germanization of liturgical practices and hagiographic canons, it appears that the success of such a world-view transformation effort was limited. This may be attributed to the general stability of societal world-views, the relatively high level of solidarity within Germanic societies, and the vitality of Germanic religiosity during this period.[78] To the extent that Christian

---

[76] Green, *The Carolingian Lord*, p. 322. See ch. 6, "The Vocabulary of the *Comitatus*," for a detailed discussion of other Germanic terms associated with the *comitatus* which Green believes were Christianized, that is, *triuwa*, *trôst*, *huldi*, *milti*, and *êra*. Matthew Schoffeleer's article "Folk Christology in Africa: The Dialectics of the Nganga Paradigm," describes a similar process currently underway among those involved with Christianization efforts in Africa: "We are regularly told by missiologists, social scientists and African writers that Africans find it difficult to integrate the person of Jesus Christ in their belief system, either because he is automatically associated with the west and the colonial past, or because his very essence is supposed to be incompatible with autochthonous religious conceptions. That view seems implicitly confirmed by African Theology, which has remained remarkably silent about this pivotal symbol of the Christian faith. At one time it has even been authoritatively stated that in traditional African cultures christological conceptions are non-existent. . . . Although several christological studies have appeared since, a feeling of crisis persists because those involved in christological research appear unable to reach even a modicum of consensus with regard to a suitable paradigm for Christ. Some prefer to cast him as Victor or Chief; others as Ancestor, without any party being able to establish a convincing claim. . . . At the level of folk theology, there exists at least one christological paradigm which is made use of over large areas of sub-Saharan Africa. The paradigm referred to is that of the medicine-person, known in many Bantu languages by the noun *nganga* or one of its cognates" (pp. 157–58).

[77] Green, *The Carolingian Lord*, p. 303. An additional, more direct rationale for the attribution of *dryhten* to Christ may be that the lordship of the *comitatus* was probably the social function most admired by Carolingian society. Green believes that the Church did not seek to assimilate the terminology of kinship, the other major source of ethical values in Germanic society, because of its close association with the obligation of revenge embodied in the blood feud (pp. 308–11).

[78] Summarizing the view of Christianity expressed in the only extant eighth-century Frankish historical text, Richard Gerberding, *The Rise of the Carolingians and the "Liber Historiae*

notions of sin and salvation were assimilated by the Germanic peoples
during the early Middle Ages, they may be said to have been Christianized;
to the extent that Christianity became more religiopolitical and magicoreligious during this period, it may be said to have been Germanized.

Francorum" (Oxford: Clarendon Press, 1987), states: "For the *LHF*-author, Christianity, its
God, and its Church are the source of holy clairvoyant men, magic relics, ritual, and patron
saints—all offering aid, advice, or protection and then usually for the pursuits of battle. . . . For
the *LHF*-author there was no dichotomy between military ideals and Christianity. . . .When
describing the founding of Saint Peter's Church in Paris by Clovis and Clothild, he put the
following words in Clothild's mouth—words all the more significant because he did not find
them in Gregory [Gregory of Tours' *Historia Francorum*]: '. . . let us build a church in honour of
the most blessed Peter, prince of the apostles, in order that he may be your helper in battle' "
(pp. 160–61). Also, Lynn White, Jr., "The Life of the Silent Majority," in Robert S. Hoyt, ed.,
Life and Thought in the Early Middle Ages (Minneapolis: University of Minneapolis Press, 1967),
has observed: "Even when there was external conformity with the new faith, the essence of
popular religion long remained little affected. Merovingian archaeology reveals horrifyingly
primitive religious attitudes. Scholars have not yet examined in adequate detail one of the most
significant chapters in European history: the gradual spread of the parish system out of the tiny
cities into the rude countryside. Not until church towers rose above cultivated fields [about the
tenth century] did the new religion begin to modify the minds and emotions of most men"
(pp. 98–99).

Conclusion

Throughout this inquiry, a number of religious, historical, social, political, and linguistic developments have been associated with the Germanization of early medieval Christianity. Some of the more notable developments discussed in previous chapters were the growth of the *Eigenkirchensystem* and *Eigenklostersystem*, the development of *Adelsheilige* hagiographic canons, the legitimation of the concepts of sacral kingship and crusade, the advance of religiopolitical complementarity, the development of a dramatic-representational liturgical form, and generally, the emergence of a heroic, folk-centered, magicoreligious reinterpretation of Christianity. Not only have the effects of Germanization and Christianization been identified, but an effort has been made to understand the process of religious transformation which occurred.

It has been argued that the degree of inherent disparity between Germanic and early Christian social structures and world-views led Christian missionaries to employ a policy of initial accommodation. They assumed that more rigorous ethical and doctrinal formation would soon follow and eliminate incompatible Germanic ideological elements. However, the decline of the catechumenate, combined with the vitality of Germanic folk-religiosity, resulted in the adherence of the Germanic peoples to a Germanic folk-religious reinterpretation of Christianity. As a consequence of the religiopolitical influence of the Ottonian emperors in Rome during the tenth and eleventh centuries, this Germanic reinterpretation eventually became normative throughout western Christendom.[1]

[1] K. J. Leyser, "Sacral Kingship," part 3 of *Rule and Conflict in an Early Medieval Society: Ottonian Saxony* (Oxford: Basil Blackwell, 1989), notes that the Ottonian Emperors "made themselves thoroughly at home in the *Reichskirche* and were really its centre giving it what solidarity it possessed. . . . It is thought by a formidable body of scholars that they [manifestations of medieval kingship] coexisted with the much older, archetypal and magical components of sacrality. This kind of kingship, or at least elements of it, were not dissolved by Christianity; on the contrary, they lived on to contaminate and to compromise the new religion" (p. 80).

Derek Baker has summarized the process by which the Christianization efforts of the early Middle Ages bore Germanized fruits:

> Indeed, when the composite character of the Christian message that was preached is examined, it becomes difficult to see what opposition could have been aroused to it, except from the vested interests of priestly or bardic castes, for the Church was seeking to incorporate much that was pagan into Christian life. . . . It was perhaps the corruption of Christians by pagan practice rather than the continuing paganism within Christendom which menaced the faith more. . . . Pagan magic had to be countered by Christian, as Columba demonstrated in his contest with the Pictish magician Briochan, and when the Christian God seemed to fail, men returned to the old ways. . . . Christianity had, in fact, been established on the same footing as the cults that it sought to displace. . . .
>
> Europe may have seemed Christian in the year 1000, but it was only "the shadow of the Christian symbol" which had been cast.[2]

The relative absence of ethical instruction and the greater absence of doctrinal inculcation and theological speculation among the Germanic peoples between the fourth and eighth centuries was countered by the omnipresence of religiopolitical unity and magicoreligious piety. The religiopolitical effects of the Germanization of Christianity appear to have endured longest, embodied in the European ideal of Christendom. Even after the official political disengagement of most European nations from Christianity, the Euro-Christian religiocultural fusion which had developed over a millennium remained strong within Western Christianity. Opposition to this fusion, especially as it might interfere with notions of universalism and ecumenism, was expressed in several of the documents of the Second Vatican Council.[3] Opposition to a magicoreligious interpretation of Christianity, particularly to the extent that it may obscure a full appreciation of the soteriological and eschatological mysteries of Redemption, was also expressed by the Council.[4] Nevertheless, Eurocentric religiocultural sentiment remains strong among Catholic traditionalists, and some of the magicoreligious effects of the Germanization of Christianity, such as Masses

---

[2] "The Shadow of the Christian Symbol," in G. J. Cuming, ed., *The Mission of the Church and the Propagation of the Faith,* SCH, vol. 6 (Cambridge: Cambridge University Press, 1970), pp. 25–28. For a detailed discussion of both pagan survivals and new adaptations, see Valerie I. J. Flint, *The Rise of Magic in Early Medieval Europe* (Princeton, N.J.: Princeton University Press, 1991), especially pp. 68–84.

[3] These Council documents include *Lumen Gentium* (Dogmatic Constitution on the Church), *Gaudium et Spes* (Pastoral Constitution on the Church in the Modern World), *Unitatis Redintegratio* (Decree on Ecumenism), and *Ad Gentes* (Decree on the Church's Missionary Activity). The apotheosis of the Roman Catholic Church's dissociation from its European heritage came on October 28, 1974 when the Vatican Congregation for Divine Worship officially forbade the celebration of the Tridentine Latin Mass. This act was rescinded by Pope John Paul II on July 2, 1988, two days after Archbishop Marcel Lefebvre consecrated three traditionalist bishops.

[4] See *Sacrosanctum Concilium* (Constitution on the Sacred Liturgy).

offered at the shrines of saints for special intentions, remain formidable elements of contemporary Catholic religiosity.

Some reflection on the nature of the missionary policy of accommodation is in order. The term "accommodation" itself is far too benign for the radical modification of beliefs, attitudes, values, and behavior (BAVB) that this policy encompassed. It almost implies that the missionaries were doing the Germanic peoples a favor by modifying Christianity to conform to their world-view. Yet this is hardly what the missionaries intended. Tacit compromises with the existing Germanic world-view were expected to constitute only the first temporary step in a gradual process of radical BAVB modification. Whereas straightforward preaching often resulted in the rejection of an alien world-view and coercion usually provoked resentment toward the new religion, by obscuring the substantial inherent disparity between Christian and Germanic world-views, the policy of accommodation allowed the missionaries to make inroads into the Germanic ethos and world-view. This deliberate misrepresentation of Christianity in Germanic terms, followed by a program of gradual, barely perceptible BAVB modification might have completely transformed Germanic religiosity into a replica of early Christianity had it not been for the contemporaneous decline of the catechumenate, and the vitality of the Germanic ethos and world-view.

The Christian effort to modify the Germanic BAVB construct did not end with the early Middle Ages. After the influence of the Ottonian emperors and their successors in Rome during the tenth and eleventh centuries helped to make a Germanized form of Christianity normative throughout Western Europe, Christianization efforts continued as movements of reform and renewal. To restore the ideal of the *ecclesia primitiva* was the goal of the Gregorian, Cistercian, and Franciscan reform movements of the later Middle Ages, as well as the Protestant Reformation and the Second Vatican Council. Implicit (and sometimes explicit) in this goal has been the de-emphasis, if not the repudiation, of the early medieval Germanic influence on Christianity. The recently accelerated, and hence more perceptible dissociation of the Roman Catholic and other Christian churches from their European heritage may have contributed toward a reciprocal dissociation of many Christians of European descent from these churches, and possibly from Christianity altogether. Alienation appears most likely to occur among those Euro-Christians for whom religiosity and cultural identity are closely related.[5]

---

[5] A study of the institutions, if any, to which these alienated Euro-Christians transfer their allegiance would be of interest. C. J. T. Talar, "Dieu, est-il anti-semite? The French Catholic Right," *Continuum* 1:1 (1990): 63–77, provides an overview of the situation in France where it appears that such individuals of a Catholic background are likely to be attracted to Catholic traditionalist churches and/or nationalist political movements. Perhaps the increasing popularity of neopagan organizations may also be derived from a reaction against the cultural self-criticism engaged in by many Christian churches in Europe and North America.

At the end of Part I, an outline of a model of religious transformation for encounters between folk-religious societies and universal religions was presented. In Part II, this model has been applied to the encounter of the Germanic peoples with Christianity. A summary of the conclusions from this application is presented below:

1. The prevailing social structure from which early Christianity emerged was urban, heterogeneous, and anomic, with a sizable underclass, whereas the prevailing social structure within Germanic societies from the fourth through the eighth centuries was rural and homogeneous, with a high level of group solidarity and a warrior aristocracy.

2. The world-view of early Christianity was predominantly world-rejecting and soteriological, whereas the world-view of Germanic societies during the early middle ages was predominantly world-accepting and sociobiological.

3. To advance the process of Christianization among the Germanic peoples, its advocates sought to accommodate the religiopolitical and magicoreligious elements of Germanic religiosity.

4. In attempting to demonstrate the superior power and reliability of the Christian God, and in employing terms derived from the *comitatus* institution to convey Christian concepts, advocates of Christianization were implicitly reinterpreting Christianity in accordance with the world-view of the Germanic peoples.

5. The continued reliance of the Church upon Frankish political and military force—from the Gallo-Roman episcopacy in the fifth century to St. Boniface and the papacy in the eighth century—contributed toward the adaptation of Christianity to Germanic political and military ideals.

6. The world-accepting Indo-European and Germanic tradition of religiopolitical complementarity was manifested in the attempt by the Goths and other Germanic peoples to preserve their ethnocultural identity in the midst of the Roman Empire by adhering to Arianism. Religiopolitical complementarity is also evident in the early medieval Germano-Christian development of the *Eigenkirchensystem* and *Eigenklostersystem,* as well as in the concept of *Geblütsheiligkeit,* and in the *Adelsheilige* hagiographies.

7. Advocates of Christianization were unable to accomplish more than a "superficial" or "nominal" Christianization of the Germanic peoples, at least prior to the reign of Charlemagne (768–814), for the following reasons:

    a. the decline of the catechumenate and a shortage of other qualified personnel;

b. a sense of eschatological urgency which prioritized the quantity of those baptized over the degree of their Christianization;

c. the substantial inherent disparity between Christian and Germanic religiosity;

d. the vitality of indigenous Germanic religiosity.

8. Gallo-Roman bishops, Irish monks, and Anglo-Saxon missionaries accomplished all that was possible, given the socioreligious environment in which they operated. Had they not adopted a methodology of accommodation, and instead focused on directly resolving the fundamental distinctions between traditional Germanic and traditional Christian world-views, they would probably have made no permanent inroads at all.

9. Although the decline of the catechumenate seriously impeded the process of Christianization, the accommodation of Germanic religiosity provided a foundation for later efforts which sought to advance Christian doctrine and ethics.

10. In their implementation of a policy of accommodating Christianity to Germanic religiosity, Christian missionaries generally misrepresented the high degree of inherent disparity that existed between Germanic religiosity and Christianity. The missionaries also tended to withhold the extent of ethos, world-view, and behavior modification which they ultimately hoped to achieve.

11. A result of the implementation of this policy of accommodation was a perception among the Germanic peoples that one became a Christian merely by including Christ and his saints in one's pantheon, and by relating to them in a Germanic magicoreligious and religiopolitical fashion, without substantial ethical or doctrinal requirements.

12. Some additional factors which affected the expansion of Christianity among the Germanic peoples during this period were:

a. the association of Christianity by non-Frankish Germanic peoples with the political aims of the Franks;

b. a historically inaccurate causal association of Christianity with Roman grandeur;

c. the coincidental similarity between certain Germanic myths, rituals, and symbols and certain Christian religious beliefs, rituals, and symbols.

Throughout this inquiry, the term "Christianization," when applied to the early medieval Germanic peoples, has been qualified by the word "attempted." It is now appropriate to consider whether, by the time of St. Boniface's death in 754, the Germanic peoples had indeed been Christianized. Given the rigorous, objectivist definition of Christianization adopted at the outset of this inquiry, with its requirement of a conscious acceptance of the soteriological essence of Christianity,[6] it is concluded that the Germanic peoples had not been Christianized by the middle of the eighth century. If, instead, a relativist or subjectivist definition of Christianity is adopted, in which the essence of Christianity is not considered immutable, or in which religious affiliation is determined primarily by self-identification, it may be argued that the Germanic peoples were Christianized by this time. But it would be necessary to specify that the form of Christianity with which they became affiliated was a Germanized one.

---

[6] See above, pp. 34–35. Clebsch's view of a "variety of Christianities," although held in abeyance earlier, appears quite valid in view of the evidence developed in this inquiry. Also, it seems that the concept of religious universality itself may benefit from a re-evaluation, given the wide diversity in BAVB constructs among cultures and the fundamental nexus between religiosity and culture.

Bibliography

Primary Sources

Avitus of Vienne. *Alcimi Ecdicii Aviti.* MGH AA Vol. 6, part 2. Edited by Rudolf Peiper. Berlin: Weidmannsche Buchhandlung, 1883.

Bede. *Historia Ecclesiastica.* PL Vol. 95.

Bernard of Clairvaux. *De laude novae militiae.* In Jean Leclercq, C. H. Talbot, and H. Rochais, eds. *Sancti Bernardi Opera.* Vol. 3. Rome: Editiones cistercienses, 1959, 213–39.

Boniface. *S. Bonifatii et Lulli epistolae.* MGH Ep. sel. Vol. 1. Edited by Michael Tangl. Berlin: Weidmannsche Buchhandlung, 1916.

Caesar, Gaius Julius. *Libri VII De bello Gallico.* Vol. 1 of *Commentarii.* Edited by R. L. A. Du Pontet. Oxford Classical Texts. Oxford: Oxford University Press, 1900.

Capitularia Regum Francorum. MGH Legum Sectio II Vol. 1, part 1. Edited by Alfred Boretius. Hanover: Hahn Verlag, 1881.

Columbanus. *Sancti Columbani Opera.* Edited by G. S. M. Walker. Dublin: Institute for Advanced Studies, 1957.

Concilios Visigóticos e Hispano-Romanos. Edited by José Vives. España cristiana, Textos 1. Barcelona: Instituto Enrique Florez, 1963.

Edda, die Lieder des Codex Regius. 4th ed. Edited by Gustav Neckel. Revised by Hans Kuhn. Heidelberg: Winter Verlag, 1962.

Gregory I. *Gregorii I papae Registrum Epistolarum.* MGH Epistolae Vols. 1 and 2. Edited by Paul Ewald and Ludwig M. Hartmann. Berlin: Weidmannsche Buchhandlung, 1891–99.

Gregory of Tours. *Libri historiarum.* MGH SRM Vol. 1, part 1. 2nd ed. Edited by Bruno Krusch and Wilhelm Levison. 1937–51, reprint, Hanover: Hahn Verlag, 1961.

————. *Libri de virtutibus S. Martini episcopi.* MGH SRM Vol. 1, part 2. Edited by Wilhelm Arndt and Bruno Krusch. Hanover: Hahn Verlag, 1885.

Heliand und Genesis. 9th ed. Edited by Otto Behaghel. Revised by Burkhard Taeger. Tübingen: Max Niemeyer Verlag, 1984.

Jonas of Bobbio. *Vitae Columbani abbatis discipulorumque eius libri duo.* MGH SRM Vol. 4. Edited by Bruno Krusch. Hanover: Hahn Verlag, 1902.

Leges Burgundionum. Edited by L. R. de Salis. MGH Leges Sect. 1, vol. 2, part 1. Hanover: Hahn Verlag, 1892.

Leges Visigothorum. Edited by Karl Zeumer. MGH Leges Sect. 1, vol. 1. Hanover: Hahn Verlag, 1902.

Lex Alamannorum. 2nd ed. Edited by Karl August Eckhardt. MGH Leges Sect. 1, vol. 5, part 1. Hanover: Hahn Verlag, 1966.

Lex Angliorum Werinorum Hoc Est Thuringorum. Edited by Karl von Richtofen. MGH Leges Vol. 5. Hanover: Hahn Verlag, 1875–89.

Lex Ribuaria. 2nd ed. Edited by F. Beyerle and R. Buchner. *MGH Leges* Sect. 1, vol. 3, part 2. Hanover: Hahn Verlag, 1954.

Lex Saxonum. Edited by Karl von Richtofen. *MGH Leges* Vol. 5. Hanover: Hahn Verlag, 1875–89.

Liber Historiae Francorum. Edited by Bruno Krusch. *MGH SRM* Vol. 2. Hanover: Hahn Verlag, 1889.

Martin of Braga. *Martini episcopi Bracarensis Opera Omnia.* Edited by C. W. Barlow. Papers and Monographs of the American Academy in Rome, no. 12. New Haven, Conn.: Yale University Press, 1950.

Pactus Legis Salicae. Edited by Karl August Eckhardt. *MGH Leges* Sect. 1, vol. 4, parts 1 and 2. Hanover: Hahn Verlag, 1962–69.

Pirmin. *De singulis libris canonicis scarapsus. PL* Vol. 89, col. 1029–50.

Remigius of Rheims. *Ep.* 1–4. *Epistolae Austrasicae. MGH Epistolae* Vol. 3. Edited by Wilhelm Gundlach. Berlin: Weidmannsche Buchhandlung, 1892.

Tacitus, Publius Cornelius. *Opera minora.* Edited by M. J. Winterbottom and Robertus Maxwell. Oxford Classical Texts. Oxford: Oxford University Press, 1975.

Vita Amandi episcopi. MGH SRM Vol. 5. Edited by Bruno Krusch. Hanover: Hahn Verlag, 1910.

Vita Eligii episcopi Noviomagensis. MGH SRM Vol. 4. Edited by Bruno Krusch. Hanover: Hahn Verlag, 1902.

Vita Vulframni episcopi Senonici. MGH SRM Vol. 5. Edited by Wilhelm Levison. Hanover: Hahn Verlag, 1905.

Walafrid Strabo. *Vita Galli. MGH SRM* Vol. 4. Edited by Bruno Krusch. Hanover: Hahn Verlag, 1902.

Willibald. *Vita Bonifatii auctore Willibaldo. MGH SSrG* Vol. 57. Edited by Wilhelm Levison. Hanover: Hahn Verlag, 1905.

Secondary Sources

Aberle, David. "A Note on Relative Deprivation Theory as Applied to Millenarian and Other Cult Movements." In Sylvia L. Thrupp, ed. *Millennial Dreams in Action: Studies in Revolutionary Religious Movements*. Comparative Studies in Society and History, supp. 2, 209–14. The Hague: Mouton, 1962.

Adam, Adolf. *The Liturgical Year: Its History and its Meaning after the Reform of the Liturgy*. Translated by Matthew J. O'Connell. New York: Pueblo, 1981.

Adams, Robert M. *Decadent Societies*. San Francisco: North Point, 1983.

Aland, Kurt. *A History of Christianity*. Vol. 1: *From the Beginnings to the Threshold of the Reformation*. Translated by James L. Schaaf. Philadelphia: Fortress Press, 1985.

Albertson, Clinton. *Anglo-Saxon Saints and Heroes*. New York: Fordham University Press, 1967.

Ament, H. "The Germanic Tribes in Europe." In Wilson, *The Northern World,* 49–70.

Amos, Thomas Leslie. "The Origin and Nature of the Carolingian Sermon." Ph.D. diss., Michigan State University, 1983.

Angus, Samuel. *The Mystery Religions and Christianity: A Study in the Religious Background of Early Christianity.* New York: Scribner's, 1925.

Ardrey, Robert. *The Social Contract.* New York: Atheneum, 1970.

Arent, A. Margaret. "The Heroic Pattern: Old German Helmets, *Beowulf* and *Grettis Saga.*" In Edgar C. Polomé, ed., *Old Norse Literature and Mythology: A Symposium,* 130–99. Austin: University of Texas Press, 1969.

Athanassiadi-Fowden, Polymia. *Julian and Hellenism: An Intellectual Biography.* Oxford: Clarendon Press, 1981.

Babcock William S. "Macmullen on Conversion: A Response." *The Second Century* 5:2 (1985/86): 82–89.

Baetke, Walter. *Das Heilige im Germanischen.* Tübingen: J. C. B. Mohr (Paul Siebeck), 1942.

_____. *Die Aufnahme des Christentums durch die Germanen: Ein Beitrag zur Frage der Germanisierung des Christentums.* Special ed. Darmstadt: Wissenschaftliche Buchgesellschaft, 1962.

Baker, Derek. "Sowing the Seeds of Faith: Theory and Practice in the Mission Field." In Baker, ed., *Miscellanea Historiae Ecclesiasticae,* vol. 3.

_____. "The Shadow of the Christian Symbol." In Cuming, ed., *The Mission of the Church and the Propagation of the Faith,* 25–28.

_____. *The Church in Town and Countryside.* SCH, no. 16. Oxford: Basil Blackwell, 1979.

Baker, Derek, ed. *Miscellanea Historiae Ecclesiasticae.* Vol. 3. Louvain: Publications Universitaires de Louvain, 1970.

Barber, Richard. *The Knight and Chivalry.* New York: Harper & Row, 1982.

Barker, Eileen. "Who'd Be a Moonie? A Comparative Study of Those Who Join the Unification Church in Britain." In Bryan Wilson, ed. *The Social Impact of New Religious Movements.* New York: Rose of Sharon Press, 1981.

_____. *The Making of a Moonie: Choice or Brainwashing?* London: Basil Blackwell, 1984.

Barnes, M. H. "Primitive Religious Thought and the Evolution of Religion." *Religion* 22:1 (1992): 21–46.

Batiffol, Pierre. *Primitive Catholicism.* Translated from the 5th ed. by Henri L. Brianceau. New York: Longmans, Green, 1911.

Baus, Karl. *From the Apostolic Community to Constantine.* Vol. 1 of *History of the Church.* Hubert Jedin and John Dolan, eds. New York: Crossroad, 1982.

Bauschatz, Paul C. *The Well and the Tree: World and Time in Early Germanic Culture.* Amherst: University of Massachusetts Press, 1982.

Bede. *A History of the English Church and People.* Translation and introduction by Leo Sherley-Price. Harmondsworth: Penguin, 1955. Revised by R. E. Latham, 1968.

Bellah, Robert. "Religious Evolution." In Roland Robertson, ed., *Sociology of Religion: Selected Readings,* 262–92. Baltimore: Penguin, 1969.

_____. *Tokugawa Religion: The Cultural Roots of Modern Japan.* New York: Free Press, 1985.

Belloc, Hilaire. *Europe and the Faith.* London: Constable, 1920.

Benko, Stephen. *Pagan Rome and the Early Christians*. Bloomington: Indiana University Press, 1984.

Benveniste, Emile. *Indo-European Language and Society*. Translated by Elizabeth Palmer. Coral Gables, Fl.: University of Miami Press, 1973.

Benz, Ernest. "On Understanding Non-Christian Religions." In Mircea Eliade and Joseph M. Kitigawa, eds., *The History of Religions: Essays in Methodology*, 115–31. Chicago: University of Chicago Press, 1959.

Betz, Hans Dieter. "Cosmogony and Ethics in the Sermon on the Mount." In Robin W. Lovin and Frank E. Reynolds, eds., *Cosmogony and Ethical Order: New Studies in Comparative Ethics*, 158–176. Chicago: University of Chicago Press, 1985.

Betz, Werner. "Lehnwörter and Lehnprägungen im Vor- und Frühdeutschen." In vol. 1 of *Deutsche Wortgeschichte*, 3rd rev. ed., ed. Friedrich Maurer and Heinz Rupp, rev. Heinz Rupp, 135–60. Berlin: Walter de Gruyter, 1974.

Bianchi, Ugo. *The History of Religions*. Leiden: E. J. Brill, 1975.

Bianchi, Ugo, ed. *Le Origini dello Gnosticicsmo: Colloquio di Messina 13–18 Aprile 1966*. Numen Supplement, no. 12. Leiden: Brill, 1967.

Binchy, D. A. "A Pre-Christian Survival in Medieval Irish Hagiography." In Dorothy Whitelock, Rosamond McKitterick, and David Dumville, eds., *Ireland in Early Medieval Europe: Studies in Memory of Kathleen Hughes*. Cambridge: Cambridge University Press, 1982.

Blake, E. O. "The Formation of the 'Crusade Idea.' " *JEH* 21 (1970): 11–31.

Blalok, Herbert M. "Status Inconsistency, Social Mobility, Status Integration, and Structural Effects." *ASR* 32 (1967): 790–801.

Bloch, Marc. *Feudal Society*. Translated by L. A. Mayon. With a foreword by M. M. Postan. Chicago: University of Chicago Press, 1961.

Blumenfeld-Kosinski, Renate, and Timea Szell. *Images of Sainthood in Medieval Europe*. Ithaca, N.Y.: Cornell University Press, 1991.

Blumenthal, Uta-Renate. *The Investiture Controversy: Church and Monarchy from the Ninth to the Twelfth Century*. Philadelphia: University of Pennsylvania Press, 1988.

Böhmer, Heinrich. "Das germanische Christentum." *Theologische Studien und Kritiken* 86 (1913): 165–280.

Bömer, Franz. *Untersuchungen über die Religion der Sklaven in Griechenland und Rom*. 4 vols. Mainz: Steiner, 1957.

Bonus, Arthur. *Zur Germanisierung des Christentums*. Jena: Eugen Diederichs, 1911.

The Book of Pontiffs ("Liber Pontificalis"): The Ancient Biographies of the First Ninety Roman Bishops to A.D. 715. Translated with an introduction by Raymond Davis. Liverpool: Liverpool University Press, 1989.

Bosl, Karl. "Die germanische Kontinuität im deutschen Mittelalter: Adel, König, Kirche." In *Antike und Orient im Mittelalter*, ed. Paul Wilpert and Willehad Paul Eckert, 1–25. Miscellanea Mediaevalia, no. 1. Berlin: Walter de Gruyter, 1962.

————. "Der Adelsheiliger." In *Speculum Historiale: Geschichte im Spiegel von Geschichtsschreibung und Geschichtsdeutung. Festschrift für Johannes Spörl aus Anlass seines 60. Geburtstages,* ed. Clemens Bauer, Laetitia Boehm, and Max Müller, 167–87. Munich: Alber, 1965.

Bostock, J. Knight. *A Handbook on Old High German Literature.* 2nd rev. ed. Oxford: Clarendon Press, 1976.

Bouchard, Thomas J., Jr. "Twins Reared Together and Apart: What They Tell Us About Human Diversity." In Sidney W. Fox, ed., *Individuality and Determinism: Chemical and Biological Bases.* New York: Plenum, 1984.

Bouchard, Thomas J., Jr., David T. Lykken, Matthew McGue, Nancy L. Segal, and Auke Tellegen. "Sources of Human Psychological Differences: The Minnesota Study of Twins Reared Apart." *Science* 250 (12 October 1990): 223–28.

Boudriot, Wilhelm. *Die Altgermanische Religion in der amtlichen kirchlichen Literatur des Abendlandes vom 5. bis 11. Jahrhundert.* 1928; reprint, Bonn: Ludwig Röhrscheid Verlag, 1964.

Bowsky, William R., ed. *Studies in Medieval and Renaissance History.* Vol. 3. Lincoln: University of Nebraska Press, 1966.

Boyer, Régis. *Le Christ des Barbares: Le Monde nordique, IXe–XIIe siècles.* Paris: Cerf, 1987.

Bradley, Keith R. *Discovering the Roman Family: Studies in Roman Social History.* New York: Oxford University Press, 1991.

Brandon, S. G. F. *Man and His Destiny in the Great Religions.* Manchester: Manchester University Press, 1962.

————. *The Savior God: Comparative Studies in the Concept of Salvation Presented to Edwin Oliver James.* 1963; reprint, Westport, Conn.: Greenwood Press, 1980.

————. *History, Time and Deity.* Manchester: Manchester University Press, 1965.

Branley, Brendan R. *Christianity and the Japanese.* Maryknoll, N.Y.: Maryknoll Publications, 1966.

Branston, Brian. *Gods of the North.* New York: Thames and Hudson, 1980.

Brechter, Suso. "Das Apostolat des heiligen Bonifatius und Gregors des Grossen Missions-Instruktionen für England." In *Sankt Bonifatius: Gedenkausgabe zum zwölfhundertsten Todestag,* 22–33.

Bromley, David G., and Anson D. Shupe. *"Moonies" in America: Cult, Church, and Crusade.* Beverly Hills, California: Sage Publications, 1979.

Brown, Lawrence. *The Might of the West.* Washington, D.C.: Joseph J. Binns, 1963.

Brown, Peter. *Religion and Society in the Age of Saint Augustine.* New York: Harper & Row, 1972.

————. *The Cult of the Saints: Its Rise and Function in Latin Christianity.* Chicago: University of Chicago Press, 1981.

————. *Society and the Holy in Late Antiquity.* Berkeley: University of California Press, 1982.

Browning, Robert. *The Emperor Julian.* Berkeley: University of California Press, 1976.

Buchholz, Peter. "Perspectives for Historical Research in Germanic Religion." *History of Religions* 8 (1968): 111–38.

Buchholz, Peter. "Odin: Celtic and Siberian Affinities of a Germanic Deity."
    Mankind Quarterly 24 (1984): 427–37.
_____. "Religious Sculpture in Roman Germania and Adjacent Regions." *JIES*
    12 (1984): 31–75.
Bultmann, Rudolf. *Faith and Understanding*. Edited by Robert W. Funk. New
    York: Harper & Row, 1966.
The Burgundian Code. Translated by Katherine Fischer Drew. Foreword by Edward
    Peters. Pennsylvania Paperback edition. Philadelphia: University of Pennsyl-
    vania Press, 1972.
Burkert, Walter. *Homo Necans: The Anthropology of Ancient Greek Sacrificial
    Ritual and Myth*. Translated by Peter Bing. Berkeley: University of California
    Press, 1983.
_____. *Greek Religion*. Translated by John Raffan. Cambridge, Mass.: Harvard
    University Press, 1985.
_____. *Ancient Mystery Cults*. Cambridge, Mass.: Harvard University Press, 1987.
Burns, Edward McNall. *Western Civilizations: Their History and Their Culture*. 7th
    ed. New York: W. W. Norton, 1969.
Burns, Thomas. *A History of the Ostrogoths*. Bloomington: Indiana University Press,
    1984.
Bury, J. B. *History of the Later Roman Empire*. 2 vols. 1923; reprint, New York:
    Dover, 1958.
_____. *The Invasion of Europe by the Barbarians*. Norton Library edition. 1928;
    reprint, New York: W. W. Norton, 1967.
Byrnes, Joseph F. *The Psychology of Religion*. New York: The Free Press, 1986.
Caesar, Gaius Julius. *The Conquest of Gaul*. Translated by S. A. Handford. New
    York: Penguin, 1951.
Caldwell, Larry. "The Indo-European Context of *Beowulf*." Ph.D. diss., University
    of Nebraska, 1983.
Campbell, Joseph. *Occidental Mythology*. Vol. 3: *The Masks of God*. Harmonds-
    worth: Penguin, 1964.
Carrier, Hervé. *The Sociology of Religious Belonging*. Translated by Arthur J.
    Arrieri. New York: Herder and Herder, 1965.
Carson, Neil R. *Psychology: The Science of Behavior*. Boston: Allyn and Bacon,
    1984.
Casel, Odo. "Das Mysteriengedächtnis der Meßliturgie im Lichte der Tradition."
    JL 6 (1926): 113–204.
Cattell, Raymond B. "Cultural and Political-Economic Psychology." In Cattell, ed.,
    Handbook of Multivariate Experimental Psychology. Chicago: Rand-McNally,
    1966.
_____. *A New Morality from Science: Beyondism*. Pergamon General Psychol-
    ogy Series, no. 32. New York: Pergamon Press, 1972.
_____. *Beyondism: Religion from Science*. New York: Praeger, 1987.
Chadwick, Henry Munro. *The Heroic Age*. Cambridge: University Press, 1912.
Chaney, William A. *The Cult of Kingship in Anglo-Saxon England: The Transition
    from Paganism to Christianity*. Berkeley: University of California Press, 1970.
Clark, Walter Houston. "William James: Contributions to the Psychology of
    Religious Conversion." *Pastoral Psychology* 26 (1965): 29–36.

Clarke, H. B., and M. Brennan, eds. *Columbanus and Merovingian Monasticism*. British Archaeological Reports, International Series, no. 113. Oxford: British Archaeological Reports, 1981.

Clawsey, Mary Crawford. "The *Comitatus* and the Lord-Vassal Relationship in the Medieval Epic." Ph.D. diss., University of Maryland, 1982.

Clebsch, William A. *Christianity in European History*. New York: Oxford University Press, 1978.

Coens, Maurice. "S. Boniface et sa mission historique." *Analecta Bollandiana* 73 (1955): 462–95.

Cohn, Norman. *The Pursuit of the Millennium*. Revised and expanded edition. New York: Oxford University Press, 1970.

Cole, Penny J. *The Preaching of the Crusades to the Holy Land, 1096–1270*. Medieval Academy Books, no. 98. Cambridge, Mass.: Medieval Academy of America, 1991.

Colgrave, Bertram, and R. A. B. Mynors, eds. *Bede's Ecclesiastical History of the English People*. Oxford: Clarendon Press, 1969.

Congar, Yves. "The Idea of Conversion." Translated by Alfeo Marzi. *Thought* 33 (1958): 5–20.

Conn, Walter. *Christian Conversion: A Developmental Interpretation of Autonomy and Surrender*. New York: Paulist Press, 1986.

Conquerors and Chroniclers of Early Medieval Spain. Translated with notes and introduction by Kenneth Baxter Wolf. Liverpool: Liverpool University Press, 1991.

Copleston, Frederick. *Medieval Philosophy*. Vol. 2 of *A History of Philosophy*. Garden City, N.Y.: Doubleday, 1950.

Covell, Ralph A. "The Conflict of the Gospel and Culture in China: W. A. P. Martin's Answer." In Kraft and Wisley, *Readings in Dynamic Indigeneity*, 428–38.

Crollius, Ary Roest. "What Is So New About Inculturation?" In Crollius, ed., *Inculturation: Working Papers on Living Faith and Cultures*, no. 5. Rome: Centre "Cultures and Religions," Pontifical Gregorian University, 1984.

Crossland, R. A. "Indo-European Origins: The Linguistic Evidence." *Past and Present* 12 (November 1957): 16–46.

————. "Immigrants from the North." In *Cambridge Ancient History*. 3rd ed. Vol. 1, part 2, ch. 27. Cambridge: Cambridge University Press, 1971.

Cuming, G. J., ed. *The Mission of the Church and the Propagation of the Faith*. SCH, vol. 6. Cambridge: Cambridge University Press, 1970.

Cumont, Franz. *The Oriental Religions in Roman Paganism*. 1911; reprint, New York: Dover, 1956.

Davenport, William. "The 'Hawaiian Cultural Revolution': Some Political and Economic Considerations." *American Anthropologist* 71 (1969): 1–20.

Davidson, Andrew R., and Elizabeth Thomson. "Cross-Cultural Studies of Attitudes and Beliefs." In *Social Psychology*, edited by Harry C. Triandis and Richard W. Brislin. Vol. 5 of *Handbook of Cross-Cultural Psychology*. Boston: Allyn and Bacon, 1980.

Davidson, H. R. Ellis. *Gods and Myths of Northern Europe*. Baltimore: Penguin, 1964.

Davidson, H. R. Ellis. *Pagan Scandanavia*. Ancient Peoples and Places Series, vol. 53. New York: Frederick A. Praeger, 1967.

_____. *Myths and Symbols in Pagan Europe*. Syracuse, N.Y.: Syracuse University Press, 1988.

Davies, Oliver. *God Within: The Mystical Tradition of Northern Europe*. Foreword by Rowan Williams. New York: Paulist Press, 1988.

Dawkins, Richard. *The Selfish Gene*. New York: Oxford University Press, 1976.

Dawson, Christopher. *The Making of Europe: An Introduction to the History of European Unity*. 1932; reprint, New York: World, 1952.

_____. *Religion and Culture*. New York: Sheed & Ward, 1948.

_____. *Religion and the Rise of Western Culture*. 1950; reprint, Garden City, N.Y.: Doubleday, 1958.

_____. "The Sociological Foundations of Medieval Christendom." In Dawson, ed., *Medieval Essays*. New York: Sheed & Ward, 1954.

_____. "The Problem of Metahistory." In *The Dynamics of World History*, edited by John J. Mulloy. New York: Sheed & Ward, 1956.

de Benoist, Alain. *Comment peut-on être païen?* Paris: Albin Michel, 1981.

de Clercq, Carlo. *La Législation religieuse franque de Clovis à Charlemagne: Etude sur les actes des conciles et des capitulaires, les statuts diocésains et les règles monastiques, 507–814*. 2nd series, no. 38. Louvain: Bureaux du Receuil, Université de Louvain, 1938.

Deichmann, F. W. "Frühchristliche Kirchen in antiken Heiligtümern." *Jarhbuch des Deutschen Archäologischen Instituts*, 54 (1939): 105–36.

Delaruelle, Etienne. *La piété au moyen âge*. Turin: Bottega d'Erasmo, 1975.

Delbono, Francesco. "La Letteratura catechetica di lingua tedesca (Il Problema della lingua nell'evangelizzazione." *Settimane* 14 (1967): 697–742.

Delbrück, Hans. *The Barbarian Invasions*. Translated by Walter J. Renfroe. History of the Art of War, vol. 2. 1980; reprint, Lincoln: University of Nebraska Press, 1990.

Della Volpe, Angela. "On Indo-European Ceremonial and Socio-Political Elements Underlying the Origin of Formal Boundaries." *JIES* 20:1/2 (1992): 71–122.

Delumeau, Jean. *Sin and Fear: The Emergence of a Western Guilt Culture, 13th–18th Centuries*. Translated by Eric Nicholson. New York: St. Martin's Press, 1990.

Desroche, Henri. "Areas and Methods of a Sociology of Religion: The Work of G. Le Bras." *Journal of Religion* 35 (1955): 34–47.

de Vries, Jan. "Der heutige Stand der germanischen Religionsforschung." *Germanisch-romanische Monatschrift*, series 2 (1951–52): 1–11.

_____. *Altgermanische Religionsgeschichte*. 2nd ed. 2 vols. Berlin: Walter de Gruyter, 1956–57.

_____. "Das Königtum bei den Germanen." *Saeculum* 7 (1956): 289–309.

_____. *Heroic Song and Legend*. 1963; reprint, Salem, N.H.: Ayer, 1988.

_____. *Perspectives in the History of Religions*. Translation and introduction by Kees W. Bolle. Los Angeles: University of California Press, 1967.

Dickinson, G. Lowes. *The Greek View of Life*. Preface by E. M. Forster. [1896]; reprint, Ann Arbor: University of Michigan Press, 1958.

Dill, Samuel. *Roman Society in Gaul in the Merovingian Age*. London: Macmillan, 1926.

Dirksen, Aloys H. "The New Testament Concept of *Metanoia*." Ph.D. diss., Catholic University of America, 1932.

Dodds, E. R. *Pagan and Christian in an Age of Anxiety: Some Aspects of Religious Experience from Marcus Aurelius to Constantine*. 1965; reprint, New York: W. W. Norton, 1970.

The Dream of the Rood. Edited by Bruce Dickins and Alan S. C. Ross. New York: Appleton-Century-Crofts, 1966.

Dressler, William W. *Stress and Adaptation in the Context of Culture: Depression in a Southern Black Community*. Albany: State University of New York Press, 1991.

Drew, Katherine Fischer. "Another Look at the Origins of the Middle Ages: A Reassessment of the Role of the Germanic Kingdoms." *Speculum* 62:4 (1987): 803–12.

_____. *Law and Society in Early Medieval Europe: Studies in Early Medieval History*. London: Variorum Reprints, 1988.

Drews, Robert. *The Coming of the Greeks: Indo-European Conquests in the Aegean and the Near East*. Princeton, N.J.: Princeton University Press, 1988.

Drinkwater, John, and Hugh Elton, eds. *Fifth Century Gaul: A Crisis of Identity?* Cambridge: Cambridge University Press, 1992.

Duby, Georges. *The Chivalrous Society*. Translated by Cynthia Postan. Berkeley: University of California Press, 1980.

_____. *The Three Orders: Feudal Society Imagined*. Translated by Arthur Goldhammer. Foreword by Thomas N. Bisson. Chicago: University of Chicago Press, 1980.

Duchesne-Guillemin, J. *The Western Response to Zoroaster*. Oxford: Clarendon Press, 1958.

Duggan, Robert D. *Conversion and the Catechumenate*. New York: Paulist Press, 1984.

Dulles, Avery. "The Emerging World Church: A Theological Reflection." *Proceedings of the Catholic Theological Society of America* 39 (1984): 1–12.

_____. *The Catholicity of the Church*. Oxford: Clarendon Press, 1985.

Dumézil, Georges. *Aspects de la fonction guerrière chez les Indo-Européens*. Bibliothèque de l'Ecole des Hautes Etudes, Section Religieuse, vol. 68. Paris: Presses Universitaires de France, 1956.

_____. *L'Idéologie tripartie des Indo-Européens*. Collection Latomus, vol. 31. Brussels: Latomus, 1958.

_____. *Archaic Roman Religion*. Translated by Philip Krapp. Foreword by Mircea Eliade. 2 vols. Chicago: University of Chicago Press, 1970.

_____. *The Destiny of the Warrior*. Translated by Alf Hiltebeitel. Chicago: University of Chicago Press, 1970.

_____. *Gods of the Ancient Northmen*. Edited and translated by Einar Haugen. Berkeley: University of California Press, 1973.

_____. *Les Dieux souverains des Indo-Européens*. Bibliothèque des Sciences Humaines. Paris: Gallimard, 1977.

Dumézil, Georges. *Camillus: A Study of Indo-European Religion as History*. Translated by Anette Aronowicz and Josette Bryson. Edited with an introduction by Udo Strutynski. Berkeley: University of California Press, 1980.

_____. *The Stakes of the Warrior*. Translated by David Weeks. Edited with an introduction by Jaan Puhvel. Berkeley: University of California Press, 1983.

_____. *Mitra-Varuna: An Essay on Two Indo-European Representations of Sovereignty*. Translated by Derek Coltman. New York: Zone Books, 1988.

Durkheim, Emile. *The Elementary Forms of the Religious Life*. Translated by Joseph Ward Swain. 1915; reprint, New York: Free Press, 1965.

Eichoff, Jürgen, and Irmengard Rauch. *Der Heliand*. Darmstadt: Wissenschaftliche Buchgesellschaft, 1973.

Elbern, Victor H. "Heilige, Dämonen und Magie an Reliquiaren des frühen Mittelalters." *Settimane* (1989) 36: 951–80.

Eliade, Mircea. *The Myth of the Eternal Return or, Cosmos and History*. Translated by Willard R. Trask. Princeton, N.J.: Princeton University Press, 1954.

_____. *The Sacred and the Profane*. Translated by Willard R. Trask. New York: Harper & Row, 1959.

_____. *The Quest: History and Meaning in Religion*. Chicago: University of Chicago Press, 1969.

_____. *A History of Religious Ideas*. Vols. 1 and 2 translated by Willard R. Trask. Vol. 3 translated by Alf Hiltebeitel and Diane Apostolos-Cappadona. Chicago: University of Chicago Press, 1978–85.

Eliade, Mircea, ed. *Encyclopedia of Religion*. New York: Macmillan, 1987.

Ellard, Gerard. *Master Alcuin, Liturgist*. Chicago: Loyola University Press, 1956.

Elliott, Ralph W. V. *Runes: An Introduction*. 2nd ed. New York: St. Martin's Press, 1989.

Ellis, Hilda Roderick. *The Road to Hel: A Study of the Conception of the Dead in Old Norse Literature*. 1943; reprint, New York: Greenwood Press, 1968.

Erdmann, Carl. *The Origin of the Idea of Crusade*. Translated by M. W. Baldwin and Walter Goffart. Princeton, N.J.: Princeton University Press, 1977.

Evans, G. R. *The Thought of Gregory the Great*. Cambridge: Cambridge University Press, 1986.

Ewig, Eugen. "The First Contacts of Christianity with the Germans and the Conversion of the Goths." In Jedin and Dolan, eds., *History of the Church*, vol. 2.

_____. "The Conversion of the Franks and the Burgundians: Origin and Organization of the Merovingian National Church." In Jedin and Dolan, eds., *History of the Church*, vol. 2.

Ewig, Eugen, and Knut Schäferdiek. "Christliche Expansion im Merowingerreich." In Schäferdiek, ed., *Die Kirche des früheren Mittelalters*, 116–45.

Farmer, Sharon. *Communities of Saint Martin: Legend and Ritual in Medieval Tours*. Ithaca, N.Y.: Cornell University Press, 1991.

Favazza, Armando R. "A Critical Review of Studies of National Character: A Psychiatric-Anthropological Interface." *Journal of Operational Psychiatry* 6:1 (1974): 3–30.

Fell, Christine E. "Gods and Heroes of the Northern World." In Wilson, ed., *The Northern World*, 15–48.

Ferguson, Everett. *Backgrounds of Early Christianity.* Grand Rapids, Mich.: Eerdmans, 1987.

Ferguson, John. *The Religions of the Roman Empire.* Ithaca, New York: Cornell University Press, 1970.

Festinger, Leon. *A Theory of Cognitive Dissonance.* Stanford: Stanford University Press, 1957.

Fichter, Joseph H. "Christianity as a World Minority." In Phan, ed. *Christianity and the Wider Ecumenism,* 163–180.

Fink-Dendorfer, Elisabeth. *Conversio: Motive und Motivierung zur Bekehrung in der Alten Kirche.* Regensburger Studien zur Theologie, no. 33. Frankfurt am Main: Verlag Peter Lang, 1986.

Finsterwalder, Paul Willem. "Wege und Ziele der irischen und angelsächsischen Mission im fränkischen Reich." *ZKG* 47 (1928): 203–26.

Fischer, Claude S. "Toward a Subcultural Theory of Urbanism." *American Journal of Sociology* 80 (1975): 1319–41.

Fisher, J. D. C. *Christian Initiation: Baptism in the Medieval West: A Study in the Disintegration of the Primitive Rite of Initiation.* Alcuin Club Collections, no. 47. London: S.P.C.K., 1965.

Fitzpatrick, Joseph P. *One Church, Many Cultures: The Challenge of Diversity.* Kansas City, Mo.: Sheed & Ward, 1987.

Flaskamp, Franz. *Die Missionsmethode des hl. Bonifatius.* Hildesheim: Franz Borgmeyer, 1929.

Fleckenstein, Josef. *Early Medieval Germany.* Translated by Bernard S. Smith. Europe in the Middle Ages: Selected Studies, vol. 16. Amsterdam: North-Holland, 1978.

Flint, Valerie I. J. *The Rise of Magic in Early Medieval Europe.* Princeton, N.J.: Princeton University Press, 1991.

Flory, Marleen B. "Family and 'Familia': A Study of Social Relations in Slavery." Ph.D. diss., Yale University, 1975.

Flowers, Stephen E. "Toward an Archaic Germanic Psychology." *JIES* 11:1&2 (1983): 117–38.

Fontaine, Jacques. "King Sisebut's *Vita Desiderii* and the Political Function of Visigothic Hagiography." In Edward James, ed., *Visigothic Spain: New Approaches.* Oxford: Clarendon Press, 1980, 93–129.

Foote, Peter, and David M. Wilson. *The Viking Achievement: The Society and Culture of Early Medieval Scandinavia.* 2nd ed. 1980; reprint, New York: St. Martin's Press, 1990.

Forey, Alan. *The Military Orders from the Twelfth to the Early Fourteenth Centuries.* Toronto: University of Toronto Press, 1992.

Fouracre, Paul. "The Work of Audoenus of Rouen and Eligius of Noyon in Extending Episcopal Influence from the Town to the Country in Seventh-Century Neustria." In Baker, ed., *The Church in Town and Countryside,* 77–91.

Fox, Robin Lane. *Pagans and Christians.* New York: Knopf, 1987.

Fredriksen, Paula. "Paul and Augustine: Conversion Narratives, Orthodox Traditions, and the Retrospective Self." *Journal of Theological Studies* 37:1 (1986): 3–34.

Frend, W.H.C. "The Missions of the Early Church: 180–700 A.D." In Baker, ed., *Miscellanea Historiae Ecclesiasticae*, vol. 3.

_____. *The Rise of Christianity*. London: Darton, Longman and Todd, 1984.

Friedrich, P. "Proto-Indo-European Kinship." *Ethnology* 5 (1966): 1–23.

Fruin, Robert. *Histoire en métahistoire*. Leiden: E.J. Brill, 1952.

Fuller, W. Harold. *Mission Church Dynamics: How to Change Bicultural Tensions into Dynamic Missionary Outreach*. Pasadena: William Carey Library, 1940.

Gager, John G. "Proselytism and Exclusivity in Early Christianity." In Marty and Greenspahn, eds., *Pushing the Faith: Proselytism and Civility in a Pluralistic World*, 67–77.

Gamkrelidze, Thomas V., and V. V. Ivanov. *Indoevropejskij jazyk i Indoevropejcy*. 2 vol. Tbilisi: Publishing House of the Tbilisi State University, 1984.

_____. "The Early History of Indo-European Languages." *Scientific American* 262:3 (March 1990): 110–16.

Garnsey, Peter. "Religious Toleration in Classical Antiquity." In W. J. Sheils, ed., *Persecution and Toleration*, 1–28. SCH, no. 21. Oxford: Basil Blackwell, 1984.

Garnsey, Peter, and Richard Saller. *The Roman Empire: Economy, Society and Culture*. Berkeley: University of California Press, 1987.

Geary, Patrick J. *Aristocracy in Provence: The Rhône Basin at the Dawn of the Carolingian Age*. Philadelphia: University of Pennsylvania Press, 1985.

_____. *Before France and Germany: The Creation and Transformation of the Merovingian World*. New York: Oxford University Press, 1988.

_____. *Furta Sacra: Thefts of Relics in the Central Middle Ages*. Rev. ed. Princeton, N.J.: Princeton University Press, 1990.

_____. "Saints, Scholars, and Society: The Elusive Goal." In Geary, *Living with the Dead*. Ithaca, N.Y.: Cornell University Press, forthcoming.

Geertz, Clifford. *The Interpretation of Cultures*. New York: Basic Books, 1973.

Gerberding, Richard A. *The Rise of the Carolingians and the 'Liber Historiae Francorum.'* Oxford: Clarendon Press, 1987.

Gerth, H. H., and C. Wright Mills, eds. *From Max Weber*. Oxford: Oxford University Press, 1946.

Gillespie, V. Bailey. *Religious Conversion and Personal Identity: How and Why People Change*. Birmingham, Ala.: Religious Education Press, 1979.

Gimbutas, Marija. "Proto-Indo-European Culture: The Kurgan Culture During the Fifth, Fourth, and Third Millennia B.C." In George Cardona, Henry M. Hoenigswald, and Alfred Senn, eds., *Indo-European and Indo-Europeans: Papers Presented at the Third Indo-European Conference at the University of Pennsylvania*. Philadelphia: University of Pennsylvania Press, 1970.

_____. *The Goddesses and Gods of Old Europe: 6500–3500 B.C.: Myths and Cult Images*. Berkeley: University of California Press, 1982.

_____. *The Language of the Goddess: Unearthing the Hidden Symbols of Western Civilization*. Foreword by Joseph Campbell. New York: Harper & Row, 1989.

Glock, Charles Y., and Rodney Stark. *Religion and Society in Tension*. Chicago: Rand McNally, 1965.

Goffart, Walter. *The Le Mans Forgeries: A Chapter from the History of Church Property in the Ninth Century.* Cambridge, Mass.: Harvard University Press, 1966.

―――. *Barbarians and Romans: A.D. 418–584: The Techniques of Accommodation.* Princeton, N.J.: Princeton University Press, 1980.

―――. *The Narrators of Barbarian History (A.D. 550–800): Jordanes, Gregory of Tours, Bede, and Paul the Deacon.* Princeton, N.J.: Princeton University Press, 1988.

―――. "The Theme of '*The* Barbarian Invasions' in Late Antique and Modern Historiography." In Goffart, *Rome's Fall and After,* 111–32. London: Hambledon Press, 1989.

Goffman, Irwin. "Status Inconsistency and Preference for Change in Power Distribution." *ASR* 22 (1957): 275–81.

Göhler, Hulda. "Das Christusbild in Otfrids *Evangelienbuch* und im *Heliand.*" *Zeitschrift für deutsche Philologie* 59 (1935): 1–52.

Gordon, Ernest. "A Thousand Years of Caesaropapism or the Triumph of the Christian Faith?" *The World & I* 3:8 (August 1988): 681–98.

Grant, Frederick C. *The Economic Background of the Gospels.* London: Oxford University Press, 1926.

Graus, František. "Die Gewalt bei den Anfängen des Feudalismus und die 'Gefangenenbefreiungen' der merowingischen Hagiographie." *Jahrbuch für Wirtschaftsgeschichte* 1 (1961).

―――. *Volk, Herrscher und Heiliger im Reich der Merowinger: Studien zur Hagiographie der Merowingerzeit.* Prague: Nakladatelství Ceskoslovenské Akádemie Ved, 1965.

Gray, Richard. *Black Christians and White Missionaries.* New Haven, Conn.: Yale University Press, 1990.

Green, D. H. *The Carolingian Lord: Semantic Studies on Four Old High German Words: Balder, Frô, Truhtin, Hêrro.* Cambridge: Cambridge University Press, 1965.

Green, Henry A. *The Economic and Social Origins of Gnosticism.* Dissertation Series, Society of Biblical Literature, no. 77. Atlanta: Scholars Press, 1985.

Greenhouse, Carol J. "Just in Time: Temporality and the Cultural Legitimation of Law." *Yale Law Journal* 98 (March 1989): 1631–1651.

Greenway, George. "Saint Boniface as a Man of Letters." In Reuter, ed., *The Greatest Englishman: Essays on St. Boniface and the Church at Crediton,* 33–46.

Gregory of Tours. *The History of the Franks.* Translated and introduced by O. M. Dalton. 2 vols. Oxford: Clarendon Press, 1927.

―――. *The History of the Franks.* Translated and introduced by Lewis Thorpe. Harmondsworth: Penguin, 1974.

―――. *Glory of the Confessors.* Translated with an introduction by Raymond Van Dam. Liverpool: Liverpool University Press, 1988.

―――. *Glory of the Martyrs.* Translated with an introduction by Raymond Van Dam. Liverpool: Liverpool University Press, 1989.

―――. *Life of the Fathers.* 2nd ed. Translated with notes and introduction by Edward James. Liverpool: Liverpool University Press, 1991.

Grimm, Jacob. *Teutonic Mythology*. Translated by J. S. Stallybrass. 4 vols. New York: Dover, 1966.

Grosjean, Paul, and Margaret Deanesley. "The Canterbury Edition of the Answers of Pope Gregory I to St. Augustine." *JEH* 10 (1959): 1–49.

Grundmann, Herbert. "Neue Beiträge zur Geschichte der religiösen Bewegungen." *Archiv für Kulturgeschichte* 37 (1955): 129–82.

————. *Religiöse Bewegungen im Mittelalter*. 3rd ed. Hildesheim: Georg Olm Verlagsbuchhandlung, 1961.

————. *Ketzergeschichte des Mittelalters*. 2nd ed. Göttingen: Vandenhoeck & Ruprecht, 1967.

Guthrie, W. K. C. *The Greek Philosophers: From Thales to Aristotle*. New York: Harper & Row, 1960.

Hamilton, W. D. "The Evolution of Altruistic Behavior." *American Naturalist* 97 (1963): 354–56.

Hanson, Richard P. C. "The Transformation of Pagan Temples into Christian Churches in the Early Christian Centuries." In Hanson, ed., *Studies in Christian Antiquity*, 347–58. Edinburgh: T. & T. Clark, 1985.

Hartmann, Wilfried. *Die Synoden der Karolingerzeit im Frankenreich und in Italien*. Paderborn: Ferdinand Schöningh, 1989.

Hauck, Albert. *Kirchengeschichte Deutschlands*. 4th ed. Vol. 1. 1904; reprint, Berlin: Akademie Verlag, 1954.

Hauck, Karl. "Geblütsheiligkeit." In *Liber Floridus: Mittellateinische Studien. Paul Lehmann zum 65. Geburtstag am 13. Juli 1949 gewidmet*, ed. Bernhard Bischoff, 187–240. St. Ottilien: Eos Verlag der Erzabtei St. Ottilien, 1950.

Head, Constance. *The Emperor Julian*. Boston: Twayne, 1976.

Head, Thomas. *Hagiography and the Cult of the Saints: The Diocese of Orléans, 800–1200*. Cambridge Studies in Medieval Life and Thought, no. 4. Cambridge: Cambridge University Press, 1990.

Heather, Peter. "The Crossing of the Danube and the Gothic Conversion." *Greek, Roman and Byzantine Studies* 27:3 (1986): 289–318.

————. *Goths and Romans: 332–489*. Oxford: Clarendon Press, 1991.

Heather, Peter, and John Matthews. *The Goths in the Fourth Century*. Liverpool: Liverpool University Press, 1991.

Hechter, Michael. *Principles of Group Solidarity*. Berkeley: University of California Press, 1987.

Heimskringla: History of the Kings of Norway. 2nd rev. ed. Trans. Lee M. Hollander. Austin: University of Texas Press, 1964.

Heinzelmann, Martin. "L'Aristocratie et les évêchés entre Loire et Rhin jusqu'à la fin du VIIe siècle." *Revue d'histoire de l'église de France* 62 (1975): 75–90.

————. *Bischofsherrschaft in Gallien: Zur Kontinuität römischer Führungsschichten vom 4. bis zum 7. Jahrhundert. Soziale, prosopographische und bildungsgeschichtliche Aspekte*. Beihefte der Francia, vol. 5. Munich: Artemis Verlag, 1976.

The Heliand: The Saxon Gospel: A Translation and Commentary. Translated by G. Ronald Murphy. New York: Oxford University Press, 1992.

The Heliand: Translated from the Old Saxon. Translated by Mariana Scott. University of North Carolina Studies in the Germanic Languages and Literatures, no. 52. Chapel Hill: University of North Carolina Press, 1966.

Herrin, Judith. *The Formation of Christendom*. Princeton, N.J.: Princeton University Press, 1987.

Herwegen, Ildefons. *Antike, Germanentum und Christentum*. Salzburg: Verlag Anton Pustet, 1932.

Hess, Davis J. *Spirits and Scientists: Ideology, Spiritism, and Brazilian Culture*. University Park: Pennsylvania State University Press, 1991.

Hexman, Irving, and Karla Poewe. *Understanding Cults and New Religions*. Grand Rapids, Mich.: Eerdmans, 1986.

Hick, John, and Paul F. Knitter, eds. *The Myth of Christian Uniqueness: Toward a Pluralistic Theology of Religions*. Maryknoll, N.Y.: Orbis, 1987.

Hiebert, Paul. *Anthropological Insights for Missionaries*. Grand Rapids, Mich.: Baker Book House, 1985.

————. *Cultural Anthropology*. 2nd ed. Grand Rapids, Mich.: Baker Book House, 1983.

Hillgarth, J. N., ed. *Christianity and Paganism, 350–750: The Conversion of Western Europe*. Rev. ed. of *The Conversion of Western Europe, 350–750*. Philadelphia: University of Pennsylvania Press, 1986.

————. "Popular Religion in Visigothic Spain." In Edward James, ed., *Visigothic Spain: New Approaches*. Oxford: Clarendon Press, 1980.

Hobbs, Edward C., and Andrew P. Porter. "The Trinity and the Indo-European Tripartite World-View." Unpublished.

Höfler, Otto. "Der Sakralcharacter des germanischen Königtums." In *The Sacral Kingship: Contributions to the Central Theme of the VIIIth International Congress for the History of Religions (Rome, 1955)*. Studies in the History of Religions, no. 4. Leiden: E. J. Brill, 1959.

Holdsworth, Christopher. "Saint Boniface the Monk." In Reuter, ed., *The Greatest Englishman*, 47–68.

Holmes, Urban T. *History of Christian Spirituality: An Analytical Introduction*. New York: Seabury Press, 1980.

Hommages à Georges Dumézil. Collection Latomus 45. Brussels: Latomus, 1960.

Hornung, Carlton A. "Social Status, Status Inconsistency, and Psychological Stress." *ASR* 42 (1977): 623–638

Howe, John McDonald. "Greek Influence on the Eleventh-Century Western Revival of Hermitism." Ph.D. diss., University of California, Los Angeles, 1979.

————. "The Nobility's Reform of the Medieval Church." *AHR* 93:2 (1988): 317–39.

Huber, Wolfgang. *Heliand und Matthäusexegese*. Munich: Max Hueber Verlag, 1969.

Hultgren, Arland J. *Christ and His Benefits: Christology and Redemption in the New Testament*. Philadelphia: Fortress Press, 1987.

Hunke, Sigrid. *Europas eigene Religion: Der Glaube der Ketzer*. Bergisch Gladbach: Gustav Lübbe Verlag, 1983.

Hus, Alain. *Greek and Roman Religion.* Translated by S. J. Tester. New York: Hawthorn Books, 1962.

Hutton, Ronald. *The Pagan Religions of the Ancient British Isles: Their Nature and Legacy.* Oxford: Basil Blackwell, 1991.

Imbert, Jean. "L'Influence du christianisme sur la législation des peuples francs et germains." *Settimane* 14 (1967): 365–96.

Iserloh, Erwin. "Die Kontinuität des Christentums beim Übergang von der Antike zum Mittelalter im Lichte der Glaubensverkündigung des heiligen Bonifatius." In Klaus Wittstadt, ed., *Verwirklichung des Christlichen im Wandel der Geschichte.* Würzburg: Echter Verlag, 1975.

Jackson, Elton F. "Status Consistency and Symptoms of Stress." *ASR* 27 (1962): 469–480.

Jackson, Elton F., and Peter J. Burke. "Status and Symptoms of Stress: Additive and Interaction Effects." *ASR* 30 (1965): 556–64.

James, Edward. *Visigothic Spain: New Approaches.* Oxford: Clarendon Press, 1980.

_____. *The Origins of France: From Clovis to the Capetians, 500–1000.* New Studies in Medieval History. London: Macmillan, 1982.

_____. *The Franks.* Oxford: Basil Blackwell, 1988.

James, William. *Varieties of Religious Experience.* New York: 1902; reprint, New York: New American Library of World Literature, 1958.

Jedin, Hubert. "General Introduction to Church History." In Jedin and Dolan, eds. *History of the Church.* Vol. 1, 1–56.

Jedin, Hubert, and John Dolan, eds. *History of the Church.* Vols. 1–3. Translated by Anselm Biggs. New York: Crossroad, 1982–87.

Jeremias, Joachim. *Jerusalem in the Time of Jesus.* Translated by F. H. and C. H. Cave. Philadelphia: Fortress Press, 1969.

Jonas, Hans. *The Gnostic Religion: The Message of the Alien God and the Beginnings of Christianity.* 2nd rev. ed. Boston: Beacon Press, 1963.

Jones, A. H. M. *The Later Roman Empire, 284–602: A Social, Economic, and Administrative Survey.* 2 vols. 1964; reprint, Baltimore, Md.: Johns Hopkins University Press, 1986.

Jones, George Fenwick. *Honor in German Literature.* Studies in the Germanic Languages and Literatures, no. 25. Chapel Hill: University of North Carolina Press, 1959.

_____. "Rüdeger's Dilemma." *Studies in Philology* 57 (1960): 7–21.

_____. *The Ethos of the Song of Roland.* Baltimore: Johns Hopkins Press, 1969.

Jordan, Mark D. "Philosophic 'Conversion' and Christian Conversion: A Gloss on Professor MacMullen." *The Second Century* 5:2 (1985/86): 90–96.

Joris, André. "On the Edge of Two Worlds in the Heart of the New Empire: The Romance Regions of Northern Gaul during the Merovingian Period." In Bowsky, ed., *Studies in Medieval and Renaissance History,* 1–52.

Judge, A. "The Social Identity of the First Christians: A Question of Method in Religious History." *Journal of Religious History* 11 (1980): 201–17.

Jung, Carl Gustav. *Collected Works.* 2nd ed. Vol. 9. Edited by Herbert Read, Michael Fordham, and Gerhard Adler. Princeton, N.J.: Princeton University Press, 1964.

Jungmann, Josef. *The Mass of the Roman Rite: Its Origin and Development* (*Missarum Sollemnia*). Translated by Francis A. Brunner. 2 vols. New York: Benziger Brothers, 1951.

————. *Handing on the Faith: A Manual of Catechetics*. Translated by A. N. Fuerst. Freiburg: Herder and Herder, 1959.

————. "The Defeat of Teutonic Arianism and the Revolution in Religious Culture in the Early Middle Ages." In Jungmann, *Pastoral Liturgy*. New York: Herder and Herder, 1962.

————. *The Place of Christ in Liturgical Prayer*. Translated from the 3rd German ed. by A. Peeler. New York: Alba House, 1965.

Kahl, Hans-Dietrich. "Bausteine zur Grundlegung einer missionsgeschichtlichen Phänomenologie des Hochmittelalters." In *Miscellanea Historiae Ecclesiasticae*, vol. 1, 50-90. Louvain: Publications Universitaires de Louvain, 1961.

————. "Die ersten Jahrhunderte des missionsgeschichtlichen Mittelalters: Bausteine für eine Phänomenologie bis ca. 1050." In Schäferdiek, ed., *Die Kirche des früheren Mittelalters*, 11-76.

Karras, Ruth M. "Pagan Survivals and Syncretism in the Conversion of Saxony." *Catholic Historical Review* 72 (1986): 553-72.

Katz, Solomon. *The Decline of Rome and the Rise of Mediaeval Europe*. Ithaca, N.Y.: Cornell University Press, 1955.

Kee, Howard Clark. *Christian Origins in Sociological Perspective: Methods and Resources*. Philadelphia: Westminster Press, 1980.

————. *Miracle in the Early Christian World: A Study in Sociohistorical Method*. New Haven, Conn.: Yale University Press, 1983.

Kee, Howard Clark, et al. *Christianity: A Social and Cultural History*. New York: Macmillan, 1991.

Keep, David. "Cultural Conflicts in the Missions of St. Boniface." In Stuart Mews, ed., *Religion and National Identity*, 47-57. SCH, no. 18. Oxford: Basil Blackwell, 1982.

Kelly, J. N. D. *Early Christian Doctrines*. 2nd ed. New York: Harper & Row, 1960.

Keresztes, Paul. "The Phenomenon of Constantine the Great's Conversion." *Augustinianum* 27 (August 1987): 85-100.

Kerr, Hugh T., and John M. Mulder. *Conversion: The Christian Experience*. Grand Rapids, Mich.: Eerdmans, 1983.

Kiev, Ari. *Transcultural Psychiatry*. New York: Free Press, 1972.

Kinder, Hermann, and Werner Hilgemann. *Anchor Atlas of World History*. Vol. 1. Translated by Ernest A. Menze. Garden City, N.Y.: Doubleday, 1974.

King, Anthony. *Roman Gaul and Germany*. Exploring the Roman World, no. 3. Berkeley: University of California Press, 1990.

Kitto, H. D. F. *The Greeks*. Harmondsworth: Penguin, 1957.

Klauser, Theodor. "Die liturgischen Austauschbeziehungen zwischen der römischen und der fränkisch-deutschen Kirche vom 8. bis zum 11. Jahrhunderts." *Historisches Jahrbuch der Görresgesellschaft* 53 (1933): 169-89.

Klausner, Joseph. *Jesus of Nazareth: His Life, Times and Teaching*. Translated by H. Danby. 1929; reprint, New York: Macmillan, 1959.

Klausner, Joseph. *The Messianic Idea in Israel: From Its Beginning to the Completion of the Mishnah*. Translated by W. F. Stinespring. New York: Macmillan, 1955.

Klerman, Gerald L., and Myrna M. Weissman. "Increasing Rates of Depression." *Journal of the American Medical Association* 261:15 (21 April 1989): 2229–35.

Kraft, Charles H., and Tom N. Wisley. *Readings in Dynamic Indigeneity*. Pasadena, Calif.: William Carey Library, 1979.

Krailsheimer, A. J. *Conversion*. London: SCM Press, 1980.

Kristjansson, Jonas. *Icelandic Sagas and Manuscripts*. Reykjavík: Iceland Review, 1980.

Krüger, Bruno, et al. *Die Germanen: Geschichte und Kultur der germanischen Stamme in Mitteleuropa*. 2 vols. Berlin: Akademie-Verlag, 1983.

Kuhn, Hans. "Das Fortleben des germanischen Heidentums nach der Christianisierung." *Settimane* 14 (1967): 743–57.

Ladner, Gerhart B. "The Impact of Christianity." In Lynn White, ed., *The Transformation of the Roman World: Gibbon's Problem after Two Centuries*. Berkeley: University of California Press, 1966.

————. *The Idea of Reform: Its Impact on Christian Thought and Action in the Age of the Fathers*. New York: Harper & Row, 1967.

————. "On Roman Attitudes Toward Barbarians in Late Antiquity." *Viator* 7 (1976): 2–26.

Lanternari, Vittorio. *The Religions of the Oppressed: A Study of Modern Messianic Cults*. Translated by Lisa Sergio. New York: Knopf, 1963.

La Piana, George. *Foreign Groups in Rome during the First Centuries of the Empire*. Cambridge, Mass.: Harvard University Press, 1927.

Larson, Gerald James, ed. *Myth in Indo-European Antiquity*. Coedited by C. Scott Littleton and Jaan Puhvel. Berkeley: University of California Press, 1974.

Lasko, Peter. *The Kingdom of the Franks: North-West Europe Before Charlemagne*. New York: McGraw-Hill, 1971.

Latourette, Kenneth Scott. *A History of the Expansion of Christianity*. 7 vols. New York: Harper, 1937–45.

Lawrence, C. H. *Medieval Monasticism*. New York: Longman, 1984.

Lawrence, Irene. *Linguistics and Theology: The Significance of Noam Chomsky for Theological Construction*. American Theological Library Association Monograph Series, no. 16. Metuchen, N.J.: American Theological Library Association, 1980.

The Laws of the Salian Franks: Translated and with an Introduction by Katherine Fischer Drew. Philadelphia: University of Pennsylvania Press, 1991.

Lea, Henry Charles. *The Duel and the Oath*. Introduction by Edward Peters. 1866; reprint, Philadelphia: University of Pennsylvania Press, 1974.

Le Bras, Gabriel. "The Sociology of the Church in the Early Middle Ages." In Sylvia Thrupp, ed., *Early Medieval Society*. New York: Appleton-Century-Crofts, 1967.

Leclercq, Jean. *The Love of Learning and Desire for God: A Study of Monastic Culture*. Translated by C. Misrashi. 2nd ed. New York: Fordham University Press, 1974.

Leclercq, Jean. *Monks and Love in Twelfth-Century France: Psycho-Historical Essays*. Oxford: Clarendon Press, 1979.

Le Goff, Jacques. *Time, Work and Culture in the Middle Ages*. Translated by Arthur Goldhammer. Chicago: University of Chicago Press, 1980.

_____. *The Birth of Purgatory*. Translated by Arthur Goldhammer. Chicago: University of Chicago Press, 1984.

_____. *Medieval Civilization: 400–1500*. Translated by Julia Barrow. New York: Basil Blackwell, 1988.

Lenski, Gerhard E. "Status Crystallization: A Non-vertical Dimension of Social Status." *ASR* 19 (1954): 405–13.

_____. "Social Participation and Status Crystallization." *ASR* 21 (1956): 458–64.

_____. *The Religious Factor: A Sociological Study of Religion's Impact on Politics, Economics, and Family Life*. Revised ed. Garden City, N.Y.: Doubleday, 1963.

The Letters of St. Boniface. Translated by Ephraim Emerton. New York: Farrar, Strauss, and Giroux, 1973.

Leuba, J. H. *A Psychological Study of Religion*. New York: Macmillan, 1912.

Levison, Wilhelm. *England and the Continent in the Eighth Century*. Oxford: Clarendon Press, 1946.

_____. *Aus Rheinischer und Fränkischer Frühzeit*. Düsseldorf: Verlag L. Schwann, 1948.

Leyser, K. J. *Rule and Conflict in an Early Medieval Society: Ottonian Saxony*. Oxford: Basil Blackwell, 1989.

Liebescheutz, J. H. W. G. *Continuity and Change in Roman Religion*. Oxford: Oxford University Press, 1979.

Lindow, John. *Comitatus, Individual and Honor: Studies in North Germanic Institutional Vocabulary*. University of California Publications in Linguistics, vol. 83. Berkeley: University of California Press, 1975.

Little, Lester K. *Religious Poverty and the Profit Economy in Medieval Europe*. London: Paul Elek, 1978.

Littleton, C. Scott. "Georges Dumézil and the Rebirth of the Genetic Model: An Anthropological Assessment." In Larson, ed., *Myth in Indo-European Antiquity*, 169–80.

_____. *The New Comparative Mythology: An Anthropological Assessment of the Theories of Georges Dumézil*. 3rd ed. Berkeley: University of California Press, 1982.

The Lives of the Eighth-Century Popes ("Liber Pontificalis"): The Ancient Biographies of Nine Popes from A.D. 715 to 817. Translated with an introduction and commentary by Raymond Davis. Liverpool: Liverpool University Press, 1992.

Lofland, John. *Doomsday Cult*. Enlarged ed. New York: Irvington Press, 1977.

_____. "Becoming a World-Saver Revisited." In James T. Richardson, ed., *Conversion Careers: In and Out of the New Religions*. Beverly Hills, California: Sage, 1978.

Lofland, John, and Rodney Stark. "Becoming a World-Saver: A Theory of Conversion to a Deviant Perspective." *ASR* 30:6 (1965): 862–74.

The Lombard Laws. Translated by Katherine Fischer Drew. Philadelphia: University of Pennsylvania Press, 1973.

Long, A. A. *Hellenistic Philosophy: Stoics, Epicureans, Sceptics*. 2nd ed. Berkeley: University of California Press, 1986.

Lopez, Robert S. *The Commercial Revolution of the Middle Ages, 950–1350*. Englewood Cliffs, N.J.: Prentice-Hall, 1971.

Lorenz, Konrad. *On Aggression*. New York: Harcourt, Brace and World, 1966.

Lortz, Josef. *History of the Church*. Translated and adapted from the 5th and 6th eds. by Edwin G. Kaiser. Milwaukee: Bruce Publishing, 1939.

————. "Untersuchungen zur Missionsmethode und zur Frommigkeit des hl. Bonifatius nach seinen Briefen." In Nikolaus Goetzinger, ed., *Willibrordus: Echternacher Festschrift zur XII. Jahrhundertfeier des Todes des heiligen Willibrord*, 247–83. Luxembourg: Verlag der St. Paulus-Druckerei, 1940.

Lot, Ferdinand. *The End of the Ancient World and the Beginnings of the Middle Ages*. Translated by Philip and Mariette Leon. Introduction by Glanville Downey. New York: Harper Torchbooks, 1961.

Lother, Helmut. *Die Christusauffassung der Germanen*. Gütersloh: Verlag C. Bertelsmann, 1937.

Löwe, Heinz. "Pirmin, Willibrord und Bonifatius: Ihre Bedeutung für die Missionsgeschichte ihrer Zeit." In Schäferdiek, ed., *Die Kirche des früheren Mittelalters*, 192–226.

Luckmann, Joan, and Karen Creason Sorensen. *Medical-Surgical Nursing: A Psychophysiologic Approach*. 2nd ed. Philadelphia: W. B. Saunders, 1980.

Lumsden, C. J., and E. O. Wilson. *Genes, Mind and Culture: The Evolutionary Process*. Cambridge, Mass.: Harvard University Press, 1981.

Luzbetak, Louis J. *The Church and Cultures: New Perspectives in Missiological Anthropology*. Foreword by Eugene Nida. Maryknoll, N. Y.: Orbis Books, 1988.

Lynch, J. J. *The Broken Heart: The Medical Consequences of Loneliness*. New York: Basic Books, 1977.

Lynn, Richard. *Personality and National Character*. New York: Pergamon Press, 1971.

McDonald, Edward R. "The Cultural Roots of Ideology: Hagen's Concept of Honor in the Nibelungenlied." *Mankind Quarterly* 21 (1980): 179–204.

McEvedy, Colin, and Richard Jones. *Atlas of World Population History*. Harmondsworth: Penguin, 1978.

McGinn, Bernard. "Apocalypticism in the Middle Ages: An Historiographical Approach." *Mediaeval Studies* 37 (1975): 252–86.

McKitterick, Rosamond. *The Frankish Church and the Carolingian Reforms, 789–895*. London: Royal Historical Society, 1977.

McManners, John, ed. *The Oxford Illustrated History of Christianity*. Oxford: Oxford University Press, 1990.

MacMullen, Ramsay. *Enemies of the Roman Order: Treason, Unrest and Alienation in the Empire*. Cambridge, Mass.: Harvard University Press, 1966.

————. *Roman Social Relations*. New Haven, Conn.: Yale University Press, 1974.

MacMullen, Ramsay. *Paganism in the Roman Empire*. New Haven, Conn.: Yale University Press, 1981.

———. "Two Types of Religious Conversion to Early Christianity." *Vigiliae Christianae* 37(1983): 174–92.

———. *Christianizing the Roman Empire*. New Haven, Conn.: Yale University Press, 1984.

———. "Conversion: A Historian's View." *The Second Century* 5:2 (1985/86): 67–81.

———. "'What Difference Did Christianity Make?'" *Historia* 35 (1986): 322–43.

McNamara, Jo Ann, and John E. Halborg, with E. Gordon Whatley. *Sainted Women of the Dark Ages*. Durham, N.C.: Duke University Press, 1992.

Malherbe, Abraham. *Social Aspects of Early Christianity*. Baton Rouge: University of Louisiana Press, 1977.

Mallory, J. P. *In Search of the Indo-Europeans: Language, Archaeology and Myth*. London: Thames and Hudson, 1989.

———. "Human Populations and the Indo-European Problem." *Mankind Quarterly* 33:2 (1992): 131–54.

Malony, H. Newton. "The Psychology of Proselytism." In Marty and Greenspahn, eds., *Pushing the Faith: Proselytism and Civility in a Pluralistic World*, 125–42.

Mannheim, Karl. *Ideology and Utopia: An Introduction to the Sociology of Knowledge*. Translated by Louis Wirth and Edward Shils. New York: Harcourt, Brace, 1936.

Manselli, Raoul. "La Conversione dei popoli germanici al Cristianesimo: la discussione storiografica." *Settimane* 14 (1967): 13–42.

Markey, T. L., and John A. C. Greppin, eds. *When Worlds Collide: The Indo-Europeans and the Pre-Indo-Europeans*. Ann Arbor, Mich.: Karoma Press, 1990.

Markus, R. A. "The Chronology of the Gregorian Mission to England: Bede's Narrative and Gregory's Correspondence." *JEH* 14 (1963): 16–30.

———. "Gregory the Great and a Papal Missionary Strategy." In Cuming, ed., *The Mission of the Church and the Propagation of the Faith*, 29–38.

———. "The Problem of Self-Definition: From Sect to Church." In E. P. Sanders, ed., *The Shaping of Christianity in the Second and Third Centuries*. Vol. 1 of *Jewish and Christian Self-Definition*. Philadelphia: Fortress Press, 1980, 1–15.

———. *The End of Ancient Christianity*. Cambridge: Cambridge University Press, 1990.

———. "From Rome to the Barbarian Kingdoms (330–700)." In McManners, ed., *The Oxford Illustrated History of Christianity*, 62–91.

———. "From Caesarius to Boniface: Christianity and Paganism in Gaul." In Jacques Fontaine and J. N. Hillgarth, eds., *The Seventh Century: Change and Continuity*. London: Warburg Institute, University of London, 1992.

Marrou, Henri I. *A History of Education in Antiquity*. Translated by George Lamb. New York: Sheed & Ward, 1956.

Marty, Martin E., and Frederick E. Greenspahn. *Pushing the Faith: Proselytism and Civility in a Pluralistic World*. New York: Crossroad, 1988.

Maurer, Wilhelm. "Hellenisierung—Germanisierung—Romanisierung: Bemerkungen zu den Perioden der Kirchengeschichte." In Heinz-Dietrich Wendland, *Kosmos und Ekklesia. Festschrift für Wilhelm Stählin zu seinem siebzigsten Geburtstag 24. September 1953.* Kassel: Johannes Stauda Verlag, 1953.

May, Rollo. *Man's Search for Himself.* New York: W. W. Norton & Company, 1953.

Mayer, Anton L. "Altchristliche Liturgie und Germanentum." *JL* 5 (1925): 80–96.

––––––. "Die Liturgie und der Geist der Gotik." *JL* 6 (1926): 68–97.

––––––. "Religions- und Kultgeschichtliche Züge in Bonifatianischen Quellen." In *Sankt Bonifatius: Gedenkausgabe zum zwölfhundertsten Todestag,* 291–319.

Mayr-Harting, Henry. "The West: The Age of Conversion (700–1050)." In McManners, ed., *The Oxford Illustrated History of Christianity,* 92–121.

––––––. *The Coming of Christianity to Anglo-Saxon England.* 3rd ed. University Park: Pennsylvania State University Press, 1991.

Meeks, W. A. *The First Urban Christians: The Social World of the Apostle Paul.* New Haven, Conn.: Yale University Press, 1983.

Mensching, Gustav. "Folk and Universal Religion." Translated by Louis Schneider. In Schneider, ed., *Religion, Culture and Society: A Reader in the Sociology of Religion,* 254–61.

––––––. "The Masses, Folk Belief and Universal Religion," Translated by Louis Schneider. In Louis Schneider, ed. *Religion, Culture and Society: A Reader in the Sociology of Religion,* 269–73.

Merton, Robert K. "Social Structure and Anomie." In Merton, *Social Theory and Social Structure.* Rev. ed. Glencoe, Ill.: Free Press, 1949.

Miller, David Harry. "Sacral Kingship, Biblical Kingship, and the Elevation of Pepin the Short." In Thomas F. X. Noble and John J. Contreni, eds., *Religion, Culture, and Society in the Early Middle Ages: Studies in Honor of Richard E. Sullivan.* Studies in Medieval Culture, no. 23. Kalamazoo, Mich.: Medieval Institute Publications (Western Michigan University), 1987.

Minaniki, George. *The Chinese Rites Controversy from Its Beginning to Modern Times.* Chicago: Loyola University Press, 1985.

Mol, Hans. *Identity and the Sacred.* New York: Free Press, 1976.

Molnar, Thomas. *The Pagan Temptation.* Grand Rapids, Mich.: Eerdmans, 1987.

Momigliano, Arnaldo. "Christianity and the Decline of the Roman Empire." In Momigliano, ed., *The Conflict Between Paganism and Christianity in the Fourth Century,* 1–16.

Momigliano, Arnaldo, ed. *The Conflict Between Paganism and Christianity in the Fourth Century.* Oxford: Clarendon Press, 1963.

Moorhead, John. "Clovis' Motives for Becoming a Catholic Christian." *Journal of Religious History* 13:4 (1985): 329–39.

Morris, Charles William. *Varieties of Human Value.* Chicago: University of Chicago Press, 1956.

Morris, Colin. *The Discovery of the Individual, 1050–1200.* Medieval Academy Reprints for Teaching, no. 19. 1972; reprint, Toronto: University of Toronto Press, 1987.

Mulago, Vincent. "Traditional African Religion and Christianity." In Jacob K. Olupona, ed., *African Traditional Religions in Contemporary Society*, 119–34. New York: Paragon House, 1991.

Muldoon, James. "Medieval Missionary Efforts—Converting the Infidels to What?" Paper presented at the Twenty-sixth International Congress on Medieval Studies, Kalamazoo, Michigan, May 1991.

————. "Conversion of the Barbarians in the Old World and the New." Paper presented at a Conference on the History of Christianity, University of Notre Dame, March 1992.

————. "Religious Conversion on the Frontier in the Old World and the New." Paper presented at the Twenty-seventh International Congress on Medieval Studies, Kalamazoo, Michigan, May 1992.

Munch, Peter Andreas. *Norse Mythology: Legends of Gods and Heroes*. Translated by Sigurd Hustvedt. Scandinavian Classics Series, vol. 28. New York: American-Scandinavian Foundation, 1954.

Munz, Peter. "Early European History and African Anthropology." *New Zealand Journal of History* 10 (1976): 33–48.

Murphy, G. Ronald. *The Saxon Savior: The Germanic Transformation of the Gospel in the Ninth-Century Heliand*. New York: Oxford University Press, 1989.

————. "Magic in the *Heliand*." *Monatshefte* 83:4 (1991): 386–97.

————. "Symmetrical Structure in the *Heliand*." *The German Quarterly* 65:2 (1992): 153–58.

Murray, Alexander Callander. *Germanic Kinship Structure: Studies in Law and Society in Antiquity and the Early Middle Ages*. Studies and Texts, no. 65. Toronto: Pontifical Institute of Medieval Studies, 1983.

Murray, Gilbert. *Five Stages of Greek Religion*. 3rd ed. Garden City, N.Y.: Doubleday, 1955.

Musset, Lucien. *The Germanic Invasions: The Making of Europe*. Translated by Edward and Columba James. University Park: Pennsylvania State University Press, 1975.

Myers, Henry A., and Herwig Wolfram. *Medieval Kingship*. Chicago: Nelson-Hall, 1982.

Nagy, Gregory. "The Indo-European Heritage of Tribal Organization: Evidence from the Greek *polis*." In Skomal and Polomé, eds., *Proto-Indo-European: The Archaeology of a Linguistic Problem: Studies in Honor of Marija Gimbutas*, 245–66.

Nakamura, Hajime. *A Comparative History of Ideas*. London: KPI, 1986.

Needleman, Jacob. *The New Religions*. Garden City, N.Y.: Doubleday, 1970.

Nelson, Janet L. "Society, Theodicy and the Origins of Heresy: Towards a Reassessment of the Medieval Evidence." In Derek J. Baker, ed., *Schism, Heresy and Religious Protest*, 65–77. SCH, vol. 9. Cambridge: Cambridge University Press, 1972.

————. *Politics and Ritual in Early Medieval Europe*. London: Hambledon Press, 1986.

Nigosian, Solomon. "Eliade, Bellah and van der Leeuw on Classification of World Religions." Paper presented at the annual meeting of the Eastern International Region of the American Academy of Religion, Toronto, April 1991.

Nilsson, Martin P. *Greek Folk Religion*. Foreword by Arthur Darby Nock. 1940; reprint, Philadelphia: University of Pennsylvania Press, 1984.

Nisbet, Robert. *The Quest for Community*. Oxford: Oxford University Press, 1953.

Njal's Saga. Translated with an introduction by Magnus Magnusson and Hermann Palsson. New York: Penguin, 1960.

Noble, Thomas F. X. *The Republic of St. Peter: The Birth of the Papal State, 680–825*. Philadelphia: University of Pennsylvania Press, 1984.

Nock, A. D. *Conversion: The Old and the New in Religion from Alexander the Great to Augustine of Hippo*. Oxford: Clarendon Press, 1933.

North, Richard. *Pagan Words and Christian Meanings*. *Costerus,* New Series, vol. 81. Amsterdam: Rodopi, 1991.

Nottingham, Elizabeth K. *Religion and Society*. New York: Random House, 1954.

O'Dea, Thomas F. *The Sociology of Religion*. Englewood Cliffs, N.J.: Prentice-Hall, 1966.

Otto, Rudolf. *The Idea of the Holy*. 2nd ed. London: Oxford University Press, 1950.

Owen, Francis. *The Germanic People: Their Origin, Expansion and Culture*. New Haven, Conn.: College & University Press, 1960.

Owen, Gale R. *Rites and Religions of the Anglo-Saxons*. New York: Dorset Press, 1985.

Pagels, Elaine. *Gnostic Gospels*. New York: Random House, 1979.

_____. *Adam, Eve, and the Serpent*. New York: Random House, 1988.

Pàroli, Teresa. "Santi e demoni nelle letterature germaniche nell'alto Medievo." *Settimane* 36 (1989): 411–90, 491–98.

Parsons, Talcott. *Religious Perspectives of College Teaching in Sociology and Social Psychology*. New Haven, Conn.: Edward W. Hazen Foundation, 1951.

Paxton, Frederick S. *Christianizing Death: The Creation of a Ritual Process in Early Medieval Europe*. Ithaca, N.Y.: Cornell University Press, 1990.

Pearson, Roger. *Introduction to Anthropology*. New York: Holt, Rinehart and Winston, 1974.

_____. *Anthropological Glossary*. Malabar, Fla: Robert Krieger, 1985.

_____. "Chieftainship as an Evolutionary Stage in the Transition from Tribal to Feudal Society." *Mankind Quarterly* 28:2 (1987): 139–50.

Pelikan, Jaroslav. *The Emergence of the Catholic Tradition (100–600)*. Vol. 1 of *The Christian Tradition: A History of the Development of Doctrine*. Chicago: University of Chicago Press, 1971.

_____. *Jesus Through the Centuries: His Place in the History of Culture*. New York: Harper & Row, 1985.

Persinger, Michael A. *Neuropsychological Bases of God Beliefs*. New York: Praeger, 1987.

Peters, Edward, ed. *Monks, Bishops and Pagans: Christian Culture in Gaul and Italy, 500–700*. With an introduction by Edward Peters. Philadelphia: University of Pennsylvania Press, 1975.

Pettazzoni, Raffaele. "Les deux sources de la religion grecque." *Mnemosyne* 4 (1951): 1–8.

Philipson, E. A. *Die Genealogie der Götter in germanischer Religion: Mythologie und Theologie.* Illinois Studies in Language and Literature 37, no. 3. Urbana: University of Illinois Press, 1953.

Phillpotts, Bertha S. *Kindred and Clan in the Middle Ages and After.* Cambridge: Cambridge University Press, 1917.

Phan, Peter C., ed. *Christianity and the Wider Ecumenism.* New York: Paragon House, 1990.

————. "Are There 'Saviors' for Other Peoples? A Discussion of the Problem of the Universal Significance and Uniqueness of Jesus Christ." In Phan, ed., *Christianity and the Wider Ecumenism,* 163–80. New York: Paragon House, 1990.

Pickering, Frederick P. "Historical Thought and Moral Codes in Medieval Epic." In Scholler, ed., *The Epic in Medieval Society,* 1–17.

Poblete, Renato. "Puerto Rican Sectarianism and the Quest for Community." M.A. thesis, Fordham University, 1959.

Poblete, Renato, and Thomas F. O'Dea. "Anomie and the 'Quest for Community': The Formation of Sects Among the Puerto Ricans of New York." *American Catholic Sociological Review* 21 (1960): 18–36.

The Poetic Edda. 2nd ed. Translated with an introduction and explanatory notes by Lee M. Hollander. Austin: University of Texas Press, 1962.

Polomé, Edgar C. "The Indo-European Component in Germanic Religion." In Puhvel, ed., *Myth and Law,* 55–82.

————. "Approaches to Germanic Mythology." In Larson, ed., *Myth in Indo-Eoropean Antiquity,* 51–68.

————. "The Gods of the Indo-Europeans." *Mankind Quarterly* 21 (1980): 151–64.

————. "Indo-European Culture with Special Attention to Religion." In Polomé, ed., *The Indo-Europeans in the Fourth and Third Millennia,* 156–72. Ann Arbor, Mich.: Karoma Publishers, 1982,

————. "Some Thoughts on the Methodology of Comparative Religion, with Special Focus on Indo-European." In Polomé, ed., *Essays in Memory of Karl Kerényi,* 9–27.

————. "Germanic Religion and the Indo-European Heritage." *Mankind Quarterly* 26 (1985): 27–55.

————. "Germanentum und religiöse Vorstellungen." In Heinrich Beck, ed., *Germanenprobleme in heutiger Sicht,* 267–97. Berlin: Walter de Gruyter, 1986.

————. "Who are the Germanic People?" In Skomal and Polome, eds., *Proto-Indo-European: The Archaeology of a Linguistic Problem. Studies in Honor of Marija Gimbutas,* 216–44.

Polomé, Edgar C., ed. *Homage to Georges Dumézil.* With an introduction by the editor. *JIES,* Monograph Series, no. 3. Washington, D.C.: Institute for the Study of Man, 1982.

————. *Essays in Memory of Karl Kerényi. JIES,* Monograph Series, no. 4. Washington, D.C.: Institute for the Study of Man, 1984.

Polomé, Edgar C., ed. *Essays on Germanic Religion. JIES,* Monograph Series, no. 6. Washington, D.C.: Institute for the Study of Man, 1989.

Pontal, Odette. *Histoire des conciles mérovingiens.* Paris: Cerf, 1989.

Powell, Elwin H. *The Design of Discord: Studies of Anomie.* New Brunswick, N.J.: Transaction Books, 1988.

Price, James L. *Interpreting the New Testament.* 2nd ed. New York: Holt, Rinehart and Winston, 1971.

Prinz, Friedrich. *Frühes Mönchtum im Frankenreich: Kultur und Gesellschaft in Gallien, den Rheinlanden und Bayern am Beispiel der monastischen Entwicklung (4. bis 8. Jahrhundert).* Munich: R. Oldenbourg Verlag, 1965.

_____. "Heiligenkult und Adelsherrschaft im Spiegel merowingischer Hagiographie." *Historische Zeitschrift* 204 (1967): 529–44.

Puhvel, Jaan. *Comparative Mythology.* Baltimore: Johns Hopkins University Press, 1987.

Puhvel, Jaan, ed. *Myth and Law Among the Indo-Europeans.* Berkeley: University of California Press, 1970.

Quigley, Carroll. *The Evolution of Civilizations: An Introduction to Historical Analysis.* 2nd ed. Indianapolis, Ind.: Liberty Press, 1979.

Rahner, Hugo. *Greek Myth and Christian Mystery.* Translated by Brian Battershaw. Introduction by E. O. James. 1963; reprint, Cheshire, Conn.: Biblo & Tannen, 1971.

Rahner, Karl. "What is a Dogmatic Statement?" In Rahner, *Theological Investigations,* vol. 5, 42–66. Translated by Karl Kruger. Baltimore: Helicon, 1966.

Rambo, Lewis R. "Current Research on Religious Conversion." *Religious Studies Review* 8 (1982): 146–59.

Ratofer, Johannes. *Der Heliand: Theologischer Sinn als tektonische Form.* Niederdeutsche Studien, vol. 9. Cologne: Böhlau Verlag, 1962.

Rawson, B. M., ed. *The Family in Ancient Rome: New Perspectives.* Ithaca, N.Y.: Cornell University Press, 1986.

Reitzenstein, Richard. *Hellenistic Mystery Religions: Their Basic Ideas and Significance.* Translated by John E. Steely. Pittsburgh: Pickwick Press, 1978.

Reuter, Timothy. "On the Aristocratic Character of Early Frankish Society." Translated by Timothy Reuter. In Reuter, ed., *The Medieval Nobility: Studies on the Ruling Classes of France and Germany from the Sixth to the Twelfth Century.* Europe in the Middle Ages, vol. 14. Amsterdam: North-Holland, 1978.

_____. "Saint Boniface and Europe." In Reuter, ed., *The Greatest Englishman: Essays on St. Boniface and the Church at Crediton,* 69–94.

Reuter, Timothy, ed. *The Greatest Englishman: Essays on St. Boniface and the Church at Crediton.* Exeter: Paternoster Press, 1980.

Reynolds, V., and R. E. S. Tanner. *The Biology of Religion.* London: Longman, 1983.

Richards, John W. "The Evolution of the Spartan Social System." *Mankind Quarterly* 20 (1980): 331–43.

Richardson, James T. "Proselytizing Processes of the New Religions." In Marty and Greenspahn, eds., *Pushing the Faith: Proselytism and Civility in a Pluralistic World,* 143–54.

Riché, Pierre. *Education and Culture in the Barbarian West from the Sixth Through the Eighth Century*. Translated by John J. Contreni. Foreword by Richard E. Sullivan. Columbia: University of South Carolina Press, 1976.

_____. *The Carolingians: A Family Who Forged Europe*. Translated by Michael Idomir Allen. Philadelphia: University of Pennsylvania Press, 1993.

Rivière, Jean-Claude. *Georges Dumézil à la découverte des Indo-Européens*. Paris: Copernic, 1982.

Rollason, David. *Saints and Relics in Anglo-Saxon England*. Oxford: Basil Blackwell, 1989.

Rose, H. J. *Religion in Greece and Rome*. New York: Harper & Row, 1959.

Rosenwein, Barbara. *Rhinoceros Bound: Cluny in the Tenth Century*. Philadelphia: University of Pennsylvania Press, 1982.

Rosenwein, Barbara H., and Lester K. Little. "Social Meaning in the Monastic and Mendicant Spiritualities." *Past and Present* 63 (1974): 4–32.

Rostovtzeff, Mikhail. *Social and Economic History of the Roman Empire*. 2 vols. 2nd rev. ed. Revised by P. M. Fraser. Oxford: Clarendon Press, 1957.

Rubin, Zeev. "The Conversion of the Visigoths to Christianity." *Museum Helveticum* 38 (1981): 34–54.

Rückert, Hanns. *Die Christianisierung der Germanen: Ein Beitrag zu ihrem Verständnis und ihrer Beurteilung*. 2nd rev. ed. Tübingen: J. C. B. Mohr (Paul Siebeck), 1934.

Rupp, George. *Christologies and Cultures: Toward a Typology of Religious Worldviews*. Religion and Reason: Method and Theory in the Study and Interpretation of Religion, vol. 10. Berlin: Walter de Gruyter, 1974.

Rupp, Heinz. "Leid und Sunde im *Heliand* und in Otfrids *Evangelienbuch*." *Beiträge zur Geschichte der deutschen Sprache und Literatur*. Part 1, 78 (1956): 421–69; part 2: 79 (1957): 336–79.

_____. "The Adoption of Christian Ideas into German, with Reference to the *Heliand* and to Otfrid's *Evangelienbuch*." *Parergon* 21 (1978): 33–41.

Russell, Jeffrey Burton. *The Devil: Perceptions of Evil from Antiquity to Primitive Christianity*. Ithaca, N.Y.: Cornell University Press, 1977.

The Saga of the Volsungs: The Norse Epic of Sigurd the Dragon Slayer. Translated by Jesse L. Byock. Berkeley: University of California Press, 1990.

Sankt Bonifatius: Gedenkausgabe zum zwölfhundertsten Todestag. Fulda: Parzeller, 1954.

Sasiki, M. S. "Status Inconsistency and Religious Commitment." In Robert Wuthrow, ed. *The Religious Dimension: New Directions in Quantitative Research*, 135–56. New York: Academic Press, 1979.

Saunders, George R., ed. *Culture and Christianity: The Dialectics of Transformation*. Westport, Conn.: Greenwood Press, 1988.

Sawyer, Birgit, Peter Sawyer, and Ian Wood, eds. *The Christianization of Scandinavia: Report of a Symposium Held at Kungälv, Sweden, 4–9 August 1985*. Alingås, Sweden: Viktoria Bokförlag, 1987.

Sawyer, Peter H., and Ian N. Wood, eds. *Early Medieval Kingship*. Leeds: The School of History, University of Leeds, 1977.

Scardigli, Piergiuseppe. "La conversione dei Goti al Cristianesimo." *Settimane* 14 (1967): 47–86.

Schach, Paul. *Icelandic Sagas*. Boston: Twayne, 1984.

Schäferdiek, Knut. *Die Kirchen in den Reichen der Westgoten und Suewen bis zur Errichtung der westgotischen katholischen Staatskirche*. Berlin: Walter de Gruyter, 1967.

———. "Ein neues Bild der Geschichte Chlodwigs?" *ZKG* 84 (1973): 270–77.

———. "Die geschichtliche Stellung des sogenannten germanischen Arianismus." In Schäferdiek, ed., *Die Kirche des früheren Mittelalters*, 79–90.

———. "Gab es eine gotisch arianisch-christliche Mission im südwestdeutschen Raum?" *Zeitschrift für bayerische Landesgeschichte* 45 (1982): 239–57.

———. "Remigius von Reims: Kirchenmann einer Umbruchzeit." *ZKG* 94 (1983): 256–78.

———. "Zur Frage früher christlicher Einwirkungen auf den westgermanischen Raum." *ZKG* 98:2 (1987): 149–66.

Schäferdiek, Knut, ed. *Die Kirche des früheren Mittelalters*. First half of vol. 2 of *Kirchengeschichte als Missionsgeschichte*. Munich: Chr. Kaiser Verlag, 1978.

Schieffer, Theodor. *Winfrid-Bonifatius und die christliche Grundlegung Europas*. 1954; reprint with updated bibliography, Darmstadt: Wissenschaftliche Buchgesellschaft, 1972; reprint with coerrections, 1980.

Schmidt, Kurt Dietrich. *Die Bekehrung der Germanen zum Christentum*. 2 vols. Göttingen: Vandenhoeck & Ruprecht, 1939–42.

———. *Germanischer Glaube und Christentum*. Göttingen: Vandenhoeck & Ruprecht, 1948.

Schmitt, Jean-Claude. *The Holy Greyhound: Guinefort, Healer of Children Since the Thirteenth Century*. Cambridge: Cambridge University Press, 1983.

Schneider, Louis, ed. *Religion, Culture and Society: A Reader in the Sociology of Religion*. New York: Wiley, 1964.

Schnürer, Gustav. *Church and Culture in the Middle Ages*. Vol. 1. Translated by George J. Undreiner. Paterson, N.J.: St. Anthony Guild Press, 1956.

Schnusenberg, Christine Catharina. *The Relationship Between the Church and the Theatre: Exemplified by Selected Writings of the Church Fathers and by Liturgical Texts Until Amalarius of Metz: 775–852 A.D.* Lanham, Md.: University Press of America, 1988.

Schoeps, Hans-Joachim. *The Religions of Mankind*. Translated by Richard and Clara Winston. Garden City, N.Y.: Doubleday, 1966.

Schoffeleers, Matthew. "Folk Christology in Africa: The Dialectics of the Nganga Paradigm." *Journal of Religion in Africa* 19:2 (1989): 157–83.

Scholler, Harald, ed. *The Epic in Medieval Society*. Tübingen: Max Niemeyer Verlag, 1977.

Schubert, Hans von. *Staat und Kirche in den arianischen Königreichen und im Reiche Chlodwigs*. Munich: R. Oldenbourg, 1912.

———. *Geschichte der christlichen Kirche im Frühmittelalter*. Tübingen: J. C. B. Mohr (Paul Siebeck), 1921.

Scobie, Geoffrey E. W. *Psychology of Religion*. New York: Wiley, 1975.

Seward, Desmond. *The Monks of War: The Military Religious Orders*. Hamden, Conn.: Archon, 1972.

Shorter, Aylward. *Toward a Theology of Inculturation*. Maryknoll, N.Y.: Orbis Books, 1988.

Simon, Edith. *The Piebald: A Biography of the Knights of Templars*. Boston: Little, Brown, 1959.

Simpson, John. "Comparative Structural Analysis of Three Ethical Questions in *Beowulf*, the *Nibelungenlied* and the *Chanson de Roland*." *JIES* 3 (1975): 239–54.

Skomal, Susan Nacev, and Edgar C. Polomé, eds. *Proto-Indo-European: The Archaeology of a Linguistic Problem: Studies in Honor of Marija Gimbutas*. Washington, D.C.: Institute for the Study of Man, 1987.

Sladden, John Cyril. *Boniface of Devon: Apostle of Germany*. Exeter: Paternoster Press, 1980.

Smalley, William A., ed. *Readings in Missionary Anthropology*. Tarrytown, N.Y.: Practical Anthropology, 1967.

Smart, Ninian. *The Religious Experience of Mankind*. 3rd ed. New York: Scribner's, 1984.

Smith, John Clark. "Conversion in Origen." *Scottish Journal of Theology* 32 (1979): 217–40.

Smith, John Holland. *The Death of Classical Paganism*. New York: Scribner's, 1976.

Smith, Julia M. H. "Early Medieval Hagiography in the Late Twentieth Century." *Early Medieval Europe* 1:1 (1992): 69–76.

Smith, Noel W. "The Ancient Background to Greek Psychology." *Psychological Record* 24 (1974): 309–24.

_____. "Belief Systems—A Psychological Analysis." *Mankind Quarterly* 25:3 (1985): 195–225.

_____. "Indo-European Psychological Conepts and the Shift to Psychophysical Dualism." *Mankind Quarterly* 30:1/2 (1989): 119–27.

_____. "Psychological Concepts under Changing Social Conditions in Ancient Egypt." *Mankind Quarterly* 30:4 (1990): 317–27.

_____. "The Evolution of Psychophysical Dualism in Ancient India: From the *Rig Veda* to the *Sutras*." *Mankind Quarterly* 31:1/2 (1990): 3–15.

Smyth, Alfred P. *Warlords and Holy Men: Scotland A.D. 80–1000*. London: E. Arnold, 1984.

Snow, David A., and Richard Machalek, "The Sociology of Conversion." *Annual Review of Sociology* 10 (1984): 167–90.

Spengler, Oswald. *The Decline of the West*. Translated by Charles Francis Atkinson. 2 vols. New York: Knopf, 1926.

Stancliffe, C. E. "From Town to Country: The Christianisation of the Touraine, 370–600." In Baker, ed., *The Church in Town and Countryside*, 43–59.

_____. *St. Martin and his Hagiographer: History and Miracle in Sulpicius Severus*. Oxford: Oxford University Press, 1983.

Starbuck, Edwin D. *Psychology of Religion*. New York: Scribner's, 1915.

Stark, Rodney. "Christianizing the Urban Empire: An Analysis Based on 22 Greco-Roman Cities." *Sociological Analysis* 52:1 (1991): 77–88.

Steklis Horst D., and Alex Walter. "Culture, Biology and Behavior: A Mechanistic Approach." *Human Nature* 2:2 (1991): 137–69.

Stephenson, Carl. *Medieval Feudalism*. Ithaca, N.Y.: Cornell University Press, 1942.

Strutynski, Udo Maria. "Introduction, Part II." In Dumézil, *Gods of the Ancient Northmen*, xix–xliii.

_____. "History and Structure in Germanic Mythology: Some Thoughts on Einar Haugen's Critique of Dumézil." In Larson, ed., *Myth in Indo-European Antiquity*, 29–50.

_____. "Georges Dumézil and the Study of the Indo-European Component in Germanic Mythology." Ph.D. diss., University of California, Los Angeles, 1975.

_____. "Introduction." In Dumézil, *Camillus*, 1–39.

Sturluson, Snorri. *Heimskringla: The Olaf Sagas*. 2 vols. Translated by Samuel Laing. Revised with an introduction and notes by Jaqueline Simpson. Everyman's Library, nos. 717 and 722. London: J. M. Dent, 1964.

Stutz, Ulrich. "The Proprietary Church as an Element of Medieval Germanic Ecclesiastical Law." In *Medieval Germany (911–1250): Essays by German Historians*. Translated and edited by Geoffrey Barraclough. Studies in Mediaeval History, vol. 11. Oxford: Basil Blackwell, 1961.

Sullivan, Richard E. "The Carolingian Missionary and the Pagan." *Speculum* 28 (1953): 705–40.

_____. "Early Medieval Missionary Activity: A Comparative Study of Eastern and Western Methods." *Church History* 23 (1954): 17–35.

_____. "The Papacy and Missionary Activity in the Early Middle Ages." *Mediaeval Studies* 17 (1955): 46–106.

_____. "Carolingian Missionary Theories." *Catholic Historical Review* 42 (1956): 273–95.

_____. "Khan Boris and the Conversion of Bulgaria: A Case Study of the Impact of Christianity on a Barbarian Society." In Bowsky, *Studies in Medieval and Renaissance History*, 53–139.

_____. "The Carolingian Age." *Speculum* 64 (1989): 267–307.

Sykes, Stephen. *The Identity of Christianity: Theologians and the Essence of Christianity from Schleiermacher to Barth*. Philadelphia: Fortress Press, 1984.

Tacitus, Cornelius. *The Agricola and the Germania*. Translated with an introduction by H. Mattingly. Revised by S. A. Handford. New York: Penguin, 1970.

Talbot, C. H. *The Anglo-Saxon Missionaries in Germany*. New York: Sheed & Ward, 1954.

_____. "St. Boniface and the German Mission." In Cuming, ed., *The Mission of the Church and the Propagation of the Faith*, 45–57.

Talley, Jeannine E. "Runes, Mandrakes, and Gallows." In Larson, ed., *Myth in Indo-European Antiquity*, 157–68.

Tarn, W. W. *Alexander the Great*. 1948; reprint, Boston: Beacon Press, 1956.

Tessier, Georges. "La Conversion de Clovis et la christianisation des Francs." In *Settimane* 14 (1967): 149–89.

Thompson, Claiborne W. "Moral Values in the Icelandic Sagas." In Scholler, ed., *The Epic in Medieval Society*, 347–60.

Thompson, E. A. "Christianity and the Northern Barbarians." In Momigliano, ed., *The Conflict Between Paganism and Christianity in the Fourth Century*, 56–78.

Thompson, E. A. *The Early Germans*. Oxford: Clarendon Press, 1965.

————. *The Visigoths in the Time of Ulfila*. Oxford: Clarendon Press, 1966.

————. *Romans and Barbarians: The Decline of the Western Empire*. Madison: University of Wisconsin Press, 1982.

Timerding, Heinrich, ed. *Die christliche Frühzeit Deutschlands in der Berichten über die Bekehrer*. 2 vols. Jena: Eugen Diederichs Verlag, 1929.

Tippett, Alan R. "Christopaganism or Indigenous Christianity?" In Kraft and Wisley, *Readings in Dynamic Indigeneity*, 400–21.

Tomasson, Richard F. *Iceland: The First New Society*. Reykjavík: Icelandic Review, 1980.

Toynbee, Arnold. *The Hannibalic War's Effects on Roman Life*. 2 vols. Oxford: Oxford University Press, 1965.

————. *An Historian's Approach to Religion*. 2nd ed. Oxford: Oxford University Press, 1979.

Troeltsch, Ernst. *The Social Teaching of the Christian Churches*. Vol. 1. Translated by Olive Wyon. Introduction by H. Richard Niebuhr. 1931; reprint, New York: Harper & Row, 1960.

Turville-Petre, E. O. G. *Origins of Icelandic Literature*. Oxford: Clarendon Press, 1953.

————. *Myth and Religion of the North*. New York: Holt, Rinehart, and Winston, 1964.

————. "Professor Dumézil and the Literature of Iceland." *Hommages à Georges Dumézil*, 209–14.

Ullmann, Walter. *The Individual and Society in the Middle Ages*. Baltimore: Johns Hopkins University Press, 1966.

————. *The Carolingian Renaissance and the Idea of Kingship*. London: Methuen, 1969.

————. *The Growth of Papal Government in the Middle Ages: A Study in the Ideological Relation of Clerical to Lay Power*. 3rd ed. London: Methuen, 1970.

Van Dam, Raymond. *Leadership and Community in Late Antique Gaul*. Berkeley: University of California Press, 1985.

————. "Images of Saint Martin in Late Roman and Early Merovingian Gaul." *Viator* 19 (1988): 1–27.

Van Engen, John. "The Christian Middle Ages as an Historiographical Problem." *AHR* 91 (1986): 519–52.

Väth, Alfons. *Das Bild der Weltkirche: Akkomodation und Europäismus im Wandel der Jahrhunderte und in der neuen Zeit*. Hanover: Verlag Joseph Giesel, 1932.

Vereno, Matthias. "On the Relations of Dumézilian Comparative Indo-European Mythology to the History of Religions in General." In Larson, *Myth in Indo-European Antiquity*, 181–90.

Vergote, Antoine. *Guilt and Desire: Religious Attitudes and Their Pathological Derivatives*. Translated by M. H. Wood. New Haven, Conn.: Yale University Press, 1988.

Verkuyl, Johannes. *Contemporary Missiology: An Introduction*. Translated and edited by Dale Cooper. Grand Rapids, Mich.: Eerdmans, 1978.

Vermaseren, Maarten J. ed. *Etudes préliminaires aux religions orientales dans l'Empire romain.* Leiden: Brill, 1967–1981.

Victor of Vita: A History of the Vandal Persecution. Translated with notes and introduction by John Moorhead. Liverpool: Liverpool University Press, 1992.

Voegelin, Eric. *Order and History.* 5 vols. Baton Rouge: Louisiana State University Press, 1956–87.

Vogel, Cyrille. "Les échanges liturgiques entre Rome et les pays Francs jusqu'à l'époque de Charlemagne." *Settimane* 7 (1960): 185–295.

_____. *Le pontifical romano-germanique.* 3 vols. Studi e Testi, nos. 226, 227, and 269. Vatican City: Biblioteca Apostolica Vaticana, 1963–72.

_____. *Medieval Liturgy: An Introduction to the Sources.* Translated and revised by William Storey and Niels Rasmussen. Washington, D. C.: Pastoral Press, 1986.

Wallace, Ruth Ann. "Some Social Determinants of Change of Religious Affiliation." Ph.D. dissertation, University of California, Berkeley, 1968.

Wallace-Hadrill, J. M. *The Barbarian West: The Early Middle Ages, A.D. 400–1000.* Harper Torchbook Edition. New York: Harper & Row, 1962.

_____. *The Long-Haired Kings.* Medieval Academy Reprints for Teaching, no. 11. 1962; reprint, Toronto: University of Toronto Press, 1982.

_____. *Early Germanic Kingship in England and on the Continent.* Oxford: Clarendon Press, 1971.

_____. *Early Medieval History.* Oxford: Basil Blackwell, 1975.

_____. *The Frankish Church.* Oxford: Clarendon Press, 1983.

Waller, Niels G., Brian A. Kojetin, Thomas J. Bouchard, Jr., David T. Lykken, and Auke Tellegen. "Genetic and Environmental Influences on Religious Interests, Attitudes, and Values: A Study of Twins Reared Apart and Together." *Psychological Science* 1:2 (1990): 138–42.

Wallis, R. T. *Neoplatonism.* New York: Scribner's, 1970.

Wallis, Roy. *The Elementary Forms of the New Religious Life.* London: Routledge & Kegan Paul, 1984.

Ward, Donald. *The Divine Twins: An Indo-European Myth in Germanic Tradition.* Folklore Studies, vol. 19. Berkeley: University of California Press, 1968.

Wardman, Alan. *Religion and Statecraft Among the Romans.* London: Granada Publishing, 1982.

Wattenbach, Wilhelm, and Wilhelm Levison. *Deutschlands Geschichtsquellen im Mittelalter: Vorzeit und Karolinger.* 5 parts. Weimar: Herman Böhlaus Nachfolger, 1952–73.

Weber, Max. *The Sociology of Religion.* Translated by Ephraim Fischoff. Introduction by Talcott Parsons. Boston: Beacon Press, 1963.

_____. *Wirtschaft und Gesellschaft: Grundriss der verstehenden Soziologie.* Edited by Johannes Winckelmann. Tübingen: J. C. B. Mohr (Paul Siebeck), 1956.

White, L. Michael. "Adolf Harnack and the 'Expansion' of Early Christianity: A Reappraisal of Social History." *The Second Century* 5:2 (1985/86): 97–127.

White, Lynn, Jr. "The Life of the Silent Majority." In Robert S. Hoyt, ed., *Life and Thought in the Early Middle Ages,* 85–100. Minneapolis: University of Minnesota Press, 1967.

Wilken, Robert L. *The Christians as the Romans Saw Them.* New Haven, Conn.: Yale University Press, 1984.

Willibald. *The Life of Saint Boniface.* Translated by George W. Robinson. Cambridge, Mass.: Harvard University Press, 1916.

Wilpert, Paul. *Universalismus und Partikularismus im Mittelalter.* Miscellanea Mediaevalia, no. 5. Berlin: Walter de Gruyter, 1968.

Wilson, Bryan. *Religion in Sociological Perspective.* Oxford: Oxford University Press, 1982.

Wilson, David M., ed. *The Northern World: The History and Heritage of Northern Europe, A.D. 400–1100.* New York: Harry N. Abrams, 1980.

Wiltgen, Ralph M. *The Rhine Flows into the Tiber: The Unknown Council.* New York: Hawthorn Books, 1967.

Wissig, Otto. *Iroschotten und Bonifatius in Deutschland: Eine kirchengeschichtlich-urkundliche Untersuchung.* Gütersloh: C. Bertelsmann, 1932.

Wolfram, Herwig. *History of the Goths.* Translated by Thomas J. Dunlap. Revised from 2nd German ed. Berkeley: University of California Press, 1988.

Wood, Ian N. "Early Merovingian Devotion in Town and Country." In Baker, ed., *The Church in Town and Countryside,* 61–76.

———. "The Conversion of the Barbarian Peoples." In Geoffrey Barraclough, ed., *The Christian World,* 85–98. New York: Harry N. Abrams, 1981.

———. "Gregory of Tours and Clovis." *RBPH* 63 (1985): 249–72.

———. "Administration, Law and Culture in Merovingian Gaul." In Rosamond McKitterick, ed., *The Uses of Literacy in Early Medieval Europe.* New York: Cambridge University Press, 1990.

Wormald, Patrick. "Bede, Beowulf, and the Conversion of the Anglo-Saxon Aristocracy." In Robert T. Farrell, ed., *Bede and Anglo-Saxon England,* 32–95. British Archaeological Reports, no. 46. Oxford: British Archaeological Reports, 1978.

Wuthnow, Robert. *Rediscovering the Sacred: Perspectives on Religion in Contemporary Society.* Grand Rapids, Mich.: Eerdmans, 1992.

Wynne-Edwards, V. C. "Ecology and the Evolution of Social Ethics." In J. W. S. Pringle, ed., *Biology and the Human Sciences.* Oxford: Oxford University Press, 1972.

Young, Jean I., ed. *The Prose Edda of Snorri Sturluson.* Introduction by Sigurdur Nordal. Berkeley: University of California Press, 1966.

Yutang, Lin, ed. *The Wisdom of China and India.* New York: Modern Library, 1942.

Zirkel, Patricia McCormick. "The Divine Child in Paschasius Radbertus' *De Corpore et Sanguine Domini,* Chapter XIV." Ph.D. diss., Fordham University, 1989.

Index

Accommodation, missionary policy of, 4, 7, 38, 43, 121, 131, 163, 181, 187, 189, 206, 211, 213
Acculturation, 12
Adams, Robert M., 128
Adelsheilige, 168
  hagiographic canons of, 209, 212
Aesir and Vanir, 111
Æthelbert of Kent (king), 184–86
Aland, Kurt, 73
Alaric (Visigothic king), 137
Alcuin (abbot and liturgist), 44
Alexander the Great, 50, 59, 63, 70, 84, 100
Alienation, 4, 78, 211
  and Hellenistic mystery cults, 67
  cultural, 11
Altruism, in-group, 53, 69, 204
Amalar of Metz (liturgist), 44
Amand (missionary), 164
Amos, Thomas Leslie, 158, 195, 199, 201
Angus, Samuel, 63
Anomie, 4, 6, 20–22, 66, 91, 131
  and world-rejecting religiosity, 57
  in Hellenistic society, 63
  in the Roman Empire, 97
Antoninian Constitution, 72
Apocalypticism, Jewish, 75
Arianism, Germanic. *See* Christianity: Arian: Germanic
Asoka (Indian emperor), 50
Astrology, 69
Athanaric (Visigothic chieftain), attitude toward Christianity, 136
Athaulf (Visigothic king), 137–38
Audoenus of Rouen (bishop), 158
Augustine of Canterbury (missionary), 183, 185–86, 192
Augustine of Hippo (bishop), 163
Augustus (emperor), 71
Avitus of Vienne (bishop), 152, 159, 165, 175

Baetke, Walter, 171–72, 202–6
Baker, Derek, 166, 210
Balthildis (Frankish queen), 160
Baptism, 36
  temporal rewards for, 195
Barker, Eileen, 93
Batiffol, Pierre, 89
Baus, Karl, 67, 74
Bauschatz, Paul, 177
BAVB
  definition of, 13
  modification of, 12, 211
Bede (English historian), 185
Belisarius (Byzantine general), 145
Bellah, Robert, 19, 49–51, 53, 177
Bernard of Clairvaux (abbot), 40
Bible, 199, 206
Biological solidarity, 66
Bloch, Marc, 130
Blood feud, Germanic institution of, 122
Bömer, Franz, 88
Boniface (Anglo-Saxon missionary), 7, 122, 132, 135, 166, 183, 185, 187, 192–94, 196, 212
  and Gregory's missionary policy, 192–93
  and secular support, 196
Brandon, S. G. F., 76
Branley, Brendan, 19
Brown, Peter, 31, 91, 176–77
  review of Dodds's "Age of Anxiety", 92
Buddhism, 19, 46, 50
Burgundians, 135
Burkert, Walter, 14, 68, 71
Burns, Thomas, 141
Bury, J. B., 64, 127, 135, 152

Caesar, Gaius Julius, 108, 114
Caesarius of Arles (bishop), 161
Campbell, Joseph, 162
Caracalla (emperor), 72
Cassiodorus, 143

Catechetical instruction, 131
  post-baptismal, 188
  medieval status of, 198, 211
Catechumenate, decline of, 211
Catholic traditionalists, viii, 210
Chaney, William A., 172
Charlemagne (emperor), 192
Charles Martel (Frankish ruler), 196
Childeric (father of Clovis), 146–47,
  175
Chivalry, 6, 18
Christendom
  concept of, 190
  European ideal of, 210
Christianitas, 133
Christianity, 46
  and anomic conditions, 94
  and civic cohesion, 88
  and Germanic political ideals, 212
  and Hellenistic mystery cults, 67
  and magic, 201
  and natural kinship structure, 81
  and politics, 135
  and Roman culture, 135
  and sociobiological relationships, 81
  and the accommodation of Germanic
    religiocultural attitudes, 40
  appeal of, 89
    and salvation, 100
    and socialization, 100
  Arian, Germanic, 7, 42, 134, 137–40,
    142, 149, 212
    and ethnocultural identity, 50
    and group solidarity, 141
    and Romanization, 142
    as a national religion, 141
  as a deviant subculture, 86
  as a European folk religion, 39
  as a salvation religion, 6, 76
  Catholic, Frankish, 134
  compared with Hellenistic religiosity, 73
  compromises with Germanic religiosity,
    201
  contemporary attitude toward Germanic
    influence, 211
  definition of, 33, 35
    belief in individual redemption, 35
  disparity between Germanic religiosity
    and, 213
  dissolution of the family unit and, 88
  early, 52
    appeal of as an alternative community,
      90–91, 93, 102
    eschatological orientation of, 82

Indo-European Greek influence on,
  62
  messianic and apocalyptic
    expectations of, 91
  organic relation to the declining
    Roman Empire, 102
  social solidarity in, 89
  social structure of, 155
  sociopolitical environment of, 98
  socioreligious and sociopsychological
    environment of, 91
early Christian model of, 191
egalitarian re-socialization and, 88
element of belief, 180
essence of, 33, 35
Eurocentric particularization of, 190
European, vii
expansion of, 50, 60, 89, 133
  factors affecting success of, 97, 100–1
folk-religious reinterpretation of, 135,
  180
Germanic, vii, 131
Germanic reinterpretation of, 188, 209,
  212
Greek and Roman influences on, 133
Hellenistic heritage of, 76
heroic reinterpretation of, 6
Indo-Europeanization of, 59, 133
  pre-Germanic, 61
Judaic heritage of, 76
magicoreligious aspects of, 162, 164
magicoreligious reinterpretation of, 6,
  154, 189, 191, 208, 209, 210
mass conversion to, 136
Merovingian, as a " 'cult' religion", 158
misrepresentation of, 23, 101, 202, 211,
  213
misunderstanding of, 202, 203
notion of Redemption in, 52
notion of the Incarnation in, 52
objectivist definition of, 132
original Judeo-Hellenistic sociocultural
  environment of, 101
pagan survivals in, 152
relativist approach to, 214
religiopolitical aspects of, 157
religiopolitical reinterpretation of, 154,
  189, 190, 208, 209
Roman, and social cohesion, 50
soteriological essence of, 36, 214
world-rejecting orientation of, 77
Christianization, 3, 6, 26, 36, 132, 134,
  162, 212–13
  "superficial" or "nominal", 212

and city size, 86
and ethics, 202
and ethnic heterogeneity, 86
and social cohesion, 158
and temporal rewards, 195
and the reputation of "brotherly love",
  88
and warfare, 40
Anglo-Saxon approach, 183
  and Iro-Frankish approach
    compared, 164
appeal to power, 212
attempted, 179
concept of, 31
definition of, 36
examples of, 16–24
  Africa, 16
  evaluated, 24–25
  Hawaii, 22
  Japan, 19
  Jews for Jesus, 22
  South Korea, 21
Greco-Roman, 4
in Gaul, 176
in Roman Empire, 183
Iro-Frankish approach, 158
  and Anglo-Saxon approach
    compared, 164
mass mode of, 135
Merovingians and, 154
metaphysical aspects of, 177
objectivist definition of, 213
of Egypt, 80
of the Germanic peoples, 46, 123, 132
of the Touraine, 181
policies of, 39
primary-phase approach, 164
process of, 13
  disparity between in classical and
    Germanic societies, 98
secondary phase, 200
  approach of, 164
  Columbanus and, 159
sociopsychological factors, 80
through semantic transformation, 163
Christians
and unworldly equality, 89
as a disruptive social phenomenon,
  81
as a threat to the Roman system, 82
as an artificial kin group, 91
early
  social solidarity among, 89
  social status of, 84

Christus Victor, 170
Civilizational dynamics, 98
Clawsey, Mary Crawford, 118, 121–22,
  131
Clebsch, William A., 34
Clement of Alexandria (theologian), 133
Clovis (Frankish king), 17, 146–48,
  150–53, 159, 165, 175, 205
  baptism of, 151
  conversion of, 33
Clovis II (Frankish king), 160
Cluny, 124
Coercion, missionary policy of, 211
Cognitive dissonance, 88
Cohesion, sociocultural, 24
Columbanus (Irish missionary), 154,
  156, 158–61, 164–65
  Penitentials of, 160
Comitatus, 7, 117–19, 128, 167, 204, 206
  and honor, 119
  and kinship bonds, 121
  and vassalage, 129
  compared with general Roman
    social structure, 119
  in Indo-European society and
    mythology, 117
Commercial Revolution, 44
Commodus (emperor), 72
Congar, Yves M.-J., 13
Constantine (emperor), 50
Constantius II (emperor), 136
Conversion, 13, 26–27, 135
  ambiguity of the term, 27
  and alienation, 84
  and anxiety, 87
  and cognitive dissonance, 84
  and loneliness, 87
  and religious belief, 29
  and repentance, 27
  and status inconsistency, 83–84
  individual, 27
    and radical personal change, 28
  mass, 202
  resocialization of, 81
  societal, 28, 31
Copleston, Frederick, 61
Cosmopolitanism, 64
Council of Constantinople (381), 140
Council of Orléans (511), 153
Crusade ideology, 6, 167–68, 190,
  209
Cullmann, Oscar, 176
Cumont, Franz, 69
Cyrus (Persian king), 50

Dagobert I (Frankish king), 154, 158, 160, 164
Daniel of Winchester (bishop), 196
  advice to Boniface, 193–94
Davidson, H. R. Ellis, 190
Dawson, Christopher, 15, 31
De Bello Gallico, 108
De correctione rusticorum, 142
De laude novae militiae, 40
De singulis libris canonicis scarapsus, 199
de Vries, Jan, 173, 204
de-Europeanization, viii
de-Indo-Europeanization, 6, 58, 76
Dead Sea Scrolls, 77
Death, attitude toward, 162
Decadence, definition of, 128
Delaruelle, Etienne, 36
Delumeau, Jean, 37
Dickinson, G. Lowes, 65
Dirksen, Aloys, 26
Dix, Gregory, 199
Dodds, E. R., 91
Dream of the Rood, The, 24, 170
Drew, Katherine Fischer, 43, 128
Duby, Georges, 132
Dumézil, Georges, 59, 98, 107, 173
  methodology of, 111, 114
  on Indo-European ideology, 112
  on Indo-European parallels, 113
  on Indo-European social structure and mythology, 113
  on the Aesir and Vanir myth, 111
  on the *comitatus,* 117
  on the tripartite structure of Indo-European ideology, 114
  on the warrior function, 117
Durkheim, Emile, 20, 131

Ecclesia primitiva, 211
Ecumenism, 210
Eddas, 110
Eigenkirche, 6, 18, 142
Eigenkirchensystem, 154, 171, 209, 212
Eigenklostersystem, 154, 159, 171, 209
Eliade, Mircea, 85, 90, 100, 125
Eligius of Noyon (bishop), 158–59, 161
Erdmann, Carl, 167–68
Erigena, Johannes Scotus (philosopher), 163
Essenes, 77
Ethical reorientation, 204
Ethnocultural destabilization, 88
Ethos
  attempts to transform, 13

change in, 100
classical and Germanic compared, 99
Germanic, 42, 121
  vitality of, 122
late Roman, 100
of the *comitatus,* 117, 132
warrior
  in hagiographies, 125
  sublimation of, 124
world-accepting, 103
Euric (Visigothic king), 148–49
Euro-Christian religiocultural fusion, 210
Euro-Christians, alienation among contemporary, 211
Eurocentric religiocultural sentiment, 210
Ewig, Eugen, 136, 154

Fate, Celto-Germanic notions of, 162
Ferguson, John, 89
Feudalism, 6
Fleckenstein, Josef, 130
Flint,Valerie I. J., 32
Florilegia, 203
Folk religion. *See* Religion: folk
Folk religiosity. *See* Religiosity: folk
Folk-religious societies, 3, 46, 108
Fouracre, Paul, 158
Fox, Robin Lane, 88–89
Franks. *See* Germanic peoples: Franks
Fritigern (Visigothic commander), 140

Gallo-Roman aristocracy, 149
Gallo-Roman episcopacy, 7, 148–52, 212
  Arian threat to, 148
  Merovingian appointees to, 153
Geary, Patrick J., 33, 149–50, 158, 196
Geblütsheiligkeit, 157
Genetic factors, in religious attitudes, 14
Gens, 100
Germania, 108
Germanic ethos. *See* Ethos, Germanic
Germanic kingship, 152, 172–74
Germanic law codes, 43
Germanic peoples
  accommodation of religiocultural attitudes by Christianity, 40
  affinity for Roman grandeur, 148
  and Roman culture, 146
  Arianism of, 144
    Ostrogoths, 145
    Visigoths, 145
  attitude of the Romans toward, 184
  attitude toward Roman culture, 143, 147
  cohesive social structure of, 102

doctrinal inculcation of, 210
ethical instruction of, 210
ethical standards of, 204
first contact with Christianity, 134
Franks
  and Roman culture, 147, 150
  and Romans, 151
  early history of, 151
  paganism of, 153
Indo-European heritage of, 102, 118
laws of, 147
Lombards, 196-97
Ostrogoths, 175
paganism of, 145
religious affiliation of, 138
  Alamanni, 164
  Ostrogoths, 141
  sources for, 108
Tervingi Goths, 135
theological speculation among, 210
Visigoths
  "mass conversion" of, 136
  and Romans, 134, 151
  encounter with Christianity, 135
  group identity of, 151
Germanic religiosity
centrality of power in, 7
sources for, 110
vitality of, 4, 7, 188, 207
Germanic world-view. *See* World-view:
  Germanic
Germanization, 43, 134, 207
ideological aspects of, 209
of Arian Christianity, 142
of Christian religious culture, 131
of Christianity, 3–4, 16, 38–39, 44, 46,
  51, 123, 131, 133, 153, 162, 167, 171
approach to the study of, 5
and the Crusade ideology, 167
and the *Eigenkirchensystem,* 154, 171
and the *Eigenklostersystem,* 154
effects on hagiography, 125, 168
effects on the liturgy, 41–43, 192
factors contributing toward, 183
magicoreligious effects of, 210
normative for the West, 4
religiopolitical effects, 210
of medieval religious culture, 41
of the Roman army, 127
process of, 124
Glock, Charles Y., and Rodney Stark, on
  conversion, 28
Gnosticism, 78, 79
versus Indo-European religiosity, 78

Gradualism, missionary policy of, 188, 211
Green, D. H., 188, 206
Greenhouse, Carol J., 176
Gregory of Tours (bishop), 148, 181
Gregory the Great (pope), 161, 183
apocalyptic vision of, 184
correspondence of, 193
missionary policy of, 183, 186–88, 192
Group solidarity, 4, 6, 167, 171, 212
and concepts of immortality, 65– 66
and Germanic Arianism, 141
and in-group altruism, 69
and world-rejecting religiosity, 57
Germanic, 126, 128–30
  compared to late Roman, 126
  contrasted with early Christian, 131
versus individualism, 100
Grundmann, Herbert, 36
Guilt feelings, 160
Guntram (Frankish king), 154
Guthrie, W. K. C., 59

Hagiography, medieval, 125, 157, 168–69
Harnack, Adolf von, 47, 155
Havamal, 121
Heather, Peter, 135–36, 140
Hechter, Michael, 126
Heil, concept of, 205–6
Heliand, 23, 206
Hellenic culture, 63
Hellenic rationalism, 133
Hellenistic mystery cults, 67, 71, 84
Hellenistic philosophical schools, 68
Hellenistic religiosity. *See* Religiosity,
  Hellenistic
Hellenistic transformation, 62, 76, 172
and de-Hellenization of native Greek
  culture, 85
and loss of cultural identity, 85
demographics of, 84
effects of, 64
  ideological, 72
  on Indo-European religiosity, 72
heterogenization and, 86
religious syncretism and, 86
role of immigration in, 85
Herwegen, Ildefons, 99
Heterogenization, social, 6, 20, 66, 84, 86
Hiebert, Paul G., 17, 132, 192
Higgins, George, 22
Hillgarth, J. N., 144, 152–53
History of the English Church and People,
  185
Hollander, Lee M., 121

Holmes, Urban T., 43
Homogeneity, social, 60
Honor
    Christian notion of, 120–21
    Germanic contrasted with Christian, 124
    Germanic notion of, 120
Howe, John McDonald, 125
Huns, 134, 138, 151
Hutton, Ronald, 32

Ideological transformation, 204
Imperial expansion
    and universalist religions, 67
    destabilization following, 66
Inculturation, 39, 121
Individualism, 69
Indo-European religiosity. *See* Religiosity:
    Indo-European
Indo-Europeanization of Christianity, 133
Indo-Europeans
    religiosity of, 115
    social structure of, 114
    uniqueness of, 116
    warrior ethos among, 118
Industrial Revolution, 44
Irish monasticism, folk-centered structure
    of, 158
Irish monks, 156
    as missionaries, 159
Irish penitentials, 156
Irsigler, Franz, 168
Islam, 46, 50

Jesus, and the Essene community, 77
Jones, George Fenwick, 119, 121–22
    Germanic parody of the Beatitudes, 120
Jordanes (Gothic historian), 138
Julian (emperor), 12
Julianism, definition of, 12
Jungmann, Josef A., 4, 39, 42, 191, 198

Kahl, Hans-Dietrich, 32
Kamehameha II (Hawaiian chief), 22
Kapus, 22
Katz, Solomon, 72
Kee, Howard Clark, 87
Kelly, J. N. D., 78
Kerényi, Karl, 180
Kerr, Hugh T., and John M. Mulder, on
    conversion, 28
Kiev, Ari, 95
Kingship, Germanic, 152, 172–74
Kinship, 7, 121
Kitto, H. D. F., 65

Kleingoten, 138
Kleinstück, Johannes, 180
Knights Templars, 40
Kokutai, 19
Krailsheimer, A. J., on conversion, 28

La Piana, George, 86
Lanternari, Vittorio, 76, 79
Lasko, Peter, 146
Latourette, Kenneth Scott, 15, 89, 97, 166
Le Bras, Gabriel, 37
Le Goff, Jacques, 37, 44, 161–62, 176
Lea, Henry Charles, 128
Leclercq, Jean, 36
Lefebvre, Marcel (archbishop), vii
Lenski, Gerhard E., 83
Lenteildis (sister of Clovis), 149
Leovigild (Visigothic king), 144
Liber Evangeliorum, 206
Life after death, 64
Littleton, C. Scott
    on the centrality of the warrior figure in
        Indo-European ideology, 117
    on the Indo-European tradition in the
        Middle Ages, 118
    on the uniqueness of Indo-European
        tripartition, 116
Liturgical uniformity, benefits of, 192
Lombards. *See* Germanic peoples:
    Lombards
Lönnroth, Lars, 123
Lord-man relationship, 129
Loyalty to one's lord, versus individual
    salvation, 121
Luckmann, Joan, and Karen Creason
    Sorensen, 96
Luxeuil, 156

MacMullen, Ramsay, 29–30, 32–33,
    47–48, 98
Magic, 69
Magicoreligious reinterpretation of
    Christianity. *See* Christianity: magico-
    religious reinterpretation of
Markus, Robert A., 32, 186–87, 202
Martin of Braga (bishop), 142, 201
Martin of Tours (bishop), 177, 181
Mayr-Harting, Henry, 32
McKitterick, Rosamond, 200, 202–3
McNally, Robert E., 199
Meeks, Wayne A., 81, 83–84, 87
Mellitus (missionary), 185–88
Mensching, Gustav, 49, 51
Messianism, Jewish, 76

Metanoia, 26–27
Miller, David Harry, 153, 175
Missionary methodologies (*See also*
  Accommodation; Gradualism;
  Coercion)
  Anglo-Saxon, 7, 163, 183, 195, 206
  appeal to temporal concerns, 194
  Iro-Frankish, 158, 160, 164–65
  summarized, 197.
Moorhead, John, 146, 148–49, 152
Moral values, 202
Muhammad, 56
Munz, Peter, 32
Murphy, G. Ronald, on the *Heliand,*
  23–24, 171, 191
Murray, Gilbert, 64, 90
Myers, Henry A., and Herwig Wolfram,
  174
Mystery cults, 70
  Cybele, 46, 71
  Dionysus, 46
  Eleusis, 46
  Isis, 46, 71
  Mithras, 46
  opposed by the Roman Senate, 71
  Sarapis, 46, 71–72
Mythologem, 107, 112

Nagy, Gregory, 66
Nakamura, Hajime, 54
Neoplatonism, 62
New religious movements, parallels with
  the early Christian Church, 93
Njal's Saga, 122
Nock, Arthur Darby, definitions of
  adhesion and conversion, 29, 30
Nordal, Sigurdur, 110
Nothelm of Canterbury (bishop), 192
Novus Ordo Missae, vii

O'Dea, Thomas, 20, 22, 79, 131
Odo of Cluny (abbot), 124
Oikoumene, 64
Origen, on conversion, 27
Ostrogoths. *See* Germanic peoples:
  Ostrogoths
Otfrid of Weissenburg, 206
Otto, Rudolf, 48
Ottonian emperors, 4, 209, 211

Pagan religious practices, 109, 201
Pagan temples, 185, 187, 190
Pagels, Elaine, 78, 82
Paul (apostle), 70

Pelagius, 163
Pelikan, Jaroslav, 170
Peloponnesian Wars, 63, 84
Pepin the Short (Frankish king), 192, 197
Pericles (Athenian statesman), 65
Persian Empire, 63
Philosophy of history, 98
Pickering, Frederick P., 178
Piggott, Stuart, 116
Pirmin (missionary), 199–200
Polis, 64, 65, 85
Political religiosity, 157
Polomé, Edgar, on Indo-European social
  structure and religion, 114–16
Powell, Elwin H., 97
Prinz, Friedrich, 156–57
Procopius (Byzantine historian), 144
Protestant Reformation, 211
Proto-Indo-Europeans, 113
Punic Wars, 71
Purgatory, idea of, 161

Quigley, Carroll, 98

Radbod (Frisian duke), 195
Rambo, Lewis R., on conversion, 27
Recared (Visigothic king), 144
Reform movements, 211
Relics, 6
Religion (*See also* Religiosity)
  and group identity, 82, 140
  archaic, 51
  Arianism, Germanic. *See* Christianity:
    Arian: Germanic
  as a response to social stress, 94–95
  Buddhism, 54–55
  Catholicism, Frankish, 134
  Chinese, ethnic component in, 19
  Christianity. *See* main entry
  Confucianism, 55
  doctrinal beliefs, 48
  folk, 45, 192
    and universal compared, 47–48
    ethnocultural aspects of, 48
    sacrality of the community in, 48
    structure of, 108
  Germanic, 27, 47
  Greek, Hellenic, 59, 63
  Hellenism, 58, 76
  Indo-European, 37, 46
  Islam, 55, 56
  Japanese, ethnic component in, 19
  Judaism, 49, 76
    Palestinian, 58, 75–76

Religion (*continued*)
  national
    Germanic Arianism, 141
    sociopolitical benefits of, 144
  primitive, 50
  Roman
    Hellenization of, 74
    Republican, 60
  Shintoism, 55
  Unification Church, 93
  universal, 3, 24, 45–46, 51, 102
    folk-religious reinterpretation of, 50
    in a folk-religious society, 103
    indigenous reinterpretation of, 142
    structure of, 108
    and folk compared, 47–48,
    urban, Christianity as, 155
    use of the term, 108
    world-accepting, 50
    Zoroastrianism, early, 49
Religiopolitical complementarity, 175,
  209, 212
Religiopolitical reinterpretation of Christianity. *See* Christianity: religiopolitical
  reinterpretation of
Religiosity (*See also* Religion)
  and stress, 96
  disparity between Christian and
    Germanic, 213
  dualist, 51
  folk, 51, 188
  Germanic, 111–12
    ethics and, 202
    socio-politico-religious synergy of,
      171
    structure of, 108
    vitality of, 7,188, 207, 209
  Greek, 58
  Hellenic, 64
  Hellenistic, 64, 74
    acceptance in Roman Republic, 70
    forms of by class, 70
    influence on Christianity, 73, 75
  immanent, 52
  Indo-European, 5, 102, 115
    ancestor worship, 63
    decline of, 75
    religiopolitical unity of, 60
    sociopolitical character of, 171
    traditional, 60
  magicoreligious, 189
  messianic, 51
  transcendental, 51
  universal, 50–51

  use of the term, 107
  world-accepting, 49, 51
    defined, 52
  world-rejecting, 49–51
    and anomie, 57
    defined, 52
    factors contributing to, 80
Religious attitudes, and genetic factors, 14
Religious evolution, 49
Religious instruction. *See* Catechetical
  instruction
Religious sects, and a feeling of belonging,
  95
Religious transformation
  associated with de-Hellenization, 85
  general model of, 3, 45–46
    fundamental postulates, 102
  of folk-religious societies, 48
  of universal religions, 48
  preliminary model of, 24
  principles of, 96
  proto-Christian, 45
  societal, 132
  sociopsychological aspects of, 81
Remigius of Reims (bishop), 148, 150,
  159, 165
Repentance, and conversion, 27
Riché, Pierre, 142–44, 147
Robinson, James M., 78
Roman Empire, viii
  anomie in, 97
  ascendancy of "un-Roman" elements in,
    98
  foreign groups in, 86
  from rationalism to religious enthusiasm
    in, 72
  heterogeneity of, 98
  organic relation to early Christianity of,
    102
  social stress in, 94
  urban centers, dissolution of, 100
Roman Republic
  Hellenistic religiosity in, 70
Romanitas, 133
Romanization, 146
Rose, H. J., 60
Rupp, Heinz, 205
Russell, Jeffrey Burton, 34

Sacral kingship, 167, 205, 209
  in the Merovingian-Carolingian contest,
    196
Saints, lives of, 6
Salvation, 50–52, 76, 100

and early Christianity, 4
appeal of
  and predisposition to a universal
    religion, 102
  related to level of group solidarity,
    102
Christian message of, 79
group, Judaic, 76
individual, 49, 63–64, 66, 68, 121, 162,
  204–5, 208
  and mystery cults, 64
  concept of in Frankish society, 161
  desire for, 203
  Hellenistic quest for, 71
  in Christianity, 73
  in Hellenism, 73
  versus loyalty to one's lord, 121
universal, Christian, 76
Salvation history, 178
Salvation religions. *See* Religion: universal
Saunders, George R., 141
Schmitt, Jean-Claude, 37
Schoeps, Hans-Joachim, 203
Schweitzer, Albert, 170
Scripture, status of, 199
Second Vatican Council, vii, 210–11
Semantic transformation, 204–5
Shintoism, 19
Simpson, John, 178
Sin, concept of, 27, 161–62, 188, 203, 205,
  208
Smart, Ninian, 55–56
Smith, Noel W., 80
Snorri Sturluson (Icelandic author), 110
Social destabilization, 6, 66, 78, 88, 95
  of the Mediterranean region, 84
Social dominance, religious rationalization
  of, 63
Social status
  of the Arian Germanic peoples, 143
  of the early Christians, 84
Social structure
  and ideological structure, 102
  and mythology according to Dumézil, 13
  conduciveness to Christianity of
    in Germanic societies, 79
    in the declining Roman Empire, 102
  contemporary and Hellenistic
    compared, 93
  disparity between classical and
    Germanic, 98
  disparity between early Christian and
    Germanic, 209, 212
  early Christian, 4

family structure, Roman and modern,
  126
general Indo-European, 4
Germanic, 4, 102, 167
Germanic kinship, 126
heterogeneous, 212
homogeneous, 212
Indo-European, 58–59, 114
non-urban, 101
of early Christianity, 155
  and urban environment of, 86
of Germanic peoples, and rural
  environment of, 86
Socialization, and early Christianity, 4
Society of Saint Pius X, vii
Sociobiological relationships, 128
Sociobiology, 53, 69, 204
Soteriology, Christian, 76
Sparta, 66
Spengler, Oswald, 66
Stancliffe, C. E., 32, 181–82
Stark, Rodney, 86
Status inconsistency, 83–84, 87–88
  and stress, 83, 96
Stephen II (pope), 197
Stoicism, 69, 85
Storey, William G., and Niels Krogh
  Rasmussen, 180
Strauss, Gerald, 37
Stress
  social effects of, 96
  and religious attitudes, 96
  and religious behavior, 6
  and status inconsistency, 83, 96
  and urbanization, 89, 96
  present in the Roman Empire, 97
Sullivan, Richard E., 31, 197, 199
Syagrius (Gallic ruler), 148, 150–51
Syncretism, 11, 85
  Christo-Germanic, 18
T'ang dynasty, 50
Tacitus, Cornelius, 108, 173
  description of the *comitatus,* 118–19
Tarn, W. W., 70
Tessier, Georges, 154
Theodoric (Ostrogothic king), 143, 147,
  174
Theodosius the Great (emperor), 140
Thomas, Keith, 37
Thompson, Claiborne W., 122–23
Thompson, E. A., 136, 138–39
Thucydides (Athenian historian), 65
Time, Christian and Germanic senses of,
  176–77

Tippett, Alan, 25
Toynbee, Arnold, 57
Tripartition, Indo-European, 114, 116
Troeltsch, Ernst, 51

Ulfila (Arian bishop), 135, 206
Ullmann, Walter, 128
Umayyad Dynasty, 50
Unification Church, 93
Universal brotherhood, notion of, 69
Universal religions. See Religion:
  universal
Universalism, 69, 210
Urbanization, 6, 87–88, 95
  and stress, 96
  socioreligious dynamics of, 86

Valens (emperor), 135, 140
Valentinian (emperor), 128
Value systems, transformation of, 202
Values
  disparity between Germanic and
    Christian, 120
  Germanic, 124
    Christian redefinition of, 121
Van Engen, John, 36, 44
Vassalage, 130
Venantius Fortunatus (bishop of Poitiers),
  170
Vengeance, Germanic concept of, 122
Visigothic missionaries (*"Kleingoten"*), 138
Visigoths. *See* Germanic peoples:
  Visigoths
Vita Sancti Geraldi, 124

Voegelin, Eric, 78–79
Vogel, Cyrille, 41, 180, 192
Völkerwanderungszeit, 130, 173–74
Votive Masses, 180
Vridu (bond of kinship), duties associated
  with, 121

Wallace-Hadrill, J. M., 40, 159–60
Warrior(s)
  aristocracy of, 212
  ethic of, 118
  ethos of, 155–56
  in Indo-European ideology, 117
Weber, Max, 131, 155
Wergild, 204
Wilfrid (Anglo-Saxon missionary), 183
Wilken, Robert L., 82
Willibrord (Anglo-Saxon missionary), 195
Wolfram, Herwig, 140
World-view(s), 4, 132
  attempts to transform, 13
  Christian, 131, 199
    soteriological-eschatological, 36
  disparity between Christian and
    Germanic, 131, 176, 178, 200, 204,
    211, 213
  disparity between pre-Christian and
    Christian, 177
  dualism, 76, 80
  early Christian, 4, 58
  factor in missiological approach, 24
  folk-religious, 50, 192
  Germanic, 4, 42, 121, 131, 189, 211
    vitality of, 4, 122, 182, 211
  Greek, Hellenic, 80
  Indo-European, 4, 58, 133
    warrior ideology, 59
  Judeo-Hellenistic, 133
  transformation of, 132, 167, 200, 202,
    207
  world-accepting, 4, 76, 103, 212
  world-rejecting, 4, 63, 73, 76, 89, 133,
    212
Wulframm (Frankish missionary), 195,
  196

Zachary (pope), 195, 197
Zoroastrianism, 50